Making Time

Making Time

Lillian Moller Gilbreth—A Life Beyond "Cheaper by the Dozen"

JANE LANCASTER

NORTHEASTERN UNIVERSITY PRESS • *Boston*

Northeastern University Press

Library of Congress Cataloging-in-Publication Data
Lancaster, Jane.
Making time : Lillian Moller Gilbreth, a life beyond "Cheaper by the
dozen" / Jane Lancaster.
p. cm.
ISBN 1-55553-612-3 (cloth : alk. paper)
1. Gilbreth, Lillian Moller, 1878–1972. 2. Women industrial
engineers—United States—Biography. I. Title.
T55.85.G64 M54 2004
658.5′4′092—dc22   2003021862

Designed by Gary Gore

Composed in Sabon by Graphic Composition, Inc., Athens, Georgia.
Printed and bound by Sheridan Books, Ann Arbor, Michigan. The
paper is House Natural, an acid-free stock.

MANUFACTURED IN THE UNITED STATES OF AMERICA
08   07   06   05   04   5   4   3   2

For Tony, who helped me make time

Contents

Illustrations

Acknowledgments

I would not have been able to complete this book without the help and friendship of members of the Gilbreth family. Robert Moller Gilbreth, Ernestine Gilbreth Carey, Daniel Bunker Gilbreth, Irene Gilbreth, Jack Moller Gilbreth, Lillian Gilbreth Johnson, and Jane Gilbreth Heppes talked to me and helped me round out a picture of their mother. My conclusions are, however, my own.

Many other people who shared their memories of the Gilbreths are listed below—my apologies to any who are inadvertently omitted. I would like thank librarians and archivists on four continents—my friends and colleagues—and, most of all, my family.

For permission to quote from published sources, I would also like to thank the Institute of Industrial Engineers; Ernestine Gilbreth Carey and Daniel B. Gilbreth for *As I Remember;* the Society of Women Engineers for *The Quest of the One Best Way;* and HarperCollins for *Cheaper by the Dozen;* and the Rhode Island Historical Society for permission to reprint material in chapter 12, which appeared in a different form as "Frank and Lillian Gilbreth Bring Scientific Management to Rhode Island," *Rhode Island History* 55, no. 2 (1998). The Gilbreth papers at Purdue University and the Ernestine Gilbreth Carey Papers and the Lillian Moller Gilbreth Papers at Smith College are copyright 2004 by Ernestine Gilbreth Carey and reprinted with the permission of McIntosh and Otis, Inc. *Belles on Their Toes* is copyright 1950 by Frank B. Gilbreth Jr. and Ernestine Gilbreth Carey, reprinted with permission of McIntosh and Otis, Inc. I also wish to acknowledge, with many thanks, support given in the form of research fellowships at the John Nicholas Brown Center for the Study of American Civilization at Brown University and at the Newell B. Goff Institute for Ingenuity and Enterprise Studies at the Rhode Island Historical Society.

I talked to many people about Lillian. They include Edith Folger Andrews, Eileen McGrath, Jane Richmond, and Walter Boyd in Nantucket; Eddie Chen in Taiwan; Mary Sissons Barrett, Marion Dunlop, Jonathon Farnum, Anne Freeman Giraud, Louise Aldrich Hoge, Martha Mitchell, Sarah Morenon, Eleanor Peckham, Robert Piacitelli, Betty Selle, and Edward Winsor in Providence; Susan Englander, David Ferguson, William Roberts, and Bebe York in California; N. Wesley Haynes on the telephone in New Hampshire; Joseph Juran and Julie Johnson Lindquist in Connecticut; Mary Brown Lawrence both in California and on Prudence Island; and Peter Liebhold and Carlene Stephens in Washington, D.C.

I also want to thank the many friends and colleagues who read the manuscript, talked to me, and encouraged me. First on the list must be Mari Jo Buhle and Jim Patterson at Brown University, and Susan Porter Benson at the University of Connecticut. They taught me to be a clearer thinker and a better writer, and without them this book may not have happened. The process of turning a dissertation into a book (which was the original intention, but I got sidetracked) was helped by conversations with Gretchen Adams, Joyce Botelho, Laura Briggs, Elspeth Brown, Mary Anne Bruscha, Mari Jo Buhle, Bruce Bustard, Richard Canedo, Jane Civins, Chrissie Cortina, Donna deFabio Curtin, Tom D'Evelyn, Anne Diffily, Eleanor Doumato, Susan Englander, David Ferguson, Sheila ffolliott, Gale Goodwin Gomes, Laurel Graham, Mary Hollinshead, Ulle Holt, Marita Hopmann, Janet Howell, Hester Kaplan, Susan Kepner, Christy Lamarr, Sarah Leavitt, Pam MacFarland, Laura Mack, Pam McColl, Joanne Melish, John Meyers, Carol Mills, Martha Mitchell, Marie Myers, Adam Nelson, Victoria Nelson, Janice Okoomian, Jeanne O'Malley, Ann Parsons, Louise Poole, Mary Lynne Poole (who also provided invaluable technical assistance), Laura Prieto, Sarah Purcell, Cynthia Pyle, Ed Rafferty, Joan Richards, Eric Simonoff, Eve Sterne, Kathryn Tomasek, Julia and Bill Walsh, and Eileen Warburton.

Hidden in that alphabetical list are members of the Female Mutual Improvement Society, without whom I might not have survived graduate school, and the Biography Group, without whom Lillian might not have seen the light of day. They know who they are, and my undying thanks go to them. I also want to thank Elizabeth Swayze, my heroically patient editor at Northeastern University Press, who waited with me while a long, drawn-out permission process tried our souls.

Finally, I want to thank my family. My mother, who did not live to see the end product, read some of the early chapters in spite of her failing eyesight. I remember her sitting at a machine in my kitchen, reading the magnified type page by page. I want to thank my son Tom, who unearthed some important documents for me at Berkeley, my son Rob for his good humor, and especially my husband Tony, whose support kept me going through my long quest for Lillian, which, like any other biography, was also a quest for myself.

Introduction: Wasn't She the Mother in *Cheaper by the Dozen?*

Lillian Moller Gilbreth was a working mother on a grand scale. She was also one of the most celebrated women in America in the middle of the twentieth century. She was admired both as an engineer and for the way she seemed to combine marriage, career, and family into a seamless whole. Contemporaries honored her: universities gave her honorary degrees and engineering societies gave her gold medals. She was described in 1952 as "The World's Greatest Woman Engineer" because of "her impact on management, her innovations in industrial design, her methodological contributions to time and motion studies, her humanization of management principles, and her role in integrating the principles of science and management." She appeared on numerous lists of the most influential women in America, and one admirer even suggested she was "Presidential Timber."[1]

Colleagues admired her. In 1937, a few days before she left on her last flight, Amelia Earhart declared that the most rewarding part of working at Purdue University was "my connection with Lillian Gilbreth." Herbert Hoover, in whose administration she served, believed she was "the most heroic woman in America" and told two of her children, "Your book should make her an immortal in the life of our country and I shall indeed be glad."[2]

There's the rub. If Lillian Gilbreth *is* immortal, it is for the wrong reason, because most people nowadays only know her as the long-suffering Mother in *Cheaper by the Dozen.* Published late in 1948 and continuously in print, the book is still read with pleasure and delight in junior high schools all over America, and the movie, which stars Clifton Webb and Myrna Loy, appears on TV from time to time. Both tell the story of a dozen children (hence the title) growing up with efficiency expert parents. Many readers have fond memories of the scene where father shows a bemused school principal how to take an efficient bath. Father is the dominant character; Mother is sweet and supportive in the background. The book is very much a product of its period; 1948 was not the best time to be celebrating nondomestic women.[3]

The book's success was ironic, as Lillian was both an agent and a representative of one of the most important social changes of the twentieth century, namely the movement of married women into the labor force. *Cheaper by the Dozen,* however, reinforced traditional gender roles by presenting her as a nonworking mother, making it difficult to take Lillian seriously as a "foremother" in the first wave of women's history. Lillian as engineer and career woman was submerged in the image of Lillian as mother.

Cheaper by the Dozen did Lillian an injustice; she disliked it and was embarrassed by it. Although she was undoubtedly a mother on a grand scale, she was more importantly a *working* mother, sufficiently distinguished to appear on a U.S. postage stamp as a "famous American." Whether we realize it or not, she influenced the way we work, the way we arrange our houses, and our attitude toward time. An enthusiastic participant in the early-twentieth-century effort to make business more efficient and management more scientific, she was an engineer, a management consultant, a professor, and a government adviser. She was one of the first people to incorporate psychology into industrial planning, by advocating educational techniques to gain the cooperation of the worker: modern management techniques are based on ideas she put forward nearly a century ago. For the last four decades of her sixty-year professional life she concentrated on women's work in shops and factories, in offices, and in the home, and she did important pioneering work for women with disabilities. She also became a role model to a generation of women who read about her balancing act between family and career. She was professionally active into extreme old age, finally retiring just before her ninetieth birthday.

I knew none of this when I read and enjoyed *Cheaper by the Dozen* as a child; indeed, I thought it was fiction. Many years later, while creating a bibliography of women scientists, I came across Lillian Gilbreth being praised to the skies by the eminent psychologist Erik Erikson. Curious, I investigated a little further and found her sharing a platform with the architect Frank Lloyd Wright and appearing on a panel with Helen Keller and Eleanor Roosevelt. She certainly moved in exalted circles and I wondered what she had done, apart from having so many children.

I then read the outline biography in *Notable American Women,* which detailed her rich professional life, and I wondered why she had failed to feature in the women's history books I read.[4] The short answer is that Lillian did not fit easily into the mainstream of American women's history. As a perceptive journalist wrote in 1971 just before Lillian died: "If Women's Lib opponents and Women's Lib advocates could agree on a patron saint, they might choose Lillian Moller Gilbreth."[5]

Lillian was a paradox and hard to categorize. She was late Victorian, upper middle class, Californian, white, a lifelong Republican, nonconfrontational, and apparently happy to be almost continually pregnant or nursing for almost twenty years. She was also fiercely intelligent, innovative, and professional and had extraordinary stamina. She was regarded by friends and children alike as a delightful, if sometimes exhausting, person. She is also much more than a list of achievements or an example of female firsts. As a colleague once wrote, "Attempting to pay homage to Dr. Lillian M. Gilbreth by merely listing her biographical data" would be "both exceedingly lengthy and woefully inadequate."[6] This book is not an attempt to pay homage, but rather an examination of the intersections between public and private, life and work, family and society.

While Lillian was undoubtedly a professional woman, she was also a mother, and the two elements of her life are almost inextricably intertwined. Accordingly, I interweave Lillian's public and private life from her birth in 1878 to her death in 1972. I use a wide range of published and archival sources, as well as numerous interviews with family and friends, to trace her transformation from a shy and self-effacing Victorian daughter to a world-famous management expert and adviser to presidents. I was also interested in how Lillian presented herself; how her peers, the press, and her children presented her; and how these representations reflect changes in the public and private role of women over her long lifetime. I believe Lillian consciously used her public image: she and Frank were early practitioners of public relations techniques.[7]

She was not, however, always able to manage social assumptions, and society's expectations of girls and women affected Lillian throughout her life. Notions of "proper" female behavior dominated her California childhood in the 1880s, her college years in the 1890s, and her years as a wife and mother in the early 1900s. Lillian also confronted gender issues in the 1920s and 1930s when she was trying to make a living in a decidedly male world, that of industrial engineering, and in the 1940s when *Cheaper by the Dozen* made her professional identity a victim of the "Feminine Mystique."

Nevertheless, Lillian Moller Gilbreth faced, and to some extent solved, one of the central dilemmas of modern American women, namely how to combine family and work. She was born a year after the end of Reconstruction and died just before the Watergate scandal started to unfold, and she lived through a period that saw enormous changes in the lives of women. Family size decreased by half while the proportion of married women working increased tenfold and the proportion of married mothers of young children in the labor force climbed from almost none to one in three. Lillian's work contributed to many of the changes in women's working habits, while her strategies for coping with the dual role of working mother were frequently presented as a model to harassed housewives.[8]

As I read Lillian's letters, I began to see that the sunny, tranquil mother in

Cheaper by the Dozen was only part of the picture. She undoubtedly loved babies and was a calm and competent foil to her brash husband, but Lillian was also a complex, driven character. While clearly ambitious, she would modestly say, "I owe it all to Frank" as a way of disarming criticism of pushy women; had she had her way, this book would have been about her husband. He was a larger-than-life character, full of energy and ideas. He was also almost unnaturally devoted to his mother and saw nothing wrong with loading his wife with work while keeping her almost constantly pregnant. Lillian loved him. There is no other way to explain why, in spite of the heavy burden of being Mrs. Frank Gilbreth and mother to his strenuous children, she would and could hear no criticism of him, and after his death she tried to carry out what she thought Frank would have wanted. Later, however, as she modified her adherence to Frank's wishes, she nevertheless disclaimed any personal ambition, preferring to get her way without offending the men with whom she had to work.

Her first biographer, Edna Yost, found it necessary to write a joint biography, as Lillian argued that their work was inseparable. Yost, who knew Lillian well, tried to deal with their personal relationship, but concluded that the Gilbreths "remain a phenomenon that increases, even as it eludes, human understanding. They fit no preconceived pattern." Lillian's marriage was certainly unusual, as was the intensity of her professional partnership with Frank, but even before she met him she longed to escape from what she perceived as her wealthy parents' stiflingly domestic environment. She wrote a master's thesis on *Bartholemew Fair* the year before she met Frank, and in it she described, with evident approval, the men of Ben Jonson's England. They were not "one-sided, atropied [*sic*] specimens," she wrote, "but passionate, hot-headed natural men."[9]

Frank Bunker Gilbreth was very much a "hot-headed natural man," and Lillian's life was far from peaceful during the twenty years of their marriage. Many people were critical of her almost permanent state of pregnancy, and she often felt professionally embattled. She and Frank were involved in disputes with other scientific management pioneers where they tried hard to present themselves in the best possible light. Thus, the huge quantity of documents in the Gilbreth Collection at Purdue University—some two hundred archival boxes—has to be approached with caution. Lillian deposited her papers there in 1940 and spent the next year arranging them. They include family scrapbooks, numerous press cuttings, hundreds, perhaps thousands of photographs, mostly of factory interiors, and manuscripts of articles for the engineering press. The archive also holds hundreds of letters from Frank written from the time they met and became engaged in 1903 to just before his sudden death in 1924. Blue pencil in hand, Lillian edited some of the letters before asking her secretary to retype them. Some of the alterations were minor and personal, such as the excision of impolite references to third parties or Frank's terms of endearment to her. She also deleted Frank's overenthusiasm for the Germans before 1917. (1941 was not the best time to be proGerman.) Nevertheless, she kept both versions; the unedited letters remained in a restricted file for many years, though they are now available to researchers. Lillian's blue pencil was also at work on her own letters to Frank; she crossed out details of her health or of weaning the latest baby, items that she thought too personal to be of "general interest."[10] More important, Lillian arranged the papers to tell the Gilbreths' side of a dispute with Frederick W. Taylor and his supporters, a dispute that split the scientific management community in two.

Lillian organized her papers with a view to posterity, and as this became clear to me, the need to consider her self-representation became obvious. She deliberately prepared "all the material which would make it possible for an adequate biography of Frank to be written" as part of a strategy to foreground her husband and minimize her own claims to ambitions and creativity. Nevertheless, the papers show her to have possessed a strength of purpose and a toughness that women of her generation (and many other generations) were trained to disguise. Sifting through her papers inspired Lillian to write her own memoir. She called it *As I Remember* and wrote it entirely in the third person and mostly in the passive voice, thereby distancing herself from overt ambition or pride in achievement while making space for her husband and his work to be seen. She represented herself primarily as Frank's helper and wrote "she had realized before she married him, that her best job would be as a 'tender' and that nothing was so important as to make it possible for him to work and help him in every way she could."[11]

Lillian made little effort to publish her memoir; it finally appeared in 1998. The way she presents herself, however, confirms the findings of feminist scholars who have described women's self-effacing autobiographical strategies. Jill Ker Conway, discussing Jane Addams, Margaret Sanger, and the athlete Babe Didrickson, could have been describing Lillian when she wrote,

> The narratives they wrote cultivate the image of the romantic female, nurturant, peace loving and swayed only by positive emotion, rather than the driven, creative high achievers we see when we study their behavior. By presenting themselves in terms consistent with romantic imagery they created their own myth about female achievement in America. . . . Their stories are about conversion experiences, about being swept along by events as the romantic heroine is swept off her feet by her lover, about being carried by events towards moments of intuitive insight and emotional truth.[12]

The emotional center of Lillian's memoir was her loyalty to Frank, her conversion experience was meeting him, and her version of the myth of female achievement was to attribute much of her success to him. Her public visibility during her forty-five-year career after Frank's death does, of course, belie this myth.

Lillian's modesty is echoed in her children's book *Cheaper by the Dozen*, which is very much in tune with the popular "back to the kitchen" conception of post–World War II attitudes to women. The primary focus of their book is father. They represent Lillian watching quietly, wisely, and supportively while Frank, portrayed as a bombastic motion study expert, tries to organize his twelve children along the most efficient lines. The book ignores Lillian's professional activities and emphasizes her warmth, nurturance, and motherliness. It gives no indication that by the early 1920s, when the action takes place, Lillian had a Ph.D. in psychology, had already written several technical books and dozens of articles, was Frank's partner in a management consulting firm, and frequently lectured to colleges and professional groups. Instead, *Cheaper by the Dozen* celebrated "old-fashioned" values of family life, with mother apparently content to be at home surrounded by babies, father apparently in charge, and the older daughters doing nothing more rebellious than bobbing their hair. At a time of national nervousness in the early 1950s, the book must have seemed very reassuring. Contemporary reviewers were conscious of this; as one pointed out, "At times like this, when parent delinquency is so rightly being screamed at us from our radios and newspapers, it is a breath of fresh air to read of at least two undelinquent parents."[13]

Cheaper by the Dozen was not, however, read in a vacuum. In the late 1940s and early 1950s, at the height of the book's popularity, Lillian was frequently celebrated in the press for both her family and her career, often in the same sentence. Many of those who enjoyed *Cheaper by the Dozen* also saw press accounts of Lillian's professional activities. They read about her continuing consultancy work, about her gold medals and her latest honorary degrees—she received fourteen during the 1950s alone. Press accounts that began with a reference to her as "Mother" went on to applaud the normality of her children as well as her professional achievements.[14]

Thus, *Cheaper by the Dozen* both reinforced and contradicted traditional gender roles. Although her children echoed Lillian's self-representation as a supportive, unambitious woman, those who read it in conjunction with press reports stressing Lillian's public achievements could conclude that she had successfully combined career and family while staying feminine and ladylike. Although it is always difficult to know how people react to a particular book, conversations with some people who read it in the 1940s and 1950s suggest that they were not misled by the emphasis on Lillian's domesticity. A woman who was running the radiology lab at Stanford University in 1948, the year *Cheaper* was published, recalled that when she and her colleagues had a big job to do, they would say, "Let's do a Lillian." She continued: "To do a Lillian was to use the production line—time and motion approach and efficiency techniques which were invented as we went along. . . . It was done with great good humor but as I look back on it—it was quite meaningful in getting an enormous amount of work done with the optimum efficiency. It was a team approach."[15]

Lillian's ability to combine a remarkable public and professional life with the raising of eleven children made her an icon for those who wanted to show that middle-class mothers could work without its adversely affecting their families. Press treatment of Lillian supports the view that women's individual excellence and success were celebrated in the late 1940s at the same time as domesticity and the joys of motherhood were extolled.[16]

The story of Lillian's life is very relevant to women in the twenty-first century. Lillian was in many ways a Victorian; she was modest to a fault, unwilling to appear ambitious, unable to talk about sex or bodily functions—yet she manufactured and managed her own publicity, selling herself and her vision of work and family to Americans through countless articles and speeches while rearing an abnormally large family and becoming known as the "First Lady of Engineering." Her relationship to her children is problematic, bearing as it does an ideological slant. There is no doubt that she loved babies and that none of her surviving children will say a bad word about her. Nevertheless, the reason she and Frank had such a large family was partly their inability to talk about birth control, but was mainly the Gilbreths' contribution to the eugenics movement—the creation of better humans. It was also an effort to show that educated women could work and parent at the same time—a discussion in the early 1900s just as it is a century later. Although some of her children would prefer this book to concentrate on their mother's career—they had enough publicity in their youth to last a lifetime—Lillian's life would be incomprehensible without the intermingling of public and private. Part of her motivation for having so many children was to prove a point—that educated women need not abandon family life. Her career decisions were affected by the need to provide for her children, while publicity about her family and how well everyone was coping (whether or not this was true) provided advertising for her work as a consultant on women's work.

William Shakespeare wrote of the seven ages of man. Had he been writing about women, he would have needed a dozen. As feminist critics have noted, the conventional biographical model of education, career, and decline does not fit women's lives, which tend not to follow a neat symmetrical curve. Their lives are more likely to be affected by family concerns such as children or aged parents, and they often experience bursts of energy in middle age just as men are starting to slow down.

This book starts at almost exactly the midpoint of Lillian's long life, with the death of her husband. It goes on to explain how shy, timid, literary Lillie Moller became Dr. Lillian Gilbreth, celebrated as both the "First Lady of Engineering" *and* "Mother of the Year." Although Lillian's situation was unusual—few women want to produce a baby every fifteen or so months or go on working until they are ninety—the way the media dealt with her as mother *and* engineer was emblematic of the twentieth-century confusion over woman's proper place. Lillian may have found it, so here is the story of a woman who tried to "have it all" and largely succeeded.

·   ·   ·

A word about names: In common with other biographers of women, I have chosen to call my subject by her first name. This is partly because there are so many Gilbreths in this story that to do otherwise would simply lead to confusion. It is also because this is the story of my understanding of Lillian Gilbreth. To further complicate matters, she was christened Lillie by her parents and changed her name to Lillian when she graduated from Berkeley, because she felt it sounded more dignified. When I use her memoirs of her childhood, where she often refers to herself in the third person, I, too, call her Lillie, unless I am talking about her later representation of herself, when I say "Lillian believed . . ."

PART I

There Was
Only One Consolation,
and That Was Work

For years I believed that my mother worked
only because she had to. I now know that I was wrong.
She did have to work, but she loved her work.

Martha B. Gilbreth, "A Large Family Is Fun" (1936)

I   Gone West

Suddenly, on June 14, 1924, Frank went,
not abroad as he had planned, but "West,"
as soldiers go. The Quest goes on!

Lillian Moller Gilbreth, *The Quest of the One Best Way* (1925)

I T WAS THURSDAY, June 19, 1924, a hot summer's day, when Lillian Gilbreth sailed for England. She was in her mid-forties and when she smiled she was a very attractive woman, but she did not smile much; she looked very tired and her pale face peeped out from under an unflattering cloche hat. Unlike the rest of the passengers, a group of eminent American engineers and their wives, she did not stand and wave to friends or relatives on the dockside. There was no one to see her off —she had insisted that they all stay home. Unlike the rest of the women, she was not dressed in her summer whites; instead, she was clutching a black linen coat around her thin body as if she was cold. She went straight to her cabin while the other passengers greeted each other and arranged the social events that would pass the time until they docked in Liverpool. Lillian had traveled to Europe with a party of engineers before, and she knew full well that the week would be spent in shuffleboard and deck tennis and invitations to dine at the captain's table. This time, however, she wanted no part of it.[1]

As the S.S. *Scythia* slowly pulled out of New York harbor, Lillian thought over the events of the last six days and how much had changed. The previous Friday, June 13, had been a day of celebration for her and for her husband Frank, for that was when their sixteen-year-old daughter Ernestine graduated from Montclair High School. Like most of her brothers and sisters, Ernestine had skipped a grade: her father, Frank Bunker Gilbreth, believed that there was no need for *his* children to be held back by a school system geared to "ordinary" children with ordinary parents. He was bursting with pride as the second of his large brood graduated. Everyone except the eldest daughter was there; Anne was in the middle of her sophomore exams at Smith College, more than a hundred miles away. The rest of the children, however, turned out in force. Next in line was fourteen-year-old Martha, then Frank Jr., who was thirteen, followed by eleven-year-old Bill, ten-year-old Lill, seven-year-old Fred, Dan, who was six, Jack, who was five, Bob, who was nearly four, and the baby, two-year-old Jane.

The Gilbreths' big old house in Montclair, New Jersey, was fuller than ever. Aunt Jane Bunker, Frank Gilbreth's dentist cousin, had come from Brooklyn specially for the great event, and some of the children had doubled up to give her a bedroom. Tom Grieves, the man-of-all-work, who was never without a cigarette drooping from his lips, was complaining more than usual: "Lincoln freed the slaves, all but one, all but one," he liked to mutter while he dropped ash into whatever dish he was helping Mrs. Cunningham, the cook, prepare.

There was a celebratory tea after the commencement exercises with ice cream all around, but Frank Gilbreth left early to attend a meeting. He drove his big Pierce Arrow car down to the Lackawanna Railroad station, a mile or so from the house, and took the train into New York City, half an hour away. He felt he had to go to this meeting, the final planning session before he, Lillian, and the other engineers set sail for the Prague International Management Conference (PIMCO). Frank was one of the prime movers for this conference and had been working on it for more than two years.[2]

Frank was not his usual ebullient self at the meeting; one of his engineering friends recalled thinking that he seemed worn out and offered to carry his bulging briefcase to the taxi. "Later I wished I had insisted," Charles Lytle wrote, adding, "Perhaps I was his last friend to see him alive."[3] Nevertheless, Frank arrived home safely, and rejoined Ernestine's graduation celebrations.

The next day, Saturday, Lillian was up early, as usual: unlike her husband, who liked to work till all hours of the night, she was a morning person. When Frank was finally up and about, he decided to return to New York to collect the visas and do some last-minute shopping. Lillian was arranging some syringa she had picked earlier that morning for Ernestine to take to her class day. Frank walked through the hall, remarking that the flowers looked like a funeral bouquet, then left for the station. A little while later the telephone rang. It was Frank to say that he had missed the train "by a good many minutes." Lillian replied, "Never mind. It must be almost time for the next one," to which he said, "Good old optimist!" Frank then confessed that he had left without the passports and asked Lillian to check if they were in his desk, telling her, "I'll wait." She went to look for them, but when she returned there was no one on the line, so she assumed he had gone on the next train. An hour or so later a police officer arrived and broke the terrible news to Lillian: Frank was dead. He had collapsed in the phone booth at the Lackawanna Railroad station, and by the time his doctor arrived there was nothing to be done. He was only fifty-five years old.[4]

Lillian had feared for several years that this might happen. Frank had been suffering from heart disease since 1919, but it was, nonetheless, a terrible shock. She bore it in numbed silence. Ernestine remembers, "I was just standing there, ready for my class day. And mother didn't cry at all." Martha and Lill were in Montclair shopping; a neighbor was dispatched to find them and bring them home. Frank Jr. and Bill were playing baseball and had to be told. The younger children were playing in the yard; after they were told, six-year-old Dan sat on the front steps of the house sobbing, "My daddy's dead."[5]

Lillian tried to console herself with the thought that his last words had probably been when he said to her, "I'll wait," and that as Frank died "without pain and without even knowing he was going," this was "the One Best Way." There was, however, little time for reflection; relatives and colleagues had to be telephoned. The next few days passed in a blur, as telegrams and letters arrived and the house filled with people and flowers. Anne boarded the next train home from Northampton, exams abandoned. Anne Gilbreth Cross, Frank's elder sister, came down from Providence, where she ran a music school, and Lillian's aunt, Dr. Lillian Powers, a Freudian psychoanalyst, arrived with her husband from Westchester County.[6]

Through all the chaos Lillian remained almost unnaturally calm. She telephoned her California relatives about Frank's death, but followed the call almost immediately with a cable telling them not to come to the funeral; she had decided to go to the PIMCO meeting in Europe as planned, so she wanted to hold the funeral as soon as possible. The delay while her parents, brothers, and sisters made the long transcontinental train journey would make it impossible for her to sail with the rest of the engineering group.

Lillian would not be going simply as Frank's widow, but as an industrial engineer in her own right. The Gilbreths had had a professional as well as a private partnership, though in public, at least, Lillian tended to downplay her own contributions. On her way to the boat—the only time she could make for an interview—she told a young woman journalist how blessed she felt to have known Frank: "I have had more in twenty years with Frank than any other woman I have known has had in twice that time," she said.[7] Her statement was nothing less than the truth. Her husband had expected a great deal of her. She had borne more children, done more work, and shouldered more

responsibility than most women of her generation, or indeed of any generation, and by the early 1920s she had become a celebrity for the way she combined motherhood and a career. Now that Frank was dead, she felt both
compelled and able to carry on their work alone.

The ship was not due to sail for five days; in the meantime, Lillian busied
herself carrying out Frank's wishes. He wanted his brain to go to the Harvard
Medical Museum. Four years earlier he had taken several of the children to
the psychiatric hospital in Boston where his old friend and former summer
school student Dr. Myrtelle Canavan worked. Ernestine, who was twelve at
the time, had gazed with fascination at a row of jars with brains preserved in
formaldehyde, and Frank had told her, "One day my brain will be in one of
those jars." Dr. Canavan quickly conducted an autopsy, which revealed that
Frank had died of arterial sclerosis.[8]

Later that evening the funeral directors brought Frank's body home. They
had dressed him in his major's uniform and carefully carried the open coffin
into the family living room. It seemed incongruous, somehow, that he was
lying there so quietly in the midst of the bookcases and armchairs where the
family had spent so many hours reading and talking and discussing. Frank
had been a large, noisy man, the life and soul of every occasion; now he was
silent. His tranquility was, however, in marked contrast to the weather. It had
been a hot summer's day and as if to underline the drama of his death, the return of Frank's body was greeted by a violent thunderstorm. Lillian remembered, "In spite of everything that had happened, the wonderful, beautiful
and startling electrical display held them spell-bound. Finally, small Bill
spoke up and said, 'Gee, I'm sure that daddy is there! Isn't it exactly like him?'
and everyone agreed that he was there, perhaps participating and certainly
enjoying."[9]

Frank's funeral took place at 2:30 P.M. on Sunday, June 15, 1924, only a
day after his death. He had served in World War I and the local American Le-
gion post helped arrange the service; his simple coffin was now draped with
an American flag. He and Lillian had talked about their funeral arrangements; she knew that he wanted a military tone to his funeral, but no flowers,
no music, and no mourning, and he wanted her to help the children feel "that
Death was as simple as Birth and as natural."[10]

Ernestine sat next to her spinster Moller great-aunts who were dressed in
rustling black taffeta. One of them said, "Well, what is poor Lillie going to
do now? This is going to be dreadful for her." The Moller aunts were in a position to help out, for they had inherited all of Lillian's father's money when
he died eleven months earlier. William Moller had made a small fortune in his
California hardware business, but reasoned that since Lillian had a wealthy
husband and his other eight children were well provided for in his wife's will,

the money he had inherited from his own parents should help his two unmarried sisters. Tillie and Hansie Moller did not, however, return the compliment to their widowed niece. Ernestine believes they disapproved of the Gilbreths: "I think they thought we were gypsies or something." Relations became very strained over the next few years as Lillian struggled to pay eleven college tuitions while the aunts lived in luxury just down the road.[11]

Frank had wanted to be cremated and Lillian carried out his wishes, though with a slight amendment; he had wanted his ashes scattered on Eagle Rock, near their home, but Lillian decided that this might upset the children, who often played there. She chose to return his ashes to the water—he loved sailing—and finally, accompanied only by her aunt and her sister-in-law, she scattered Frank's remains in the Hudson River.[12]

After rejecting her aunt's offer of psychotherapy, Lillian called a family council. Her four eldest children were there. Two of them, Ernestine and Frank Jr., wrote about this meeting more than twenty years later in their humorous family memoir *Cheaper by the Dozen*. They portray a very determined mother announcing that she wanted to go to the European conferences and give the speeches Frank had planned to make in London and Prague. "I think that's the way your father wants it," she added. "But the decision is up to you." More recently, Ernestine stressed her mother's clever management of the situation. "I think we had a sense of very great value that we had helped her to do it. You see, she was so smart, handling us. We had a vote which made this possible."[13]

Lillian wanted to continue with the industrial engineering work she and Frank had been doing for the last dozen years, and the children wanted to help her do so. Lillian had several reasons for this plan. Frank had not left much money; the large consulting fees he and Lillian earned went to keeping the house and family, and any excess was poured back into new equipment. She needed to make enough to keep the family together and see all the children through college; in addition, she wanted the Gilbreth work in motion study analysis to continue under her name rather than be buried under other branches of industrial engineering. She was still smarting from a dispute between Frank and Frederick Winslow Taylor, the so-called father of scientific management, and although Taylor had been dead for nine years, some of his followers would be only too pleased if the Gilbreths' unique contribution was allowed to disappear. She also wanted to expand her and Frank's research into what was later called ergonomics, but what she called "Fatigue Elimination." This was the part she really enjoyed, even though for public consumption she modestly categorized it as "Frank's research."[14]

These goals may do much to explain Lillian's decision to go to Europe in June 1924. In so doing she informed the engineering profession that she intended to continue the Gilbreth work; she also reassured the international community that she was fully competent to speak for "The One Best Way." The support of these two groups would do much for her continued financial success and thereby the children's well-being. Thus, what seemed the most extraordinary decision of Lillian's life may have been a rational choice. She had been intending to go to Europe anyway, she had no other jobs lined up for the next two months, and she needed the distraction of work. Although she left her children to fend for themselves less than a week after their father's death, their accounts of the period do not reproach their mother for not being there; they stress instead their own resilience.

And resilient they seem to have been. Unlike the five children of Eleanor Roosevelt, a contemporary working mother, who among them had nineteen marriages, the eleven Gilbreth children had only twelve; unlike the Roosevelts, they never voiced public anger at parental neglect. Numerous press accounts reported Lillian's decision to go to Europe; none of them suggested that she was in any way mistreating her children. The *Providence Journal Bulletin* described her as "determined that her misfortune would neither keep her from the trip nor her husband's plans from their fruition," while the *New York World* noted that although she "sailed four days after he succumbed to attend power conference in his place," she still "fulfills all of her domestic duties most carefully."[15]

Part of the explanation for the children's determination and their subsequent success was the way they were brought up. Their parents encouraged them to be independent and cooperative at the same time, and they were very conscious that they were part of a family experiment in living and working together. The Gilbreths were practicing what the famous educator John Dewey had proposed a generation earlier. By participating in household activities the child would, believed Dewey, get "habits of industry, order and regard for the rights of others and the fundamental habit of subordinating his activities to the general interest of the household."[16]

The Gilbreth children all had regular household chores, and the older ones had responsibility for younger family members; in addition, they had all been roped in as research assistants on several motion study projects. One summer, for example, they turned their Nantucket holiday cottage into a laboratory where they experimented with methods of packing soap for Lever Brothers. Another year Frank filmed them picking blueberries on the Nantucket moors in order to find the "One Best Way" of doing so. As Lillian wrote soon after Frank died, she was determined that "the Quest must go on." The Gilbreths' "Quest" was twofold, a deliberate melding of work and family, to find the most efficient way of working and the best way of raising well-rounded children and have the two aims interact and assist each other.

Lillian believed that their effort to combine their work and family was still in the experimental stage and "the real value of such a Quest will be its effect on future generations."[17]

The future generation was put to the test much earlier than she had anticipated. Nineteen-year-old Anne took the children to the family's Nantucket cottage, helped by her slightly older cousin Carol Cross, while Tom Grieves and Mrs. Cunningham did most of the hard work. The chores were divided among the children, and a network of Nantucket friends was on hand if necessary. It had been planned as an experiment to see if their family system really worked. "It will be a test summer for everyone," Lillian wrote. "Can the children, with the help and counsel provided, show themselves capable of managing the summer and making a success of it?" The children were certainly prepared to try, even though the circumstances were so drastically changed, and Lillian's desire to carry on was reinforced by the support of some of her engineering colleagues. The Society of Industrial Engineers sent her a telegram "expressing the hope that she would carry on the work in which she had so ably assisted her husband" and transferred Frank's credentials to her, making her chairman of their delegation to PIMCO.[18]

Thus, on Thursday, June 19, 1924, only five days after Frank's death, Lillian left her children in Montclair. Sitting upright and still in the taxi, not crying, or at least not while her children could see, Lillian must have reflected on how much more testing the summer would be than they had planned. Some of her children waved good-bye as the taxi crunched down the gravel drive, but she insisted that none of them go to the Lackawanna Railroad station to see her off; it would have been too painful, as it was there that Frank had suffered his fatal heart attack the previous Saturday. As if it was not enough to leave her eleven fatherless children, eight of them were sick in bed. Many years later, Lillian described their illness as a welcome distraction during the immediate aftermath of Frank's death. "Perhaps it was fortunate," she later wrote, "that the children were coming down with a combination of measles and chicken pox and that the whole household procedure had to be adapted to their needs."[19]

Four of the children developed chicken pox on the day of the funeral and two more joined in the next day. On June 17 toddlers Bob and Jane also broke out in spots, and almost as soon as Lillian was out of the house they also contracted measles. (Six of the older children had had measles four years earlier, causing, according to the family doctor, a significant blip in the Essex County public health statistics.) The doctor came and said there was no real danger, but then Fred came down with measles. Anne insisted that her mother not be told; there was nothing she could do anyway, two days out in the Atlantic. Instead Anne wrote cheery letters to Lillian, describing imaginary picnics.

Lillian had never traveled alone; this time, needing company and not wanting to waste a steamer ticket, she had invited Elizabeth (Pos) Sanders, a school friend of her eldest daughter, to join her. When Lillian got to the boat, however, she told her young traveling companion that she wanted to be alone for a while.

Lillian Gilbreth was a most unusual engineer; before she met Frank, she had started a doctoral program in English literature, and at difficult moments she tended to retire to her room and compose a sonnet. It is, perhaps, a fitting style for so controlled a woman; the sonnet is the most disciplined form of poetry but at the same time can be the most passionate. Lillian described the plans she and Frank had made "to travel hand in hand" and her determination to carry on after his death. The poem concludes:

> Go on, My Dear, I shall not faint or fall,
> I cannot know, but I can sense your way
> God speed! You must not swerve or wait for me.[20]

It would be a difficult and painful journey, but now nothing could upset her, because, as her children wrote, "the thing that mattered most had been upset." They never saw her cry again.[21]

PART II

Dear Lillie Was Always a Remarkable Person

We can't say we have ever been surprised
at her becoming famous. We always knew, even as children,
that dear Lillie was a remarkable person.

Two of Lillian's sisters, interviewed in the *Oakland Tribune*
(1949)

2   Once Upon a Time

*"Once upon a time" two couples met each
other on a steamer crossing the Atlantic. All four
people had been born in Germany; it was the thrill
of each summer, now they were middle-aged
and prosperous, to go back home.*

Lillian Moller Gilbreth describing her grandparents,
As I Remember (1998)

LILLIAN MOLLER GILBRETH was sixty-three years old when she wrote her memoir (though it had to wait nearly sixty years for publication). Frank had been dead for seventeen years and her children were all married or in college. Her husband had been at the center of her life for twenty years and he cast a long shadow, but by 1941 it seemed as if she wanted to show that she had a life before she met Frank and that she was not merely his creation.

Lillie Evelyn Moller was born in her parents' house in Oakland, California, on May 24, 1878. (She changed her name to Lillian when she was a student, believing it sounded more dignified.) She met Frank Gilbreth twenty-five years later, in late June 1903, and during that quarter century she had changed from a nervous and cosseted baby into an intelligent and accomplished young woman, able and willing to challenge her parents' expectations. She was exceptionally well educated for her class and her time; she also had well-formed opinions. Most of all, she was seeking what people at the turn of the twentieth century called "the strenuous life."

Lillian's childhood and her intellectual development are unusually well documented. Her mother wrote chatty letters to her younger sister Lillie (the young Lillie's godmother) away at boarding school, and Lillian later wrote at length about her education. She began her memoir with the time-hallowed phrase "Once upon a time," as if to suggest that her childhood was like a fairy

tale. In some ways it was, as her family was wealthy and she grew up surrounded by great material comfort. A perfect childhood is rare, however, and
though Lillie was born with the proverbial silver spoon in her mouth, she described that silver spoon as belonging to a very nervous young person, subject to frequent nightmares and fears about death. The adult Lillian was very
much in control of her emotions, but she wanted to present a very different
picture of her childhood. Much of her nervousness was connected with the
dynamics within her family. Relations between her father and mother and between her parents and her grandparents were often strained and her mother
was often ill—or at least claimed to be.

In May 1879, Annie Delger Moller celebrated Lillie's first birthday in
style, but the only guests were the baby's father and two Japanese servants.
The baby's Delger grandparents were on their way to Europe, escorting their
depressed youngest daughter Lillie (who eventually became the Freudian psychoanalyst Dr. Lillian Powers) to boarding school in Germany. Her never-
mentioned and disowned Aunt Matilda was in Japan, where she had eloped
with an English sea captain. Her Uncle Ed was at Harvard, doing anything
but studying. The Moller grandparents were three thousand miles away in
New York, missing their son, the baby's father, who was having business
problems, while Lillie's mother hated being financially dependent on her parents. It is somehow not surprising that the day ended in tears.[1]

Annie's relationship with her parents was complex; though she was close
to her mother, a buxom, friendly countrywoman, she frequently clashed
with her father. Frederick Delger, tall, black-bearded, and stern, was a self-
made man. A bootmaker by trade, his fortune came from real estate specu-
lation. Delger was born in Saxony in 1822; he never lost his thick German accent and was far from comfortable speaking in English. He emigrated to
New York in 1847, where he met and married his equally shrewd German-
born wife, Ernestine. Three years later they sailed to San Francisco with their
infant daughter Matilda, with only one dollar to their name, or at least that
was the family story. Delger made his fortune quickly. In gold rush California it was easier to get rich by supplying the needs of the miners than by pan-
ning for gold, and after picks and shovels the great need was for sturdy work
clothes and strong boots. Levi Strauss supplied the former and Frederick Delger the latter. Local craftsmen could not meet the demand for footwear, so
Delger invested his savings in a consignment of eastern factory-made boots,
which he sold at a handsome profit. He then invested in land, which was ap-
preciating fast, and moved into real estate development full time. In 1860 he
purchased ten acres in what soon became downtown Oakland and moved
there with his young family. Oakland was quiet in those days and almost suburban compared with the hustle of San Francisco. It seemed a good place to

bring up a family. It was also a good opportunity to become a big fish in a small pond.[2]

By the time Lillie knew her grandfather he owned one of the grandest houses in Oakland—with its magnificent gardens it occupied practically the whole of a city block—and was reputed to be the town's first millionaire. When Delger died in 1897 the local newspaper estimated that the "deceased capitalist" had left an estate worth an incredible "three and a half million dollars, likely to be more rather than less."[3]

The Delgers gave their four children the best education that money could buy, though this education was very gender specific. While Edward was prepared for Harvard and the law, the three girls were taught how to be ladies. Despite their firmly Lutheran background, they went to convent schools. The nuns taught Annie to sing, play the piano and the harp, speak and write "a cultured English," read "discriminatingly," and sew. It is clear from the memories of Annie's children and grandchildren that she also became expert in getting others to do exactly as she wanted, without appearing anything less than feminine.[4]

After school there was little for the Delger girls to do but wait for a suitable man to propose marriage. Matilda, the eldest daughter, rebelled in her late teens and eloped, but Annie was not quite so bold. She left the convent soon after Matilda's elopement, but she hated being at home, where the atmosphere was grim and silent. Annie was a very beautiful seventeen-year-old, tiny, buxom, with brown curls cascading down her back, but to her horror she was supervised night and day. She was not even allowed into the garden unless her mother was with her. Despite, or perhaps because of, her parents' watchfulness, Annie developed a "crush" on a local boy, so her parents decided to send her to finishing school in Germany to keep her out of harm's way.

The Delgers escorted her there themselves, and before setting sail for Europe they spent a few days in New York where they called on the Mollers, a German couple they had met on a previous transatlantic voyage. John Moller was the head of the American branch of the family's sugar refining business, and he and his wife lived in quiet luxury on Thirty-seventh Street, just around the corner from Charles Tiffany's store. Although both couples were wealthy, the Mollers came from a moneyed background; there were considerable class differences between them, especially in the way the women dressed, and the Delgers seemed very nouveau riche in comparison.[5]

Annie was silent, perhaps a little overwhelmed, when a maid showed them into the Mollers' parlor. She did not, however, need to say much. Twenty-six-year-old William Moller, son and heir to the family fortune, took one look at her and fell in love at once, or so he always claimed. Annie looked at him and saw a tall, trim, sandy-haired young man with a quiet smile. Flattered by his attentions, Annie quickly realized that William Moller provided a golden opportunity to escape from her father. He was wealthy, he was German, their parents already knew and liked each other, and, best of all, his work and his home were three thousand miles away from California.[6]

Despite the nine-year difference in age, the parents approved of William's plan to marry Annie. The wedding did not, however, take place right away; Annie spent the next year at finishing school, though she was more interested in her trousseau than in German grammar. Her mother, having been denied the pleasure of shopping for her eldest daughter's wedding, spared no expense and purchased down quilts, huge quantities of linens onto which tiny initials were sewn, enough clothes to last for years, and so much silk that a whole bolt was left over and was handed down in the family for generations. Finally, on May 21, 1873, the young couple was married in a simple ceremony at a Lutheran church in Hamburg. Annie was eighteen-and-a-half years old and William was twenty-eight. It was a very Moller wedding. Though Annie's parents were there during their annual visit to Germany, the rest of the guests were Mollers, whose German links were very strong. One of them, cousin George, even joined the newlyweds on their honeymoon.[7]

Annie was already pregnant when she and William returned to New York in the early fall of 1873 and moved into a suite of rooms in the Moller house. Living there suited her husband very well: there was little change in his life, as he returned to his much-loved job in the sugar refinery and saw his parents every night at dinner. Annie, on the other hand, had nothing to do and she was lonely and bored. After shivering throughout the New York winter, in April 1874 she gave birth to her first child, whom she named Anna Adelaide (called Addie for short), after her mother-in-law. At last Annie had a role in the Moller household. Annie's baby was welcomed as one more addition to the family, which already included five young children. William's youngest sisters, Tillie and Hansie, who became the Moller aunts who inherited all his money, were very young, three years and one year old, respectively. They were late babies, born when their mother was in her forties, and became the family pets, loved and teased by their elder brother. In addition, William's sister Lizzie Moller Fliedner lived with her husband and three young children on the fourth floor.[8]

The heat of a nineteenth-century New York summer was, however, hard on babies, and the Moller children suffered along with the children in the tenements. Annie was slow to recover from childbirth, and both she and Addie suffered from gastric problems as the summer wore on. William took mother and baby out of town to Dobbs Ferry, hoping to find some relief from the heat, but it was useless: Addie died on August 15, 1874, at the age of four months. Annie was inconsolable and spent most of her waking hours at the baby's graveside at the Green-Wood Cemetery in Brooklyn. Her worried husband consulted the best doctors in New York, one of whom suggested that a change of climate might do her good. William agreed to take her to California for a visit, but once there she told him she wanted to stay. This put William in a difficult situation. If he wanted the marriage to continue, he would have to uproot himself and make his life where his wife could be happy. Reluctantly he sold his share in the refinery and invested in a plumber's store in Oakland. His family was sad to see him leave New York. His father mourned the loss of his only son and business partner, his mother feared she would rarely see him again, and his little sisters cried at the thought of his going so far away. William Moller missed New York, but he seldom complained, and despite his reservations, he prospered. He was a good accountant and a well-run builders' supply business was almost bound to do well, given the population growth in the Bay Area.[9]

Despite her husband's sacrifice, Annie was not completely happy. Nor did her return to California improve her relationship with her father. Her discontent and her related illness were among the formative influences on her children, especially on Lillian, who grew up terrified of her grandfather, determined never to let illness prevent her from working and searching for a more forceful husband than her father proved himself to be—although she never said so, or at least in not so many words. In the meantime, however, Lillie had what appeared, on the surface at least, to be a charmed childhood. For her first two years she was loved and cosseted by two doting parents. Lillie was very fond of her father, despite what she later saw as his almost feminine submission to his Delger relatives. He was a gentle and loving parent, and as his relationship with his in-laws deteriorated, he was to find much consolation in his children.[10]

Annie Moller spent a lot of time with baby Lillie, although she had plenty of servants. She didn't want to lose her as she had lost Addie. Weeks after Lillie's first birthday Annie was still nursing her and finding weaning very difficult, and both mother and baby shed bitter tears before the process was completed. Lillie was finally weaned in mid-July at the age of fourteen months; the next baby, Gertie, was conceived six weeks later.

Lillie was a bright little girl and an early talker. She slept in a cot in Annie and William Moller's bedroom, and one morning she woke her astonished parents with a loud rendition of "Jesus Loves Me." It would seem her father was less than delighted by the recital and scolded Annie, who was hard-pressed to convince him that Lillie had picked it up on her own. Even if he was unhappy about being awakened at dawn by a hymn-singing toddler, William Moller was nevertheless a conscientious father. Sometimes he took Lillie into town with him; they either went to his shop or simply to buy a Sunday paper. Sometimes they went on family outings; one day, just before Lillie's first birthday, William hired a horse and buggy. The three of them went for a drive, with Lillie holding the reins of the quiet old horse part of the time. Lillie was not an easy child, however, and when she tired she was often fractious, so this outing came to an abrupt end.

Lillie's second year was peaceful, partly because the Delger grandparents were away. Things started badly, however, for Annie, who was unwell. She called in Li Po Tai, one of the best-known Chinese doctors in San Francisco, and spent forty dollars a month on medicines from him. To put that amount in some kind of perspective, Annie rented out a suite of rooms in one of the buildings her father had given her as a wedding gift to a (Western) doctor for fifty dollars a month and felt very generous when she raised her two Japanese servants' wages from fifteen to twenty dollars a month between them. Annie continued to use Dr. Li for many years, as did her father and her brother; she also took Lillie to him from time to time. When her daughter was three, Annie asked Dr. Li to try to cure her "nervousness," and when Lillie had a stomach upset that the family doctor seemed unable to cure, Annie sent her husband over to San Francisco to get medicines from Li Po Tai.

Lillian recalled being fascinated by Chinatown. Holding tight to her mother's hand and surrounded by mysterious smells and unfamiliar noises, she would climb up some narrow stairs into a small room where she and her mother came face to face with the famous Dr. Li. He was tiny and wrinkled and seemed to the young Lillie as old as the hills. She had a strong visual memory, describing his black gown and cap and his long queue tied with a black silk cord; she also remembered the veins on his hands and his long painted nails. He would feel the pulses in Annie's wrist, study her face and look her up and down. After a few moments of silent thought he would write something in elegant Chinese letters on a piece of rice paper, hand it to an assistant, bow, and leave the room. Minutes later the assistant returned with some flat packages containing dried leaves, herbs, licorice, and other roots that Annie boiled up and drank when they got home. It was probably neither adventurousness nor desperation that persuaded Annie to rely on Dr. Li. Licorice is still given for "womb problems," which she claimed to have had since getting out of bed too soon after the birth of Addie. Drinking an herbal remedy was much less unpleasant and at least as effective as some of the mainstream treatments for menstrual difficulties available at that time.[11]

Annie Moller liked to see herself as delicate and she described a variety of symptoms but was convinced that Li Po Tai's medicines helped. Her letters are full of complaints about feeling unwell and tiring at the slightest effort. She may have suffered from migraines; sometimes she claimed her eyes were weak and that she could hardly see. Often she complained of exhaustion. She spent a week in bed after putting together a parcel of commissions for Matilda in Japan (a correspondence that was carried on behind their father's back). A few days later, however, she was up and about, directing the gardener and agitating for her husband to take her to the Oakland fair and the races, which he did. She could and did exert herself when she wanted; one July day in 1879 she and her friend Mrs. Buck put up vast quantities of red currant jelly (forty-six jars, to be precise), then rewarded themselves with chocolate cake and a chat.

In matters of health Annie Moller was typical of her class and her time: many nineteenth-century middle-class women believed they were unwell. Sometimes their problems were real, but elements of this Victorian epidemic of ill health resulted from the frustrations felt by women who, like Annie, had too little to do. As men went "out" to work, their wives found themselves restricted to the so-called separate sphere of home and childbearing. Some women enjoyed this and devoted themselves to raising large families, but others, consciously or unconsciously, tried to avoid the danger and discomfort of repeated pregnancies by claiming ill health and (metaphorically) closing the bedroom door. Annie's maladies had a profound effect on her whole family, as her husband became overprotective and her eldest daughter suffered from anxiety bordering on neurosis. Lillian recalled that her father was so concerned that his wife might become ill that he "waited on her by inches," and if she was late returning from a call he would pace restlessly up and down the floor, "unaware that Lillie thought he feared Mama was dead." Lillian later wrote that she lived under the constant fear of losing her mother. If Annie went to call on Grandma Delger, an almost daily occurrence, Lillian recalled that she waited at the garden gate "in agony if she was delayed." This was Lillie's short-term reaction to her mother's illness; her long-term response was to enjoy robust health for most of her life and avoid inactivity at all costs.[12]

In 1879 Annie decided to build a new house. She bought a plot of land at Nineteenth and Grove Streets from her father and planned to pay him off in installments from her rents on the properties he had given her as part of her dowry. The Mollers moved in six months later, in May 1880, two weeks before Lillie's second birthday and three weeks before the birth of Annie's next child. Although Annie described it as a "cottage," it was a twelve-room house.

Meanwhile, Annie was having servant problems: like many late Victorians, her letters are full of complaints about the "help." Her domestic arrangements were a little unusual. For Lillie's first two years the live-in couple were Japanese: Tony, a nursemaid, and Stozzy, her husband, who did everything else, even the cooking. At first everything went well and Tony and baby

Lillie were inseparable, but there was an argument and the Japanese couple left suddenly, just before Gertie was born. Lillie heartily disliked the new Irish nursemaid her mother hired and reacted by clinging to her mother's skirts. Within a week the nursemaid had been told to pack her bags and a new one, by the name of Katie, was hired. Katie lasted only four days, but her replacement, Julia McCarthy, came and stayed. Lillian remembered this as a great misfortune, for the new nursemaid was hired at the same time as the new baby was born, and Julia always seemed to regard that baby as her special charge.

The birth of Gertrude Wilhemina Moller on June 3, 1880, just ten days after her elder sister's second birthday, was a great blow to Lillie. As soon as her initial curiosity about the baby was satisfied, she became even more demanding of attention than before. Annie reported that Lillie was into all kinds of mischief. She was a great climber; her mother discovered her clambering onto a bureau and a hat stand and was scared to death that she might fall. Lillie had been the center of attention for the first two years of her life, but the arrival of Gertie changed all that. Her jealousy was compounded by the servant upheavals and probably by some parental insensitivity. Annie remarked rather casually in August that she had sent Lillie's puppy away when the baby was due and now, two months later, when it was brought back, it was no longer a fluffy little creature but a long-legged dog. A little later she forgot to cover Lillie's guinea pigs one frosty night and they froze to death. We can only guess how Lillie might have felt.[13]

Lillie sat for a portrait in September 1880 when Gertie was three months old. Photography was a slow process in those days; the subject had to sit still for a minute or more while the plate was exposed; nevertheless, two-year-old Lillie looks unusually solemn and serious. Perched on a fringed velvet chair with her hair scraped up into a little white bow, she is staring into the middle distance; there is a slight pout, a turning down of the mouth, and she does not look very happy. A photograph taken a year later shows a more tranquil, smiling Lillie. Perhaps she was used to having Gertie around by this time; perhaps the photographer was better with children. In later years Lillian tended not to dwell on discord and unpleasantness, but she admitted that she and Gertie often disagreed, and there were years of squabbles over territory and possessions.[14]

It also rankled that everyone gushed over Gertie's beauty, though Lillie was far from plain; numerous photographs show her regular features, firm chin, and thoughtful eyes. Lillian claimed that she thought herself unattractive and for this reason decided she had to excel at school. "If I couldn't be pretty, then instead I could be clever," she wrote. By perpetuating the myth that one could not be pretty and clever and that cleverness was somehow a substitute for more traditional feminine attributes, Lillian justified to herself her rejection of much of what her mother and her sisters stood for.[15]

Lillie's Auntie Brown was everything her mother was not. Determined, energetic, forceful, she and her daughters provided young Lillie with a strenuous alternative to her neurasthenic and perpetually pregnant mother. Lillian was three years old when she first met her Auntie Brown, who returned from Japan after two tragic accidents: the death of a five-year-old son, followed six months later by the death of her husband. Matilda Brown gathered up her five surviving children, her possessions, and the embalmed body of her husband and took the first steamer back to Oakland. A letter arrived by a faster boat giving the family in California less than a week's notice of their arrival. Lillian remembered her mother rushing around, buying and borrowing beds and directing the servants to prepare for the arrival of six extra people. Shortly before the Browns' boat was due to dock, however, another letter arrived, saying that all the children had developed whooping cough. Annie agonized over what to do, but for once in his life William Moller was bold and decisive. "Of course they must come!" he declared. "Perhaps the Lord will keep Lillie and Gertie from catching it!" Annie was less sanguine; rather morbidly she took Lillie and Gertie to the photographer's, explaining that she was so worried about their dying of whooping cough that she needed to have their pictures taken. There was, however, little else she could do, as her father was still furious with his eldest daughter and would not allow her in his house.[16]

When the great day finally arrived, Lillian stayed at home looking through the window while her mother and father went down to the dock. Annie always insisted her daughters be well dressed, and Lillie had a little blue cashmere cloak trimmed with white lace, which always attracted admiring glances from other mothers. On this particular day she wore a white embroidered dress, stiff with starch, white stockings, and shiny kid shoes. Her fine straight hair had been braided the night before and now "stood up in a pleasing fuzz" topped by a pale blue ribbon. Eventually the carriages drew up outside the Mollers' house, and as Lillie watched a small woman and five young children entered the house. Either the Lord—or the long sea voyage from Japan—ensured that the Browns were no longer infectious when they arrived in Oakland, but nevertheless they whooped alarmingly.[17]

Over the next few weeks Lillie got to know her cousins. Tillie, the eldest, was the dependable one who wanted to help her mother. Annie Florence was bookish and as time went on she often read aloud to Lillie. The youngest daughter, Elsie, became Lillie's closest friend: they were nearly the same age and they played for hours in the Mollers' yard. Sometimes they played house with their dolls, but on other days the sloping lawn was simply too tempting and they would roll over and over, squealing with delight.[18]

The Mollers' family grew steadily, as did Lillie's responsibilities, in a pattern she was to follow with her own children. Ernestine, born when Lillie was four years old, soon followed Gertie. Another two years passed and then Elinor Matilda was born. She soon became her father's pet, making Lillie extremely jealous. The fifth Moller daughter (or sixth, if Addie is included), Josephine Elizabeth, was born in 1886, three weeks after Lillie's eighth birthday. Josie became Lillie's favorite sister, as well as her special responsibility, and she became closer to Josie than to any of her other siblings. Mabel, the last of the Moller girls, was born in 1888, when Lillie was ten.[19]

The Mollers were no different from most families, then and now. They wanted a son, a child who could continue the "family name." With six girls, William Moller may have thought his chances of having a son were slim, but according to his daughter, "he never acted disappointed as the babies came, or as if he had one girl too many." Nevertheless, when Mabel was three years old Annie finally gave birth to a boy. He was named Frederick John after his grandfathers. He looked like his mother and became "everyone's idol." Lillie was thirteen years old by this time and her mother marked the event by taking personal charge of little Frederick, handing responsibility for the two youngest girls to their eldest sisters. Lillian recalled that her mother asked her and Gertie to come into her room and said, "Girls, I shall be very busy with this little brother. I am giving Josie to Lillie and Mabel to Gertie, to help bring up. You shall each have a room and a small crib next to your bed for your little sister. Shall you like that?" Lillian commented, "And, of course, they did."[20]

A few months before Frederick's birth the Mollers had moved to a grand seven-bedroom mansion on Prospect Avenue, atop "Lawyer's Hill." The new house was a jumble of architectural styles. Steps led up to a Greek-pedimented porch, while on the second and third floors bays, towers, and turrets competed for attention. It was, however, very much to the taste of the 1890s: a local newspaper thought it was "probably the most elegant home in this city" and that Mr. Moller must be "Oakland's happiest man." The house boasted a passenger elevator and "other up-to-date conveniences" and an extensive garden. There was also a staff of Chinese cooks, maids, and gardeners to see that all ran smoothly.[21]

The large bedroom that Lillie and Josie shared for the next dozen years, until Lillie finally left home to marry, had a big bay window and a tower. There was a screened-off washstand, a large closet, bookcases, and a worktable. Lillie read, studied, and sometimes daydreamed as she sat at the table looking out over the Bay. She did not, however, have unlimited time for studying or for daydreaming, as her mother continued to produce babies. Lillie's responsibilities extended to Billy Jr., who was born in June 1895. He was a pale, delicate baby and often woke in the night, crying pitifully, and fourteen-year-old Lillie, who was in high school by this time, would get up to walk with him or cuddle him until he was ready to sleep. The last Moller child, Frank, was born when Lillie was a college freshman, but, although she was still living at home, she had less to do with him. Annie's repeated pregnancies exerted a cost on the family, notably on Lillie, who was trained to take on family responsibilities. What female contemporaries such as the social reformer Jane Addams knew (and rejected) as the "family claim" was instilled into Lillie Moller from a very early age.[22]

In her memoir, Lillian described herself as "a shy child" who was "easily frightened," adding that she entered her teens taking "a burden of fear with her, carefully secreted, but real and at times shattering." Her mother's frequent confinements contributed to Lillie's nervousness, for however large the house, Lillie was never out of earshot of her mother's bedroom. She could see doctors, nurses, and midwives coming and going and hear her mother's cries as the latest baby was born. Lillie suffered recurring nightmares and was unable to tell anyone what made her so afraid. Many of her nightmares concerned the death of her mother, herself, or loved ones.[23]

It is perhaps significant that several nightmares Lillian described were related to strong women in her family, namely her Aunt Lillie and Auntie Brown. Soon after her return from her German boarding school, Lillie Delger married Harry Trowbridge, an Oakland druggist. She bore two children, but in November 1888 her three-year-old daughter, Violette, died suddenly of "convulsions," and her death became part of another recurring nightmare for Lillie. Auntie Brown bustled over to the Mollers' house to tell the dreadful news and asked for some ribbon to put in Violette's hair. Annie Moller asked Lillie to give her the new hair ribbons she had not yet worn, promising to buy her some more. Sixty years later, Lillian recalled how much she loved those ribbons. She had only had them for a few days and kept them carefully rolled in her bureau. She remembered opening the drawer a dozen times a day, admiring them and feeling their silky smoothness. Very reluctantly, she gave them up. Then Auntie Brown suggested that Lillie go and see her dead cousin. Annie Moller demurred, saying that Lillie was still very young "and I hate to have her shocked." Auntie Brown was made of sterner stuff and replied, "She isn't too young to know what death is. Besides, I think Sister Lillie will be hurt if she doesn't go—after all, she is her God-child." So Lillie was taken to see her cousin lying in a white box, "so pale and stiff, so different, so fearsome." She was terrified; she "felt cold to her very soul and frightened." Then she saw her white ribbons in Violette's hair, a "never to be forgotten horror . . . a terrible sight. Never, so long as she lived, could she see such ribbons without a shudder."[24]

Violette was buried in Mountain View, one of the most beautiful cemeteries in America. Laid out on a hillside by Frederick Law Olmsted, already famous for his work in New York's Central Park, it commanded a view over Oakland and across the shimmering Bay to San Francisco. Frederick Delger had been one of the cemetery's founders back in 1863 and his Gothic mausoleum, complete with its spire and its stained glass window, stood at the crest of the hill, on what soon became known as Millionaires' Row. Violette was in good company, for the next plot contained the enormous rotunda of Charles Crocker, founder of the Southern Pacific Railroad and the Crocker Bank, and the Ghirardelli family, of chocolate fame, was nearby.[25]

Lillie was frightened of the living as well as the dead. She was terrified of the Mollers' gardener, Mr. Helke, whom she described as a "Prussian." One day he was planting a tree and young Lillie got in his way. After telling her several times to run along, he lost patience with her and threatened to bury her "in this hole." Seeing how frightened the child was he added, "And if you ever tell anyone, I'll surely do it." She never told anyone, but she had, she recalled, recurrent nightmares about being buried alive. The connections with the suffocating environment within the Moller family seem transparent. She was also frightened of her stern grandfather, who, despite his American fortune and his pride in his American citizenship, remained very German. The Mollers spoke English at home, but Delger insisted that his granddaughters should have German lessons. When he tested them they panicked: "We stammered and blushed and I'm afraid hung our heads and shivered 'til he said, 'Go to your grandmother.' Then we silently fled houseward."[26]

As an adult Lillian Gilbreth was inclined to see the bright side of almost everything, so the way she dwelt on her unhappiness when she wrote her memoirs is quite remarkable. Nevertheless, many of her childhood experiences *were* happy and in spite of her fear of her grandfather, she had fond memories of his house and garden, though she was careful to call when she knew he would be out. She remembered the wide, airy halls and high-ceilinged rooms filled with flowers and with pictures and furniture imported from Germany. There were mirrors in heavy gilt frames, stiff black sofas stuffed with horsehair, and wax flowers under glass domes. As an adult, Lillian tried to simplify her life, and having a house perpetually full of young children meant that the good china was put safely out of reach. As a child, however, she thought going to her grandmother's was better than going to a museum, because she was allowed to touch some beautiful things. She was particularly entranced by two Swiss music boxes: one was a simple gilt roll in an inlaid box, but the other she remembered as much larger with bells and little drums. Grandma also had a huge set of Meissen china, enough for twenty-four people to sit down for dinner, though they seldom did, for Frederick Delger hated entertaining.[27]

Lillian always loved flowers and her grandfather had a magnificent garden where he grew every variety of tree and shrub, flower and vegetable he could buy in California. One year he decided to buy plants in Europe, and thereafter each time he went to Germany he came back with "red beech, lillies [sic] of the valley, ferns" and even the soil to plant them in. The Delgers also kept a cow and Lillian remembered watching as her grandmother—still a countrywoman at heart—made cheese.[28]

For the most part, however, Lillian remembered being at home, for the Mollers kept themselves to themselves. Like many other wealthy late-nineteenth-century families, the parlor was the center of their life. It was filled (William Moller might have said "cluttered") with display cabinets for Annie's collections of china and Japanese lacquerware, of ivory and jade and Tiffany vases. The windows were covered by lace curtains, with heavy garnet-colored drapes over them; corners were filled with potted plants and vases of flowers picked in the garden. In the evenings the family gathered around the table, reading or knitting by the light of the green-shaded oil lamp.[29]

Despite the late-Victorian abundance of objects, the Mollers had an exceptionally tidy house. William Moller liked everything to be in its place; even the gardening tools, which shared space in the basement with the laundry and Lillie's tricycle, were kept neat and tidy by order of her meticulous father. Lillian depicted an almost neurotic love of order. Pictures had to be straight and window blinds had to be level. She recalled that her father "suffered even when all the shades were not drawn to exactly the same level and measured a housewife's efficiency by the evidence he saw as he passed their house." Annie also tried to teach Lillie neatness and how to care for clothes; she had to polish her mother's shoes and brush the dust from the hem of her skirts. Much later, Lillian wrote that she would "never care enough for clothes to house and care for them so carefully!" Her career in scientific management was, however, to display much of her father's attention to detail and love of order, though her own household regime was to be much more relaxed. Indifference to clothes and fashion is a recurrent theme in Lillian's memoirs; it may serve as a way of distancing herself from "female" preoccupations and, by implication, from her mother and sisters.[30]

Annie did not do much around the house: the Mollers always had plenty of servants. Lillian recalled that her mother was "never strong or well enough to do what the family needed done," so she seldom worked with her maids or the cook, as other women did. Annie had, however, plenty of energy for shopping. She sent Lillie on errands to the little stores around the corner on San Pablo Avenue and often took her on shopping expeditions in downtown Oakland. Occasionally they took the ferryboat *Oakland* across the Bay to San Francisco, a great treat. Lillian remembered the rainy days when she went downstairs with the carriages and wagons and watched the businessmen smoking and talking, and the sunny days when she sat on deck watching the forest of masts in San Francisco harbor growing nearer and larger. As the boat passed Alcatraz she would wonder if there were any mysterious prisoners like the Count of Monte Cristo lying forgotten in its cells, while she thought the cormorants drying out their wings on the rocks looked like broken umbrellas.[31]

Young Lillie's life was certainly not all fears and nightmares. One of her particular joys was travel, and she journeyed across America at least three times before she went to college. The first time was when she was six and she went with her parents to visit the Moller grandparents. She went east again when she was twelve and accompanied her father on a business trip to Boston. They stayed at the Parker House, a luxurious hotel just off Boston Common, and after his business was completed, they crossed the river to Cambridge to visit Harvard. After a train ride to Concord to see the homes of Louisa May Alcott and the New England poets, they continued their literary pilgrimage by riverboat down the Hudson, discussing Washington Irving and James Fenimore Cooper.

Lillie's third trip was in 1893, when she was fifteen and a school friend invited her to go with her and her father to the World's Fair in Chicago. Lillie was flattered to be asked, for Paula Rued was one of the most popular girls in the class. Lillie's hair was long at this time and she wore it braided and wound into a bun on her neck; photographs show her looking very serious, almost severe. Her cousin Elsie Brown, who sat behind her in class, loved to tease her by pulling out her hairpins, much to Lillie's embarrassment. Paula was never embarrassed. Earlier that year she had been very ill with a fever and had all her hair shaved off. Her mother had bought her a very lifelike wig, thinking this would make it easier for her daughter to return to school. But every time the teacher's back was turned Paula would take off her wig—to the great amusement of the class—then replace it before the teacher could discover the cause of the mirth. Lillian recalled being very impressed by such boldness.[32]

When they arrived in Chicago, Mr. Rued met with business colleagues while the girls paid their fifty-cent admission to the fair and toured the educational exhibits. As loyal Oaklanders they probably visited the California building, where they would have seen a statue of a medieval knight on horseback made entirely of prunes, which the official World's Fair brochure noted was "distinctly a unique departure in statuary."[33]

Given Lillian's later career in time and motion study, it would be fitting if she had bought *The Time-Saver*, a guidebook that claimed to name and locate "5,000 Things at the World's Fair Which Visitors Should Not Fail to See." The guide used a three-step rating system of "1: interesting, 2: very interesting and 3: remarkably interesting." The small fraction of the exhibits rating a 3 formed an eclectic group and included a Japanese iron eagle, two feet high, with three thousand individually crafted feathers; a twenty-six-foot section of California redwood with a stairway through it; the guns that fired the first and last shots of the Civil War; the original manuscript copy of the Declaration of Independence; and the couch upon which General U. S. Grant sat at Appomattox.[34]

Mr. Rued took the girls to the Midway on several occasions: it was by far the most popular part of the fair. There were sideshows and restaurants, theaters and shops, and exhibits from exotic parts of the world. Its most notable exhibit was "Little Egypt" dancing what became known as the hootchy-kootchy. *The Time-Saver,* as a proponent of genteel culture, was less than enthusiastic about the Midway. The only item earning a 3 was the newly invented and immensely popular Ferris Wheel.[35]

Diversions such as travel and shopping did little, however, to alleviate the stifling atmosphere in the Moller household, and behind the luxurious facade there was considerable anxiety. Although by the 1890s William Moller was widely perceived as being "quietly happy" because of his wealth, his house, and his large family, it took him some time to reach that state of contentment. As a way of showing that he was master of something, William, separated from his own family by three thousand miles, estranged from his father-in-law, and living in a house paid for by his wife, exerted a firm control over his children. He liked to see them all around the table at every meal, including breakfast. No child was allowed out on a school night and his daughters were never permitted to sleep away from home. Lillian's memoirs depict a close, almost claustrophobically close, family and most of the Moller children found it impossible to break away. Only one of her five sisters ever married, while all three of her brothers married late. All eight of them lived at home with their parents well into middle age. Lillian was to be the notable exception.[36]

3

The "Athens of the Pacific"

She developed a passion for study. . . . She didn't care much for going to other girls' houses—and if they came to hers, preferred to show them her books, rather than whisper and giggle. No wonder she wasn't popular.

Lillian Moller Gilbreth, *As I Remember* (1998)

LILLIE FOUND reading very easy and learned young. Learning to spell was more difficult, and Lillian commented that it had been a great comfort to marry a man who "thought only stupid people spelled well." She portrayed herself in her memoirs as a real bookworm, implying that her childhood love of reading helped her to imagine different possibilities for herself. Although she lacked her own physical space within the Moller household, the young Lillie found a psychological space through literature and used these books to create a new personality for herself as an independent-minded woman. Many of the books Lillian recalled reading challenged middle-class beliefs about woman's "place" and helped her understand and even overcome some of the constraints of her gender and her class.[1]

Lillie's parents bought her all the books she wanted, so she made little use of public libraries and failed to meet Oakland's remarkable librarian, the poet Ina Donna Coolbrith, who was to inspire local teenagers as varied as Gertrude and Leo Stein, Isadora Duncan, and Jack London. Instead, Lillie's personal library grew rapidly. Writing half a century later, Lillian recalled the appearance, the color, and the texture of many of the books she owned and claimed that by the time she was nine she "had practically memorized the complete and unabridged works of Louisa May Alcott." She regretted, in retrospect, that some of the bindings were red, while some were green. ("Why couldn't they all be the same color?") Lillie moved from children's literature to the nineteenth-century classics. She particularly enjoyed Sir Walter Scott and acquired a cheap edition of the Waverley novels, which she recalled as "a dull red set of many volumes, none too good print, on poor paper, but magic in each one!" Lillie, like many of her contemporaries, devoured his stories of adventure and chivalry.[2]

Lillie's reading was both a public and a private activity. The habit of reading aloud persisted in the Moller family, and Lillian continued the practice with her own children. Her eldest son later recalled that "all eleven of us would go up to Mother's room and sit around her bed while she read to us. She thought the most basic training of all, in rearing a family, was to instill an appreciation of good books." This appreciation came primarily from her father and she loved to hear him read. After her baby sister was sleeping peacefully, Lillie would slip out of bed, open the door a crack, and settle down to listen while her father read to her mother. Annie loved being read to: she claimed her eyes were too weak to read, though she *could* see to tat and to make beautiful patchwork quilts. William Moller was an excellent reader, according to Lillian, "dramatizing at times, stopping at the end of each chapter to discuss it." Lillie heard her father read both the classics and recent bestsellers, and she also heard snatches of books her parents thought "risqué" and hid at the back of the bookshelves.[3]

Not all the books Lillie heard presented her with usable heroines. Some of the most popular books of the period depicted independent-minded women who were eventually subdued by strong, domineering men and happily resumed their "proper" role. These books incorporated conventional gender characteristics, depicting women as subordinate, emotional, and incapable of serious thought. Alternatives did, however, exist, and some of the novels Lillie heard or read reinforced her desire for more education and her resistance to marriage. When Lillie was about sixteen, for example, she heard her father read George du Maurier's novel *Trilby,* in which the far from respectable heroine is described in masculine terms: "'Why, she's as upright and straight and honorable as a man!'"[4]

Lillie read, but later claimed she wished she hadn't, the "women's" novels that her mother favored; her true literary preferences reflected her father's. She read *The Three Musketeers* and *The Count of Monte Cristo,* both of which her mother considered racy. Annie Moller preferred to read romantic novelists such as Augusta Jane Evans, whose best-known work, *St. Elmo,* was published in 1866. It was one of the most popular novels of the nineteenth century, outsold only by *Uncle Tom's Cabin* and *Ben Hur.* Lillian later described such books as "twaddle," though she was reluctant to criticize her mother too harshly; she added that perhaps they acted as a balance to all the serious literature she was reading.[5]

Lillie devoured numerous Victorian novels, including William Makepeace Thackeray's *Vanity Fair,* which she particularly enjoyed: its heroine, Becky Sharp, was the archetype of a woman who lived by her wits. She also read George Eliot, whose novels are full of strong, if often misguided, heroines. None of this reading was required by any of Lillie's teachers, but it provided a whole range of alternatives. She later described it as a refuge from a frightening world for an introverted and imaginative child, claiming in her memoirs that books permitted her to escape into a world of her own, where she was "never lonely or unhappy, except when she was called out of some other world to buy clothes, meet people, be part of any social life."[6]

Lillie Moller was always a bright child and became an excellent student. Her intelligence and her passion for education eventually provided a way out of her family and its stultifying values. Her formal schooling was late starting, however, and she was educated at home until she was nine years old. School attendance was not yet compulsory, so Lillie was not unique. Oakland was home to some extraordinarily creative young people in the 1880s and 1890s, and they had similarly irregular schooling. Isadora Duncan, who was exactly the same age as Lillie, started giving her friends dancing lessons from the age of six and left school completely at age ten in order to help her mother run her dancing school. Jack London, who was a couple of years older, dropped out of Oakland High School to hang around the city's docks and canneries. Gertrude Stein, two years older still, who had moved to Oakland in 1879 when she was five years old, found school "dull" and spent her time wandering around the Oakland hills with her brother and marveling at the "eucalyptus trees . . . so tall and thin and savage and the animal life very wild."[7]

Lillie's life was very domestic and quiet. Her parents certainly did not let her explore the hills or the docks on her own; instead, they set up a schoolroom for her at home. William Moller brought some paper home from his store and carefully cut it into strips, on which Annie wrote lists of words or sums in her neat, convent-school handwriting. William taught his daughter, too, but in a less formal way. On Sundays, after morning church and a big traditional lunch of soup, roast, and homemade ice cream, he looked after Lillie and her sisters while his wife took a nap. Filling his pocket with cigars, he would put on his hat, carry his cane, and walk with his children through the empty Sunday streets toward Lake Merritt. In those days, there were only a few houses around the lake and cattle grazed at the water's edge. William Moller and his daughters made for the weeping willow trees whose drooping branches almost touched the ground. It seemed a magical and very private place to Lillie, a place where she and her sisters could have their father all to themselves. Lillian remembered being fascinated by the differences between her father's life and her own. It was not only a matter of New York versus Oakland, but also how different a boy's life was from a girl's. He made it clear that he had always known he would have a career in the family sugar refinery, and Lillie started to realize that work outside the home could be very satisfying.[8]

Lillie tried to start school when she was eight, but her heart was not really in it. She had enjoyed her lessons at home with her mother. She had her younger sisters and her cousins for company, her piano teacher and her German teacher came to the house, and she could see no good reason to go to school. Her parents decided she was ready, nevertheless, and sent her to Miss Snell's Female Seminary, which was considered one of the best schools in Oakland. Lillie's few days at Miss Snell's were not a success. She found the other girls alarming and was convinced they were laughing at her hair or her clothes. When she was called on to recite, her knees trembled so much she could hardly stand, and she could not raise her voice above a whisper. She would run home sobbing uncontrollably and became so ill with "nine o'clock headaches" each morning that her parents relented and kept her home, warning her she would have to start the following year. Lillian recalled being very miserable that year, for she worried continually about what was ahead.[9]

Eventually, in the fall of 1887, when Lillie was nine years old, she went to a public elementary school. The principal insisted she start in first grade. Daunting as it sounds, this may have been good psychology, since Lillie became an unofficial teacher's aide, though she commented later that it was "very humiliating" to be in with children so much younger than herself. She was used to small children, however, as she already had four younger sisters, and having a responsible "position" in the classroom eased Lillie's transition from home to school. Although the buildings were more crowded, the classes larger and the books more tattered than at Miss Snell's, she soon settled in. She was rapidly promoted through the grades, though she remained a nervous, bookish child who preferred cleaning the blackboard or sitting in the seat of honor on the platform next to the teacher's desk to playing with the other children. Her parents were delighted by her good report cards and her teachers said she was a credit to everyone, but as Lillian reflected later, her position as "teacher's pet" did not endear her to the other students.[10]

School was not always a comfortable place for Lillie. Lillian recalled St. Valentine's Day as perhaps the worst, the most embarrassing day of the school year. Each classroom had a box where cards for teachers and classmates were deposited and then distributed just before school was out for the day. Annie tried to help, buying pretty valentines for Lillie to send; she even sent a few to the school for her daughter, who was not deceived by her mother's efforts. Lillian remembered being reduced to tears by some of the "comic" valentines sent by boys who thought it fun to tease the "little blue-stocking."[11]

Lillie was a worrier. She was anxious about being late for school. After her parents moved to Prospect Avenue, she had to walk down the hill to catch a streetcar, then walk several blocks through crowded business streets to the school. The son of one of her neighbors was in her class, but she was afraid of boys in general and him in particular, after he had laughed at her one rainy day when, clutching her schoolbooks, she fell off a plank into a gutter. Her journey to or from school was even longer if she went around the block to avoid him or some other boy who had teased her.[12]

Lillie enjoyed the academic component of school, though she disliked the extracurricular activities her parents insisted upon. One winter her mother sent her to a gymnastics class, which she hated; she was never much of a sportswoman. Another year Lillie took calisthenics, which she also disliked. She was a clumsy, self-conscious child and, feeling neither strong nor grace-ful, spent the hour wishing it would end. She watched the "big boys showing off, small boys trying to imitate them, strong girls competing, graceful girls being helped" with more embarrassment than envy. Yet another year she went to dancing class. Her parents probably did not think Isadora Duncan and her mother were respectable enough, so Lillie was sent to a Miss Daroshe, who concentrated on deportment. Lillie managed without too much discomfort, but later wished someone had taught her to "concentrate on the others and not on my shy, unhappy self."[13]

Other extracurricular classes were more enjoyable. Lillie loved her piano lessons and was invited to join a musical society; unfortunately, this involved occasional recitals, which she found "agony." One winter Lillie studied Del-sarte, a then-fashionable system of dramatic training, which involved learn-ing prescribed movements to accompany and represent certain sentiments and emotions. One of its early supporters praised it in terms that resembled the way enthusiasts were to describe scientific management: "This is an age of formulation. What Comte has done for exact science, Buckle and Mill for history, Spencer for culture and Ruskin for painting, Delsarte has tried to do for action, for expression. . . . surely an art like acting should have some higher standard than the empirical caprices of its exponents. 'Trusting to the inspiration of the moment, is like trusting to a shipwreck for your first lesson in swimming.'" Lillie liked Delsarte classes much better than dance or gym-nastics: they suggested the "One Best Way" to express emotion.[14]

Lillie thus survived elementary school with a lot of help from her parents and outside teachers, and she started at Oakland High School in the fall of 1892. Oakland liked to call itself the Athens of the Pacific, and its public schools were a source of civic pride. Lillian had fond memories of her high school days and remembered that some of her teachers brought energy and enthusiasm to their classes. Her English teacher, Elsie Lee Turner, was a particular favorite. Many years later Lillian pictured her standing at the front of the class in her crisp white shirtwaist and blue serge skirt, a "lovely clean-looking person and her costume always looked as though she had just stepped from a bandbox." While Lillie was at high school Miss Lee married. Many school districts expected married teachers to resign, but this was not the case in Oakland. Mrs. Turner taught all her life, even while she was raising her two children. Lillian Gilbreth was explicit about Elsie Lee Turner's influence on her. As well as being an inspiring teacher who made a subject "so interesting that you wanted to go exploring for yourself," she recalled that Mrs. Turner was "simple but intellectual, had a high forehead and a warm and friendly personality. She was a fine person, the kind of person that a studious quiet girl would want to be." Lillie may have had the same English teacher as Gertrude Stein, since both claimed to enjoy diagramming sentences. Lillian simply recorded "careful instruction" while Stein was quite lyrical, writing that it "has been to me . . . the one thing that has been completely exciting and completely completing. I like the everlasting feeling of sentences as they diagram themselves."[15]

Lillie enjoyed Oakland High much more than Gertrude Stein, but when she looked back even Lillian saw some shortcomings. She complained about a lack of connection made between the subjects, but her cousin, Annie Florence Brown, who was studying at the University of California, helped fill some of the gaps and broaden Lillie's education. On sunny Saturday afternoons the two serious young women would take their books out into the Oakland hills and sit beside a stream. Lillian remembered that her cousin read to her and fired her imagination with the words of Emerson, Milton, and Tennyson and by the heroic deeds in the *Trial and Death of Socrates*.[16]

Lillie gained confidence and started to blossom in high school. In her senior year she was elected vice president of her class. As the (female) class historian wrote in the yearbook, "We have had a few very exciting times this term during the election of class officers. Some of the girls, sad to say, have acquired quite a taste for and ability in, the political contests." Lillie was one of only two female class officers; the other was the secretary, Helen Campbell, who wrote a piece in the school magazine, the *Aegis*, prophesying what would have become of the class of '96 twenty years thence. She referred to Lillie as "the poetess, Miss Moller, who (in strictest confidence) lives mainly on crackers and cheese and fame."[17]

Lillie Moller graduated with straight As in her senior year, and she had also begun to write. Three of her pieces were published in the *Aegis* in 1896, two poems and a prose essay, "The Beauty of the Bay." A very pious piece on the pleasures of study was selected as class poem. The last two stanzas read:

> Till our loves grown nobler, better,
> Shall present examples clear,
> That there is a good in study
> And no evil one need fear;

> Till each one that chanced to meet us
> Shall have cause and need to say,
> "They have profited by study,
> They have wisely used each day."[18]

In spite, or perhaps because of this, Lillie's graduation day was a nightmare. The other girls—who she had assumed were her friends—told her that they were all going to wear flowered dimity dresses for commencement, then turned up in the traditional white. Nearly fifty years later she remembered her humiliation. Writing, as usual, in the third person, she recalled, "Choking back tears, she had sat there on the stage, a conspicuous blob of color in a sea of billowing white gauze." There was more embarrassment to come. Her family had provided a great luxury for her graduation party, namely, homemade strawberry ice cream. Unfortunately, the berries were frozen solid, and a male guest took it upon himself to be the life and soul of the party by placing a frozen strawberry between his teeth, positioning his chin on the edge of the dining room table, and then hitting the top of his head with his fist. The Mollers were not amused. Lillie, whose first instinct was to deny any unpleasantness, went to her room and wrote on her commencement program: "The end of a dreadful day!"[19]

4

In Search of the Strenuous Life

There was no prejudice against women. Consequently it was a surprise and a painful one, to aim for a Phi Beta Kappa key, only to learn that there would be no girls on the list because "when it came to finding a good job, men needed the help of this honor more than women did."

Lillian Moller Gilbreth, on her student days at Berkeley (1970)

LILLIE MOLLER graduated from Oakland High School in May 1896 and accepted Frank Bunker Gilbreth's proposal of marriage in December 1903. The seven and a half years between those two milestones were tumultuous for her, for American women, and for the American nation. During those years Lillie tried and rejected upper-middle-class ladyhood, academia, and the "family claim" and chose an apparently respectable and conventional option, namely marriage. Lillie wanted to please her parents and be useful to them, but she also wanted a wider role outside the home and domestic life.[1]

For three of Lillie's four years at high school the United States had been in the midst of a major economic crisis. Triggered by the panic of 1893, it was the longest and worst depression in American history. The 1890s also saw political and social upheavals, with labor problems, strikes, and the rise of the Populists. Meanwhile, middle-class American girls became "new women" attending college, riding their bicycles, and rejecting their mothers' notions about separate spheres. The social, economic, and political crises of the decade gave rise to a mood described later by historians as "American nervousness"—a shift in attitudes whereby the complacent materialism of the Gilded Age was replaced by a culture of strenuous youth. Such cultural changes are never stress-free, and Lillie's efforts to find a role for herself reflected this.[2]

43

In the summer of 1896 Lillie Moller was just eighteen years old. She was
tall and slim, perhaps a little too thin for the curvy Gibson Girl ideal of the
period. She wore her reddish-blonde hair off her face and piled up on top of
her head, which, combined with the high-collared blouses of the period, accentuated the length of her neck. She dressed in the outfits her mother and her
mother's dressmaker thought most suitable for the granddaughter of one of
Oakland's wealthiest men, never forgetting her hat and her gloves. One of
the precepts her mother had drilled into her was that "decent women dressed
quietly. . . . A lady's aim was to be inconspicuous."[3]

Lillie wanted to go to college. She first broached the subject in her sophomore year of high school, but unlike the fathers of some of her contemporaries, who encouraged their daughters' academic ambitions, William Moller
was firmly opposed. His opposition was based on class and gender consider-
ations. As a wealthy citizen he assumed he would provide for his daughter,
and he saw a degree as simply a meal ticket for women who had little option
but to become schoolteachers. It is also possible that he feared that his close-
ness with his eldest daughter would be threatened if she saw more of the
world and became more independent. In old age Lillian was still angry about
this, recalling him saying, "Your mother, aunts, grandmothers never went to
college—yet they are cultivated gentlewomen. Your place is here at home,
helping your mother and learning to be like her. You can devote yourself to
your music—read a lot—travel perhaps. College is only necessary for women
who have to make their living. No daughter of mine will have to do that. I can
support them—I want to!" It seemed a compelling argument at the time. Lillie's mother was a supreme example of the Victorian ideology of separate
spheres: she had married straight out of school and her life revolved around
her husband and her children. Lillie was a good daughter; she chose not to
take some of the college preparatory courses her high school offered, thereby
resigning herself to the idea of not attending college.[4]

In spite of what Lillie's father said, there *were* several educated women in
the family. Annie Flo was at Berkeley and Elsie Brown was planning to follow
her brother David to Stanford. The most dramatic example was, however, her
newly divorced Aunt Lillie, who was embarking on what was to become a remarkable career. She started college in her early thirties and graduated near
the top of her class at the Cooper (later Stanford) Medical School. She
changed her name to Lillian, as her niece was to do, thinking that "Lillie" was
much too frivolous a name for a physician. After marrying a fellow doctor,
Swazey Powers, she studied in Vienna with Freud. She practiced psycho-
analysis in New York City for many years, retiring in 1953, only two years before her death at the age of eighty-seven. Lillie's cousin Tillie Brown, on the
other hand, set an unfortunate example. An eldest daughter, she did not at-

tend college, believing it was her responsibility to help her widowed mother. Lillie was similarly an eldest daughter, with a semi-invalid mother and a house full of younger brothers and sisters, but she resisted Tillie's precedent and tried to find a compromise. Self-sacrifice was a fate she wished to avoid.[5]

By her senior year Lillie had managed to persuade her father to change his mind. He reluctantly conceded that she should "try it for a year." Annie Moller may have played a role in her husband's change of heart as she blamed too early motherhood for years of ill health. She saw college as a kind of finishing school that would delay marriage and possibly make her daughter a better wife. Lillie was delighted, but her determination to attend college came at the cost of abandoning her musical ambitions. John Metcalf, who was well known locally as a composer, refused point blank to continue teaching her, saying, "You could play well—if you devote full time to it.—You'll do mediocre work at college *and* your music if you attempt both." This was a blow to Lillie, who was very proud of the fact that Metcalf had written the music to accompany *Sunrise,* one of her poems. Nevertheless, she decided that college was more important than music and that perhaps she could continue to play on her own.[6]

When August arrived, Lillie was ready to sign up for classes. The University of California was a raw, unfinished place in 1896: it had only four buildings and they stood like isolated monuments on the hills outside the village of Berkeley. It was seriously underfunded compared with Stanford, newly created by railroad magnate Leland Stanford some thirty miles down the Camino Real in Palo Alto. Contemporaries regretted that none of Berkeley's buildings "compare in beauty" with Stanford; and "there is no comprehensive plan of them; they are even of unpleasantly differing shades of brick." The lack of a "comprehensive plan" was something that Phoebe Apperson Hearst was trying to remedy. Mrs. Hearst, who was to be appointed regent in 1897, during Lillie's sophomore year, was the widow of the millionaire U.S. senator George Hearst and mother of the newspaper publisher William Randolph Hearst. A Missouri schoolteacher before her marriage, she was interested in education and gave a large amount of money to the University of California. In addition to new buildings, she was particularly involved with the women students and funded scholarships to "worthy young women and needy."[7]

Lillie was one of nearly three hundred students who entered Berkeley as the "class of naughty naught." There were no tuition fees at the university, which tried to provide an education for any Californian who matriculated. This generous policy resulted in budget deficits, and there was so little classroom space that many lectures were given in tents donated by Mrs. Hearst. Other facilities were poor; as the university president complained in 1894, the "laboratories are becoming insufficient. . . . The Museum is choked with undisplayed treasures. The health-giving Gymnasium has but half the needed space and appliances." More important from Lillie's point of view was his last criticism: "The hundreds of young women have for a day-home only one room in a basement."[8]

Facilities for women students were, indeed, limited. All the students, male and female, lived either at home or in lodgings, for the university's founders believed, along with many other nineteenth-century educators, that dormitories were "incubators of student disorder." (This policy was abandoned in the 1920s.) While men found it relatively easy to persuade their parents to allow them to live in boardinghouses near the campus, a majority of the women students lived at home and faced a daily commute. If they lived in San Francisco, as many did, their traveling time by ferry and bus or horsecar could be easily three hours a day. Once on campus, finding a place to eat was problematic. A lunchroom was provided in the basement of North Hall for commuters to eat their bag lunches. It soon became a disgrace and was not a place where the gently raised Lillie Moller wanted to spend any time: "benches were broken in roughhousing, walls were stained in evidence of fiercely fought apple-core battles and other equipment in the room was in general disarray."[9]

Sororities provided a social base for some of the middle-class women, and Lillie was invited to join the newly founded Theta House. Sororities served only a small proportion of the women students, however, and most of them continued to have problems with housing and eating places. Sororities also increased social divisions among the female students since they excluded those of the "wrong" class or ethnicity.[10] Lillie declined the invitation to join, later explaining that her father disliked all secret societies. She was anxious not to give him any more excuses for his opposition to her college career, but she became friendly with some of the sisters anyway.

Lillie's enrollment at the University of California was part of a trend; over a twenty-year period, when the number of college places had increased by about 20 percent, the proportion of female students had risen by about 75 percent.[11] This increase did not go unchallenged by male students, particularly as coeds of Lillie's generation tried to combine some of the Victorian ideals and rhetoric about women's "place" with the more active, expansive ideas of the "new woman" of the 1890s. Lillian's Berkeley contemporaries tried to disarm criticism, claiming: "We do not make our advent with the idea of 'raising the tone of the University' or taming with gentle presence our brother of the book. Not at all." Not wanting to be classed "Pelicans," the name given to the "dried-up schoolma'am" type of female student, these young women embraced the possibility of career *and* marriage. "We come to study," they wrote, "to learn, to enjoy, to meet the nicest men, to take a degree and go forth prepared for work, in or out of the home, as Providence decrees." And that is precisely what Lillie Moller proceeded to do.[12]

She had to work very hard in her first semester at the university, for although she was a top student at Oakland High, she had not taken the pre-college Latin course and was admitted to Berkeley on condition that she fulfill the Latin requirement by the end of her first semester. In addition, she took the required math and science courses and advanced German. Lillie's second semester was easier and she soon rose to near the top of her class. Her German instructor, the stern, bearded professor Albin Putzker, who played billiards with her father, told him that his eldest daughter was a fine student with "one of the best minds in the freshman class." Putzker's remark was a great help in Lillie's campaign to win her father over: William Moller relented and permitted Lillie to continue at Berkeley. Eventually he became proud that his clever daughter was a student at the university.[13]

Lillian was a student when the feminization of the university and the baleful effect of women on the curriculum were frequently deplored, but she did not threaten any conventional gender assumptions in her choice of subjects. She majored in English, received a good grounding in philosophy, and studied some psychology, which was still included in philosophy departments. She also studied French drama and German and took enough education courses to earn a teacher's certificate. She was a conscientious student; she often rose early to complete her assignments, and after lectures she usually went to the library. "It was such a *welcoming* place," she later wrote. Then she carried her books home, riding the streetcar back down Telegraph Avenue. She spent some of her evenings assisting her mother and supervising her younger brothers' and sisters' homework. She read late into the night, then rose early to study again. She met other students on the streetcar, and as she pointed out, being a serious student had some social advantages, since "lazy boys as well as girls caught one's car" and asked her for help with their assignments. It was a bold young man who actually came to call on the Mollers, however, since the younger children would lie on the landing to listen, or even crawl halfway down the stairs in their eagerness to see the visitor. Lillian remembered these occasions as agonies of embarrassment.[14]

Lillie's growing interest in her studies started to divide her from her parents. She felt lonely and wanted to find a new place for herself, which was not easy at Berkeley. Classes were very large; the administration's response to the budgetary crises of the late 1890s was to cut the number of classes available. During Lillian's senior year eight classes contained more than one hundred students and a further forty-eight had more than fifty. It was hard to be noticed among such large groups and as she recalled, "anything that made a professor interested in one was a help to an ambitious student." Lillie *was* ambitious and managed to make an impression. She won a prize for the "best undergraduate verse" in 1899, and she started to act in the Charter Day plays. Lillian recalled that she forgot her shyness and felt she actually looked pretty in her eighteenth-century costume complete with powdered wig. These performances were a turning point in her relationship with her parents, as well as with the university community, but her mother heartily disapproved. She had a perfect excuse for nonattendance at Lillie's first public performance in 1897 as she was home giving birth to her tenth and last child, but according to Lillian's reminiscences, Annie Moller disliked her daughter appearing in so public a place and getting her name in the papers.[15]

Lillian recalled that her fear of boys—now men—started to evaporate. Fellow actors from the Charter Day plays invited her to their fraternities, most often to Phi Delta Theta, which she remembered as an especially pleasant place to go. The house contained, she later wrote, "a studious crowd, where brains, even in a girl, were not a great handicap." In this experience she may have been unusual, as this second generation of college women had to endure many "jokes" about the supposed ill effects of too much education. Student newspapers and yearbooks displayed an ambivalent, if not hostile, attitude to clever women. Cartoons in the *Pelican,* the campus humor magazine, showed women chewing cigars, wearing men's suits, proposing marriage to men, and even serving in the army in high heels: it was clearly not possible to be clever *and* feminine. Other cartoons depicted women students as skinny old maids and suggested that no man would want to marry a clever woman, since intelligence was inevitably accompanied by plainness. The college yearbook warned incoming women students that if they worked too hard it would make their "pretty little nose[s] very red," their "rosy cheeks" jaundiced, and their hair thin. The 1895 edition had a cartoon showing a pretty young thing "when she comes" transformed into a sour-faced, bespectacled woman "when she leaves." A college education had, however, the opposite effect on young men. The same cartoon showed the entering freshman poorly dressed and squinting at his books, while four years later he left college as a handsome, polished gentleman.[16]

Many years later Lillian's youngest daughter, Jane, recalled that her mother always worked well with men, and it is clear that her comfort in mixed society went back to her college days. In spite of the misogyny rampant at Berkeley, Lillie was not interested in separatist organizations; she wanted to be treated as an equal. Unlike those of an earlier generation of women, who created their own necessarily women-friendly institutions, Lillie's extracurricular activities seem to have been coeducational; there is no evidence that she was involved in any way with the Associated Women Students or other "separate but equal" organizations. Like many other women educated around the turn of the century, Lillie confronted gender-related problems as an individual, rather than by joining with other women in a group strategy for changing the political order.[17]

Lillie also wanted to be treated as an academic equal. In her senior year she nursed a secret ambition to win a Phi Beta Kappa key and was bitterly disappointed when her name did not appear on the list. Lillian recalled that she heard from a reliable source that she had tied with one of the men, but that someone had said, "He needs it more," or "It will be more useful to him." She wrote, in old age, that there were no girls on the list because, "'when it came to finding a good job, men needed the help of this honor more than women did.'" Lillian's memory here was a little selective, for there *were* two women on the list of nine honorees. The key was not, however, permanently denied. She was elected in 1913, on the recommendation of Minnie Bunker, Class of '89, who had also been elected years after her graduation and who was, by then, Lillian's cousin by marriage. Nevertheless, in 1900 Lillian was not happy, though she was careful not to let her feelings show. Many years later she wrote: "She had wanted 'The Key'—had worked hard for it. It was a bitter disappointment not to get it. Fortunately her family knew nothing of this—so she did not have the added ordeal of breaking the news to them. She bore her disappointment quietly."[18]

Lillie was to receive consolation a few days later, after she got off the Telegraph Avenue streetcar and walked up the hill to her parents' house. Her feet dragged a little because she was tired; it had been a long day and she still had a lot of reading to do for tomorrow's classes. She was wondering whether all this studying was worth it; her failure to get the key left her feeling very discouraged. When the maid opened the front door Lillie could hear her large family enjoying themselves; only two of her sisters, Ernestine and Mabel, showed any academic inclinations, and the rest of them could not understand why Lillie felt the need to work as hard as she did. Her mother was, as usual, stretched out on the sofa; her nineteen-year-old sister, Gertie, who had not bothered to go to college, was reading poetry as a break from her needlepoint; sixteen-year-old Elinor was playing the piano and thinking about the party she had been invited to; and thirteen-year-old Josie was chatting with some school friends. Lillie's little brothers were there, too; eight-year-old Fred was practicing his violin, while four-year-old Billy and the toddler Frank were playing with their toys. As Lillie walked into the parlor her mother looked up from her tatting and told her that there was a telephone message; she was to stop by university president Benjamin Ide Wheeler's office at ten the following morning.[19]

Lillie wondered what it was about; she knew Wheeler and had taken a course from him earlier in the year. He was new to Berkeley, having arrived the previous September like a breath of fresh air. He succeeded a series of weak presidents and had lost no time in promoting student self-government and involving students in disciplinary committees. Wheeler was a firm believer in coeducation and resolutely resisted calls for the sexual segregation of classes. He believed it was not the presence of women but rather the vocational needs of the male students that led them to choose mining, engineering, agriculture, business, and law, rather than literature or history. Wheeler's attitudes toward women were, nevertheless, traditional and he believed that women's education was designed to fit them for marriage and domesticity. He told his women students that they were "not like men and you should recognize the fact. . . . You may have the same studies as the men, but you put them to different use. You are not here with the ambition to be schoolteachers or old maids; but you are here for the preparation of marriage and motherhood. This education should tend to make you more serviceable as wives and mothers."[20]

Wheeler was, then, no radical feminist. Perhaps that was why he decided to ask Lillie Moller, who was both able and nonconfrontational, to represent the women students at commencement and give one of the addresses. Lillie was amazed and secretly delighted. She knew this was a singular honor and that it would more than make up for her Phi Beta Kappa disappointment, for she would be the first woman ever to speak at the University of California's commencement since its foundation in 1868. Times were changing and as a local newspaper noted, "This innovation will undoubtedly be the precedent for years to come." That Wheeler was not altogether comfortable with this precedent and still had some reservations about women speaking in public was evident in his next remarks. He felt constrained to tell Lillie to be feminine, advising her to be "womanly" in her presentation. He even told her what to wear, saying, "Don't wear a stiff dress, wear one that is soft and has ruffles." He also advised the experienced actress: "Don't scream. Don't give an oration—read what you have to say. And not from 8½ x 11, but from small pieces of paper, easier to handle. Don't try to imitate a man—speak as a woman." Lillie took this advice calmly, whether or not it was necessary, and set off to visit her dressmaker and write her speech.[21]

Eventually it was May and time for commencement, and Lillie was involved in a whirl of activities. There was a farewell banquet across the Bay at the Palace Hotel in San Francisco, a baccalaureate sermon preached by Dr. Brown, her minister from Oakland Congregational Church, and an afternoon at Mrs. Hearst's palatial new home, the Hacienda del Pozo de Verona, in the hills some thirty miles southeast of Berkeley. Lillie was back in time to attend the final meeting of the Philosophical Union, where George Stratton, one of her favorite professors, presented a paper, "Spiritual Implications of Psychological Experiments," which was much more to her taste than frolics in the hills. More festive was the senior class party, held in Hearst Hall, with Mrs. Hearst, resplendent in black silk and pearls, heading the list of chaperones. Dinner was served and dancing began at nine o'clock.[22]

Class day was light-hearted, at least on the surface, but a number of the activities involved implicit critiques of women's ambiguous role on campus. The graduating class walked in procession around the campus, bidding farewell to the various buildings. The librarian found "some good even in Coeds who use one dictionary and sit on two at the same time," while President Wheeler beseeched the class to give generously to the university library. In the afternoon, the whole class took part in an *Extravaganza* in the university amphitheater. The terraced hillside was packed with a large crowd of parents and friends, when promptly at two o'clock the class, more than two hundred strong, "a flashing, jingling, radiant throng," entered the stage, singing as they marched. The play itself reflected the sometimes strained gender relations and expectations on campus. Written by Lillie's friend and classmate Alice Humphreys '00, it showed Medea rescuing a male student with an "unfulfilled condition" and, by outwitting the bureaucratic dragon, which she tied up in his own red tape, enabling the unfortunate young man to get his degree. Most of the watching students, well versed in Greek mythology, would have known that Medea was a witch and an unnatural mother who killed her own children. The *Extravaganza* therefore contained a very mixed message.[23]

The graduation festivities concluded with the commencement exercises, held on May 16, 1900. It was a beautiful California spring day; the morning fog had cleared and the sky was a cloudless blue as promptly at ten o'clock the students, faculty, and alumni processed into the gymnasium to the popular march from Gounod's *The Queen of Sheba*, played by the orchestra. Lillie carried a big bunch of lilies of the valley, her favorite flower, and was very conscious that the dressmaker had excelled herself; the "soft dress with ruffles" contrasted admirably with the severe black gown. There were only two women in the platform party, Lillie Moller and Mrs. Hearst. They sat with faculty members and regents, distinguished-looking men, solemn in their academic gowns. The stage was decorated with a profusion of flowers and potted plants, vines and branches of greenery, as well as the Stars and Stripes and the university flag. Lillie looked out over the sea of faces in front of her. She reflected that she was glad the exercises were taking place in the Harmon Gymnasium, for although she thought it was an ugly building, it was small enough that she could see her family and friends.[24]

Lillie waited, a little nervous in spite of her theatrical experience, as three male students took turns to speak. Finally it was her turn, and President

Wheeler gave her a smile of encouragement as she walked past him to the lectern. She was poised as she read her speech: the shy teenager of a few years before had developed into a confident young woman. In her talk, which was entitled "Life: A Means or an End," she discussed nothing less than the purpose of life and how that purpose was to be discovered. Her remarks show the influence of two of the most important cultural leaders of the day, the philosopher/psychologist William James and the vice president of the United States, Theodore Roosevelt.[25]

Lillie's speech is one of very few contemporary examples of her thought. She did not describe it in her memoirs, beyond a rueful remark: "It is to be feared that a sense of humor and the light touch were not her strong points— at this point in her life, at any rate." The local newspaper, however, printed a long and detailed summary, which is a very important clue to what she was thinking years before she met Frank. Her wish to avoid what she called a "narrow, one-sided life" can be read both as a desire for a career and as a reaction to the unthinking luxury and comfortable domesticity of her family. She deplored the materialism of the age and, by implication, of her grandfather and her parents. "We see rich men working that they may become rich or powerful or famous," she declared. "At first glance some seem to be heaping up gold, not that they may use it, but that they may enjoy the satisfaction of having more than their neighbors." Lillie then backtracked a little; having no wish to be too controversial, she did not take her attack on materialism too far, adding, "If one takes a closer view he sees that, while many men seem to be striving to better their surroundings, yet on the whole the end is not selfish."[26]

Many of Lillie's statements reflect James's essay "What Pragmatism Means," the subject of a lecture he gave at the University of California in 1898.[27] It is unthinkable that the serious-minded Lillie Moller would not have gone to hear the great man speak. She asserted that everyone needed a goal in life that was both honorable and immediate. "Let us scorn to strive for unworthy things," she declaimed, "or to toil, unheedful of the present, for a future which is like a far-off dream." She stressed strenuousness, activity, and effort. She applied James's ideas about the purpose of life, which she argued must be judged by its practical results, which should not be material things, or glory, or "that will-o'-the wisp, fame." Life was an end in itself and should be lived actively and unselfishly, one day at a time. Lillian did not concern herself with moral certainties or universal values. Like all pragmatists, she had problems talking about ideals.

Lillie's remarks were also strongly influenced by Theodore Roosevelt's widely publicized "Strenuous Life" speech, in which he saw such a life as one of "toil and effort, of labor and strife."[28] Like the vice president, Lillie believed that life was all about activity: "Life is acting, doing," she said. "When we act our many-sided natures, we bring all of the past to the present and are all that we are, then we live. For we must be our whole selves. It is what we are and do that counts." She declared that life should be "for life's sake and nothing else. . . . Let us refuse to lead narrow, one-sided lives. Let us push forward in the path of progress by living out each day as it should be lived." She concluded, "We believe that life is its own end. There is no break. The future grows from the present. We must 'be what we are and say what we think.'"[29]

It was a very earnest oration; the local paper reported, "Miss Lillie Moller of Oakland made the most interesting speech of the day—that is it contained more original ideas and was not so much the stereotyped graduating essay." President Wheeler smiled again as she sat down; her family beamed and her pastor later told her father, "Lillie ought to be in the pulpit instead of me." Lillie's parents were very proud of her; they did not register the implied criticism of their lives, though her mother was distressed by all the newspaper coverage her daughter received. Nevertheless, even she admitted that if Lillie's photograph *had* to appear in the newspapers, "I'm glad it was in such a dignified way." Everyone made such a fuss of Lillie that she became embarrassed by all the attention and was relieved to go home, get out of her ruffled dress, and return to her normal, everyday life.[30]

She did not plan to stay home for long, however, for during her years at Berkeley she had started to think about a professional career. Like many intelligent women of her generation, she had entered college assuming that her liberal education was to be a preparation for "life" (meaning marriage and motherhood) rather than for a career, but now she realized that four years were not enough and that she wanted "all the education she could get—travel, meeting interesting people, a job to do."[31]

It is hard to imagine Lillian's role models; she was estranged from her Aunt Lillie, as she disapproved of her divorce, and apart from her there were few professional women close at hand. The university had as yet no women faculty. There were two women pursuing doctorates at Berkeley while Lillie was a student. One was Millicent Washburn Shinn (1858–1940), who became, in 1898, the first woman to earn a doctorate at the university. Shinn worked on the sensory development of infants, a topic of interest to Lillie as a psychology minor as well as the eldest of nine children. She retired from the university in 1899 (at the very young age of forty-one) to look after her brother's children. She was not, then, the best of role models for a would-be career woman. The second female to earn a Ph.D. was Jessica Peixotto, daughter of a wealthy Portuguese Jewish merchant, who entered the university over her father's objections at the age of twenty-seven and received her Ph.D. in 1900, the year Lillie was the commencement speaker.[32]

Wherever Lillie found her inspiration, she was certainly looking for alternatives to staying home and waiting for marriage. Toward the end of her senior year her mother had begun putting none too subtle pressure on her eldest daughter to resume her familial duties full time. Lillie's sisters were starting to go to parties and dances and needed chaperones, but Annie Moller made it clear that she was "too delicate" for such activities, or for much household management. Lillie decided, in spite of this pressure, to take a master's degree, and the college she chose on the advice of her literature professor, Charles Gayley, was Columbia University, which was about as far away from Oakland and her parents as she could get.[33]

Thus, in September 1900 twenty-two-year-old Lillie Moller, now wishing to be called Lillian, as befitted her dignity as a graduate student, left home for the first time. Her mother had spent the previous weeks ensuring that her daughter's wardrobe was filled with new clothes, and though she felt a little guilty leaving her family responsibilities behind, Lillian's main feeling was one of exhilaration. She was looking forward to pursuing her education. Her parents were not quite ready to let her travel unchaperoned, however, and her father took the opportunity to make a business trip to New York.[34]

Lillian took a room in the Fiske dormitory at Barnard, the women's college, and registered as a student in philosophy and comparative literature at Columbia. To her dismay she discovered that James Brander Matthews, the scholar most particularly recommended by Gayley, refused to have women in his classes. "It sounds naive," she later commented, "but neither [Gayley] nor any of the other faculty people with whom she talked knew that Professor Matthews refused to take women students." Columbia was restricted to male undergraduates, but nearly half the graduate student body of 412 was female, so although Matthews was a well-known playwright, author, and friend of Theodore Roosevelt, his stance meant that the administration confined him to teaching undergraduates. Matthews would not change his mind, however, even to admit a star student from the West, who had reportedly traveled three thousand miles to take his course. Lillian later reported that he said, "And I don't care if she *did* make the commencement speech out there. She is *not* going to distract my classes or me. I'm still old-fashioned enough to believe that a woman's place is in the home."[35]

Lillian was too much of a lady to make a fuss and she soon found "wonderful courses to take," namely comparative literature, music, and psychology. She found her literature professor, George Edward Woodberry, inspiring, in a restful kind of way; "one came away from his seminars serene and uplifted." Her music classes with Edward Alexander MacDowell were, however, much less tranquil. She was still annoyed about her Oakland music teacher's refusal to teach her if she became a college student. MacDowell was not, unfortunately, the right person to help her with her ambition to combine study with composition, as he was an angry and frustrated man: few students were up to his expected standard of dedication. A distinguished composer in his late thirties, he taught at Columbia from 1896 until his abrupt resignation in 1904. Lillian remembered him as "a restless genius" pacing up and down the lecture room, sitting at the piano to illustrate some point he was making, and stopping suddenly, as if he had forgotten what he wanted to do. The class "sat hypnotized—whatever happened—recognizing a master."[36]

Though Lillian still thought of herself as a literature student, the most influential of her professors was to be the psychologist Edward Thorndike. In 1900 he was twenty-six years old and a newly appointed adjunct instructor, though within four years he became a full professor, beginning a distinguished forty-year career. In 1902 he was coteaching an introductory course called the Elements of Psychology and an advanced course in genetic psychology, and although Lillian's student records have not survived, it seems more than likely that she studied the latter. Lillian's few weeks with Thorndike were more influential than the brevity of the encounter would suggest, since he not only became a major figure in American psychology, but also was important in the development of eugenics in the United States. Eugenic beliefs were instrumental to Frank and Lillian Gilbreth's later decision to have twelve children.[37]

Lillian was very much impressed by Thorndike's energy and enthusiasm. She recalled his classroom presence as "like a strong wind" and that he was a "person of tremendous vitality physical and intellectual—he had no use with fussiness and no patience with pretense." He was good with his students; "he encouraged the shy," she remembered, "quizzed the assured, flattened out pretensions." Lillian, like many of his other students, was devoted to him. "Once his student," she wrote, "you remained so all your life and could carry your little failures and successes to him sure of encouragement and appreciation." She maintained contact with Thorndike for the next four decades, cited him in the two doctoral dissertations she was to write, and was strongly influenced by his functionalist approach to learning. Thorndike believed that people were capable of learning new skills and finding new sources of satisfaction. He taught Lillian two concepts that became fundamental to her later work in scientific management: that individuals were shaped by their environment and that satisfactions varied from person to person.[38]

Lillian was not, however, under Thorndike's direct influence for long, as she became terribly homesick. Like her mother a quarter century earlier, she missed the familiar sights and sounds and tastes of California. There were few facilities for the graduate students at Columbia: the Morningside Heights campus was new and unfinished, and though New York was moving inexorably northward, there were windy gaps between construction sites. At least at Berkeley Lillian could escape to a comfortable house at the end of each day, but at Columbia all she had was a bleak dormitory room. Lillian found it difficult to make friends: few of the graduate students lived in the dormitories. Some were New Yorkers who commuted, while others lived in boardinghouses. Many were older teachers taking time for advanced study at Teachers College before returning to their classrooms.[39]

Lillian made strenuous efforts to overcome her homesickness; she did not want to admit defeat. She drew up a list of all her New York Moller cousins—and there were a great many of them, since her grandfather had been one of six brothers—and invited all those in her age group to tea. She also made an effort to meet her grandfather's pastor, Armand Miller. An evangelical Lutheran from Virginia and a published poet, he was in charge of the Church of the Holy Trinity and in the middle of building a grand new church on Central Park West at Sixty-fifth Street. Lillian spent happy afternoons visiting the Millers and their three young sons, who treated her like a big sister. That was almost like being at home. She also may have been involved in the Vienna Ladies' Tailoring Institute on West Fourteenth Street; an anonymous booklet in the New York Public Library is indexed under her name. The ninety-four-page booklet comprises many pages of dress patterns and a few pages of text, which includes the following sentences: "It is the first impression on the mind that is most lasting. Therefore it is important that the right beginning be made," which is a phrase that Lillian later used many times.[40] By November Lillian was gradually starting to get used to New York. She found Columbia's library, an imposing, domed structure in the middle of the campus, even more conducive to study than the one back in California. She started to meet a few of her fellow students, at least two of whom became very important to her later in life. Dorothea Canfield (later Fisher), the author, was to write the introduction to one of Lillian's child-rearing books, and Susan Kingsbury, later a Bryn Mawr sociologist, was to collaborate with Lillian on a survey of working women. That was many years in the future, however. But though Lillian's life and her studies were progressing reasonably well, a crisis occurred when the weather started to get cold.

Lillian was spending long hours at her books; she neglected to eat properly and did not have warm enough clothes. She caught a cold, which developed into a severe attack of pleurisy. Thoroughly miserable, she lay coughing in her room, worrying that she was getting behind in her classes. Her roommate was no help; Lillian shared with a freshman she described as "unattractive, odd and extremely untidy." According to Lillian's recollections, she left food around and "mice scratched around her tea set and cookie jar." Lillian's aunts Tillie and Hanna Moller heard she was unwell and descended upon her dorm room. Unmarried society women in their early thirties, they were far from convinced that higher education for women was a good thing. Alarmed by Lillian's condition, they wired their brother in California. He boarded the next train east, and refusing to listen to her arguments, took Lillian back home to Oakland. It seemed, for a while, that her father was to get his way. He was convinced that his daughter had now had enough education and felt that she need not expose herself to illness and squalor in a strange city so far from her family. As soon as Lillian recovered, however, she started to "mourn and grieve" for her uncompleted work and felt that to abandon her graduate studies seemed "more than she could possibly bear!" These are strong statements from Lillian; her recollection in her sixties suggests that her return to Oakland was a kind of death.[41]

A few months at home living the well-chaperoned life of a wealthy young woman convinced Lillian that she wanted to resume her studies, and she persuaded her parents to let her return to Berkeley. Professor Charles Gayley advised her to start with a master's degree. She knew that this would mean writing two theses instead of one, but perhaps doubting whether her family would permit her to finish a doctorate, or even doubting her own resolve, she reasoned that "if one did *not* go on—one had accomplished a definite stint, in a year's time." In August 1901 Lillian Moller returned to the Berkeley campus. She registered for courses in linguistics "intended for prospective teachers of languages" with President Wheeler. She also studied comparative literature and, under Gayley's guidance, selected Ben Jonson's play *Bartholemew Fair* as the subject of her thesis. This was an unusual choice for a Victorian gentlewoman, however strenuous. Jonson's play, first performed in 1614, was dismissed by most critics as crude and vulgar and was virtually ignored for more than two centuries. It was rediscovered in the 1850s and hailed as one of the great works of the Renaissance stage. Lillian studied it as "a product of its time, place and moment" and claimed to feel "more Elizabethan than 1901 American." Despite aspects of the play that embarrassed her as a rather prim young woman, she later wrote that she enjoyed "its roughness—its frankness, which would have been abhorrent to her in real life" and saw them as part of "an exploratory age."[42]

Lillian's thesis contains many echoes of her Berkeley commencement speech. She portrayed the Elizabethan period in England as a very strenuous time when "everyone did, everyone felt, everyone lived or desired to live with every fibre of his being." She saw many parallels with turn-of-the-century America. "There were new lands to discover, houses to build, trades to regulate, plays to write, schools to found, great opportunities everywhere. There was the Currency problem, the Immigration problem, the Labor problem, the Export problem, all demanding men of quick wit and wide resources." The men Lillian described meeting these challenges were very different from her father or from the young men she met at society functions in Oakland. The Elizabethans were "not one-sided, atropied [*sic*] specimens, but passionate, hot-headed, natural men."[43]

Lillian was preparing herself to meet Frank Bunker Gilbreth, who was just such a man.

PART III

The One Best Partnership

It is extremely difficult to assert with
any degree of certainty which, for scientific
management, was the more important event of
the year 1903; the June meeting of the American
Society of Mechanical Engineers at Saratoga, where
Frederick Taylor presented his classic paper, SHOP
MANAGEMENT, or the meeting that same
month between Lillian Moller and Frank
Gilbreth near the Abbey Murals in
the Boston City Library.

William Jaffe, *The Gilbreth Story* (1962)

5 Not Like Any Boys We Know

He isn't a bit like any of the boys we know,
in fact I'm afraid he would call them kids.

Lillian Moller to Josephine Moller (June 29, 1903)

L ILLIAN RECEIVED her master's degree in the spring of 1902. Around the same time she heard that Minnie Bunker, a local school-teacher, was planning a trip to Europe the following June and would chaperone any young ladies wanting to take a "Grand Tour." Lillian jumped at this opportunity to travel: she was not convinced she wanted to go on with her studies, and a trip to Europe would give her time to decide. It also seemed the perfect opportunity to get away from her parents. Miss Bunker, forty-five years old, was the ideal chaperone. She was well educated and well traveled: she had recently returned from Athens, where she had spent a year at the American School of Classical Studies; she was knowledgeable about art and she was socially acceptable. She was even a member of the First Congregational Church, which Lillian attended. She taught Latin and Greek at Oakland High but was itching to return to Europe. Another extended tour was beyond her means, so like other impecunious female travelers, she decided to cover her expenses by chaperoning some young ladies. Eva Powell and Mary Susan Barker completed the party, and the three sets of parents met with Miss Bunker to work out the financial arrangements. Eva, a member of another wealthy Oakland family, had been friendly with Lillian through high school and college. She was engaged but in no hurry to marry (and as it turned out, she never did), while Mary Susan was unsure whether to accept "a very fine offer" of marriage, so her parents encouraged her to travel while she made up her mind.[1]

Meanwhile, Lillian returned to the university and started preparations for her doctorate. She registered for advanced courses in French and English, gaining a grade 1 in the former and "no report" in the latter. Her heart was not in it; she did not register for the second semester and devoted herself entirely to preparations for her European tour. In light of her earlier determination to study, Lillian's decision to drop out of graduate school is odd, to say the least, but there are some hints in her memoirs. On her return to Oakland she had resumed her friendship with Alma Brown, a college friend and serious shopper. Alma had numerous charge accounts and taught Lillian "that there were other things to spend money for besides books." They patronized the best shops and bought the things fashionable young women required: Dana Gibson drawings and the latest novels at Smith's, bunches of violets at Sanborn's, eau de cologne at Bowman's. They spent a great deal of time at Lehnhardt's devouring oyster cocktails, ice cream, and candy. It was a rather aimless existence, enlivened by Saturdays when Lillian and Alma took the ferry to San Francisco to lunch at the Golden Pheasant before taking in a matinee at the Tivoli.[2]

Perhaps Lillian started to enjoy being a young lady about town; perhaps she began to doubt whether the "strenuous life" was worth the struggle. Perhaps the Mollers had persuaded her that she could learn more by traveling, and she simply gave in to parental pressure; the European tour was a reward for withdrawing from graduate school. Whatever the reason, Lillian was not the only late-Victorian woman to see travel as an antidote to study. A notable voyager was Jane Addams, who, after she dropped out of medical school, wrote to her friend Ellen Starr, "It seems quite essential for the establishment of my health and temper that I have a radical change and so I have accepted the advice given to every exhausted American 'go abroad.'"[3]

Lillian and her friends were part of a mass movement of middle-class Americans, an estimated one hundred thousand of whom were traveling to Europe each year in the early 1900s. They went for many reasons: for culture, for cures, for "conspicuous consumption," or for personal or sexual liberation. Freud suggested that there was a connection between the longing to travel and the guilty desire to escape from home and family; a desire to escape was one of Lillian's main motives, whether or not she was able to admit it.[4]

In a halfhearted attempt to keep up her studies, Lillian joined the Ebell Society, an elite women's club in Oakland. Founded in 1876 by a feminist man, its members were at the forefront of many progressive causes; they helped finance the Oakland Public Library and were interested in woman suffrage and racial justice. Guest speakers included Julia Ward Howe, Susan B. Anthony, and Booker T. Washington, the first major black leader to visit California. The Ebell Society ran a number of weekly classes; Lillian attended one where she and the other members read and discussed "culture," and she conscientiously read books on painting, on legends, and on the lives of the saints in preparation for her trip to Europe.[5]

The tour was meticulously planned: train and boat schedules were studied, tickets secured, hotel reservations made. More new clothes were bought and even Lillian managed to show a little interest, though she later claimed she found the guidebooks they purchased much more enthralling. There was no shortage of such books, some of which were specifically intended for women travelers. While these preparations were under way, Lillian tried to fit the model of upper-middle-class ladyhood. She made social calls as her mother expected and went to society teas. She contemplated spending her time in more constructive ways such as settlement work or teaching Sunday school in a Chinese mission, but did not do so; instead, she drifted through the next six months becoming increasingly irritable.[6]

The atmosphere in the Moller house was fractious. Lillian always claimed that she had a hot temper, though in later years it was so much under control that only her closest associates could detect her seething fury at some slight. As a young woman, however, her family felt her temper was "an awful calamity" and tried everything they knew to teach her to be patient. They were not very successful in the spring of 1903; Lillian acknowledged her irritability in an apologetic letter just before her steamer left Boston. She told her parents, "When I come home I shall . . . be oh so good and never be cross at all." A letter to her sister Josephine echoed the same theme: "Do try and make everybody keep the peace," Lillian wrote; "it ought to be easy with one away. Perhaps I shall learn somewhere to do it myself."[7]

Lillian left Oakland in the middle of June 1903. She and Eva had arranged to meet Mary Susan Barker and Miss Bunker in Boston. As the train pulled out of the station, Lillian breathed a sigh of relief: she was on her way to a great adventure. It was her ninth transcontinental train journey and she felt very sophisticated compared with her friend, who had never "been east" before. Lillian had great fun showing Eva the ropes as they dealt with the porters and ordered their meals in the parlor car. Although both women were college graduates in their twenties, this was the first time they had traveled so far without chaperones and, as Lillian recalled, "the trip across the country was too fast to suit them." After a few days in New York, they set off for Boston. They had a rather disagreeable journey. The train was full of "true believers" traveling to a Christian Science convention and the parlor car was full, so the two young women had a hot and dirty trip in a regular coach. Minnie Bunker met them at the station and escorted them to the Parker House Hotel, where Lillian had lodged with her father ten years earlier. Minnie was staying with relatives in the Back Bay area of Boston and was expecting her brother Fred to come from Maine to see her off.

After lunch Lillian and Eva took a short subway ride to the Boston Public Library to see the recently installed murals. They climbed the imposing
marble stairs and walked into a dark, wood-paneled room. They were craning
their necks to admire Edward Abbey's paintings of Sir Launfaul in pursuit of
the Holy Grail when Miss Bunker appeared. To their surprise, she invited
them to join her for a ride in her cousin Frank Bunker Gilbreth's new car. Lillian reluctantly turned away from medieval chivalry and reentered the twentieth century. Outside the library, however, was a big red Winton Six Coaching Car that rapidly replaced Sir Launfaul in Lillian's affections. Frank's car
was one of the most expensive models available in 1903; it cost three times as
much as a Model A Ford or even a Cadillac. Lillian was deeply impressed. She
told her family it was the "most gorgeous automobile" she had ever seen; it
was "three times as big as Mr. McWilliams's" and was "beautiously upholstered in black leather."[8]

Lillian's first impression of Frank Bunker Gilbreth was of a jovial man
in his mid-thirties wearing a well-cut suit and the "most stylish automobile
cap and glasses you ever saw." He was heavy-set, "not fat, but pretty heavy,
'chunky' Miss Bunker calls it." She noticed his curious, triangle-shaped eyes,
which sloped down at the outside corners and that he had "*plenty* of brown
hair!" She soon found out that he was a building contractor and told her family that he had "heaps of money which he has made all himself." Lillian assured her parents that his lack of a college education was not necessarily a
drawback, since he was "well read and talks agreeably." She noted again, "He
really has money to spare." Lillian was very much taken with Frank, as well
as with his car, and she wanted her parents to approve. Similarly, Frank
needed his mother's approval, and the first thing he did after meeting Lillian
and Eva was to take them home to see his mother and aunt. Lillian noticed
that family ties were strong and that Frank was the center of his mother's life.
The visit was short, however, and Lillian had little time to take in all the details of the apartment and Frank's adoring relatives, as Fred Bunker, Minnie's
brother, was due to arrive at North Station any minute.

Frank parked outside the station. "I took charge of the auto," Lillian reported. "I had to keep the engine running and it was great fun." When Frank
returned, she asked him "something about the machinery" and Frank "took
off the whole of the front part to let me see it." Lillian admired it enthusiastically, though as she later commented, "It is doubtful whether their host was
much deceived or in the least impressed." Deceived, no; impressed, perhaps,
for Frank started to take an interest in his guest. She reported gleefully, "Mr.
Gilbrith [*sic*] must have been impressed by our interest in machinery for he
asked if we would like another ride," adding, "of course, we simply were
wild for one." They spent the afternoon touring the countryside before

Frank dropped them off at the Parker House. It had been a long and interesting day.

The next morning Lillian and Eva rose early and breakfasted on coffee
and the famous Parker House rolls. Then, wearing their best silk dresses, they
walked the short distance to the Old South Church. In the afternoon they
took another, longer look at the Abbey murals, which, Lillian remarked enthusiastically, were "the beautifulest I ever did see!" Returning to the hotel to
change at about four in the afternoon, they had just ordered dinner when a
waiter appeared bearing a card from Frank Gilbreth that said, "F.B.G. and the
Buzz-Wagon." Eva sensibly suggested sending a message back telling him to
return after they had eaten, but Lillian would not hear of it; she canceled their
order and went out at once. It was a beautiful June afternoon and Frank took
Lillian and Eva, plus Minnie Bunker and her brother Fred, on a tour of modern Boston. On Lillian's previous visit she and her father had walked across
Harvard Yard and viewed the homes of the New England writers she enjoyed
so much. This time, it was only on the insistence of Minnie Bunker that they
went anywhere near Harvard, and Frank agreed to drive past the college
merely because his contracting firm had built some of the dormitories. They
did take in the Bunker Hill Monument, which made Lillian "giggle inter-
nally" as she recalled her sisters' irreverent nickname for their Latin teacher.
Like most of the Bunkers, Minnie was rather stout.

Lillian had never taken much interest in building before and tried desper-
ately to make sense of what she was seeing and to respond intelligently. She
was eager to make a good impression, and she was dismayed to find that there
were so many things she knew nothing about. Frank spoke of speed building
and reinforced concrete; Lillian recalled years later, "It was a whole new
world, vital and challenging and it made a deep impression on at least one
member of the group." Frank was no better off when she discussed her interests. He listened politely to Lillian's comments on the history and literature
of Boston, but she soon realized that they were speaking different languages.

In the early evening the car had a flat tire. Lillian was not completely surprised, for she felt the vehicle had been "more like a mountain goat than an
automobile" as they drove around Frank's building sites. As the two men
tried, without success, to repair the damaged tire, a large number of small
boys appeared, apparently from nowhere, making "frank and caustic remarks" on both the car and its driver. Lillian saw how embarrassed Frank
was and as the eldest of nine, not to mention someone who was certified to
teach in the California public schools, she knew how to divert the attention
of the young. So she took the children onto an adjoining vacant lot and
started to tell them Hans Christian Andersen's story "Tinder Box." "They
came like little lambs," she told her parents. "I sat on a rock and they pressed

so close that I was glad I had been a sensible girl and left my silk dress at the hotel."

After a few minutes Lillian noticed that Frank was sitting behind the children, listening intently. There was only one thing for it, and that was to spin out the stories for as long as possible. When her stories were exhausted, she got the children to sing their school songs to her. Eventually, Fred returned with a new tire, the car was ready, "and we sailed off in triumph" just as the sun was setting. Frank was full of compliments and told Lillian she was "The Hypnotist." He said he had counted forty-two children and a dog in her audience. Lillian told her parents that "Mr. Gilbrith presented neat compliments in public and told Miss Bunker in private that 'I was a brick' and could have him and his automobile for four cents, so I grew comforted." As they set off again, Frank discovered "with a groan" that Lillian and Eva had not dined. They all had a late supper and then the young women returned to the Parker House, Lillian wishing, as she fell asleep, that she had spent "less time on literature and more on science and current events."

Lillian was clearly attracted to her chaperone's cousin. She had reached the age of twenty-five with no serious attachments and when she met Frank she was overwhelmed by him. He was very different from all the young men she had met before. She found him very challenging, but she held her own in the verbal sparring that went on. She told her sister that Frank took delight in having the last word. His "favorite remark is 'Now I guess that will hold you for a while,'" when we try to make a smart remark and he adds a smarter one." Frank was also impressed by Lillian. He later wrote, "You had a way of directing the conversation to things that the one you were talking to was most interested in," and he went on to complain, "In fact you did this so well that it annoyed me, because I couldn't retaliate in the same line to save me— and when I got a good start I found that you invariably switched it back the other way."[9]

This mutual attraction did not escape Minnie Bunker's sharp chaperone's eye. She hinted to Frank that Lillian was, like her friends Eva and Mary, "spoken for," if not actually engaged, and as Frank later wrote to Lillian, this "made it very necessary that I should keep off the grass." This was difficult, however, as he found Lillian Moller hard to resist and resolved to find out how "*hard* and *fast*" she was engaged.[10]

Lillian found her few days in Boston very unsettling and told her parents that she wished she could have stayed there longer, "as we are having such a grand time." The Mollers can hardly have found the rest of the letter reassuring, as she described all the invitations she had received and her desire to travel. "What would you say," she asked, "if I didn't come home at all, but just went around and around paying visits until there was nothing at all left of me?" She was careful to add, "But you needn't be afraid, my dear own people,—you seem even dearer than ever as I get ready to go far away from you." Nevertheless, she was beginning to see a possible escape from home.

It rained much of the following day. Lillian watched the raindrops getting larger and more persistent and was bitterly disappointed when the planned ride in Frank's car was canceled. She spent a very quiet afternoon, but they met for dinner and Lillian was able to get a good look at Frank's family. His mother, Martha Bunker Gilbreth, was a tall, stout woman in her late sixties; his "duplicate mother," Aunt Caroline, was thirteen years younger and only a little less stout. They seemed to think Frank could do no wrong and hung on his every word.

It was a very simple meal: Lillian was worried about seasickness and ate very little. She told her sister that she had been "taking that old Brush's Sea Sick Cure faithfully. It is horrid, but I want to do all I can then if I'm sick it wasn't my fault. Mr. Gilbrith says if I can only take a good long nap soon after we sail I shall become adjusted to the motion without realizing it. Well, I don't care—I shall at least have a grand send off to look back to." Lillian spent most of the evening talking to Frank, though she found much of his conversation disconcerting. He described his interest in ancient Egypt, in the transmigration of souls, and in the influence of the past on the present. He also talked about the future and the things he hoped to do with his life, but when he suggested that she might write about his experiences, he "left her entirely at a loss as to how to reply."

Lillian rose next morning still rather bewildered by Frank's words. Dressing carefully in her "beauteous blue linen waist" and donning a long coat, she felt she looked "quite stylish," especially when she added an "off my face hat." Lillian had experienced difficulties with hats in the past, particularly one that never looked right when she got it back from the shop. She eventually returned it, complaining "I thought this was becoming when I bought it, but I never have since." The milliner took one look at the hat and said, "Well, Miss Moller, it would help if you wore it right side to," whereupon she marked the front with an X of white thread and set it back on Lillian's head. Perhaps Lillian's traveling hat had a white X; it was certainly perched at a jaunty angle.[11]

Frank had promised to drive them to the boat, but he was very late and Lillian paced the room as she wondered whether he would come in time. When he eventually arrived, he explained that he had been in court, having been arrested some days earlier for exceeding the ten-miles-per-hour speed limit. He drove them to the dock at a stately pace, but to Lillian's delight they and the Winton Six were "the observed of all observers." Frank saw the women to their stateroom and almost spoke to Lillian about his feelings, but he hesitated "and all was lost, but only for a few months." He later said that he wished that they could have been married in June 1903. Lillian was equally attracted to Frank but told him later that if he had spoken to her it would have ruined her whole summer. Frank promised to meet the party when they returned in November, and just before the ship sailed he posed for a photograph with Lillian, who was wearing her large hat and an even bigger smile.[12]

The Atlantic crossing was foggy, and Lillian spent most of the time sitting quietly in her steamer chair. In her own words she was "living over every moment of her Boston stay, a thousand times." Her friends assumed she was feeling a little seasick and left her alone, but sharp-eyed Minnie Bunker was feeling responsible for Lillian's emotional welfare and tried to find out what kind of impression Frank had made. Lillian said very little, and finally the chaperone decided to warn her off. Describing Frank as invariably "gallant to ladies," Minnie said he was devoted to his work and had little time for anything else, and she stressed that he would be unlikely to leave his mother. She added that he had no reason to marry since his mother and aunt provided "a perfect home, unlimited devotion, everything done for him." In addition, his married sister lived nearby and if he was interested in children, he had Anne's two "beautiful children to enjoy." As a final reason she added, untruthfully, that Frank had been "deeply attached to a beautiful girl who died," and his faithfulness to her memory meant that he would never marry. Although Lillian later claimed she was not deceived by the dead rival, she never quite forgave Minnie Bunker for "almost wrecking romance."[13]

6

Even Quest Makers Change Their Minds

In laying out his life's plan Frank had decided among other things that in all likelihood he would not marry. Why marry when his home life was so ideal? However, he changed his mind, as even Quest Makers do and made two trips, one to become engaged and the second, married.

Lillian Moller Gilbreth, *The Quest of the One Best Way* (1925)

LILLIAN AND HER PARTY docked in Liverpool in early July 1903 and set off immediately for the Lake District. Minnie Bunker had organized a whistle-stop tour of the major literary sites of England and Scotland. Lillian described her impressions in a daily journal, which, unfortunately, has not survived; when she wrote about her "grand" tour many years later, her memories amounted to little more than a list of places visited. Remarkably, perhaps, for someone who protested for most of her life that she did not care for shopping, she included numerous references to clothes and to souvenirs she purchased.

They started with Wordsworth's cottage in Grasmere and then paid flying visits to Edinburgh (Sir Walter Scott), Stratford-upon-Avon (Shakespeare), and Canterbury, where they visited the cathedral and thought about Chaucer. They spent a longer period in London, where they visited the Old Curiosity Shop, a delight to Lillian with her long-standing love of Dickens. Minnie Bunker's schedule was tightly packed with lectures or museum visits in the mornings, excursions in the afternoons, and plays or concerts at night, though she also allowed them occasional breaks for shopping or rest. The group stayed together most of the time, but "bookish and studious" Lillian wrote later that she visited more museums than the others cared for. Sometimes, however, they "dragged" her to shops and fashionable restaurants, whereupon she found "that she had latent capacities for enjoying both that she had never suspected!" The high point of Lillian's visit to England came when she stood in Westminster Abbey and saw the stone with the inscription "O rare Ben Jonson!" It took her back to her old life, to her Berkeley thesis on *Bartholemew Fair* and to the promise—or threat—of a life with Frank Gilbreth, which gave her pause for thought. The evening before she left Boston Frank had asked her about herself. She had explained something of her interest in English literature, to which he replied, making it very clear that her interests were not his, "I don't know anything about Ben Jonson or Samuel Johnson, but I know all about the Johnsons who are prize fighters and builders!" With her thesis still fresh in her mind, however, Lillian had found a twentieth-century example of her energetic Jacobean hero.[1]

Lillian tried to put thoughts of Frank to one side and concentrate on her travels and her shopping. After crossing the English Channel, they spent a few days visiting Dutch and Belgian galleries. In Brussels she bought some lace, which she stowed in her travel bag along with the Scottish plaid and the beautiful silks bought at Liberty's London store. When they arrived in Paris, there was little time for shopping, as Minnie Bunker had filled every moment with visits to museums and galleries and drives in the Bois de Boulogne.

After Paris, while the others went to Switzerland, Lillian "dashed" to Berlin to visit her German relations: her cousin Emma had married a son of Bismarck's secretary. Lillian, with her mind full of Frank Gilbreth, recalled seeing Adolph von Tiedemann as a wholly unsuitable kind of husband. He was small, slim, and nervous and seemingly a "domestic tyrant." Her cousin, however, "seemed accustomed to his dictatorial ways" and was prepared to drop everything when he pointed to the piano and commanded, "Emma, play!" His children seemed afraid of him, too, and they all tiptoed around the house when father was home but "became merry and almost noisy when he went to his office." Lillian particularly disliked what she saw as von Tiedemann's "imperious nature." One evening, after she had dressed for the opera in what she described as a "conservative evening gown," he sent her back upstairs to change. He stipulated that she wear a blouse "long as to sleeve and high as to throat" and a black skirt, since "only light ladies wear evening dresses to the opera!" Lillian was a well-behaved guest and did as she was told, but she fumed inwardly "and resolved that no girl of her generation would marry a German and above all, a German officer!"

Lillian rejoined her traveling companions in Munich, where they heard Wagner's *Ring* cycle in its entirety. She had studied some Wagner pieces with her piano teacher, Mr. Metcalf, but now heard the "thrilling" music "for the first time sung as it should be sung." She enjoyed the experience so much that "the entire trip would have been justified by that all-too-short stay in Munich." Their next stop was Vienna, where, Lillian recalled, "the shopping contingent took over." Minnie Bunker, with Yankee frugality, was convinced that Viennese styles were comparable to those in Paris but with much lower prices. Lillian bought a suit and a hat and felt herself very stylish. Between fittings and trips to the milliner's, the party still had some energy left to visit museums, drink chocolate, and spend their evenings at the theater. Their last stop was Italy, with trips to Pompeii, Rome, and Florence, "every hour of every day an excursion into the past." The Italian part of the journey was rather a letdown, as they were all exhausted; they had been traveling for nearly five months and were eager to return home.

The four women arrived in the United States in late November 1903. The seas were rough but the travelers were too tired to mind. They spent their time making lists of their purchases for the customs inspectors, checking that they had gifts for all their relatives, and making sure that their journals were up to date. As the steamer approached New York, Lillian's spirits rose, and while the whole party was excited to see the Statue of Liberty raising her arm in salute, she was looking for a particular welcome. As the boat slowly edged its way into the harbor, she stood on the deck scanning the crowds gathered below and to her great delight saw Frank Gilbreth standing near her parents on the quay. Frank later recalled to Lillian that she "turned around and hugged someone, either Miss Powell or Miss Barker (just to show me how you *could* do it) and then you danced up and down." He pushed his way through the crowd to the bottom of the gangway and shook the travelers' hands as they came off the boat. There was an enormous amount of luggage but Frank did not help to carry any of it, explaining that he had had his appendix removed a few weeks earlier. Major abdominal surgery was far from routine in 1903, when an appendectomy was a life-threatening procedure. Frank went into the hospital with some foreboding and later told Lillian he had thought of writing her a long letter telling her of his feelings but decided not to. He felt that "if anything happened to him it was better not to have complicated her life," so his only communication had been a few brief postcards addressed to the whole party.[2]

Lillian was delighted to see Frank. Her family agreed to meet him for dinner and later they all went to a show, the London production of *Ben Hur*, which was playing to packed houses. The next day Frank took her to the Metropolitan Museum of Art to see his beloved Egyptian wing, but he arrived at her hotel so late that she almost refused to go. What he did not tell her at the time, but confessed later, was that he had stopped to quiz one of her friends about Lillian's feelings for him. Mary Susan Barker was encouraging, according to a teasing letter from Frank, saying, "you thought I was not-so-bad and that if I really spoke to you in New York before you went back west I would take advantage of the only chance to win you . . . but if you got back

to your own home it would be all up with me. . . . That your mother had noticed that I was the victim of spooney infatuation and that she (your mother)
(Ha!Ha!) had hauled you over the coals to see just where *you* stood and that
you had been court-martialled for one or more hours on the subject."[3]

Lillian's mother was indeed suspicious. She was concerned about Frank
Gilbreth's intentions, and although a daytime visit to a museum was permitted, she vetoed Frank's plan to take her twenty-five-year-old daughter to the
theater without a chaperone. As Frank commented to Lillian, "The things
your 'mother would never let you do' may fill a volume." Frank could, however, be very persuasive when he wanted, and although the Mollers had
planned to take Lillian back with them to California almost immediately, he
convinced them to postpone their return for a few days. His ostensible reason
was to show Lillian's sisters Elinor and Ernestine the sights of Boston; the real
reason was to get his mother's approval of his courtship.[4]

While Lillian's mother was cautious, Frank's mother was a formidable
obstacle; Lillian's first few encounters with her were an ordeal. Frank was
practically worshiped by his mother and his aunt. Lillian later described him
as "a family idol, waited on by inches, never asked to raise a finger, from
whom all household problems and complexities were to be carefully concealed, who found always a smiling welcome, a bountifully spread table, keen
admiration." Female control of domestic arrangements was, of course, normal in Victorian America, as was "keen admiration" for the male head of the
household. What was unusual was the degree of idolatry and Frank's continuing and total dependence on his mother to provide this support.[5]

Frank was most eager to gain his mother's approval. He told her of his
wish to marry weeks before he actually proposed; he later told Lillian that his
realization of "*that's the* girl, but *how?*" had been followed by a "quiet declaration to my family that they'd better make *their* plans accordingly." Those
plans would include his mother and his aunt, as well as Lillian, for he was determined that his marital home would also include them, and the two women
were more than happy to agree. Lillian had less choice in the matter, but the
strength of her feeling for Frank overrode any worries about such an unusual
arrangement.[6]

Lillian visited Frank's office while the Mollers were seeing the sights of
Boston. She wore her up-to-the-minute Vienna-tailored suit and a big new
hat with a fluffy chiffon veil, which she very soon realized was an "inappropriate and foolish" outfit for such a visit. Meeting Frank's secretary made Lillian more uncomfortable. Anne Bowley was a very competent woman who
"could do anything from extend a note at the bank to keeping her boss's
crowded schedule in order," and she was dressed sensibly in a neat shirtwaist.
Lillian wanted Frank to take her seriously, not see her as an idle society

woman, which was what her outfit proclaimed. She felt even more over-dressed when Frank took her to visit some of his construction sites, though her host seemed oblivious to her discomfort. She made the best of it, deciding that since everything was "so interesting," clothes were "as usual, a slight thing to mention."[7]

That evening Lillian and her parents dined with Frank's mother and aunt, then they all went to the theater to see *The Wizard of Oz*. Frank found two seats well away from the rest of the party, but as Lillian remarked later, "Nobody seemed to think that that presented any difficulty!" Finally, the Mollers left for home, taking Lillian with them. Still Frank had said nothing, though he mentioned that he had business in the West and would try to follow on a later train. He caught up with them in Chicago. It was a cold and windy December day, and icy rain was falling when he appeared at the Mollers' hotel. After a little shopping—Frank needed sturdy shoes for the slushy pavements and could not resist looking in camera shops—he took Lillian out. Annie Moller's attitude was starting to soften; she allowed Lillian to go to the theater without a chaperone for the first time in her life. Frank told Lillian that he would visit her in Oakland, but by this time she was a little overwhelmed by her "strenuous and insistent" friend and looked forward to a few days' peace before he reappeared. The first she knew of his presence was when her mother told her that someone claiming to be the White Rabbit was on the telephone. Lillian remembered that she had talked to him about *Alice in Wonderland* and guessed that Frank was letting her know he had now read it.[8]

Lillian's mother was warming to Frank. She fussed over him, not letting him carry his own suitcase or play with the young Moller boys because it was too soon after his appendectomy. She relaxed her surveillance and as Frank commented to his mother, she was the ideal chaperone who "knows just how to keep out of the way at the right time." He went with Lillian, her father, "and a fine he-cousin" to a Christmas football game, helped Lillian decorate the tree on Christmas Eve, then put on his "glad rags" and sat down in the Mollers' grand dining room with all eleven Mollers and seven Browns. Frank was very conscious that he was "on exhibition" to "sort of 'see what Lilly [sic] found in her travels.'" He showed off a great deal and survived the inspection, and although Lillian remembered the occasion as "rather an ordeal," Frank boasted that he performed "with great nonchalance and apparent enjoyment."[9]

The day after Christmas Lillian and Frank went to San Francisco. It was a beautiful California winter's day; the sun was shining and there was a light breeze. Lillian was comfortable; she was on familiar territory, and Frank's questions about building projects soon stopped as he enjoyed the sights and sounds of Chinatown. They lunched at the Cliff House, a turreted hotel perched high on the rocks overlooking the Pacific, and then took each other's photographs on Sutro Beach. Lillian was wearing a striped two-piece, which accentuated her tiny waist, and a great big smile. Her hand was raised as if to catch hold of her hat, which looked as though it was about to blow away. Frank stood, arms akimbo, his vest stretched tightly across his stomach. He wore his bowler hat at a rakish angle and looked extremely pleased with himself. Later that day they sat together on a bench overlooking the Golden Gate, and Frank asked Lillian to marry him. He explained that he had "a life filled with strenuous work ahead," that he could not leave his mother and aunt, that his business life was complicated and he had "innumerable responsibilities to face and problems to solve." Despite these apparent obstacles, Lillian was willing—indeed eager—to share his life.

Later that day Frank wrote an odd letter to his mother: he wanted to reassure her that she would always have a home with him. Almost as if it was too risky to play it straight, he wrote as if his engagement was a building contract, telling Martha that he reserved the right "to always make my new home *the home in fee simple of my mother and old aunt*—to all of which the party of the second part cheerfully and apparently by preference agreed." He went on, "I was awarded the contract to furnish all labor and materials to support a wife and family on a basis of cost plus all the usual joys and sorrows that attend that kind of a job." There was still a problem with Lillian's father; Frank noted that "the actual date of signing contract and beginning work will be delayed for some time until the frost is out of some of the people here who would think it consisted of hurriedly prepared plans—we have agreed to say nothing to *anyone* except Mamma [Annie Moller] and you." He warned his mother not to tell any of her Boston friends and even to use her discretion about informing her sister Caroline or her niece Jane. Frank insisted, "*No one is to know anything about it until I come West again.*"[10]

Frank left Oakland three days after Lillian agreed to marry him, and they did not meet again until he returned to California for their wedding nearly ten months later. In the meantime there were many obstacles to be overcome. One serious problem was the precarious state of Frank's finances; another was their very different backgrounds and personalities. The most immediate obstacle, however, was Lillian's father, who wanted to be sure his daughter would be well provided for. As a plumber's merchant he was well aware that the building trade was notoriously unstable and that whenever there was a recession the construction business was the first to suffer.[11]

The Mollers knew next to nothing about Frank and were anxious to find out about his background; they were reassured to discover that he was a Maine Yankee with a distinguished family tree. He traced his paternal grandmother's family back to 1630, when his ancestor Thomas Dudley, four-time Massachusetts governor, arrived in New England. Frank's late father had been of Scots-Irish stock: the family believed that the name was originally Galbraith, though a deaf recorder in some election misspelled it. Frank's mother, Martha, was a middle child in Daniel Bunker's family of fifteen. The original Bunkers arrived in Maine from Devon, England, in the 1640s, but by the middle of the nineteenth century there were few opportunities for ambitious people in Maine, so most of Martha's siblings left to look for work or adventure. The Bunker women were made of particularly stern stuff: two headed schools and one trained as an artist in Paris. Martha stayed in Maine; she started teaching in a village school in 1849, when she was fifteen, and left nine years later to marry. John Hiram Gilbreth ran a hardware store, though Fairfield, Maine, did not offer the same business opportunities as downtown Oakland. Gilbreth was, however, an energetic salesman; photographs of his store showed advertisements "at every available place," and the back of his stationery was also covered with advertising. Gilbreth was also a stockbreeder; he tried to produce "the best Knox horse; the best Jersey Cow; the best pig." His pride and joy was his Morgan stallion, Gilbreth Knox, an outstanding trotting horse.[12]

Frank was the youngest of three Gilbreth children. He was born in July 1868, joining eight-year-old Anne and three-year-old Mary. His father was delighted, though his pride was mixed with a certain impatience that this wonderful event should happen in the middle of his busiest season. "You will be glad to know," he wrote his mother, "that Martha has a nice-looking boy, born this morning at nine o'clock. She is as comfortable as could be expected. Her babe weighs eleven pounds and has dark brown hair. I am in great haste. My business drives me. I have sold twenty three mowing machines at retail in my store within three days, so you see I am busy." Frank's early childhood was spent in Maine, playing in the winter snow and paddling in the river in the summer. He remembered his father showing him the new inventions and products in the hardware store, or lifting him up high on his shoulders to see the wonderful horse. These idyllic days came to a sudden end in November 1871, when Frank was three and a half years old. Gilbreth Knox was ill; Hiram sat with the horse through a cold Maine night, caught a chill that developed into pneumonia, and died three days later. He was only thirty eight.[13]

Martha was devastated. She became seriously ill and took little interest in life or her surroundings for almost a year. During that time her in-laws liquidated her husband's estate on her behalf. They did very well, selling Gilbreth Knox for the amazing sum of $17,000, and the four colts sired by the stallion brought in another $16,000. The store was sold and it looked as though Martha and her children were comfortably provided for. However, something happened whereby one of the Gilbreth relations lost—or stole—almost all the money. The timing of this catastrophe is unclear, but a recent account suggests that the money disappeared a few years later while Martha and her family were living in Andover, Massachusetts, and that the two most likely suspects were Ed Flint and Colonel Clayton Hale, both brothers-in-law of Hiram Gilbreth. As Martha severed all ties with the Gilbreths and refused thereafter to discuss the matter, the real culprit may never be known.[14]

Before this happened, Martha Gilbreth had left Maine in search of better schools for her children. She and her sister Caroline (always known as Kit) rented a house in Andover, sent Anne to the Abbott Academy, one of the best girls' schools in the area, and taught Frank at home until he was old enough to attend the local elementary school. They stayed in Andover until the fall of 1878, when Frank was ten. By this time Martha's money had disappeared; not only could she no longer afford to send him to Phillips Academy, as she had planned, she also had to take Anne out of school only a semester before she was due to graduate with the Class of '79.[15]

Martha Gilbreth decided to move to Boston, where there were excellent public schools. Frank was not at all happy about this, and when moving day arrived, he was nowhere to be seen. His mother went without him, though she quietly left word and train fare with neighbors. Frank followed the next day: by spending the day with his friends he avoided much of the work of moving. This story demonstrates an interesting power dynamic between mother and son, one in which each was prepared to call the other's bluff. It also marks the beginning of a pattern by which Frank Gilbreth avoided problems, both emotional and physical, by absenting himself and letting his womenfolk do the work.[16]

Like many middle-class women in reduced circumstances, Martha opened a boardinghouse. She knew that the five hundred dollars a year she could earn as a schoolteacher was insufficient to keep herself, her sister Kit, and her three children; her sister rarely sold any paintings, and Anne needed expensive piano lessons. Martha first checked where the best schools were located, then found a suitable property, a five-story building on Columbus Avenue. Unfortunately, the owner wanted a thousand dollars a year in rent, payable in advance, and Martha had only about a hundred dollars left. According to family legend, she put on her best clothes, walked into a bank, and somehow, with no security, persuaded a group of Boston bankers to lend her a thousand dollars. The bank president asked her how she knew she could run a boardinghouse, and she is said to have replied firmly, "*any* woman raised in the state of Maine could run one." Frank thus lived in a boarding house from the age of ten. His mother, assisted by a succession of Irish maids, ran a "splendid, ultra-respectable" establishment, a place that was simultaneously "a residence, a restaurant, a club, a protector of morals and a place where a respectable stranger could become acquainted." Martha made a success of the venture and invested in her daughters' education. Anne studied with noted local music teachers and later traveled to Weimar, Germany, where she took a master class from the famous pianist and composer Franz Liszt. Mary Gilbreth attended Radcliffe College, became a member of the American Association for the Advancement of Science, and was making a reputation as a botanist until she contracted consumption and died in 1893 at the age of thirty.[17]

Frank spent his childhood surrounded by a group of strong, accomplished women, with no male role models close at hand. He reacted by becoming defiantly and almost delinquently "all boy." Lillian's account of him, written for her children and the scientific management community in *The Quest of the One Best Way* (1925), presents him as the opposite of her introverted, bookish self. She described him as more interested in playing than studying and always willing to fight. Frank was a poor student and made so little progress at Boston's Rice Grammar School that Martha taught him at home for a year. He scraped by in his classes at English High School, and although he enjoyed mathematics and mechanical drawing, French, English, grammar, and spelling occupied as little of his time as he could possibly manage. He was once able to get only two correct answers out of twenty-six on a spelling test: he was so proud of this feat that he kept the test paper for the rest of his life. Frank's grades improved in his junior year, when he was top of the class in math and science. He was a first lieutenant in his high school battalion, though his captain remembered him as a less than perfect officer who only "fell in with the duties when he felt like it and there was nothing more interesting for him elsewhere." These attributes were to characterize Frank Gilbreth for the rest of his life, and Lillian had to learn to work with and around his self-centeredness.[18]

When Frank was in his senior year, his mother thought he should go to the Massachusetts Institute of Technology. To please her he followed the college preparatory course and took the entrance examinations in the spring of 1885. According to his own recollections he "passed creditably," though the college records show no reference to him. Lillian wrote, in a very common examination anecdote, "he probably furnished quite a little amusement to the examiners. One question read, 'Can you name, etc.,' and Frank, ever ready to enjoy a joke, answered briefly and to the point, 'I can.'" Frank was, however, far from eager to spend four more years studying, so when Renton Whidden, his old Sunday school teacher, offered him a position in his building firm, Frank accepted. His decision to forgo college reflects his class and status concerns. Frank wanted his mother to give up the boardinghouse, and he also felt that being a part of the emerging middle-class occupational structure was somehow less manly than working for oneself. Frank's decision was unusual, as most of his classmates were moving into white-collar jobs such as account-ing, banking, and sales. There are also gender implications in his decision to avoid office work, an increasingly feminized world, in favor of manual labor, which was seen as masculine. As a school friend noted, Frank liked to show off in front of women: "He used to delight, on his noon-day hour, to walk through the fashionable shopping district in his mortar-spattered overalls to see how many of his girl friends would recognize him. He was a great favor-ite among the ladies, being what the Hollywood people would call a real he-man."[19]

Whidden was looking for native-born Americans to serve as foremen to crews of Irish immigrants. Like many of his contemporaries, he saw foreign-ers as untrustworthy agitators, and the strikes and disorders of the 1870s and 1880s simply reinforced this view. After the Boston employers refused to con-cede the eight-hour day, there were numerous disputes: in 1886 alone more than 450 Massachusetts building projects were affected by strikes and lock-outs. There were also antagonisms between the native-born Protestant em-ployers and the many Irish members of the Knights of Labor. Whidden told Frank he would waive apprenticeship rules and promote Frank through the ranks, dangling the possibility of a partnership if he would sign on as a la-borer and learn the various trades. This offer was not as radical as it sounds; the old training system had broken down, and Frank's decision to learn on the job was not unique. Few colleges taught engineering and even fewer taught management, but the capital-less Frank Gilbreth had, in effect, enrolled in a management training program.[20]

Frank started work one hot July morning in 1885, just five days after his seventeenth birthday; his mother sent him on his way with a full lunch pail. He started as a bricklayer's helper and thereafter claimed that his interest in motion study was piqued by his very first day at work. Tom Bowler, a small, wiry, Shakespeare-loving Irishman, was assigned to show the newcomer what to do, but the instruction went badly. Frank pointed out that Bowler was us-ing three different methods to lay bricks: one when he was demonstrating; a second when he was chatting with a fellow worker; and a third, faster one when he realized he was falling behind his target. The foreman came over and told Frank he was there to learn the bricklaying trade, not to criticize meth-ods, and transferred him to another teacher who also used three methods that differed slightly from Tom Bowler's three. When Lillian wrote Frank's life story, she saw this experience as immensely significant, because by the end of that first day, she wrote, although he had not progressed far in bricklaying, Frank had found his purpose in life, "the Quest of the One Best Way." This quest for uniformity was far in the future, however, as Frank worked his way up the Whidden organization. Within five years he was a superintendent and was making enough money to persuade his mother to give up her boarding-house; he had grown even closer to her after the marriage of his sister Anne and the death of his sister Mary. After ten years with Whidden's he approached his employers and on finding them unwilling to offer him a partnership, he resigned.[21]

Frank Gilbreth and Company opened for business on April Fool's Day, 1895, and it was four months before he won his first contract. He had recently patented the Gilbreth Waterproof Cellar, a device to prevent leaks in concrete walls, and his first job was to build such a cellar. His other inventions included his Vertical Scaffold (1890), which was said to increase bricklayers' productivity by 25 percent, and a gravity-fed concrete mixer (1899), which provided him with a steady income for several years. He opened an office in London in 1900, where he employed an agent to supervise European patent applications and sales of the concrete mixer. His business grew rapidly; he built dams, canals, houses, mills and even a whole town, Woodland, Maine. In the first few years of the twentieth century Frank had many big contracts, particularly where large-scale concrete construction work was needed. He insisted on operating on a cost plus fixed sum basis, which caused disputes with other builders and clients. Frank was frequently in court, either suing or being sued.[22]

Frank became famous for speed work; in 1902, when he completed the new Lowell Laboratory for MIT in the record time of eleven weeks, he was the subject of a convocation address.[23] As Frank's business grew, he started to systematize his company. In 1899 he hired J. W. Buzzell, a graduate engineer, who acted as a calming influence on Frank, whose often grandiose claims meant that many other construction engineers of the day did not take him seriously. By the time Frank met Lillian Moller in June 1903, he was running one of the largest construction companies in the United States, but despite the expensive car that had so impressed Lillian, he was less wealthy and his business less stable than he liked to pretend. He was a good showman, however, and William Moller finally gave his eldest daughter permission to become engaged.

7 A Long-Distance Engagement

*"Miss Moller . . . does not remind you of a
college graduate at all, she is a very well-bred
girl, full of charming enthusiasms, brimming
over with fun and good humor."*

"The Meddler" gossip column (1904)

AFTER ACCEPTING Frank's proposal, Lillian contin-
ued living with her family and receiving daily letters from her fiancé. In the
first one, written on the train as he left Oakland, he told her that his mother
saw her as a new daughter in place of his dead sister Mary, who "was not only
my mother's favorite child, but also my mother's chum." Becoming Martha's
chum was a daunting prospect. More encouraging was a package containing
a large and beautiful solitaire diamond ring inscribed "FBG and LEM, Dec. 26
'03." Frank went to New York specially to buy it at Tiffany's, explaining "an
engagement ring bought at any other place would not be so binding." Lillian
was not able to wear it in public or show it off to her friends, however, until the
family was quite certain that he was a suitable husband for their daughter.[1]

Lillian returned to her old life, and the society page of the local paper
recorded some of her activities. Less than two weeks after Frank's departure
she was described as "one of the most attractive girls" at a tea, where her
"beautiful Parisian costume was much admired." Lillian seems to have been
very much part of Oakland society at this time, and her social life started to
worry Frank; he told her that he had few friends: "I am on good terms with a
lot of people, but I never call on them—or they on me. I shall certainly have
to start a new plan when you and I are married. You will be so lonesome when
you see how few friends I have." He added later, "I should not be able to furnish you any of that kind of fun unless you *create* it yourself."[2]

Lillian continued to attend classes and lectures at the Ebell Society. In late January 1904 she told Frank she had presented a paper there, which led to a long diatribe from Boston. Frank was hostile to society women who ventured to have opinions and announced that if he ever had anything to do with a women's club again "it will be one composed of inmates of a deaf and dumb factory." He believed that "there would probably be very few women's clubs and fewer members if the papers were printed and distributed instead of read. . . . it is interchange of thought on millinery instead of papers which holds them together." Frank's attitude toward women's clubs had been colored by his experiences building the Women's Club House at 13 Beacon Street, Boston, in 1898–99. It had been his most important contract to date, but he claimed that since the ladies frequently changed their minds he made little profit on the job. This makes his courtship of the highly educated and undoubtedly upper-middle-class Lillian Moller all the more unexpected and her decisions about her new life all the more problematic. She did not accept his prejudices without a fight, and Frank eventually conceded that women's clubs were "fine in theory," though he could not resist another antifeminist swipe: "Show me a woman who belongs to several clubs and is an officer in two or more and I'll show you an 'unclaimed misfortune' for any man or family to possess."

Several letters concerned religion, but unlike the Congregationalist Lillian, Frank was no churchgoer and was irreverent if not hostile toward organized religion. He never went to church— he spent his Sundays relaxing or playing and believed in "nothing except what is taught us by science."

Lillian started showing an interest in Frank's business from her earliest letters, somewhat to his surprise, though it was certainly a sensible move on her part. Frank was delighted. He wrote, "You are certainly a dear to be so interested in my possible contracts." Frank was uneasy about the effect his temporarily shaky finances would have on the timing of their marriage. He told Lillian that business was very bad and no new buildings were under contract. Financiers were being cautious because 1904 was an election year. In addition, it was a very cold winter in Boston, so cold that the harbor was frozen. Lillian decided to do whatever she could to improve Frank's business. At first he was apologetic about "bothering" her with "such commercial rot," but very soon he started to rely on her suggestions. She asked questions and gave Frank advice, and within a month of their engagement she was sending detailed critiques of his advertising brochures.

Lillian tried to impose order on Frank's ideas. She spent much of January 1904 editing his "Field System," a booklet he had written about the organization of his company. She reorganized it, corrected the syntax, and added an index. Frank was impressed. He told Lillian, "Your letters of criticism on the

Field System are really *masterly,*" adding, half-grudgingly, "most of the faults
I recognized previous to publication and after trying to straighten them myself, gave it up as a bad job." By February Lillian was taking an active role in
Frank's business; he jokingly referred to her as a "newly-hired graduate employee" and added in a postscript that as she was now "a partner in the firm,"
he would make no apologies for talking "shop." He must have received some
encouragement from Lillian, for in a later letter he added, "What fun we will
have when we can talk 'shop' every day."

Lillian's superior education was an issue in their relationship. Although
she did not return to her doctoral program at Berkeley, she had not entirely
given up her studies and continued to take advanced German classes. Frank
had grown up surrounded by accomplished women, but he was not entirely
comfortable with a better-educated wife, although he made frequent assertions to the contrary, telling her "every ambitious man longs to have a wife
who is his mental superior with also a superior education." Frank was very
sensitive about his lack of formal qualifications and said he was hoping to get
a college education "by induction." Lillian encouraged Frank to read more;
he claimed to admire Rudyard Kipling, was struggling to like Robert Louis
Stevenson, and was impressed by Lillian's championing of Tolstoy as "the
greatest man on earth."

When Lillian made some comments on his advertising techniques, Frank
wrote: "It impressed me to see how you attack the problem. That is certainly
the result of the college training. I want you to teach me that thoroughly one
day." Frank repeatedly asked Lillian for help in dealing with college audiences; when he was invited to speak at MIT, he asked Lillian to give him "the
college man's viewpoint" on his proposed remarks. If only she were there to
coach him, he added rather wistfully, "they would think I was really worthwhile."

By March Lillian and Frank were discussing a possible date for announcing their engagement, as by then her father's reservations were diminishing.
This was a great relief to Lillian, who was finding her secret engagement very
stressful. While her friends saw their fiancés regularly, she could not even talk
about Frank. The circumstances seem to have affected Lillian's health; Frank
was only half joking when he accused her of going out to "so many social affairs that her family have to send her to a sanitarium to recuperate." Given
Lillian's robust health for most of the rest of her life, her illness in the early
months of 1904 may have been neurasthenic as she struggled to find a "respectable" way to leave her family.

Finally, April 14, the day of the "announcement," arrived. Frank wrote visualizing the engagement party. "At this very moment Miss Moller is telling
swarms of Peacherinos that her personal title is to be passed to Gertrude as

she is about to consummate an alliance that she has forged with the 'People's Choice,'" he wrote, "—what a hum there must be and what excitement." He was not far wrong. Annie Moller had invited most of Oakland society to a four-o'clock "tea." It was an all-female occasion. Lillian, her mother and sisters, and forty of her cousins and closest friends, all wearing their finest afternoon dresses, received their guests in rooms elaborately decorated with festoons of cherry blossom and white wisteria. Four hundred invitations had been sent out, and local newspapers described it as "one of the largest receptions of the season." Lillian was wearing a high-necked white lace dress and carrying a cascading bouquet of ferns and flowers; photographs of Frank Gilbreth were prominently displayed. It had taken Lillian months to get these photographs, as Frank had vetoed several earlier versions that made him look too fat, too old, or just not right. The secret of the engagement had been well kept; most of the guests were unaware that this was anything more than Mrs. Moller and her eldest daughter repaying their social obligations. As soon as the engagement was announced, however, as one local paper reported, "a chorus of ejaculations . . . echoed through the Moller home, as the many different friends arrived and were told the news." Another declared that the "shower of congratulations and good wishes attest how many and how sincere are the friends of this charmingly typical 'California girl.'" Lillian wryly recalled that the surprise was not always complimentary. Miss Hilton, her high school history teacher, almost "sank to the floor" muttering, "At last my prayers are answered," and told Lillian that she had been sure that if her former student married at all "it would be a long white-bearded philosopher," and that she found the photograph of Frank "attractive and reassuring."[3]

The tea and the engagement were widely reported. While the Oakland press subscribed to negative stereotypes of college women, having earlier emphasized that "Miss Moller does not at all represent the usual University graduate," the *San Francisco Call* contented itself with reporting that Lillian was "credited with being one of the cleverest girls in society."[4]

Over the next few weeks hostesses vied to entertain Lillian at receptions and wedding showers, and as Lillian had already been a bridesmaid to six of her friends, there were many obligations to be repaid. After the excitement of the announcement, however, Lillian felt a great sense of anticlimax. She was still unable to say when the wedding would take place, as Frank claimed to be too busy to set a wedding date. Moreover, the way he was taking charge of all their future living arrangements made her feel helpless. Frank was moving his head office to New York, but Lillian had no say in the location and furnishing of their new home. He told her he wanted a house, but at this stage he could afford only an apartment since his finances were still not entirely in or-

der. Lillian may have wondered a little about his priorities; he told her that he
had paid off most of his debts and had about $5,000, even after buying a new
car for $1,600. Frank was always willing to spend on business promotion. He
rented new offices on West Twenty-sixth Street for $1,200 a year, which was
double his previous rent. They were very grand offices: the whole front was
plate glass so that it felt "like working out of doors," he told her.

Frank was always hustling work and landed plenty of contracts, though
sometimes he overextended himself and had serious cash flow problems.
During one such crisis Lillian worried that a wife would be an "expensive luxury." Frank replied indignantly—and revealingly—that she was necessary to
his business and that the expenses would take care of themselves. "I'll admit
you are a luxury," he continued, "but when figured on the dollars and cents
basis, I think we will make more money together—yes, lots more—than I
ever could without you to plot and plan schemes with me." He went on to
compare her to his beloved Winton Six: "Why, to put you down to a commercial plane, you are like the buzz wagon, you may cost money, but I've *got*
to have you for the help you will give me to do more and better work." He realized that this might sound a little less than romantic and added: "Now, how
do you like being compared to an automobile anyway? Perhaps it would
sound better if I put it in the form of a parable."

Lillian tried to pin Frank down to a wedding date in early October and to
set aside include four weeks for a honeymoon. Frank replied that he could
spare only six weeks altogether, including the coming and going and possibly
two weeks at the World's Fair in St. Louis; in any case, he suspected that he
might be called back to his office. Lillian was feeling unwell again, and Frank
was worried about her "overtaxing" her strength. Her spirits revived when
she discovered that Minnie Bunker, her erstwhile chaperone, was planning to
go east to visit her relatives and was willing to take Lillian with her. Frank was
full of plans: "We will pick out the flat," he wrote. He would even take her to
visit his cousin Fred in "Godforsaken Maine," and there would be "Buzz wagons—horses—days at the seashore—pop concerts—and—and—you know
the rest." Perhaps it was "the rest" that alarmed Annie Moller, who promptly
vetoed the plan as "unsuitable." Instead, Lillian spent the late spring sewing
her trousseau and collecting her linens—her mother believed that her daughter should have dozens of everything and that each item should be hand-
initialed—while Frank still procrastinated about the wedding day. The social
season finished in May and as the summer wore on, Lillian felt low and envious of friends who had fiancés nearby. She spent June and July looking after
her younger brothers and sisters in the family's (seven-bedroom) summer
"cottage" in Inverness and also visited friends in San Francisco.

Lillian and Frank's partnership took shape during this long-distance engagement: not only did she take on Frank's ideas, she also added ideas of her own. She wrote a form letter that Frank thought "so good" that he planned to "send it out just as you left it." He had plans for a new book on bricklaying. "Do you know what a 'bond' in masonry is?" he asked her in May 1904. He proposed that he would explain the process to her and "'mein frau' will write [about] it." Frank realized that her academic training was going to be invaluable: "It has helped me already in lots of ways and when we can talk instead of write it will help me a lot." He added, modestly, "I wish there were something I could give in return. I'll try to think of something for it isn't fair to have *it all one-sided*."

Lillian's education was helpful in Frank in at least two ways: she wrote clearly and elegantly, and her training in psychology was to provide an original and important new angle to Frank's work. She began incorporating psychology into his business when she sent Frank a copy of Northwestern University professor Walter Dill Scott's newly published book, *The Theory of Advertising*. Scott advocated using an emotional appeal to persuade (or manipulate) the customer to buy; he introduced many ideas that became standard advertising techniques, including the association of ideas, the power of suggestion, the direct command, and the "psychological value of the return coupon."[5] This marked the beginning of a shift in direction for both Frank and Lillian. He used psychology in his advertising, and she understood how she could work in business while remaining connected to the academic world she enjoyed.

Frank's financial problems were not over, and he spent much of the summer chasing contracts. Meanwhile, his mother found an apartment on Ninety-fourth Street at a rent of $1,200 a year. It was farther uptown than Frank had wanted, but as he told Lillian, "I don't believe we will find anything that will suit us for less." The building was only four years old and in good condition; nevertheless, the formidable Martha Bunker Gilbreth went to see the agent to persuade him to redecorate, "and if they will, she will close the lease at once." They agreed and Martha signed the lease. It was a symbolic signature underlining the importance of Martha to her son's marriage. Lillian, meanwhile, was making final preparations for her wedding and also doing Frank's work for him. He sent her an agitated note asking her to buy wedding gifts from him to her sisters. "Will you buy it for me out there and send me the bill or shall I send it from here and if from here, tell me *exactly* what to get. You know I'm an expert on dams but not dames and *so you must tell me explicitly*."

Finally, in early October, Frank left for Oakland, leaving numerous problems behind him; he faced several lawsuits and in late September 1904 he again had problems meeting payroll. His mother wrote Lillian an extraordinary letter telling her in an extended metaphor that she was sending "under separate cover a great diamond in the rough for your wedding day, a 'sonburst' of my own design." Martha cautioned Lillian not to try to change Frank: "I believe you could not chip off any part without seriously affecting the whole." Nor should she challenge him too directly: "I must caution you about rubbing it the wrong way. As you proceed with the polishing you will doubtless discover many small flaws. It is not unusual in gems of such value, but I have the greatest confidence in your skill and tact and know you will be able to smooth them down so that they will not detract from the Sterling worth of the original."[6]

Lillian certainly faced a challenge both from her "diamond in the rough" and from the diamond's mother, but first she had to go through what she remembered as the "ordeal" of her wedding. Annie Moller wanted the grandest ceremony that money could buy for her eldest daughter, but it did not turn out that way, for Frank suddenly wrote saying he was on his way and wanted a small wedding as quickly as possible. The Mollers were extremely annoyed, as the arrangements were, in Lillian's words, "completely made . . . that being the family custom for all plans." They acquiesced, albeit unwillingly, but when Frank *did* finally arrive, Annie Moller insisted on postponing the wedding until the following Wednesday, October 19, because it was her "lucky day." Lillian's mother was exerting what power she could.[7]

Lillian's later account of the few days before her wedding and of the wedding itself is full of remembered embarrassment. Although she had not seen Frank for nearly ten months, her first encounter with him turned out to be a public ordeal. On hearing that Minnie Bunker intended to meet her cousin Frank at the station, Lillian refused to go. She hoped that they could have a private moment when Frank arrived at her home, but Minnie came back to the house and added to Lillian's discomfort by insisting that the entire family join hands and dance around the engaged couple on the lawn. Frank was amused by the whole business, but though she was seething inwardly, Lillian said nothing.

As the wedding was now scheduled for the following week, Frank was forced to do what he dreaded, namely go to church with the Mollers on Sunday, October 16, and be paraded in front of all the friends and relatives. He imagined them saying, "My! Ain't he fat!" and "He's old enough to be her father." Frank was increasingly sensitive about his weight; he was only five feet nine and in spite of an effort to diet, he still weighed 217 pounds "with all my clothes on." Photographs taken that day show Frank and Lillian posing awkwardly in the October sunshine. Sometimes they stood alone but looking away from each other; sometimes they were in family groups with Grandma Delger in her bath chair and young Moller brothers and sisters in sailor suits.

Lillian wore an elaborately tailored outfit with a cutaway jacket over a high-necked lace blouse, and a dramatic hat. She looked much taller and slimmer than Frank.

Both bride and groom were nervous. Lillian was very uncomfortable having to explain to everyone why one of the brightest and most popular young women in Oakland society was having such a sudden and private wedding. The ceremony was set for 8:30 in the evening on Wednesday, October 19, 1904. Lillian later described the whole day as "long and distracting." Her friends came over in the morning and decorated the house with festoons of white roses, pink blossoms, and long streamers of white tulle. It was almost as if they were making up for not being at the wedding by covering almost every surface with flowers. They draped the stairway with greenery and hung yet more flowers from the chandeliers. Meanwhile, Frank was missing. He spent all day in the Southern Pacific offices in San Francisco trying to make reservations for the train journey back east. As the appointed hour drew near, there was no sign of Frank. The Mollers "became a little upset," and Lillian's eighteen-year-old sister, Josephine, was near panic. She was to be maid of honor and had spent the whole afternoon at an upstairs window, waiting for the groom to return and fearing that "the thrill of a lifetime" was to be denied her. When Frank finally turned up, Josephine was immensely relieved. Such a reaction suggests that the family was still not convinced that Frank would go through with the wedding. Lillian's account of the wedding also emphasizes the hitches and delays, which she later depicted as amusing incidents, but which could reflect the profound ambivalence of Lillian's family toward this wedding.[8]

Again the dressmaker had excelled herself. Lillian's wedding dress, which emphasized her tiny waist, was of creamy-white silk. It had a high neck, ruched sleeves, and eight yards of fabric in the skirt; a floor-length lace veil cascaded from a circlet of flowers on Lillian's head. Her five sisters, the bridesmaids, wore white silk dresses with lace inserts and sported big white bows in their hair. While the young women waited nervously upstairs, the men were worrying about their ties. Lillian's cousin Everett Brown, who was to be best man, arrived wearing a black tie to find the groom wearing a white one, but that problem was easily rectified since "Frank's collection of haberdashery was always extensive" and he lent Everett one of his. Even when the correct ties were in place, they had to wait for Grandma Delger, who had to go to the bathroom. She had had a stroke and, as Lillian later explained, was "slowed by her lameness and the excitement." Then, just as the wedding party was starting to process down the Mollers' grand staircase, Lillian's youngest brother, nine-year-old Frank, got out of step and insisted that they go back up and start again.

The wedding took place in the Mollers' drawing room. There were only two guests outside the immediate family, Lillian's old shopping companion Alma Brown and her neighbor and college friend Ethel Olney. Lillian's minister, Dr. Charles Brown, was out of town, so his predecessor at the Congregational Church, the elderly, bearded Dr. McLean, officiated. In the rush of Frank's belated arrival, however, McLean had not had the chance to meet the groom; once that was rectified, the service proceeded, vows were exchanged, and the newlyweds sat down to a wedding supper at a table as elaborately flower-bedecked as the rest of the house.[9]

Supper over, the bride and groom changed into their traveling clothes and set off on the first part of their honeymoon. Frank had reserved a suite at the grandest hotel in San Francisco, the newly opened St. Francis Hotel in Union Square. Their rooms were filled with flowers and there was a bottle of champagne waiting. Lillian, who was practically teetotal for her whole life, declined the champagne and Frank, relieved that he was no longer on show at the Mollers, ordered a beer. They posed for photographs, sitting rather self-consciously on a sofa in front of an open bedroom door. The next morning the waiter brought breakfast to their room and promptly dropped the tray. Lillian thought in retrospect he was nervous, having never served a bride and groom before; more likely she was reflecting her own embarrassment at being so obviously a newlywed. Frank was not embarrassed at all and simply sent the waiter back for more supplies.

Later that morning Lillian and Frank returned to Oakland to catch the train for St. Louis; fourteen-year-old Fred Moller came to the station to see them off, and Frank promptly invited him to visit them in New York. Despite his efforts the previous day, Frank had not been able to secure a private drawing room; Lillian was disturbed to discover that family friends were in the next section "and were obviously interested in the bridal couple." Frank was less concerned and drew little cartoons showing that all eyes in the dining car were focused on them. Although Lillian stressed her embarrassment in retrospect, in a photograph taken en route she looks almost smug and considerably more relaxed than in the wedding photographs taken only a few days earlier.

Almost as soon as the newlyweds boarded the train Frank said, "Do you realize how little we have in common?" And so they drew up a list of each other's experiences, qualifications, and interests. Some of their first discoveries were a little disconcerting. Frank announced, "You have red hair and I have always resolved I would marry a brunette. You are tall and I admire short girls. You are quick-tempered and I need someone who never gets angry." As Lillian later remarked, "This and much more leads one to wonder where a partnership will land." Ever the optimist, she countered that "red hair often stands for activity, there are sometimes advantages in being tall and a quick-tempered person is seldom monotonous to live with. So there you are!" Lillian and Frank also made a list of each other's likes and dislikes. Frank was easy to cater to since he claimed he ate "everything but onions" and drank "everything but glue," but he claimed to have second thoughts about giving Lillian a list of the things that irritated him. "Maybe you'd better tear up that list about my dislikes," Lillian claimed he said. "I'm beginning to realize I may have made a horrible mistake. How could a husband be so stupid as to deliver into his wife's hands a written recipe of exactly how to run him crazy?" Lillian's list does not survive.[10]

The Gilbreths spent part of their honeymoon at the Louisiana Purchase Exposition in St. Louis, where Frank planned to show Lillian the technical displays. He wanted them to share interests, telling her, "*You* have got to look at machinery, steam and gas engines and methods of transportation," while he was prepared to "look at tapistries [*sic*], weaving machines and embroidery." They spent several days at the fair and visited the art exhibits as well as the science buildings. They ate at a variety of restaurants—"some so gay," Lillian recalled, "they were a new sensation to the California girl, who had seen very little of night life." One even "served salad and chicken in the French fashion." The visit was cut short, however, exactly as Frank had predicted it would be, by a telegram saying he was needed in the office. They left for New York in such a hurry that Lillian's trunk was forgotten, and she arrived at her new home with only the clothes in her traveling bag. It was an inauspicious beginning to married life.[11]

8

The One Best Marriage

"It was a fifty-fifty proposition throughout. Any
woman can do it with that sort of a husband."

Lillian Moller Gilbreth, in "Who Washes the Dishes When Ma Is
Famous?" (1925)

W HEN SHE WAS middle-aged and a widow, Lillian
Gilbreth described her partnership with Frank as "the One Best Marriage"—
but the earliest months were very difficult. Marrying Frank was not an easy
option, but the "strenuous life" was a choice deliberately made. The success
of the marriage was largely due to a conscious effort on Lillian's part, and
that success did not happen overnight. Whatever Lillian wrote later and however firm her resolve at the time, the first year of the Gilbreth partnership involved her in painful geographical, social, sexual, emotional, and intellectual
adjustments. Her response to Frank's plans and his likes and dislikes was initially much less lighthearted than she later suggested.

Lillian claimed that one of their secrets was a "serio-comic pact" they
made soon after their wedding, promising that they would never become
angry at the same time. By so doing, she said they inadvertently discovered a
way of avoiding arguments. As she commented, "No quarrel can last long after the participants begin trying to decide who has the right of way on being
angry." Though Frank accused Lillian of having no sense of humor, she had
enough to find him amusing and to live "happily and appreciatively with a
man more richly endowed," so "the results were admirable."[1]

Frank and Lillian tried to work out what each could bring to their partnership. "We made," she wrote, "what was practically a job analysis of the
part each was to play in the family life in order to find out what each could do

best and with most satisfaction to himself and to the other." She was well aware that some people would find their marital job analysis "absurd" and "too much like an engineering project," adding defensively, "this is what industry does of a man or woman seeking a job."[2]

The Gilbreths represented their marriage as a business arrangement— not in the old, impersonal way of an arranged alliance between wealthy families, but one in which the family was an economic unit with the husband and wife as productive partners. They believed that tasks should be assigned rationally by skill; they aimed to maximize the efficiency and profitability (in whatever terms that was to be measured) of the family unit. They invented their own style of partnership; Frank called Lillian "Boss" while signing his letters "Your chum." Lillian explained that they preferred to "put all their assets into the partnership and meet the world as a firm." She continued:

> This was not in any way an easy thing to do. It would have been simpler, perhaps, for the man to go ahead with his world's work alone, sharing the results with his partner. For the woman, too, it would have been easier either to devote most of her time to running the home end of the project and use some free time to go on with her own work of studying and teaching, or give the bulk of the time to her own work, which was already under way and make contributions from the result to the home project just as the man did.

A more conventional approach would have been simpler, but she and Frank did not want to remain "two individuals earning and dealing with the world separately," but instead wanted "a complete partnership."[3]

Lillian brought more to the marriage than she claimed afterward, and she was always a more equal partner than Frank's critics, or her children, would allow. She was, however, a dutiful nineteenth-century daughter as well as an early-twentieth-century wife, and under both guises she was unwilling to publicly admit to a desire for power and control over her own life, so she continued to represent herself as a junior partner. She must have been convincing. When Edna Yost, who knew Lillian well, wrote a biography of the Gilbreths in the 1940s, she asserted that Lillian was Frank's creature and would not, except at her husband's instigation, have even tried "to develop the capacities which later marked her as one of the most distinguished women of her day. Their unusual quest for fulfillment was his idea alone." This is not true, as Lillian had already shown in her pursuit of the "strenuous life." She was intelligent and ambitious and wanted a life of achievement rather than a life of ease. Though the early years of the Gilbreth marriage were difficult for Lillian, she soon started to reassert her claim to the intellectual authority and business partnership that she had displayed during their engagement.[4]

When Lillian wrote about her marriage, she emphasized how the relationship changed over time. While their partnership started with conventional gender assumptions, it became an ongoing tutorial as new roles and responsibilities evolved. She wrote, "In our family, we started, on the advice of
a relative, with the rule, 'outside the house the man rules, inside the house the
woman rules.'" She added, "It worked very well as a start. Gradually, as fitness for leadership in any function showed itself, it was delegated there when
appropriate." Lillian's willingness to describe herself as the pupil is a key element of her public representation of her marriage; she wrote, "The greatest
help was found in changing the leader-follower relationship to a teacher-pupil
relationship. . . . In so far as the husband-wife relationship and the parent-
child relationship become teacher-pupil relationship, happiness is assured especially where there is that readiness which every true teacher feels to take the
role of pupil."[5]

The Gilbreth tutorial, however, became a two-way process wherein Frank
learned as much from Lillian as she did from him. A careful reading of Lillian's brief biography of Frank, *The Quest of the One Best Way*, shows that
she realized this. She recalled, "Frank *thought* his chief emphasis was on the
choice and purchasing of materials," while "unconsciously to himself, more
or less, there was coming into his work the systematic and finally the scientific handling of the human element, which is really so much more important
in getting the results desired" (italics added). Thus, she brought her academic
training to bear on ideas that Frank had developed through practical experience. These different experiences and approaches meant that the Gilbreths
were unlike contemporary husband-and-wife scientific couples, most of
whom were trained and working in the same discipline.[6]

Lillian later claimed that she and Frank made a conscious effort toward a
fifty-fifty marriage, trying to share all responsibilities. She told a journalist,
"I had a husband with a modern conception of a woman's business brains
and ability. He decided above all things, from the very start, that I have a career outside the home. Consequently he shouldered his half of the responsibilities of the home and family. There was nothing he could not or would not
do. It was a fifty-fifty proposition throughout. Any woman can do it with that
sort of a husband." Whether the Gilbreths—or anyone else—achieved
equality within marriage is another matter, but their partnership evolved into
an unusual kind of companionate marriage as each partner learned from and
depended upon the other. Neither wholly equal nor totally hierarchical, they
invented their own style of partnership. Though Frank Gilbreth may now
seem selfish and insensitive, his recognition of his wife's abilities and his desire that they should form a team was very advanced at the time.[7]

When Mr. and Mrs. Frank Bunker Gilbreth arrived at Grand Central Sta-

tion on October 30, 1904, eleven days after their wedding, Lillian was appre-
hensive. Happy as she was to be married, she did not have fond memories of
New York. As she later wrote, "There was every indication that the new life
would be rough and winding, uphill and down." Her son Frank was more direct, writing that his mother "had a fairly hellish year of it, to judge by all
accounts." Finding a way to coexist with her mother-in-law was the most immediate of Lillian's difficulties. Martha Bunker Gilbreth and her sister Kit
were already very much at home in the apartment; Lillian was the newcomer.
Martha Gilbreth's fierce and often tactless personality and Frank's dependence and unquestioning devotion to her made it hard, and Lillian later admitted, "Perhaps the ideal situation is for the young couple to start alone."
This was putting it very mildly. According to her eldest son, Lillian was terrified of Frank's mother and his aunt. He wrote that every time his mother
thought of the two women "sitting sharp-eyed and straight-backed in their
identical rockers, poised to wait on Frank hand and foot, she felt depressed
and downright frightened." Much later Lillian explained to her children—
many of whom knew their formidable grandmother well, since she lived with
the family until her death in 1920—that "it was really much more efficient
that way. So don't think you ought to feel sorry for me. It all worked out
very nicely." Frank Gilbreth Jr. was less sanguine. He commented that "very
nicely" referred to the long term—and that in the short term "the atmosphere was often strained."[8]

Lillian's bag was quickly unloaded from the train, Frank hailed a cab, and
they set off northward to West Ninety-fourth Street. Their destination was
the Norfolk Apartments, a seven-story building between Broadway and
Riverside Drive. When they arrived, Frank led the way through a little iron
gate and into the small lobby, which was dominated by an elevator placed
solidly in the middle. On the fourth floor Martha Gilbreth stood ready to
welcome her beloved son and his new bride. When Lillian saw her new home
for the first time her heart sank a little; it seemed cramped and gloomy and
much less grand than the illustration in the agent's advertisement suggested.
It was spacious as New York apartments went, but Lillian was used to a big
California house; her first glimpse was of a dark entry hall, and though the
good-sized parlor was a little more encouraging, it faced north with an unin-
spiring view—just a similar apartment building forty feet away. It seemed
claustrophobic especially when compared with the view she had left behind
in Oakland.[9]

Martha had decided, consciously or otherwise, to take control of furnishing the apartment, and Lillian acquiesced, being more sensitive to her
mother-in-law's needs than the older woman deserved. No longer young—
Martha was nearly seventy—she had left all her friends and uprooted herself

from Boston, where she had lived for almost a quarter of a century, to be with her beloved Frank, whom she now had to share with his wife. In one of her letters Martha Gilbreth had told Lillian that they were waiting for her to arrive to set her own mark on the decor, but that in the meantime she had sent all the family furniture to be repaired. Martha gave an amusing account of the furniture's adventures, which seemed further designed to establish ownership of the apartment: "Some were weak in the legs," she wrote, "some had disabled arms and some wanted new dresses . . . and they came back looking as young and fresh as if they had never seen service."[10] By the time Lillian arrived the place was full of Martha's furniture, and Kit's paintings hung on the walls; accordingly, her wedding presents, including china and some beautiful furniture, were placed in storage, where some of them stayed for half a century, until long after Martha was dead and Lillian's own children had grown up. Perhaps because Martha's touch was everywhere, Lillian never grew to like the apartment or feel really at home there.

Lillian's first dinner in the apartment was something of a battle of wills. Martha Gilbreth installed her new daughter-in-law at the head of the table so she could take over the role of carving, serving, and passing the plates, the "masculine" jobs that Frank had always entrusted to his mother. Lillian, seeing how ill at ease Martha was in handing over this responsibility and probably uncomfortable herself in assuming a traditionally male role—this was certainly not something her mother had ever done—got up and invited her mother-in-law to resume her normal place.[11]

Lillian spent her first night in her new home without Frank, who had dashed off to Boston on the sleeper. Although he was away for only a short time, those early days were very awkward as Lillian and her in-laws faced what she later described, with heroic understatement, as "difficult problems of adjustment." All three women were immensely relieved when Frank came back; as Lillian wrote, "never was a returned traveler more heartily welcomed." The place was not really large enough for three women who were home all day, and as the only interest they had in common was Frank, relations were sometimes strained. They tacitly agreed, however, to let Frank think that the arrangements were perfect. Lillian later wrote, "It must be the job of the three women to keep him feeling that way, constantly." This may have been a good way to keep the peace, but it encouraged Frank to be self-centered; he was simply oblivious to the tensions at home and assumed that all his womenfolk were as content as he was. And it did little for Lillian's peace of mind.[12]

As Lillian unpacked her clothes and her books, she wondered how on earth she was going to fill her days. Her honeymoon was clearly over; now she had to create a job for herself. Frank wanted her to work with him, although he told her it was not feasible for her to work in his office. Martha Gilbreth made it equally clear to Lillian that she and Aunt Kit would be in charge of the domestic arrangements; she already had the housekeeping well in hand. Making a biblical pun on Lillian's name, she told her daughter-in-law that like the lilies of the field, "you should not toil or spin more than you want to, while we are in such good working condition." This arrangement had some advantages: it meant that Lillian was released from all domestic responsibilities, even managerial ones, and was free to pursue other interests. Difficult as she was to live with, Martha Gilbreth made many of Lillian's professional achievements possible. Martha benefited, too; she needed to keep her place in her son's affections, and under the guise of helping Lillian, this is exactly what she proceeded to do. She had already hired a servant and installed her in the tiny room next to the kitchen. She told Lillian, "We have the nicest old lady helping us. Not much on cooking but very neat and good laundress." The servant's lack of culinary skills did not matter, for Martha was an excellent cook, devoted to providing "comfort foods" like puddings and pies for Frank, a menu that contributed to his expanding girth.[13]

Lillian soon found a role writing about Frank's business innovations, and whenever Frank was not away "hustling" business they worked together. They spent long summer Sundays in the little study off the parlor reviewing and recording ways of mixing concrete, which was a remarkable change of direction for someone who only months before had been a prominent member of Oakland society and a student of Jacobean literature. A publisher was interested in Frank's *Field System*, and Frank wanted to turn some of his other systematizing ideas into book manuscripts. Lillian collected and annotated his photographs and rewrote his notes on reinforced concrete, which resulted in *Concrete System*, which was published in 1908. She then turned her attention to bricklaying and read all the available literature, which, she claimed, could be "easily mastered" by the "trained reader," and then wrote a book directed at the apprentice bricklayer. *Bricklaying System* was published in 1909; both books appeared with Frank's name on the title page and no mention of the real author. These two books were part science, part public relations, as Frank was not yet sure whether he wanted to be a builder or a business consultant.[14]

Lillian occasionally accompanied Frank on site visits. The first of these trips, to Rochester, New York, occurred in November 1904, soon after Frank returned from Boston. Perhaps he missed her; perhaps she was so miserable in the apartment without him that even he noticed. In Rochester Lillian met Kate Gleason, probably the best-known (and almost the only) woman heading an engineering company at that time. This meeting suggested endless possibilities to Lillian. Gleason was much admired; even Henry Ford once re-

marked (erroneously) that the Gleason beveled gear planer, a vital component of automobiles, was "the most remarkable machine work ever done by
a woman" (in fact her father developed the gear planer when Kate was only
seven years old). Gleason was middle-aged and single and thought marriage
severely overrated. She enjoyed being beholden to no one and felt just a little
sorry for Lillian, who was surrounded by demanding relatives. Lillian must
have been feeling very bold. To Gleason's amusement she sat in the cab of a
small steam engine and insisted that Frank teach her how to drive it. Lillian
was very pleased with herself, which makes it odd that she never learned to
drive a car. She remembered from her previous visit to one of Frank's building sites that high fashion and construction did not mix; accordingly, she left
her corsets at home, donned loose clothing and sensible shoes, then climbed
up ladders and over scaffolding to inspect the brickwork or the concrete pouring. She repeated this feat many times over the years unless prevented by advanced pregnancy.[15]

Most of the time, however, Lillian stayed home and Frank came back
from his trips full of plans and ideas and projects to share with Lillian. She
found his enthusiasm exciting but his energy a little daunting, and she decided the only way she could keep up was to "learn to rest and relax, when he
was away, in order to be an adequate companion when he was at home."
Spending time in her room "resting" was undoubtedly an excellent way for
Lillian to get away from her in-laws. Frank's Aunt Kit was in the early stages
of diabetes and was frequently irritable and bad-tempered. Frank's mother
had become a Christian Scientist and Aunt Kit was going along with her sister's views on the treatment of illness, but perhaps prayer was as good a remedy as anything, for insulin was not to become available until the early 1920s.
Aunt Kit grew increasingly uncomfortable, and Lillian bore the brunt of her
misery, though as Frank hated the idea of anyone being ill, Kit managed to
bear her illness in silence when he was around. As Lillian wrote many years
later, with admirable understatement, she "wished she had known that the
disease affected one's nerves and one's disposition, as well as one's digestion
and had been more patient, inwardly as well as outwardly, with the devoted
aunt." This was a rare admission of impatience on Lillian's part.[16]

Lillian was determined her marriage would succeed; however demanding
and insensitive Frank might appear to others, she loved him, and despite all
the problems of adjustment (most of which was done by Lillian), it developed
into a most extraordinary partnership.

9 Planning a Family

The most famous attempt to merge
Scientific Management and eugenics was the
demonstration project of Frank Bunker Gilbreth. . . .
The principles of efficiency could make superior, Anglo-
Saxon children "cheaper by the dozen," as Gilbreth put
it. The failing intellectual and racial balance of modern
society could be restored by modern industrial
methods of mass production applied to
human breeding and education.

Judith A. Merkle, *Management and Ideology* (1980)

LILLIAN'S FIRST CHILD was conceived within six weeks of the marriage. Though it was an easy pregnancy physically, it was psychologically difficult, as she felt very much alone. Frank was often away and she felt abandoned by her parents, as they had taken several of her sisters and brothers on a prolonged tour of Europe. The baby was due in early September 1905, and as the confinement neared she busied herself with preparing the baby's clothes. She remembered, rather wryly, that she made "enough garments for half a dozen babies." Her industriousness was fortunate, as it turned out, for this was to be the first of thirteen pregnancies.[1]

Lillian wrote many years later: "Frank had decided, with his usual knowledge of exactly what *he* wanted, that they would have six boys and six girls," a prospect she said she greeted with some reservations, commenting, "This seemed an easy undertaking to a person who had practically been an only child all his life, but was a little appalling to the 'oldest of nine.'" "A little appalling" is something of an understatement. Lillian was often asked why she and Frank had so many children. The answer was a complex mix of public and private reasons, including eugenics, women's rights, and sheer love of babies, combined with a reluctance to discuss birth control. Her family became famous both for its size and for the "home training" system the Gilbreths devised.

Lillian's children were born at roughly fifteen-month intervals between

1905 and 1922. This was a period when immigration from southern and eastern Europe and Asia was causing considerable alarm in the United States, as people deemed racially and intellectually "less fit" were supposedly "breeding like rabbits." Some Americans were worried by what they called race suicide, by which they meant the declining middle-class birthrate, a decline that was thought to be particularly steep among the better educated. Numerous statistics were produced to show that college-educated women (and men) failed to marry or else produced few children.[2]

Eugenics—the term was coined by the English scientist and statistician Francis Galton and defined as "the science which deals with all influences that improve inborn qualities"—was influential in the United States through the Progressive Era and beyond. Eugenicists were heavily influenced by Social Darwinism and feared that well-meaning humanitarian reforms were interfering with the laws of natural selection. They believed charitable efforts to rehabilitate criminals and support the feeble-minded enabled them not only to survive but also produce families. As late as 1927 the Supreme Court in *Buck v. Bell* upheld a Virginia statute permitting the sterilization of inmates of state institutions. In the majority opinion Justice Oliver Wendell Holmes wrote: "We have seen more than once that the public welfare may call upon the best citizens for their lives. It would be strange if it could not call upon those who already sap the strength of the State for these lesser sacrifices . . . in order to prevent our being swamped with incompetence. . . . The principle that sustains compulsory vaccination is broad enough to cover cutting Fallopian tubes." He concluded with an infamous and much-quoted statement: "Three generations of imbeciles are enough."[3]

Like many of their contemporaries, the Gilbreths believed in eugenics, but Lillian was not an out-and-out hereditarian. While she shared many unflattering middle-class assumptions about immigrants and blacks and, like most of her contemporaries, occasionally used racial epithets that would now be considered quite inappropriate, she also believed that environment could have a positive impact. She qualified her account of the Gilbreths' investigation of their own heredity (which they clearly found adequate), insisting, "We have no right to use heredity as an excuse for failure, for no one has yet proved that environment and education cannot overcome tremendous handicaps. Nor have we any right to rely upon heredity to carry through without all the help that environment and education can give."[4]

The Gilbreths were positive eugenicists. Rather than calling for forcible sterilization of the less "fit," they applied their theories to themselves and produced their own large family. They also wanted to demonstrate by means of their family system that it was possible to rear and educate many healthy children, and do it economically and efficiently, while leaving time for the mother to be professionally active. Here they diverged from many of their contemporaries, even feminists, many of whom believed that a well-educated woman's most useful role was in raising superior children, rather than imitating men in their desire to work outside the home. Lillian, however, did not want to be *only* a mother; she also wanted to work. Theodore Roosevelt, father of six children, was another positive eugenicist. His assumptions about male and female roles were, however, much more conventional than those of the Gilbreths. He castigated modern women for their "fear of maternity." They were, he believed, shirking their duty, as were men who avoided work or preached pacifism. A nation composed of such people was "rotten to the core." Roosevelt thundered: "When men fear work or fear righteous war, when women fear motherhood they tremble at the brink of doom and well it is that they should vanish from the earth, where they are fit subjects for the scorn of all men and women who are themselves strong and brave and high-minded." Lillian and Frank certainly wanted to count themselves among the brave and high-minded, but they also wanted to avoid the rigid gender roles suggested by the president. Lillian was far from the "domestic helpmeet" recommended by Roosevelt.[5]

If support for eugenics—presidential, feminist, or otherwise—was part of the reason for the Gilbreths' dozen children, a more mundane reason was reluctance on Lillian's part to raise the issue of birth control. In the 1900s abstinence and withdrawal were the most common contraceptive methods; neither seems to have appealed to either Lillian or Frank. Their daughter Ernestine believed that Lillian "was very Victorian about birth control—felt that love should have its full expression." Lillian always said, however, that her family was planned, albeit in a very idiosyncratic way. As she became more engaged in writing, she said that her books and babies were timed to coincide. She said she could use what Frank dubbed the "unavoidable delay" surrounding a confinement, which in those days literally involved staying in bed for two weeks or more, to correct the galleys of their books. In addition, both Gilbreths liked children. Frank doted on them when he was at home, but his frequent absences meant that Lillian was the more consistent parent. Lillian liked babies (at least, if they did not cry too much), though she sometimes found her large brood very noisy and tiring. She once told a journalist who asked her which of her family was her favorite, "The last baby is always the one you love best."[6]

Lillian wanted a strenuous life, and she wanted to work with her husband. Frank wanted a large family; thus, their child-rearing methods evolved to satisfy both needs. Lillian's explanation for her acquiescence in the plan to have a dozen children certainly supports the assertion that the Gilbreths' experiment was part of the scientific management movement. Lillian wrote that "she was all for doing anything [Frank] wanted and he was sure that the same principles of efficiency that worked out on the jobs should make the running of the household and the bringing up of a family easy."[7]

Easy or not, during the early years of their marriage Frank's demands were hard on Lillian. Her almost continual state of pregnancy aroused criticism. She was often exhausted, and her friends and family were concerned she was overtaxing her strength. She had always been slender, but photographs show the once blooming bride growing thinner and more strained while surrounded by an ever increasing number of children. Few of Lillian's children were what could be called "easy babies." Anne Gilbreth certainly was not. She arrived with "loud yells" that continued for several months. Lillian had plenty of help with the baby; in addition to her mother-in-law and the maid, there was a trained nurse staying in the apartment. From time to time Lillian pushed the baby carriage with the slumbering Anne into the elevator and down to the street, aiming to get some fresh air, but her pleasure in this exercise was invariably spoiled by the fact that, however soundly asleep Anne seemed to be, "no sooner was she on the street that she cried so lustily that kind old ladies would stop and ask what her mother had done to her." Lillian would retreat, mortified, to the apartment. Frank was less bothered by Anne's crying. He had read somewhere that babies should be left to cry, so if she screamed, he "dumped her in her bed and closed the door." As soon as Frank left for work, however, Lillian picked up and cuddled Anne, braving the disapproval of Frank's mother for such insubordination.[8]

Lillian was unwell for several months after Anne was born. Her coccyx had been damaged during childbirth, making sitting very painful, and she lacked the energy to oppose Frank's child-rearing experiments until a "capable doctor patched her up." Frank knew next to nothing about babies but was anxious to try out all kinds of theories based on his reading. He resolved to investigate whether the infant Anne could swim. This scheme was based on theories of recapitulation that were widespread around the turn of the century. Scientists read Darwin and theorized that children went through all the stages of evolution; biologists had detected traces of gills in developing fetuses, so the idea of an infant's ability to swim would be, according to the eminent psychologist G. Stanley Hall, a "faint, reminiscent atavistic echo from the primeval sea." Baby Anne was just one day old when Frank tried his first experiment. Many years later Lillian recalled that she was lying in bed resting after the delivery and was more than a little surprised when Frank came into the room saying, "I read somewhere that if you put a very young baby in water, she will swim. Do you mind if I try it out?" She commented that she certainly *did* mind, but "I didn't say anything about it because I thought 'Oh, she has to get acquainted with her father.'" Frank's mother and aunt were aghast at the idea and protested vigorously, but Frank ignored them and, with the trained nurse standing by, ran the bathwater. Frank soon returned to Lillian "really chagrined" and reported that "'she sank. It wasn't true!'" Nevertheless, Lillian added, "the small daughter was none the worse for the experiment."[9]

Lillian nursed all her children. Though breastfeeding is not a totally reliable contraceptive, the spacing of Lillian's many pregnancies and occasional references in her correspondence suggest that she weaned her babies anywhere between three and nine months. When Anne was weaned Lillian was unwell; she was losing weight and felt lethargic, and the doctor diagnosed a case of jaundice. Frank finally noticed that something was amiss and "snatched her up" to accompany him on a business trip to California. Lillian was not at all anxious to take the noisy baby on the long train journey, so Anne was left at home with Grandma. The Mollers had still not returned from Europe, but Lillian spent a restful time with her Auntie Brown and her cousins and conceived her next baby while on this trip.

Soon after their return to New York in late April 1906, they heard about the San Francisco earthquake. The huge quake, which measured 8.3 on the Richter scale, lasted for less than a minute, but it cracked the water and gas mains, and two-thirds of the city was either destroyed by the fire or dynamited to stop the fire from spreading. Even the earthquake-proof St. Francis Hotel was badly damaged by the fire. More than two thousand people died and nearly a quarter of a million were left homeless: families were camped out on the hillsides waiting for shelter. There was damage across the Bay in Oakland, too, and such was the sense of excitement that the newspaper proprietor William Randolph Hearst, who was always ready to finance a publicity stunt, offered one hundred dollars to every child born in his emergency hospital there. Frank joked to Lillian, "I think there is a chance for you if you hurry."[10]

Frank saw a major opportunity for his firm and returned to "the city of ashes and strenuosity" in mid-May. This was weeks before more conservative (or more sensible) contractors, who were waiting until the city published its new building codes, began pursuing building projects. Frank erected a huge sign that read "Frank Gilbreth, Building Contractor" near his office on Market Street. It was, he boasted, "sixty feet long and thirty feet high—unparalleled, a corker, the talk of the town." His publicity methods bore fruit; by mid-June he had four smallish contracts totaling $600,000.[11]

Frank bombarded Lillian with letters, claiming, "I shall not be surprised if I landed ten, twenty, or even thirty million dollars worth of work in the next year or two." Lillian reacted cautiously, advising him to contact the engineering departments at both Berkeley and Stanford. She may have been aware of some of the criticisms of Frank's work, and that he did not have sufficient engineering expertise on staff. She was therefore urging him to do what he had started doing in the East, that is, hire big names from the top universities as consultant engineers. Frank was convinced that the future lay in the West, while Lillian, rather presciently, questioned the wisdom of concentrating so much of his effort in San Francisco; he replied, "The labor conditions may be bad for me but they are bad for the other contractors." Then she asked him, "Suppose there is a slump?" to which Frank replied, overoptimistically as it turned out (the depression of 1907 was only months away), "I have now got enough work to keep me busy." Lillian was right to be concerned. Frank's finances were still poor; his company had expanded too fast, but he resisted selling shares or borrowing too much capital from bankers or other investors. In a period of professionalization and company amalgamation, Frank was essentially a small businessman trying to maintain personal control. Had Frank listened to Lillian in 1906 and behaved more cautiously, he might have been less badly burnt, but he was full of optimism, the eternal booster. The previous year he had spent fifteen thousand dollars on advertising. While in San Francisco Frank bought a secondhand Pierce Arrow car and hired a publicity man for forty dollars a week.[12]

In the summer of 1906 Frank sent for Lillian to join him. She hesitated, although it meant seeing her siblings and her parents: the Mollers had hurried back from Europe on hearing about the earthquake, as the business opportunities for a plumber's supplier were too good to miss. The real resistance to Frank's plans came, however, from his mother and his aunt. His extraordinary dependence on their approval meant he was prepared to do without Lillian's company and even forgo the chance to rebuild San Francisco if they would not agree. Martha and Kit found it hard to deny their beloved Frank, however, and after much delay they reluctantly consented to move.[13]

Lillian, nearly four months pregnant, left for California with ten-month-old Anne in early July 1906. Frank met them at the Oakland station and then promptly returned to New York to raise more capital. Lillian, meanwhile, was enjoying the luxury of her parents' house. However restrictive she had found her old life, it was starting to seem very much better than the constant presence of Martha and Kit, though her family's implied criticism when they wondered why "dear Lillie" did not assert herself more made her very uncomfortable. None of the younger generation of Mollers was pursuing anything remotely resembling the "strenuous life." Most of Lillian's sisters had attended private schools, where they prepared to be accomplished gentlewomen like their mother, and her brothers were still at school. There were plenty of servants, which made life comfortable. Frank started to worry that

Lillian might prefer this easier life. He criticized the aimless Moller household, writing:

> Well I suppose you are sitting in my place at the table and you try to feel at
> home (and don't). Do they miss me at Beer time? (10.30 P.M.) I can see
> Gertrude dusting and sitting out on the back porch—Ernestine crocheting a
> sponge. Elinor is practicing. Josephine is worrying almost to death which
> dress she will wear. Mabel is hiding and reading under the light and behind
> the chair. Fred is skating and doing an imitation of a whirling dervish—Bill
> and Frank also. Pa is reading the Meddler [the local gossip column] and mak-
> ing believe it is the Russian insurrection and ma is entertaining some com-
> pany she wishes would go home.[14]

Two months later Lillian was still living with her parents. Although she
had done a little house hunting, good rental properties were in very short
supply in post-earthquake San Francisco. Frank wrote optimistically, "I notice you are still the same old girl of New York type and that you have not
fallen into your old Oakland views. Your letters show that you like really the
strenuous life better than the old G. G. Gobble Pink tea of yore—That's
lucky, isn't it?" He was less sanguine a few days later, however, but wrote that
he'd soon have her "back in the strenuous life" and "uncivilize" her again.[15]

On Frank's urging Lillian resumed her hunt for a house in San Francisco
in September. Although she was six months pregnant, she traveled by trolley
rather than use Frank's company car and chauffeur. Frank scolded her for being a "strenuous strong minded woman," but he was pleased with her choice,
a pretty, four-bedroom Arts-and-Crafts row house on Ashbury Street. This is
one of the few Gilbreth or Moller dwellings still standing. Built shortly before the earthquake, it has a fine walnut front door, a large entrance hall with
a staircase curving past a stained-glass window, a large paneled dining room
overlooking the backyard, and a small sitting room with an elaborate
canopied fireplace and paneled walls. Upstairs there are four bedrooms with
dressing rooms and two bathrooms; in the basement there are several large
rooms that presumably were servants' quarters. Although the Ashbury Street
house was a great improvement on their New York apartment, it was on a
steep hill and had a very small yard. Odors from a pig farm, which was a little
farther up the hill, meant that Lillian spent much of her time indoors.[16]

Lillian moved to Ashbury Street in late September and waited, without
much enthusiasm, for the arrival of her mother-in-law and Aunt Kit, though
they were in no hurry to leave the East. Meanwhile, Frank was missing his
daughter. "Do you know Boss," he wrote to Lillian, "I never really knew the
paternal instinct until this time away." He was still away when Anne took her
first steps: "I suppose she is walking and conversationing by this time." He

added, "I kind of feel as tho I was working for her as well as you." He regretted not being around for Anne's first birthday but was too busy to buy her a
present and trusted "the ever thoughtful Lillie would look after my present to
her." This was a pattern that was to continue for the rest of his life; Lillian
would fill the child-rearing deficiencies that Frank left in his frenetic wake. On
the few occasions he was at home, Frank continued educating—or training
might be a better word—baby Anne. He put marks in the closet where his
slippers belonged and taught her to fetch them and put them back. He tried
to insist that Lillian speak to her in German and that no one use baby talk.
He also tried to get Anne to do everything for herself. She learned to walk and
talk early and, according to her mother, was a "born arguer, so she and her
Daddy had some wonderful times together."[17]

Whether it was the stress of moving, anxiety over Frank's business, or
simply advancing pregnancy, Lillian was unwell in September. Frank hated
the thought of her being ill, though it did not stop his endless demands upon
her time and energy. He had written a speech on his cost plus method and
asked her to "fix it up" for him, though as ever he was a very touchy student.
He asked Lillian for her comments but warned her, "If you knock it too hard
you are knocking your most interested pupil because I have changed or at
least attempted to alter my style in accordance with your lessons."[18]

Frank's business problems were multiplying. He was trying to find work
for his men and financing to complete other projects. He spent fruitless hours
chasing bankers for loans and many tiring days traveling up and down the
East Coast as far as Montreal, Canada, in pursuit of contracts. Meanwhile,
his legal problems increased, most of them concerning the *Engineering
Record* Building in New York City. It was a reinforced concrete building, and
as both the owner's and the architects' plans had already changed several
times, costs and tempers were rising. James H. McGraw, the owner, tried to
cancel the contract unless Frank would complete the project at cost. Frank
started consulting lawyers, who said he had a strong case. Then McGraw
threatened to expose Frank as an engineering incompetent in the *Engineering
Record*, a threat that Frank, with some justification, described as blackmail.
In November McGraw canceled Gilbreth and Company's contract, and the
Engineering Record published a letter from one of Frank's strongest competitors that Frank's cost plus fixed sum method was like "taking candy from
babies," since it gave the builder little incentive to be efficient. Frank was
furious and decided to fight McGraw rather than arbitrate. He eventually
won substantial damages, but the case dragged on for years and did little for
his reputation.[19]

Although California did not make him rich, Frank got a number of attractive contracts. One, the Alameda Bank Building in Oakland, came

through his father-in-law's influence; but the profit was relatively small, only three thousand dollars. Another contract was to take six of the eight stories off the damaged Mutual Life Building in downtown San Francisco. It was an interesting job, since the steel-framed building had withstood the earthquake and fire better than many nearby structures, but it paid relatively little, with a profit of a mere two thousand dollars, most of which Frank spent on photographing, measuring, and investigating the structure at every stage of its demolition. This may not have been a good commercial decision, but it pleased Lillian. She preferred to see him as a scientist rather than simply a builder, and she worked with him on a paper on fireproof buildings, which he sent to the American Society of Mechanical Engineers (ASME) for publication in their journal. Some of the biggest contracts, however, went to his competitors, and very soon things began to go wrong.[20]

Frank was out of town for the birth of their second child. Lillian told him not to worry, as his mother and aunt had eventually arrived, Annie Moller was nearby, and a trained nurse was on hand. Mary Elizabeth Gilbreth was born in San Francisco on December 13, 1906, and Frank celebrated by giving his wife a very large diamond—"so much larger than Lillian's wedding ring," she recalled, "and the ring with three stones—which had been the present when baby Anne came—that the entire household was in an upheaval."[21] It is not hard to imagine that Lillian might have preferred more of Frank's help and his company, however huge the diamond.

Mary was a much more peaceful baby than her elder sister; the trained nurse also "brought calmness and good nature," in dramatic contrast to Frank's mother and aunt, who caused nothing but discord. The two women were miserable in California: they disliked the climate and found getting around the damaged city almost impossible. They missed their friends and found the shops, the food, and the general surroundings unfamiliar and strange. Kit was increasingly irritable and her opposition to California became more and more vocal.

Lillian was exhausted. Two babies within fifteen months had taken their toll. Getting up in the night to nurse Mary and being awakened at dawn by a lively toddler was simply hard work. The only time Lillian really relaxed was on the Sundays when Frank was in town, when they all piled into the big Pierce Arrow and took the ferry across the Bay to Oakland. Frank would play catch with her youngest brothers while the two old ladies sat in the sun. Lillian, "relieved of all responsibilities of every sort . . . drew a long breath between the end of one week and the beginning of another." Lillian was not to live close to her family for long, however; in the fall of 1907 Frank and Lillian, Martha, Kit, and the two babies took the train back east. It had not been a very successful experiment.[22]

10 Mentioned from the Platform by Taylor

*"He wasn't a nice person.
You wouldn't have liked him."*

Lillian Moller Gilbreth on Frederick Winslow Taylor (1972)

W HEN LILLIAN AND FRANK returned to New York in 1907, they leased an apartment in the brand-new Hendrik Hudson Building on the corner of Cathedral Parkway and Riverside Drive. The moment Lillian saw the imposing doorway she knew that this was going to be a great improvement on their previous apartment; entering the spacious marble lobby, with its grand furniture and wealth of potted palms, simply reinforced her view. The Hendrik Hudson resembled an Italian villa and covered almost half a city block. There was a billiard parlor, a café "for the convenience of tenants," and a barbershop and a ladies' hairdresser in the basement. Rents reflected the amenities; whereas the Gilbreths had paid $1,200 a year on Ninety-fourth Street, at the Hendrik Hudson rents ranged from $1,500 up to $3,000 a year.[1]

Martha and Kit did not go straight to New York; instead, they went to Providence to see Anne Cross, Frank's sister, leaving Lillian to get Martha's furniture out of storage and see to its arrangement. Aunt Kit died suddenly in Rhode Island in early October. She was only sixty. Martha missed her terribly, and her loneliness made her more determined than ever to be part of her son's life. That was what Frank wanted, and Lillian gradually learned to tolerate her mother-in-law, though it was an uphill struggle. Lillian realized Martha needed to feel wanted and useful and that she had no intention of sitting in the corner with her knitting. She declared, "I won't hump or scuff as long as I live and when I die I'll lie straight in my casket." She was successful in this; photographs of Martha in extreme old age show her standing ramrod straight.[2]

Lillian was pregnant again: baby number three was due in April 1908. She spent much of the winter attending meetings with Frank while Martha looked after the children. Lillian's business responsibilities increased dramatically as Frank faced bankruptcy. The 1907 depression affected construction, but during that cold, difficult winter Frank first met Frederick Winslow Taylor, the "father" of scientific management. This meeting had a profound effect not only on the Gilbreths' professional life but also on their child-rearing methods. Frank met Taylor in New York in December 1907 and for years after he pointed out the place in the lobby of the Engineering Societies' Building, declaring, "Here on this spot I met a very great man." Frank had known about Taylor's ideas for almost a decade, though he was far from convinced by Taylor's reliance on time study, preferring to improve efficiency by better motions, as he was with the bricklaying experiments he and Lillian were currently planning. Taylor was sufficiently intrigued by Frank's ideas to visit him in his office three times in the next two weeks. During the following month, January 1908, Frank paid a two-day visit to Taylor at his house near Philadelphia. He also visited the Tabor Manufacturing Company, the showpiece of the Taylor system. There he met Horace King Hathaway, whom Taylor believed to be "the best all-round man in the movement."[3]

Although Taylor was twelve years older than Frank, the two men's education and careers were remarkably similar. Both were raised by strong-minded mothers, both refused to go to college, and both worked their way up by learning a trade. Taylor graduated from the exclusive Phillips Exeter Academy in 1874 and passed the Harvard entrance exams but did not attend, ostensibly because of eyestrain. Four years later, after completing an apprenticeship as a pattern maker (hardly the most obvious trade for someone with eye problems), Taylor moved to Midvale Steel, where he advanced from a laborer to chief engineer in six years. While working full time he enrolled in the Stevens Institute of Technology, where he earned his degree in two years. Unlike Frank Gilbreth, Taylor was independently wealthy and earned another fortune from his patent on high-speed steel, which cut at twice the speed of conventional steel tools. He made so much money that he was able to retire at the age of thirty-seven and devote himself to consulting and proselytizing scientific management. He died in 1915 at age fifty-nine.[4]

Frederick Winslow Taylor and the system named after him, Taylorism, have been widely criticized as authoritarian, dehumanizing, and exploitative. His name was and is anathema to much of organized labor. He was often his own worst enemy: he once described one of his key workers as "so stupid and so phlegmatic that he more nearly resembles in his mental make-up the ox than any other type." Nevertheless, Taylor's ideas were influential and were applied, with varying degrees of thoroughness and success, to businesses, conservation projects, municipal reform, education, and housework. Scientific management has been described as a "secular Great Awakening" during a period when "efficient and good came closer to meaning the same thing . . . than in any other period of American history." The evangelical aspects of Taylorism are reflected in the terminology used by its "disciples," which includes comparisons of Frederick Winslow Taylor's "Shop Management" with the Bible or the Holy Grail and Frank Gilbreth's assertion that on time study "Taylor is the Law and the Gospel."[5]

The Gilbreths, however, were different from Taylor's other disciples. Frank's experience was on building sites rather than in machine shops, and Lillian, educated in both the humanities and psychology, was appalled at some of Taylor's ideas and what she saw as his shoddy "science." On the other hand, Frank was useful if not always trusted by the Taylorites, who agreed (somewhat ungrammatically) that "Mr. Gilbreth is not a man in whom it would be well to place a good deal of dependence upon unless there is something further in view." The "something further" was Frank's flair for publicity and his ability to speak "so convincingly about modern scientific management" that he was a useful spokesman for the movement. Frank was oblivious to this hostility and assumed that he was part of scientific management's inner circle. Taylor believed his was the only way and that any deviation from his methods was heresy and bound to lead to disaster, but the Gilbreths, particularly Lillian, became the Martin Luthers of Taylorism. Rather than follow blindly, they wanted to interpret scripture for themselves. Like Luther, they believed, at first, that they were merely removing imperfections from orthodox beliefs; but like Luther in the Reformation some four hundred years earlier, they were roundly criticized and eventually excommunicated by adherents of the true faith.[6]

It is necessary to examine Taylor's ideas in order to understand how the Gilbreths adapted and modified them. Taylor believed that money underlay all industrial disagreements and that low productivity was not always the worker's fault. Though he frequently inveighed against "soldiering" or deliberately limiting output, he also criticized management for inefficiency in not having the tools or materials in the right place at the right time. He believed he could improve labor relations and increase efficiency by simultaneously concentrating power in the hands of management and gaining workers' cooperation with a complicated system of bonus payments. Taylor wanted his management system to be "scientific," so while he was a consultant at Bethlehem Steel he carried out his most famous "experiment" to demonstrate how a combination of financial incentives and training could enable anyone (even the most stupid worker, as he put it) to be more productive. Taylor told the story of the oxlike "Schmidt" many times, describing him as "a man of the mentally sluggish type." Taylor was exaggerating for effect, as Schmidt was in fact Henry Noll, who stood at five feet seven and weighed only 135 pounds. Noll had, however, extraordinary stamina and, as Taylor himself acknowledged, "had been observed to trot back home for a mile or so after his work in the evening, about as fresh as he was when he came trotting to work in the morning." Noll was then handling twelve and a half tons of pig iron a day; Taylor decided (after some specious calculations) that a first-class workman should be able to handle forty-seven tons a day. Ten men were able to load more than the previous rate, but only three, including Noll, were able to meet Taylor's target, so the rest were moved to other, much less remunerative work. This, Taylor argued, was actually doing them a favor, since they were not well suited to pig-iron loading.[7]

Taylor outlined many of his ideas in a paper called "Shop Management," which he presented at an ASME conference in Saratoga, New York, in June 1903, the day after Lillian Moller said good-bye to Frank Gilbreth and set sail for Europe. When published, it was known as Paper 1003. Frank regarded it as holy writ, despite one glaring problem. Taylor always selected the best workers to time with his stopwatch, which made his piece rates well beyond the average worker's grasp. Taylor later asserted: "In essence, scientific management involves a complete mental revolution on the part of the working men—and on the part of those on the management side, the foreman, the superintendent, the owner of the business, the board of directors—as to their duties towards their fellow-workers in the management, toward their workmen and toward all of their problems." The problem with Taylor's mental revolution was that it was not always followed by the employers, some of whom speeded up production without acknowledging any "duties" to their workers.[8]

Taylor was not the most tactful of men; at one time or another he offended everyone. His system particularly annoyed skilled workers by shifting many of their functions to "experts" in coats and ties, and he met serious opposition from foremen, from the unions, and from some members of Congress. In August 1911 workers at the Watertown Arsenal in Massachusetts walked out to protest the introduction of scientific management, and Taylor was summoned to appear before a special subcommittee of the House Labor Committee. The committee banned the use of the stopwatch on federal projects, a ban that remained on the books until 1949.[9]

In December 1907, however, the House hearings were several years in the future, and Taylor, though well known in engineering circles, was hardly the

national figure he was to become. Nevertheless, the Gilbreths were drawn
into his circle. While Lillian was much less taken with Taylor than was Frank,
she immediately saw both the social and professional implications of scientific management. She liked to think that Frank was an engineer rather than
"just" a builder. She had been trying to teach him how to investigate "scientifically" and how to present his findings to an academic audience. Lillian was
interested in improving their social position; she saw Taylorism not only as a
blueprint for efficient work, but also as a way of entering the middle and
higher echelons of industry. Lillian and Frank started to entertain engineers,
writers, and managers in their New York apartment, particularly those who
shared their interest in scientific management. Lillian strongly preferred these
people to Frank's old building trade colleagues and his Bunker relatives. A
friend later recalled the couple as "the most delightful hosts," who displayed
a "versatility" of conversation and a "wide acquaintance with every topic of
the day." Lillian was well able to hold her own in these conversations. She had
attended meetings of the ASME since her marriage; colleagues soon realized
that Lillian "was perfectly capable of thinking with the best of us," and she
was "accepted as one of the regular members of our management group."[10]

The Gilbreths' new friends included some of the biggest names in the
world of scientific management, including James Mapes Dodge, a former
president of the ASME and president of Link-Belt Company, the first firm to
install a complete Taylor system. Lillian also admired Mrs. Dodge, "who always made it her special business to see that the strangers were properly welcomed and entertained." She described the couple as "genial, unaffected,
ideal hosts. . . . Handsome, beautifully dressed, gracious, poised, distinguished!" This was, perhaps, the way Lillian herself would have liked the
world to see her and Frank. Henry Laurence Gantt, a leading Taylorite, and
his wife, Mary, were to become the Gilbreths' closest friends—and closest
philosophically—in scientific management circles. Gantt (1861–1919) was
for several years one of Taylor's most trusted "disciples." A mechanical engineer, he invented the Gantt chart, which enables production to be planned in
terms of time rather than quantities. Like Taylor and Frank Gilbreth, Gantt
had a strong-minded mother: in his case, she supported the family after his
father lost his Maryland plantation after the Civil War. He later became a
leading revisionist with his emphasis on industrial democracy and on the importance of the human factor, and his ideas had a profound influence on Lillian Gilbreth. Lillian's description of Mrs. Gantt's attributes may also be a
clue to what kind of women she admired at this time, and even the kind of
woman she might have become except for Frank's extraordinary professional
and sexual demands. Lillian described Mary Gantt's "wonderful sense of humor," her "keen interest in everything pertaining to her husband's work," her

"large circle of friends," and her "interest in the arts," which "made her home a center for both business and personal friends drawn from every field." A third woman Lillian respected was Beulah Bancroft, the wife of a Philadelphia engineer, who represented all the roads she herself had not taken. Bancroft, who was "the center of the liveliest of circles," was, according to Lillian, "a trained musician, a wonderful singer, a student not only of literature but of rhetoric, a lover of art and of people, with a wit all her own." It is hard not to detect a little wistfulness in Lillian's voice as she wrote those words.[11]

If meeting Taylor was a conversion experience for Frank, it was also very important for Lillian. She decided to resume preparations for her doctorate, transferring her scholarly attention from English literature to educational psychology. Lillian's academic (and German) background predisposed her to value education and professional qualifications. Times were changing in industry, and many of the younger engineers she met were not content to work their way up through apprenticeships. An engineering degree would have been next to impossible for the nonmathematical Lillian or for the undisciplined mind of Frank; she chose a more unusual route to gain professional and academic respectability, and one that was more attainable to Lillian as a woman. Her choice of psychology was an inspired one. Both she and Frank recognized that skilled workers were likely to resist Taylor's techniques. Frank had experienced problems on some of his building sites, despite his usually excellent relations with the unions, and both Gilbreths believed that a better understanding of psychology was necessary. They surmised that the latest ideas in teaching would help them to devise methods of persuasion and training that would gain the workers' cooperation, or if that proved impossible, to train semiskilled men or women to take their place.

Lillian read everything on management and education she could find and accompanied Frank on his visits to scientifically managed plants. She also attended seminars at Taylor's home outside Philadelphia, an experience she did not remember with much pleasure. "We used to spend days listening to him lecture," she later told an interviewer. "The two young sons would meet you with pads and pencils and Mr. Taylor would sit down and lecture for several hours at a stretch." He hated interruptions, she recalled, and asked his audience to save their questions until the end. "Usually by the second or third hour all the questions you had in the first hour would be answered," but he always asked for questions and anticipated opposition. "Unless you said 'I would like you to expand . . .'" Lillian recalled, "he thought you were criticizing him. But if you would say, 'Mr. Taylor, how about so and so?' he was *sure* you were criticizing."[12]

The Gilbreths became steadily more involved in scientific management circles, though they still saw themselves as orthodox Taylorites. In March

1908, in her eighth month of pregnancy, Lillian was finalizing motion study experiments for Frank to use on a building contract. As he later acknowledged, "I think [my wife] has made her full share of the progress which has been made in the science of bricklaying." The experiments did not go as hoped, however, as union leaders told Frank that they would brook no Taylorite experiments. Rather than provoke a confrontation, Frank used the methods on a nonunion job. Frank claimed that by using the new methods, bricklayers could lay nearly three times as many bricks as before, though much of the increase came from a lower-paid worker doing preparation work, placing bricks the right way around and mixing the mortar to a firmer consistency. Frank's vertical scaffold, which minimized bending, also increased productivity. Frank had once belonged to a union and prided himself on being pro-labor, but Taylorism was becoming very unpopular by 1908.[13]

Lillian finished writing *Bricklaying System* in the spring of 1908, just before her third daughter was born. Ernestine Moller Gilbreth appeared in April with some difficulty and amid much disappointment that she was not a boy. Martha Gilbreth wrote to her daughter Anne Cross, "I suppose you are mentally condoling with the family who got a girl instead of a boy. Lillie was so dreadfully disappointed she looked feverish." Lillian had been to a matinée in the afternoon, as "there seemed no immediate prospect," but she went into labor shortly before midnight and produced a nine-pound baby almost exactly three hours later. Although it was a short labor, the rest of the family was clearly exhausted; all but the redoubtable Martha had a lie-in the next morning. "We all feel today as if we had had one ourselves," Martha wrote. Everyone was there to witness the disappointment, as Lillian's parents and sixteen-year-old brother, Fred, were visiting from California. There was also a nurse, a Mrs. McMahon, who, Martha Gilbreth was quick to note, was "not of that bedbug tribe, she is from N. Jersey" and, moreover, "knows her business and minds it."[14]

The new baby was, in her grandmother's words, "as fine a specimen as you could pick up . . . *for a girl* she is absolutely satisfactory." They named her Ernestine after Grandma Delger, who had died a few weeks earlier. Lillian's two-week confinement was spent reading the proofs of the bricklaying book. She found Ernestine "enchanting" and was delighted when Frank announced a business trip to the West Coast. She decided to go with him to show off the new baby to the rest of her family. Leaving Anne and Mary with their grandmother and the servants, she and Frank set off on the long train journey to Oakland. They alternated work on the proofs of their *Bricklaying System* manuscript with playing with the infant Ernestine. By the time the bricklaying book was finally published Lillian was pregnant for a fourth time, and she welcomed the book's arrival "almost as happily as a new child." She sent copies to her parents as well as to prominent engineers, professors, and even King Edward VII, though what the playboy king thought of it is anybody's guess.[15]

By September 1909 the apartment on Riverside Drive was getting a little crowded: the lease was up for renewal, and as Frank and Lillian were not convinced that New York was "the One Best Place to bring up children," they moved to the country. They leased a large house in Netherwood, a leafy suburb of Plainfield, New Jersey, where they were to live for the next three years. It was a good place to settle. Other engineers lived on the same street and some friends from the Oakland Congregational Church were nearby. Anne remembered the "ecstasy" of going for rides with them in their little straw pony cart, though Lillian was less ecstatic about life in the suburbs. She did not fit easily into Netherwood social life, mainly because she was so busy working. Some of her female neighbors disapproved of her recurrent pregnancies and the way she left the children with Grandma while she traveled with Frank. For her part, she recalled, perhaps with a little touch of superiority, that she was not involved in women's social affairs "because she had neither time nor inclination for bridge."[16]

Martha, of course, moved with the Gilbreths and continued to run the house. This was a mixed blessing for Lillian, for although it gave her plenty of time for her professional work, she was irritated by and a little envious of the close bond between Frank and his mother. Lillian had learned to accept Frank's frequent absences, but she resented the fact that every day he *was* home, he insisted on spending an hour after dinner hour with his mother. Martha and Frank would talk about everything—their relatives in Maine, his travels, his work. Sometimes the children overheard their conversations; Ernestine recalls her grandmother telling him to leave household efficiency alone, saying, "Hosh wash Frank, that isn't your area, stay out of it Frank, that's women's work." Lillian learned to displace her anger with her mother-in-law onto inanimate objects, especially if those objects happened to belong to Martha. According to a friend, "If, in inner conflict, Lillian accidentally knocked over a chair or broke a dish . . . it would be chair or cup, not Frank or Martha or the children, who felt it."[17]

Irritations notwithstanding, Martha's presence enabled Lillian to resume work on her Ph.D. While they were in California in 1908 she and Frank had talked to members of the Berkeley psychology department about her plan to apply William James's theories on habit formation to industry. She also wanted to investigate how psychology could be useful to people installing scientific management schemes, which were often resisted by the workers involved, hoping to discover what psychological techniques would best persuade the workers to accept new practices. This work could not be done from books, for no such books had yet been written; Lillian had to travel to plants where the Taylor system had been installed, most of which were in and around Philadelphia, in New Jersey, New England, or upstate New York. Her committee, which consisted of old mentors such as George Stratton and Charles Gayley and newer ones such as Jessica Peixotto, agreed that this fieldwork could not be done in California, as scientific management had not yet reached the West Coast.

Lillian was, then, necessarily away from home from time to time, but the children had plenty of adult supervision. Grandma played a very important role in their lives. She taught five-year-old Anne to read from McGuffey's Reader, dressed her cuts and stings, and reprimanded her if she went out without her sunbonnet. "Do you want freckles?" she would ask. Anne was able to outwit Grandma on occasion. Among the complement of servants the Gilbreths usually included a German nursemaid, for they wanted the children to be bilingual. Martha knew no German and Anne was often called upon to be the translator between the current Fräulein and Grandma. According to her sister Ernestine, Anne, who was "a born mischief," deliberately garbled conversations between the two women "with a sense of fun and increased power."[18]

Lillian's fourth daughter, Martha Bunker, was born in November 1909 and named after her grandmother. She was overdue, so Lillian, like many women before and since, did what she could to speed the baby's arrival as she and the nurse "made many a rapid trip around the neighborhood." The birth was very difficult, but, Lillian hastened to add, Martha "was worth waiting for." She had blue eyes and red curls and immediately became her grandmother's pet. Anne, Mary, and Ernestine, now ages four, three, and eighteen months, were pleased to have a little sister. By the following spring, when the weather got warmer, Martha's high chair became a popular gathering place on the porch.[19]

Despite her own indifference to suburban activities, Lillian made sure her daughters got all the benefits the area provided. The Gilbreth children's lives, at least at first glance, were not very different from those other upper-middle-class children in the early twentieth century, nor indeed from Lillian's own California childhood. They played with neighboring children, attended dancing classes and Sunday school, played in the sandlot, or sat on the steps of the big, wide porch. Yet the Gilbreths were not like their neighbors: for one thing, they dressed differently. Lillian had long abandoned the corseted waist shown in earlier photographs: although she was to remain slim all of her life, her repeated pregnancies necessitated looser garments. She also dressed the children simply except when they were off to dancing class, when they enjoyed wearing the clothes sent by their California grandmother: beautiful white dresses with satin sashes, and big white bows in their hair.

Lillian's indifference to clothes sometimes caused problems. Anne became jealous of Betty Fenner, who lived next door. "She was very pretty and always exquisitely dressed and Anne looked at her clothes enviously," wrote Lillian. One day Mrs. Fenner gave Anne a pair of Betty's outgrown shoes. They were white and black patent leather, and Anne thought they were the most beautiful shoes she had ever seen. Frank, however, was furious; this smelled of charity and he ordered Anne to take them back. Anne asked her mother why she couldn't have outfits like Betty's. An exasperated Lillian finally exclaimed, "Andie, we believe brains are better than clothes!"—a remark that Anne immediately ran next door to tell her friend. Lillian commented in her memoirs, "It took a little adjusting to straighten that out!"[20]

In mid-July 1910 Lillian and Frank traveled to England to attend the joint meeting of the ASME and the British Institution of Mechanical Engineers. Lillian had recently weaned seven-month-old Martha and left her and her sisters at home with their grandmother. Martha Gilbreth was seventy-six years old by this time and had a very strenuous summer looking after four children under the age of five. Meanwhile, this was the Gilbreths' first overseas visit together. They traveled with nearly 150 other engineers and their wives on the SS *Celtic*. Frank reported to his mother that "Lillie has made a hit with everybody—and the trip has done her lots of good." Lillian thought otherwise; she was a poor sailor and spent much of the time in her cabin, though according to Frank, who was always inclined to look on the bright side, "she has missed only about one meal." While Lillian lay on her bunk, Frank was the life and soul of the party. There were pillow fights and obstacle races, bridge drives and concerts, and Frank was awarded a consolation prize for coming in second in the shuffleboard contest.[21]

Frederick Taylor, who had traveled separately, welcomed the engineering group in Liverpool, and then they all took the train to Birmingham, where the lord mayor greeted them at a civic reception. It was a very large conference: a fleet of buses was chartered to take the delegates and their wives from place to place. Lillian and Frank went to a dance in the Botanical Gardens, where the exotic plants were illuminated by hundreds of Chinese paper lanterns. They also took a coach trip to nearby Stratford-upon-Avon. The most important part, indeed the main purpose of the conference, was the engineering sessions: Lillian attended them, not the ladies' teas.

Lillian was not presenting a paper, but to her amazement Frederick Taylor mentioned her work on the psychology of management in his keynote speech. Frank was delighted, writing proudly to his mother that Lillian "was mentioned from the platform by Taylor . . . much to the joy of all and to the embarrassment of Lillie." Many of the other engineers' wives were amazed: Lillian did not broadcast her work, and most of the women had assumed that she was, like them, "just" a wife, rather than a woman beginning to make her own professional contributions. When a woman buttonholed Frank and asked if his wife *really* helped him with his work, he reported to Lillian that she "was astounded when I told her, 'Yes.'" With Taylor's recognition, Lillian started to move out of the shadow of her husband and into the public gaze.[22]

Lillian enjoyed her moment of glory (though it was a little embarrassing to be singled out in such a public way), and she liked meeting the other engineers and being with Frank, but she missed the children. Three weeks after leaving them she wrote to Martha, "I am getting too homesick to *see*. It doesn't seem to me as if I can bear to be away another minute." She was, however, away from the children for nearly six weeks in all, and by the time she got home in late August she must have realized she was pregnant for a fifth time.[23]

Lillian had no time to rest on her laurels, as the fall of 1910 was important for the scientific management movement, for the Gilbreths, and especially for Fred Taylor, who suddenly found himself famous. A group of railroads had petitioned the Interstate Commerce Commission to allow them to increase freight rates. Louis Brandeis, later a Supreme Court justice but then a prominent Boston lawyer, argued that if only the railroads were run more efficiently, they would save a million dollars a day and would thus have no need of a rate hike. Brandeis held many meetings with Taylor's followers and proposed calling some of them to testify before the ICC. They were delighted by the possibility of spreading the word, and as Lillian later wrote, "small feuds were forgotten; ancient friendships revived; new members were being admitted to the cult, everything in the field that could be used to further the cause was being gathered together and prepared so that it could be best utilized."[24]

Lillian attended most of these New York meetings, despite her pregnancy and the commute from Plainfield. Brandeis wanted a clear name for the system and she was one of those who helped to choose it. Several possibilities were rejected, including the Taylor System (Taylor didn't like it), Functional Management (too cold), Shop Management (too restricted; the methods could apply to many kinds of workplace), and Efficiency (too vague). Henry Gantt was anxious to find a name that sounded respectable, and finally they agreed unanimously on "scientific management." After all, "scientific" accuracy was one of the justifications for Taylor's time study methods, and science was seen by most people as an undeniably good thing.[25]

The second major event of that fall was Frank's creation of the Society to Promote the Science of Management (later renamed the Taylor Society), which some of his colleagues saw as his greatest contribution to "the cause." It provided a forum for the examination of Taylor's methods and continued even when his ideas were in disrepute. The society met once a month among the clay pipes and the gargantuan mutton chops at Keen's Chop House on Thirty-sixth Street. The Chop House was something of a male preserve; nevertheless, Lillian attended numerous meetings elsewhere. As she modestly recalled, Frank made sure "his 'pupil' should be included . . . whenever possible."[26]

In November 1910 Frank Gilbreth was one of the dozen or so "experts" whom Brandeis called to testify at the ICC hearings, and he made quite a splash. The commissioners hung over their desks and watched, fascinated, as Frank seized law books and built them into walls to illustrate how to reduce the number of motions needed in bricklaying. The commissioners were convinced and refused to grant the railroad rate increases, but more important for the Gilbreths and their friends, the publicity engendered by the hearing galvanized the business and engineering community and resulted in an outpouring of articles in both the popular and technical press. As one writer graphically remarked, "Frank Gilbreth found himself one of the biggest frogs in a rapidly expanding puddle."[27]

Lillian also had a toe in the "puddle," but her almost continuous state of pregnancy or nursing, combined with popular prejudices about women, kept her out of the public eye. Nevertheless, she was more than a pupil; she was becoming an equal partner in the development of the Gilbreth system as her skills as a researcher and her organized mind complemented Frank's intuitive grasp of work simplification. Her great contribution to the partnership was practicality: Frank had grandiose, not always workable notions, but she brought order out of chaos. As a friend remarked in a housekeeping analogy, Lillian ensured "there were sheets on the bed."[28]

In March 1911 a long-awaited son, Frank Jr., was born. His arrival meant that they now had five children under the age of six. Frank was so delighted to have a boy after the four girls that he sent telegrams to almost everyone he knew and distributed cigars to all his friends and acquaintances. Meanwhile, Lillian spent what she called the "unavoidable delay" after the birth checking the galleys of their latest book, a volume on motion study, which had grown out of their earlier work on bricklaying. It also bore only Frank's name.[29]

The year 1911 saw the high point of the Gilbreths' relationship with Frederick Taylor. Taylor was a slow and meticulous writer, reluctant to commit himself to print, but after Brandeis's success in publicizing scientific management, he had been persuaded to submit a series of articles to the *American Magazine*. Entitled "The Gospel of Efficiency," they inspired a flood of inquiries. Taylor felt he did not have time to answer them and suggested that Frank Gilbreth be invited to respond. He and Lillian did so in a little book entitled *The Primer of Scientific Management*, which Frank wrote very quickly in longhand—almost in one session—sitting in his pajamas at his worktable.

Although Lillian claimed modestly that she did little other than provide good working conditions, this is unlikely. The *Primer* was almost certainly a joint production: they were used to bouncing ideas off one another, and one authority maintains that Lillian wrote it and that it was, as were all her previous books, simply published under Frank's name.[30]

Lillian remembered the writing of the *Primer* as one of the most pleasurable times of their married life. "If only all of life could have been as free from stress and worry as the all-too-few days spent at home!" she wrote. She tried very hard to keep her husband at home and had organized an office with "sufficient equipment for work there to keep Frank busy and happy," hoping that he would be able to "concentrate so completely that outside things were not allowed to interfere." Frank thrived on action, however, and on the publicity it brought. He was never happier than when he was at the center of things, talking all night on train journeys, gossiping on steamers, lecturing at colleges and conferences. However busy Lillian kept him at home, it was never enough; he needed the distractions of travel, of hustling, of pursuing the "strenuous life."[31]

In his absence Lillian kept herself busy. She started writing her doctoral dissertation some months before Frank Jr. was born, and the household routine was arranged to make it possible for her to write. Frank set up a Gantt chart showing how much time she could spend on each part and clarifying what had caused delays. It soon turned out that the children, who found any excuse to see their mother, caused most of them. She did not mind; she enjoyed seeing them and admiring their latest painting or examining a scraped knee. She later remarked, perhaps a little tongue-in-cheek, that she "thought it fortunate that her home and family life provided so many interruptions."[32]

Lillian did not sit and write endless drafts of her dissertation; she instead dictated it into a Dictaphone and stenographers typed it. Lillian found the Dictaphone difficult at first: "the whirring of the cylinder distracted the eye, the buzzing of the motor distracted the ear, the rubber tube leading to the mouthpiece was constantly reminding the touch that something new was being attempted." Frank suggested she prop the mouthpiece next to the telephone, and Lillian discovered that "as soon as one became interested in the dictating and one's attention was concentrated on the thought, one was able to forget the new variable . . . and dictate fluently." She became so wedded to the efficiency of the Dictaphone that she eventually had one on each floor of the house. She later told a journalist, "If I haven't but fifteen minutes to dictate, I utilize that time. By having a machine on every floor, it not only saves me from walking up and down steps but is always at hand inspiring me to work."[33]

As she wrote her dissertation, Lillian came to believe that the essential flaw in Taylorism was the lack of attention to "the human element" and that the introduction of psychology could remedy this deficiency. Her dissertation was therefore an attempt to integrate modern teaching methods with scientific management. It was titled "The Psychology of Management: The Function of the Mind in Determining, Teaching and Installing Methods of Least Waste" and was the first such effort within the scientific management movement. In it Lillian recommended psychologically based teaching techniques, better personnel management, and improved vocational guidance in order to minimize the workers' resistance to scientific management. Lillian still believed in Taylor's basic assumptions about the social harmony that would derive from the development of better management practices and fairer methods of payment.[34]

Meanwhile, Frank was working on ways to measure motion. This infuriated Taylor, who demanded complete obedience to his system and saw Gilbreth's work as almost sacrilegious. The Gilbreths were not the only early revisionists; Gantt's task and bonus payment system rewarded the worker for meeting the standard rate rather than punishing failure to do so. Toward the end of his life Gantt came to believe that science should be given priority over profit and that engineers should organize society. Lillian did not go so far; she wanted to ameliorate the existing democratic and capitalist system rather than change it. However, the sonnet Lillian wrote when Gantt died in 1919 suggests she had a great deal of sympathy with his ideas. The last lines read:

> He preached the Gospel of real leadership,
> In quiet words, with stress on facts and laws
> Showing the goal and pointing out the way,
> Nor dreamed his words would found a Fellowship
> Of those who held him Leader in a Cause, —
> The winning of a new Industrial Day.[35]

The new industrial day, Lillian came to believe, would emerge out of better, more cooperative working methods, which would come about by discussion and trial and error, rather than through Taylor's more autocratic ideas being imposed on the labor force. She started talking about this as early as October 1911, when her dissertation was half written. She and Frank were invited to attend a conference at Dartmouth College; it was designed to explore the current state of scientific management. Six-month-old Frank Jr. was not yet fully weaned, so they took him along with them on the train.[36]

Lillian was one of only thirteen women among the three hundred or so delegates to the Amos Tuck Business School Conference (most of the other women attending were wives). Frederick Taylor gave the opening address, and all the big names in scientific management were there. Among the speakers was Edwin Gay, dean of Harvard Business School, who talked about "Academic Efficiency." On the last day there was a session designed to summarize the conference. A consulting engineer, Morris Llewellyn Cooke, asked half a dozen delegates for comments, then turned to Lillian, saying, "We have all been watching the quiet work of one individual who has been working along lines apparently absolutely different from those being followed by any other worker in the scientific management field." Lillian was surprised to be asked. "I did not expect to speak in this place," she began, "but I feel as though I must. I feel that the gap between the problems of academic efficiency and industrial efficiency, which is after all only an apparent gap, can be easily closed if only we will consider the importance of the psychology of management." She spoke in a way that was to become characteristic. She tried to get people to see the similarities between different methods and get them to work together. She continued: "I spent several years examining and studying it and it seems to me that Scientific Management as laid down by Mr. Taylor conforms absolutely with psychology." She suggested practical ways of bridging their differences: "Principles of vocational guidance may be studied along psychological lines to train the individual so he will know exactly what he does want to do. It is the place of the colleges to train the man so that when he comes into his work there will be no jar. Since the underlying aim is the same and since psychology is the method by which we are all getting there, isn't it merely a question of difference of vocabulary between academic work and scientific work? Why not bridge this gap and all go ahead together?" Lillian's remarks took half a printed page in the conference proceedings. Frank, who *had* been invited to speak, followed her; his rambling anecdotes took three pages of the book.[37]

The Dartmouth conference was a turning point in Lillian's professional life. Although she was unwilling to criticize Taylor in such a public forum, she was convinced that even the best presentations were lacking "any knowledge or recognition of what teaching and the sciences that underlay it should mean in management." She became even more certain that despite the brilliance of Frederick Taylor, he "had serious shortcomings as a pedagogue and psychologist." "Serious shortcomings" is putting it very mildly, but Lillian spent the next few years trying to overcome them.[38]

PART IV

"Some Classy Bear-Cat and Cave-Woman"

Mrs. Gilbreth's influence on all her husband's work is very apparent and is probably the principal reason why he has been successful where Taylor failed, in securing the cooperation of workmen in carrying out plans.

Kenneth H. Condit, "Management Methods of Frank B. Gilbreth Inc." (1923)

II Divine Providence

Never from that day on could either parent find
the relief of speaking freely of the experience and never
could Frank answer the question, "How many children
have you?" without stopping to calculate.

Lillian Moller Gilbreth, *As I Remember* (1998)

As 1911 DREW to a close Lillian put finishing
touches on her Berkeley dissertation. She and Frank celebrated Christmas together and watched their five young children playing with their new wooden
building blocks underneath the Christmas tree. The last few months had been
very rewarding for the Gilbreths, both personally and professionally; the children were healthy, and Lillian and Frank were moving steadily to the top of
the scientific management group. However, 1912 was a dreadful year. The
combination of a family disaster and two professional setbacks changed the
direction of the Gilbreths' lives as well as their relations with their children.[1]

In late January 1912 Taylor was in Washington facing congressmen hostile to scientific management. In defending himself he denigrated Frank
Gilbreth's contributions, suggesting, among other things, that Frank's work
with the adjustable scaffold (which he had patented in 1890) was a result of
his conversations with Taylor. The Gilbreths were not in Washington to hear
what Taylor had to say, for just before his testimony started, Anne and Mary
came down with a mild fever, headaches, and sore throats. The doctor diagnosed diphtheria, which was and is a terrible disease. Although the majority
of sufferers recover, between 5 and 10 percent of cases are fatal. Diphtheria is
a horrible cause of death; a thick membrane grows in the throat and the victim can choke to death. At the same time toxins in the bloodstream injure the
heart, nervous system, or other organs, which cease functioning. Although

no antibiotics were available to kill the bacteria until after World War II, an antitoxin was readily available and, if all else failed, a tracheotomy was sometimes performed to allow the patient to breathe. Lillian had had diphtheria as a child and so assumed (incorrectly) that she was unlikely to contract it a second time. She went into quarantine with the children while Frank paced up and down outside the door. Anne had a mild case and soon recovered, but five-year-old Mary seemed unable to fight the infection. Doctors, nurses, and Lillian worked in vain: Mary was becoming weaker. Finally, in desperation, Frank performed an emergency tracheotomy. It failed and Mary died on January 31, 1912.[2]

Both Anne and Ernestine remembered Mary's illness for the rest of their lives. The two little girls reacted to their parents' tension by being naughty, bouncing on their beds and making noise. As a teenager, Ernestine wrote a strange, sad poem about it:

> "Hush," said Daddy, coming in
> With a funny smile,
> "Mary's going to try to sleep
> For a little while."
>
> Anne and I kissed Daddy hard,
> Daddy hugged us tight
> "Mother needs me now my pets,
> Pleasant dreams tonight."
>
> Anne and I played somersaults,
> One! Two! Three!
> "I guess Mary's going to die,"
> Anne said to me.[3]

Ernestine, with the single-mindedness of three and a half years, wanted Mary's scrapbook. "I figured if she was dying I would certainly get it," she recalled, and she was bitterly disappointed when all Mary's things were destroyed so that the germs would not spread. Mary disappeared, too; there was no funeral, or if there was, Anne and Ernestine were not told about it.[4]

Both parents were devastated. Photographs of Lillian taken at this time show her heavy-eyed and sad. Frank was also heartbroken: as Lillian recalled, he "for the first time in his life faced a situation he could not master." Neither parent mentioned Mary in public again, although in *Cheaper by the Dozen* she appears as one of the dozen children. Lillian stated, "It was an experience which an understanding psychiatrist might possibly have adjusted, but it was not adjusted and it left a permanent scar." Anne learned from this experience; a dozen years later, when her father died, she took her mother to one side and insisted that they all start to talk about him, because otherwise the youngest children would not remember him.[5]

A few weeks after Mary's death, the Gilbreths faced another setback. Lillian had submitted her thesis to the University of California in late 1911 with the full understanding that the university would waive the rule that the last year of a doctoral program be spent on campus. In early 1912, however, she learned that the senate had denied her the degree until she had spent another year in residence at Berkeley. Lillian found the university's conditions impossible. She could not relocate to California for a year; she had a husband and four young children and a partnership in a construction company on the East Coast. Frank was furious and wrote a series of letters to President Benjamin Ide Wheeler, but in vain. Eight years later he was still annoyed; he amused himself during a long sea journey in composing an "Ode" that, however jaunty, displays his anger with the University of California: "Why that's the College / Where they encourage / Tautology and concealed knowledge," he wrote.[6]

Lillian decided to publish her dissertation and look for another institution that would permit her to pursue a degree in applied management. It was not easy to find a publisher. Frank "shopped strenuously" but several firms turned him down, saying, according to Lillian, that the book was ahead of its time and likely to interest only a few readers. If this reaction is true, rather than a polite fiction, it was a little shortsighted, since scientific management was in the news and other books combining industry and psychology were starting to appear. The Harvard psychologist Hugo Münsterberg's popular and accessible *American Problems from the Perspective of a Psychologist* had been published two years earlier, and he was working on *Psychology and Industrial Efficiency,* which was to be published in 1913.[7]

A short-term publication solution was found whereby Lillian's dissertation was serialized in a technical magazine, the *Industrial Engineering and Engineering Digest,* which was edited by one of their Plainfield neighbors, Robert Kent. It appeared in thirteen monthly installments between May 1912 and May 1913, thus predating Munsterberg and making her book the pioneering work in the field. Eventually, Thomas Walton agreed to publish Lillian's dissertation in book form, on the condition that the author's name should appear only as L. M. Gilbreth, M.L., and the publicity should not mention that its author was a woman. Lillian later commented, "This disturbed feminist Frank more than it did Lillian." (The idea of Frank as feminist is an intriguing one. In that he believed Lillian capable of anything and especially of combining career and family, perhaps he was.) The book, titled *The Psychology of Management,* sold fairly well; the initial printing soon sold out and it was reprinted in 1917 and 1918.[8]

Lillian's dissertation does not survive, so any discussion of her ideas has to be based on the published version. Oddly, for a family that seems to have kept almost every piece of paper that passed through their hands, there is no copy of Lillian's dissertation in the Gilbreth Collection or at Berkeley. In the published version, however, Lillian combined educational psychology with scientific management. Although many of the authorities she cited were pupils of Wilhelm Wundt, the German experimental psychologist, her book did not include controlled experiments. Instead, she applied to industrial workers theories associated with progressive educators such as Montessori, Pestalozzi, and Froebel, all of whom, it should be noted, worked with young children.[9]

The heart of Lillian's dissertation was a long chapter on teaching in which she asserted that training practices under scientific management echoed current educational psychology in using all the senses, visual (drawings and photographs), oral (instruction by the teacher), and kinetic (exhibits and working models made by the student). The nub of her argument, and the place where she differed from Taylor, was her emphasis on teaching workers the correct motions. She quoted William James on habit formation and pointed out that the standardization inherent in scientific management made the acquisition of good working methods more likely, and that "there is no more important subject in this book on the Psychology of Management than this of teaching right motions first."[10]

Lillian concluded that if measurement of a fair day's work was made *truly* scientific, by means of moving pictures (which Frank was currently developing), and the best motions were taught, the workers would be so impressed by the "squareness" of it all that they would learn to cooperate willingly with management. Harmony and teamwork would follow and "the tug-of-war attitude of the management and men is transformed into the attitude of a band of soldiers scaling a wall." Class conflict would be eliminated and "true 'Brotherhood' . . . may some day come to be."[11]

In spite of this utopian view, harsh realities were facing the Gilbreths. Taylor's hostility, Mary's death, and the University of California's rejection of Lillian's dissertation helped them make up their minds about moving out of contracting and into management consultancy, a decision they had been considering for some time. Lillian believed that her knowledge of psychology and Frank's rapport with workers would mean less resistance from the reorganized and systematized workers and that between the two of them, they could install their version of the Taylor system in industry and make a good living. There were also economic and social dimensions to their decision. The Gilbreth construction firm was facing recession and possible bankruptcy, not for the first time; the solution was either to reorganize the company by seek-

ing outside funding, thereby relinquishing control to the banks or sharehold-
ers, or to wind down the business and start in another field.

Lillian was convinced that "management engineering, the new profession, was bound to rise in importance and dignity" and that by becoming scientific management consultants she and Frank would move in the "right" social as well as professional circles; moreover, these would be circles where she,
as a woman, might gain admission more easily. The Taylor Society was much
more open to women than many more traditional professional organizations. Contracting, on the other hand, was very much a masculine world;
Frank's clients entertained him in clubs where she could not go. She recalled
that "there was also a purely personal reason that made me anxious to have
Mr. Gilbreth enter this field. I could not stand having him entertained in the
club rather than the home as was the case of the consultant and I could not
stand to see Taylor and Gantt having a certain kind of social life while contracting was not having that end."[12]

In May 1912, just before Lillian celebrated her thirty-fourth birthday, the
Gilbreths moved to Providence, Rhode Island, where they were to live until
November 1919. Lillian had wanted to leave the Plainfield house, which now
held too many unhappy memories. Her pride was hurt by the Berkeley rejection; she wanted to complete her doctorate, and she and Frank both
believed that letters after her name would bring their work academic respectability. Given the similarities between Lillian's approach and that of
Hugo Münsterberg at Harvard, it is perhaps surprising that she decided to
study at Brown. However, she was probably well aware of Harvard's refusal
to grant Ph.D.'s to women: they had declined to award the psychologist
Mary Calkins the Ph.D. she had earned, despite the strong support of her
adviser, William James. Brown offered Lillian credit for earlier work and
permitted her to study the latest theories in education and psychology, write
a new dissertation, and prepare for her oral examinations there. The extra
two years' study proved beneficial; her previous dissertation had been written far from academic supervision, but the new one was much better documented, used case studies gleaned from Lillian's fieldwork, and showed fa-
miliarity with the latest research and the results of access to a university
library.

This was one of the most important periods of the Gilbreths' professional and personal lives; over the next seven and a half years their family experiment and their motion study modifications of Taylorism developed side
by side. Frank wound down his construction business and became, in partnership with his wife, a management consultant. Six Gilbreth babies were
born in Rhode Island, and Lillian found time to research and write another
doctoral dissertation. She also played a major role in the Gilbreths' shift from

being disciples of Frederick Winslow Taylor to peddling their own brand of scientific management.

Transporting the whole family from New Jersey was quite a feat, as the four surviving children were very lively. Anne was six, Ernestine four, Martha two and a half, and Frank a cheerful fifteen-month-old baby. Lillian was pregnant again; her sixth child was due in December. The household still included Frank's redoubtable mother, Martha Bunker Gilbreth, who was delighted to be returning to New England. Although she was seventy-eight years old, she was still strong and healthy and more than capable of overseeing all the domestic arrangements. Suitable accommodation was scarce, particularly for a family with so many young children, so they started with a temporary rental while they looked around for something more permanent. They leased a house belonging to a professor of Greek and archeology, "while he was off on his holidays." It was full of books and photographs of classical ruins, and Lillian wove stories for the children about the Greek and Roman heroes whose busts graced the bookshelves.

Providence was a good place for them to live. A social and family network was already in place, as Frank's sister, Anne Gilbreth Cross, had lived there for more than twenty years and knew "everybody." She ran a flourishing music school on Cabot Street, which employed a number of music teachers who among them taught most of the children of the Providence middle classes. She also taught the poor, setting up the Providence Music School Settlement in 1911. She always maintained, "If you can get a boy to practice ragtime he will finally play the Moonlight Sonata."[13]

Anne Cross was a typical Bunker, short and plump like her brother, Frank—photographs of him at his time show his jacket stretched increasingly tightly across an expansive stomach. Her students remembered her as "fat and jolly," but she was not entirely happy. She had married on the rebound after a failed romance; her husband was an insurance salesman and "not a good provider." He was younger than his wife, a ladies' man who had "personal problems." The Crosses had two children, Carol and John. The son was very much his mother's favorite, which made his sister's home life miserable. Carol spent a great deal of her time with her cousins, and Lillian came to regard her as the eldest Gilbreth child. Anne Cross had entertained high ambitions for a musical career before her marriage and had fond memories of her master class with the aging virtuoso Franz Liszt. One of her nieces felt that she was dissatisfied with being "a piano teacher for children with grubby fingers like me."[14]

The Gilbreths' first few weeks in Providence were difficult, as the two youngest children came down with mild cases of diphtheria. Mary's death was still vivid to Anne and Ernestine, who were terrified that Martha or Frank might "disappear," too. Lillian spent many hours nursing and comforting her children, which, she recalled, "did little harm except to tired bodies and emotions." Despite this shaky start, the Gilbreths settled into Providence, and at the end of the summer they moved into a clapboard house on Brown Street, which they promptly turned into both a home and an office. It was only half a block from the university campus, so though the house had a very small backyard, the children could play on the main green, at least when the students were not around. They were so close to Brown that, Frank joked, Lillian "could go to class and if a child fell out of the window, catch him before he landed on the ground."[15]

Brown Street was part of a varied, racially mixed neighborhood. A block to the west stood the mansions of Prospect Street, where mill owners and businessmen lived in style, while a block to the north on Olive Street was the Providence Shelter for Colored Orphans, which housed as many as two dozen black children at any one time. Meeting Street, a block farther north, was home to many of Providence's black families. While white middle-class children took dancing classes in Froebel Hall, catty-corner from the Gilbreths' house, their mothers sat in Laura Carr's Tearoom—which was also a source of excellent ice cream—just across the street. The Brown Street trolley, horse-drawn in those days, passed by the door, but the Gilbreths seldom used it; they were great walkers, especially Lillian when a baby was imminent. They could walk five minutes down College Hill to the Art Club or the Athenaeum and five minutes more into the center of Providence, or stroll five minutes in the opposite direction to Anne Cross's house. She had offered them the use of a large room in her music school, which Frank promptly renamed Frederick Taylor Hall.

September arrived, all the children were recovered, and it was time for Anne and Ernestine to start school. Notwithstanding her unhappy experience at Miss Snell's seminary, Lillian sent her daughters to a private school, wanting them to be "taught by gentlewomen and hearing the speech and vocabulary of cultivated homes during those first impressionable years." In spite of Frank's preference for public schools, the two eldest girls were soon enrolled at the Lincoln School on Thayer Street, about a three-minute walk from their house. Lincoln had recently appointed a new, progressive headmistress, Miss Frances Lucas, who dressed in purple or green velvet and was not afraid of "anyone or anything" and came "from away" (all the way from Lowell, Massachusetts). She was suspected of having "rather advanced" ideas and soon introduced student self-government and a parent-teacher organization. Miss Lucas's progressive ideas attracted Lillian, who respected her professionalism. They remained friends until both women left Providence.[16]

Lillian worked hard during the Providence years. In addition to producing a baby every fifteen months or so, she ran Frank's business during his frequent absences, researched and wrote an entirely new doctoral dissertation, and authored most of the books and papers that appeared under Frank's name. Although her activities and stamina seem prodigious, a typed copy of "Mother's Daily Schedule," dated July 11, 1912, may explain how she managed to do so much. It read:

INSTRUCTION CARD

Item	Detailed instructions	Continuous or running time		
1.	Arise	7.00		
2.	Breakfast	7.30	—	8.00
3.				
4.				
5.	Begin the day of work	10.00		
6.	Work on book	10.00	—	12.00
7.	With children	12.00	—	12.15
8.	Lunch	12.15	—	1.00
9.	With children	1.00	—	2.00
10.	Nap	2.00	—	2.30
11.	With baby	2.30	—	3.00
12.	Work on book	3.00	—	4.00
13.	Callers	4.00	—	5.00
14.	With children	5.00	—	6.00
15.	Miscellaneous	6.00	—	6.30
16.	Dinner	6.30	—	7.30

The schedule includes a note in Lillian's handwriting: "Important to start the family off each day—'cheerful and happy.' Eliminate *worry* and *rush* by proper planning." Although it is easy to make lists and schedules and not follow them, there is evidence that Lillian did try to pace herself by taking a nap each afternoon. She told a journalist some years later, "No matter what happens, I manage two hours of rest and quiet immediately after lunch. This is the best time for me as most of the children are at school and the little fellows are out of doors and the house is at its quietest."[17]

Lillian could not, of course, have done all this without help. She neither cooked nor cleaned, and although she scheduled much more time with her children than women who work outside the home usually manage, she had assistance with the children during the hours she spent on her professional work. In fact, hers could *almost* be seen as a leisurely schedule. In addition to

Martha Gilbreth, who acted as household manager, an English widow named Annie Cunningham did most of the cooking, and Tom Grieves, an Irishman, became the Gilbreths' man-of-all-work. Tom and Mrs. Cunningham were a couple, unable to marry because of Annie's Roman Catholicism and Tom's divorce; nevertheless, they moved in together on the top floor. Frank and Lillian turned a blind eye to this "unusual" arrangement; as Ernestine recalled, "Neither the Gilbreths nor equally Victorian Aunt Anne let themselves worry about the sleeping arrangements in the Gilbreth attic being unconventional. Who had time to be finnecky? Their 'close-friendship' was accepted without comment."[18]

Tom did the washing, ran errands, shopped, and became somehow indispensable. The older children adored him. He was a mimic, a dancer, a harmonica player, and a whistler, and he would bang his chest melodramatically and insist he had been a fool ever to permit himself and Annie to be "shanghaied" into this crazy household, where the work kept on increasing with a new baby every year. He would sigh deeply and say, "Lincoln freed the slaves, all but one, all but one."[19]

Lillian and Martha were not enamored of Tom. Lillian found him exasperating. He had, she wrote, "an unfortunate history of Jack of all trades and master of none." He would do whatever Frank asked him to do without demur, "and everything went beautifully as long as the master of the household was at home." However, as soon as Frank was away, which was a great deal of the time, "Tom wanted to make decisions, to drop any work if anything more interesting suggested itself, to forget things on one shopping trip in order to be sent on another." Martha didn't trust him, either. She "scorned his shiftlessness and refused to have him launder her clothes, or have anything to do with her room or possessions." Yet Tom stayed: his presence proved to many observers that the Gilbreths didn't always practice what they preached in terms of household efficiency.[20]

Tom and Mrs. Cunningham soon put the house in order. It was quite a large house. The front room contained a suite of Martha's furniture, which was upholstered in green velour, a number of potted ferns, and the piano. Here the children did their music practice. There was a dining room containing a table big enough to seat eighteen people for Thanksgiving dinner and a beautiful Japanese screen, given to Lillian by her mother, one of the very few of Lillian's possessions that found a place in the house. Much of the rest of the first floor was devoted to offices; two stenographers worked in one room, typing from the Dictaphones that Frank and Lillian spoke into "at any hour of day or night." The other first-floor room was their laboratory, where they created and filmed some of their motion study experiments and developed the films. The process was highly flammable: buckets of sand were placed at strategic intervals. As the children got older they worked in the darkroom; Ernestine remembers, "We would help develop [the films] with sticky little fingers and blue print them and it was a very professional place."[21]

Lillian needed more assistance with the children if she was to resume her graduate studies. She found a well-educated mother's helper, Helen Douglas, who was a student at Pembroke, the women's college at Brown. She and Frank had interviewed several young women before they found one that suited. Helen Douglas recalled walking the block from the Pembroke campus to the Gilbreths' house and meeting another student coming out, who was muttering grimly, "You won't be interested here." Frank interviewed Helen, scaring her to death with questions about teaching, playing with, and disciplining young children. "I meekly said I'm a freshman wanting to study to be an English teacher—I've never been with young children so I'd just have to do what *seemed* proper on the occasion." Frank looked so amused that Helen Douglas was convinced that she had lost the job until he called up the stairs, "Lillie, come down and meet Miss Douglas—I've just hired her because she doesn't know a damn thing."[22]

The Gilbreths wanted a helper who would follow their educational theories and not substitute her own ideas. They even sent Helen to a Montessori school to get a little training. Her job was to look after the two oldest girls every afternoon after they returned from school. "Helen's Redheads" became a familiar sight on the Pembroke campus. She took them walking if the weather was fine, or read to them on rainy days. Helen remained a family friend for the rest of her life and often reminisced about her time with the Gilbreths, describing how she stood up to Frank and was "amused by his peccadilloes." She recalled Frank as "a very difficult man, who liked to rule the roost," and she told friends that though Lillian never contradicted or opposed Frank in public, she had more to say in private—"Lillian was no doormat."[23]

With a full complement of household assistants in place, Lillian was poised to play a more public part in Gilbreth and Company, management consultants.

12 Scientifically Managing New England Butt

If anything had been needed to convince
Frank and his wife that they had chosen the right
work, that they had found the straight road, it was
found in the response of the workers to the efforts
made to conserve and foster the human element.

Lillian Moller Gilbreth, *The Quest of the One Best Way* (1925)

M ARY'S DEATH and Lillian's need for a university where she might finish her doctoral work were important factors in the Gilbreths' move to Rhode Island, but the decisive reason was their contract to introduce scientific management at the New England Butt Company (NEB). Between June 1912 and August 1913 the Gilbreths installed the Taylor system at NEB to the satisfaction of management and most of the workers. They also carried out a series of motion study experiments that Lillian designed and Frank executed. Motion study was to become Frank's major contribution to scientific management, while Lillian's was the introduction of educational psychology. The work at NEB was important in both the evolution of the Gilbreths' own ideas and in the history of scientific management, since a major quarrel between the Gilbreths and Frederick Taylor and a split in the scientific management movement were among its by-products.

The New England Butt contract had its origins in a talk given by Frank the previous winter. His lecture to the Town Criers, a Providence "booster" club, so impressed John Aldrich, vice president of NEB, that he invited Frank to install the Taylor system at the plant. The contract was very lucrative: Frank told his English agent, "They are paying me more and for less time than I would get with a $200,000 building." As Gilbreth and Company's profit margin was seldom less than 10 percent, this suggests a payment of at least twenty thousand dollars, a handsome sum in 1912.[1]

133

New England Butt was a small, progressive firm, and Aldrich hoped to increase its profitability and benefit the workers at the same time. Founded in 1842, it took its name from its original product, butt hinges for doors; in 1855 it added braiding machines to its product line. With the introduction of electricity in the 1880s, the need for braided coverings for electric wires meant a vastly increased demand for the machines. By the early twentieth century New England Butt was manufacturing a wide variety of machines for products as diverse as fishing lines, laces for shoes and corsets, cords for curtains and window sashes, clotheslines, and wicking, as well as fancier braids for dresses and military uniforms and "rickrack braids . . . square braids . . . oval braids . . . antennae wires, tire beads . . ." In 1912 the firm occupied more than two acres of floor space in their plant off Broad Street in Providence. The brick buildings included a foundry and many assembly shops. There were about three hundred employees, who were not unionized.[2]

It is difficult to disentangle Lillian's contribution at New England Butt from Frank's since they worked very closely together. John Aldrich always said NEB was fortunate to have had "the services of these two people," and Lillian insisted that the work was a joint project. She wrote, "There was a much greater chance than there ever had been of them working together and even more need of this, since the new work was an integrated application of the findings of engineering and psychology in the industrial fields"; she added that she planned to supervise "this initial work from day to day." Most of the surviving documents, however, give Frank the most public role. A particularly detailed set of daily reports by S. Edgar Whitaker, the young engineer in charge of the micro-motion studies, is addressed to Frank. In light of her husband's hectic travel schedule, however, and because he was still running the remnants of his construction company from a New York office, Lillian must have dealt with many of Whitaker's questions. She was eager to apply the insights of her recently rejected Berkeley doctoral dissertation at New England Butt. She wanted to teach scientifically determined work methods (the "One Best Way") to the workforce, though she let Frank handle the actual teaching, possibly because she was pregnant again. The Gilbreths' on-site work started in July 1912, and William Moller Gilbreth was born five months later. He was "little and delicate looking" and "took plenty of time and attention," which reinforced Lillian's preference for working at home.[3]

The Gilbreths had never handled an installation before, their earlier attempt to use Taylor's methods at a building site in Gardner, Massachusetts, having been abandoned after union objections. They therefore hired as a consultant a highly experienced engineer, Horace King Hathaway, who had worked with them on the ill-fated Gardner job. He had been trained by Taylor and remained to the end of his long professional life an ultraorthodox

Taylorite "who crossed the t's and dotted the i's according to his teacher." It turned out to be an unfortunate choice of consultant, for Hathaway's orthodoxy contributed to the split between the Gilbreths and Taylor. Frank had few alternatives in the matter, however, for Taylor insisted that only "experts" designated by him be used, or else "strikes and labor troubles" would ensue. Frank and Lillian still did not suspect how much Taylor and his followers mistrusted them. Whether the hostility was due to concerns about Frank's competence or whether they feared that he threatened their own livelihood is not clear, but Taylor started worrying almost as soon as the job began. He wrote to Hathaway that Gilbreth "had no business whatever to undertake the systemization of a large company without having any experience in this field," while Hathaway damned Frank with faint praise, telling Taylor that success *was* possible, but only if Frank proceeded "according to the rules."[4]

The Gilbreths wanted to use the New England Butt job as a blueprint for later work, as Taylor had at the Tabor Company in Philadelphia, so it was unusually well documented. In addition to instructing Whitaker to submit daily reports, Frank hired a photographer to record the machines and machinists for lantern slides to be shown at engineering meetings. The Gilbreths also made their own micro-motion films, which they planned to use to generate publicity for their new partnership.[5]

At first the installation went well. Hathaway thought the men seemed in "a receptive frame of mind" and ready to cooperate, but he warned the Gilbreths that the job would take time; it should not "be a hundred yard dash, but a long hard pull." One of the basic tenets of orthodox Taylorism was that it took three to five years to install a system of scientific management in a way that would avoid backsliding once the consultants withdrew. But the Gilbreths were in a hurry: according to Charles B. Going, an engineer, they were trying to "Out-Taylor Taylor" on this contract and installed a system in thirteen months.[6]

Frank, who still saw himself as an orthodox Taylorite, followed most of Taylor's rules faithfully; when someone proposed putting supplies next to a machine rather than in the storeroom, he protested: "Such a deviation is the beginning of the end of the Taylor system and I will never O.K. it." Problems soon developed, however, many of them due to the Taylor group's animosity. The respeeding of machines, for example, was "virtually sabotaged" by Carl Barth, who refused to let Gilbreth use his slide rule methods to calculate the new speeds. Nevertheless, the Gilbreths' team created more effective cost accounting procedures and better routing of work; they reorganized toolrooms and storerooms and set up a planning department to take over many of the functions of traditional foremen.[7]

Changes started to creep in; for example, the Gilbreths introduced a packet system based partly on Lillian's earlier systemization of bricklaying. Instead of a well-paid and highly skilled operative "wasting" his time, a low-paid tool boy would place all the necessary equipment and parts in the correct order on a vertical frame next to the workbench. The bench itself was lowered, for Frank observed that the workmen had to stretch in order to fit the last pieces. These modifications, the Gilbreths asserted and John Aldrich, vice president of NEB, agreed, allowed braider assembly time to be reduced by almost 75 percent, so a process that had taken a skilled man thirty-seven and a half minutes could now be done by a man and a boy in eight and a half minutes.[8]

The Gilbreths used a mixture of personnel management, vocational education, industrial democracy, and psychology to persuade the workers to accept what the "experts" thought was best for them. In a shrewd move they installed the new methods in the office first. As one of the shop-floor operatives recalled, "It was a matter of amusement to us men in the shop to see him start in the office and it also made us feel as we were not the only ones that needed to be taught management." They set up a messenger system to improve interdepartmental communication and created an information bureau where all documents would be kept. Rolltop desks, which were then standard office equipment, were anathema to Frank: the tops were removed and his assistants painted grids on the desks. He told the clerks, "You've got lots of stuff filed away in the pigeonholes that you can't find when you want it and no one else can find it when you are away from the office. Clean it all out and empty the drawers too."[9]

Office reorganization was only the first phase, however; changes in shop-floor practice were potentially more difficult. This was where Lillian's psychological expertise came in. She believed that the worker would cooperate if he felt that he was "a part of what is taught and that the teachers are a *means* of presenting to him the underlying principles of his own experience." The Gilbreths applied this insight at New England Butt, setting aside a place they dubbed the "betterment room" where they set up cameras and carried out experiments. They selected workers to be filmed and gained cooperation by persuading them that they were part of the investigative team. Joseph Piacitelli, recently arrived from Italy, was an office boy at New England Butt in 1912. He was a very bright lad who later trained as an engineer and worked with Lillian Gilbreth. He believed that the Providence men cooperated because the Gilbreths respected the workman's own knowledge and experience and incorporated it into the new methods. "The workmen selected to be studied were always considered not merely as workers but investigators," he wrote, "having respect for their knowledge of their own work and utilizing their experience towards the establishment of the 'ONE BEST WAY.'"[10]

Many years later, Piacitelli recalled that although the office boys were "in the lowest echelon" of the organization, Frank always kept an eye on what they were doing. One day they decided to play with the recently installed Dictaphone "and after a good deal of experimentation we managed to put the latest song on the cylinder." Immensely proud of themselves, they "left the reproducer on for him to hear our masterpiece of recording." When Frank started recording a memo, he heard the tune and summoned the boys; lecturing them on how to use "unavoidable delays," he told them to practice touch typing in their spare time. He tested them every week and gave a dollar to the one who did best, using as a text Taylor's *Shop Management*.[11]

Incentive schemes, prompt recognition of merit, and persuading workers during retraining that they are part of the solution are now, of course, standard techniques, but they did not always work at New England Butt quite as smoothly as Piacitelli suggested. In addition, labor relations were not always as sensitive as they might have been. One machinist, Harry Flynn, was apparently doing well in the betterment room until his services were needed in another department. His bonus was not transferred with him to the third floor, so after a meeting with John Aldrich he quit. Nor did an appeal to "reason" always work smoothly. Whitaker spent several days trying to organize the janitor, Aaron, who, according to the irritated engineer, "is a foreigner and does not readily understand what he is told and likes or has a natural tendency to argue matters." One of Aaron's tasks was the emptying of wastebaskets. Whitaker found much to criticize in his methods and devised a new and, he thought, more efficient scheme. What Aaron thought about the new arrangements is not recorded, but notwithstanding problems with Harry Flynn and Aaron, most of the workers accepted the changes.[12]

The Gilbreths knew how unpopular scientific management was in some circles. Positive stories appeared in the *American Machinist* and the pro-business *Providence Journal,* but the local labor press was understandably less sanguine and claimed that the Gilbreths wished to "eliminate false moves and drive the worker into a stride that would be as mechanical as the machine he tends." The Gilbreths were sensitive to criticism that they were "automating" their workers and wrote, "Those who have only an academic knowledge of perspiration as a means of earning a livelihood should be comforted by the knowledge that the 'slave of motion study' will have a pay envelope of much greater purchasing power to compensate him for his 'slavery.'" In an early exercise in public relations the Gilbreths held a series of meetings starting in July 1912. Some talks were of general interest, at least to members of the public curious about efficiency and scientific management; others were directed particularly at the New England Butt employees. Regular meetings were also held between managers, foremen, and operatives, "at which every phase of the system has been discussed." Lillian and Frank knew it was crucial to gain the cooperation of the foremen, as they had most to lose. Under scientific management the foremen's duties were broken down and divided among as many as eight people, and the organization of work, training, discipline, repairs, and clerical work was separated. Several of these new positions were "white collar" and moved off the shop floor and into a planning office. The Gilbreths were eager to convince the foremen that the new system actually increased their career opportunities, which for some of them, particularly the younger ones, it did. They also introduced their "three-position plan of promotion," whereby the person being promoted first trained his successor while being trained by the person whose job he was about to take. This was supposed to make for smoother transitions as well as promote feelings of interdependency; it was often effective. As Lillian reported, "A study was made of their capacities and abilities and at the end of one year a machinist had become an inspector; a probation messenger had become assistant in the purchasing department; another machinist had become a chart-maker; a messenger had become the head of the information bureau; a foreman had become a superintendent; a draftsman had been advanced to take charge of the discipline of the entire plant; and a skilled laborer had become a machine shop foreman."[13]

Where the Gilbreths' approach was different from most other scientific management installers was in their insistence on an improvement of the workers' environment, which included clean bathrooms, lunchrooms, and regular rest periods. It also involved education for the workers, including the provision of libraries and lectures. This was known as industrial betterment and had strong overtones of the kind of psychological thinking revealed by Lillian Gilbreth at the Dartmouth conference. Lillian was convinced that decent working conditions would lead to contented workers and greater profits. She suggested that welfare and betterment should be so integrated into the general management scheme that there would be no need for a welfare department and that "the workers must understand that there is absolutely no feeling of charity, or of gift, in having them; that they add to the perfectness of the entire establishment."[14]

Clean toilets preoccupied Edgar Whitaker for much of his first month on the job. He found "the toilets and urinals in quite an untidy condition. I have spent a good part of the day, trying to determine a practical way of cleaning the closets, without an excess of hard labor." He continued, giving a graphic example of the grim thoroughness of many scientific management people, "I recommend the issuance of a Standing Order, providing that the care of the toilet rooms be assigned to a definite person and that daily the bowls shall be swabbed out on the inside with a cloth using one circular motion and then flushed and that twice a week the outside shall be wiped over with a moist cloth." In true scientific fashion Whitaker experimented with various chemicals but found their use "somewhat risky." Dilute sulfuric acid and oxalic acid damaged the enamel, so he settled on a proprietary brand, Dutch Cleanser, which, although it required "hard rubbing," seemed safer. He also wanted to find the best method of cleaning the windows, which were coated with iron rust. Again, Dutch Cleanser seemed most satisfactory. He timed himself cleaning a large (sixty-paned) window and found it took fifty-five minutes, but he suggested that "lower-priced labor" might be less efficient. The Gilbreths' other betterment programs included ergonomically sound chairs, proper workbench height, better lighting, and regular breaks. It is not clear whether the New England Butt employees felt that clean toilets and windows added to the "perfectness" of their life, or whether they preferred the pay bonuses they received for cooperating with Gilbreth and his staff.[15]

The Gilbreths also introduced a suggestion box with monthly prizes for the best ideas, which apparently worked well; one man who had been working on a particular machine for several years suggested "various improvements on that machine, netting him $25 in prizes." Another Gilbreth effort to encourage the workers was their Home Reading Box scheme. It involved an elaborate system of young men in cars visiting households to collect old magazines, which they deposited through a window into a box at New England Butt "that the day's work might not be interrupted." The workers could take as many as they liked, then keep them or return them. Lillian recalled seeing "the fathers choosing the home or picture magazines for the wife to read or the children to cut up" and men "of a studious turn of mind selecting the trade catalogs that might have some hint as to an invention or some new idea for the Suggestion System that might win a prize." Responding to criticism that the magazines were of the "lighter variety," Frank retorted that the box's contents included *Scribner's, Century, Atlantic Monthly,* and six volumes of the *Encyclopedia Britannica.* He told a reporter he believed with all his heart "that it is the best scheme yet devised to help in educating the worker," whose two biggest problems, he asserted, were that "in the first place he has no vocabulary [and] in the second place he cannot read fast or remember what he does read." Andrew Carnegie had a better-organized—and much more expensive—scheme for workers' self-improvement, but the Home Reading Box movement was part of the optimistic Progressive spirit of the time: give the workers access to knowledge and they will use it. The Providence Public Library set up a branch at New England Butt and reported that the first book borrowed was Dante's *Divine Comedy*—checked out by an Italian employee.[16]

New management practices at New England Butt, and the interest of pro-

fessors at the Gilbreth Summer Schools in what New England Butt employees had to say, may also have enabled the workers' self-confidence and ambition to remain high even after the Gilbreths had departed. The free two-week
scientific management schools were organized by Lillian and held during four
summers, from 1913 to 1916. The curriculum consisted of morning and
evening lectures, between which the participants, who were mostly professors
of management in business schools, visited New England Butt to talk to the
operatives about the new systems.

Thus far the Gilbreths' methods had involved classic Taylorism inter-
woven with psychology. Their first technological innovation was their effort
to measure motion. They wanted to find a "scientific" way of promoting efficiency rather than using Taylor's stopwatch methods, which they believed to
be less accurate and more subject to human error. Calling the system "micro-
motion study," Frank used movie cameras and a clock calibrated in hun-
dredths of a minute to film operatives against a grid in the background. He
and Lillian examined the film frame by frame through a magnifying glass and
then synthesized the best motions into a standardized, fatigue-minimizing
method. Operatives who were willing to be filmed using the new methods
earned a bonus. Bill Slocum, a machinist, started special training in late July
and within a month he had earned generous bonuses of perhaps a third of
a day's wages for "preparing two packets correctly," which entitled him to a
dollar for each one. Bill Slocum became well known in scientific management
circles; in February 1913 Frederick Taylor, who was in Providence to speak to
the Town Criers, watched him assemble a braider. Taylor seemed impressed,
though his comments concerned the purely Taylorite elements of the installation. According to Whitaker, "He declared this method was the quickest he
had ever seen; he said that he had never seen a better Tool Room." Taylor
made no comment on the elaborate film apparatus. Frank and Lillian persisted with their motion studies and used the resulting films to train the workers. The machinists watched themselves on film using both the old methods
and the new ones. The combination of Frank's natural teaching ability and
the novelty of moving pictures made the films a success. Frank would give
a running commentary, intimating that the workmen had made the vital
motion-saving suggestions. He would say, "There's the spot Bill was able to
untangle," or ask his audience's advice: "See that snag—the work rhythm
is broken there—maybe one of you fellows can help figure out something
better."[17]

The New England Butt installation went smoothly: there were no strikes
or walkouts and productivity rose. This was partly due to Frank Gilbreth's
skillful handling of the men. Henry Hopkins, an operative who was promoted to gang boss, remembered Frank as an approachable, sympathetic

man who "tried to come into personal contact with all." Hopkins continued, "Soon he was calling the men by their first name which you know makes a man feel as though he could talk to him and ask him many things he would not do under restrained conditions. . . ." Frank was soon "considered a friend of the men." Hopkins was promoted; he benefited from scientific management. Yet Frank and Lillian won over many whose benefits were less tangible or even nonexistent. This was remarkable because throughout 1912 and 1913 there was serious labor unrest in New England. The radical labor union Industrial Workers of the World (the IWW, familiarly known as the Wobblies) was exploiting the American Federation of Labor's lack of interest in unskilled immigrant workers and won a long struggle for unionization of the mills in Lawrence, Massachusetts, early in 1912. The strike was punctuated by outbreaks of violence; three IWW leaders were arrested and charged with the murder of a young striker, though their supporters maintained that a Lawrence policeman was responsible for the shooting. The trial was set for late September, and as the time grew near there was unrest throughout industrialized New England. Wobblies, socialists, and anarchists organized a sympathy parade in Providence in early September, and the famous IWW activist Helen Gurley Flynn addressed the rally.[18]

The only potential labor problem at NEB occurred during that hot, restless summer. Steven Vose, a carpenter who had recently left NEB, spoke to IWW organizers, who called a meeting in Olneyville, a working-class area of Providence about two miles from the NEB plant. About eighty NEB employees met on August 16, 1912, but nothing came of the meeting and the IWW did not gain a foothold in the plant. The meeting had one unfortunate effect, however; Taylor got wind of it and wrote to Hathaway, "It would not in the least surprise me that Gilbreth should have a strike on his hands." So convinced was Taylor of Frank's incompetence that he refused to endorse him for a job with a manufacturing company interested in hiring him. Taylor advised Carl Barth not only to continue withholding his slide rule but also to avoid any financial involvement, as Frank had, he said, a dubious record.[19]

Nevertheless, labor relations at New England Butt remained good. Workers continued to have weekly meetings with senior management, where policies were discussed and criticized and where "the president of the company sat on the same kind of chair and had the same kind of cigar to smoke." The system itself, however, was far from perfect, and as soon as Frank's back was turned, many of the reforms he had instituted were quietly abandoned. Whitaker described a "general relaxation and slipping back into the old ways of doing things."[20]

Frank and Lillian spent part of the summer of 1913 at meetings in Europe. When they returned to Providence Frank was appalled by conditions at

New England Butt. He sent a sixteen-page report to John Aldrich listing forty deficiencies, including backsliding in the planning department, which was, he claimed, "a wild and savage orgy" until the supervisor came on duty, and problems in the information bureau, where haphazard filing meant "things are scattered all thru the factory." The toolroom was good, "the best I have ever seen," but nevertheless it needed work, as too much time was still wasted collecting tools. Many of his rules were not being enforced, and he urged the disciplinarian to start imposing fines of twenty-five cents per infraction, the money to go toward the annual works outing. Frank concluded with a pious hope that "this work be the finest example of the pure Taylor system" and enclosed a bill of two thousand dollars for his services for the preceding ten weeks, in spite of having spent six of those weeks in Germany.[21]

New England Butt paid the Gilbreths fourteen hundred dollars on this occasion, not the full sum Frank demanded; relations nevertheless remained good. In the early 1920s, even after the business fluctuations caused by World War I, the loyal John Aldrich reported that the system was "still in full force" after "10 years of eminently satisfactory operation" and that "both management and employees heartily endorse the improved methods and have no desire to abandon the plan and return to former conditions." NEB had, however, standardized their product line, something the Gilbreths had not attempted, and it is very possible that this was the main reason New England Butt had survived the economic vagaries of war and peace.[22]

13 The Good Exception

We must have our own organization and we must have our own writings so made that the worker thinks we are the good exception.

Frank Gilbreth to Lillian Gilbreth (May 9, 1914)

ALTHOUGH FREDERICK TAYLOR viewed Frank Gilbreth's work at New England Butt with alarm, the break between the two men was not immediate, and they continued to meet at professional meetings. Taylor sometimes sent Frank to speak on his behalf; one such occasion was in March 1913 when the anarchist Emma Goldman challenged the whole idea of scientific management. Taylor had bronchitis and asked Frank to address the Western Economic Society in Chicago. Lillian traveled with him, three-month-old Bill in tow. After Gilbreth had explained about functional foremen, demonstrating on a chart the eight types of foreman, all of whom were directing a worker underneath, Emma Goldman interrupted him. She pointed to the chart and said, "We want the man at the top. There is nothing in scientific management for the workman. The only scheme is to have the workman support the loafers on top of him." At this point, Lillian whispered something in Frank's ear; he said nothing but returned to the platform and turned the chart upside down to show that management supported the workers. Frank's point was greeted with applause from his engineering audience, but Goldman walked out of the hall in disgust.[1]

On their return to Providence the Gilbreths continued to work on micromotion, which they saw as the best way to make scientific management acceptable to the workers. On April 1, 1913, Frank photographed Lillian demonstrating how movement could be recorded. She sat at a desk with a painted grid, and the same grid was superimposed on the film, so the small-est movement could be measured. She wore a ring with a small electric light attached, and as she moved her hand the light created a bright line on a single, time-exposed photograph. She and Frank then analyzed the shapes in the photograph and simplified the movements. They called the system the stereo-cyclegraph and tested it at their new job, the Hermann, Aukum handkerchief company in South River, New Jersey.[2]

Frank tried on more than one occasion to explain his method to Taylor "and told him what it would do and told him I was surprised that he did not recognize its meaning. He acted so I saw he was hurt and so I changed the sub-ject." Even if Taylor was unreceptive to motion study, Frank worked hard to sell it to a wider public. He had introduced it to an engineering audience in December 1912, and a few months later he ensured maximum publicity for the Gilbreths' new and "scientific" system of measuring movement by mak-ing micro-motion films of popular sporting events. He started close to home, filming Brown University athletes running in the hundred-yard dash and play-ing baseball. Frank told the editor of the *Sunday Providence Journal*, "We studied throwing from pitcher to catcher to second, also the getaway of the batter." A little later he filmed the New York Giants playing the Phillies. Such films were advertising gimmicks, designed to refute the assertions of Emma Goldman and other critics and demonstrate that scientific management—or at least the Gilbreth version thereof—could benefit and interest the "com-mon man." Although Frank was no golfer (the only exercise he ever took was sailing), he filmed the swing of Francis Ouimet, the former draper's assistant who was the first American to win the U.S. Open, thereby suggesting that everyone could benefit from his motion study methods.[3]

By mid-1913 even the thick-skinned Frank was starting to suspect that he had offended "the father of scientific management." As Taylor controlled most of the scientific management installations in the United States, this threatened the Gilbreths' livelihood. Frank started to think about advertising his techniques elsewhere; his trip to Germany in 1913 was part of this change of direction. He and Lillian attended meetings of the Verein Deutscher Inge-nieure (VDI), the German equivalent of the ASME.[4] Leaving the four oldest children at home with Frank's mother, they took six-month-old Bill with them. The baby spent the journey either sleeping cozily in an open bureau drawer or being carried aloft on Frank's arm and petted by all the crew and passengers.

They had hired a nanny to take care of the baby once they arrived in Ger-many. Sister Clara met the Gilbreths at the quay and whisked Bill away. Lil-lian remembered that it was "a little appalling" to have him and the luggage disappear in a taxi, but the next five weeks were perhaps the most luxurious of her life. The nurse was German and Dutch "with probably a touch of Javanese," and Lillian found her "not only competent but extremely good-looking." Sister Clara also organized Lillian and Frank and made Lillian realize all over again Tom Grieves's deficiencies. Sister Clara was "valet and lady's-maid and nurse and advisor and schedule keeper and everything else." By the time the Gilbreths reached their hotel, Sister Clara had preempted the best rooms on their behalf, unpacked their bags, and ordered certified milk for the baby. She managed to get them the outside rooms with private bath everywhere they went. Lillian remembered with some amusement that she was "so tactful and so good-looking that the men of the party seconded any plan she proposed and persuaded their women-folks if not to concurrence, at least to silence!"[5]

Lillian and Frank arrived home in late July, and after a month at the shore Lillian resumed preparations for her doctorate. She was no ordinary student; she and Frank had talked to Dr. W. H. P. Faunce, Brown's president, before deciding to move to Providence, and he "helped outline the plan of work and was always ready with encouragement and interest." Lillian studied current educational problems with Walter Ballou Jacobs and took two laboratory-based courses in experimental psychology, one with Stephen Colvin and the other with Edmundo Burke Delabarre. Her fourth course, also with Professor Delabarre, was Intermediate Psychology, which dealt with "the nature and composition of consciousness"; she received grades of A and B at the end of the semester. Although Lillian's doctorate was an important credential for her and for Frank, she later wrote that she viewed her studies as relevant only insofar as they had a practical application to Gilbreth, Inc., consulting engineers. "The real purpose was not the 'Ph.D.,'" she recalled, "but the constant feeding of new material in the areas of psychology, education and personnel, into the data to be used on the jobs." Perhaps because of this she preferred not to take more courses than absolutely necessary. Although she registered for second-semester courses, she promptly withdrew and prepared "The Psychology of Management" for publication, without, of course, using her full name or suggesting in any way that it was not written by a man.[6]

While Lillian studied at Brown she also presided over a very energetic and noisy household. She and Frank followed many progressive educational ideas. Lillian was familiar with the work of Friedrich Froebel, the early-nineteenth-century pioneer of kindergartens for young children, who wrote that music, play, and activity should be at the center of a child's schooling. These all became part of the Gilbreth children's lives; despite varying degrees of musicality, they all took music lessons and dancing classes. They took piano and violin lessons at Aunt Anne's music school and their daily practices had to be supervised. Anne, who played piano and violin, seems to have been the only one who practiced willingly, while Ernestine "preferred improvising to practice" and Frank and Bill "seemed to prefer rhythms to mastering an instrument." The older children went to dancing school, over the protests of the boys. Lillian sent all the children to Sunday school, despite agnostic Frank's insistence "that it should be made optional." Frank acquiesced, if only to get the children out of the house on Sunday mornings so he could catch up on his sleep.[7]

Lillian managed to spend a lot of time with her children. Ernestine remembers going to Shepard's department store with her mother "especially when she wanted to be alone and collect herself for one reason or another." Ernestine was not always a great help in this respect, for she recalls having a tantrum on the floor of the shop because her mother was in a hurry and would not buy her a hyacinth. "I lay on the floor and kicked and screamed so people looked at mother as if to say what have you done to that child?" More than eighty years later Ernestine vividly remembered her mother's calm response. Lillian said to her, "Dear, I'm awfully sorry, I told you we have to go home and I'm going. You can follow me if you want."[8]

Lillian also had to fit in her graduate studies with running the management consultancy business. Frank was a restless, gregarious man who loved to travel. He was away from home a great deal, either working or spreading the "gospel" of scientific management; he took the evangelical aspect of his work so seriously that his diary notes show plans for a new book to be titled "The Religion of Scientific Management." When Frank was out of town Lillian supervised the workers and hired new ones; she organized the photographic processing, analyzed the data, and prepared all the reports. A typical letter from Frank listed eight things he wanted her to do. Five weeks later, in the midst of another long list of tasks for her, he remembered that she was, yet again, pregnant and warned, without any conscious irony, "There is a great necessity that you slow down. I shall not worry about anything except that you might break down. You know your condition does not usually warrant such hard work as you are doing. I think we will accomplish most if you study how to do less."[9]

The Gilbreths' trip to Germany in the summer of 1913 was the first of many, as Frank increasingly sought work outside the United States. On subsequent visits he went alone, leaving Lillian to look after the business and the children, but this was unfortunate, as Frank spoke little German, while Lillian was fluent, practically bilingual. During a twenty-five-month period between late December 1913 and February 1916 (a period that included the first nineteen months of World War I), Frank spent almost thirteen months in Germany. He worked for both Allgemeine Elektrizitäts Gesellschaft (AEG), the German equivalent of General Electric, and Carl Zeiss, the lens makers.

Scientific management was, however, extremely unpopular with the German unions and the Social Democrats. As Frank wrote to Lillian, "The Taylor System [here] is a fighting word," so AEG was trying to keep his presence at their plant as quiet as possible. Frank won a short-term contract to redesign the office system, but only after war broke out and many of the workers were drafted was Frank given free rein to reorganize the workshops. Frank's services were not cheap. As he told Lillian, "They still think I am a very great man. It is mostly because I charge such high fees." AEG paid handsomely: Frank received fifteen thousand dollars for two months' work, which is approximately three hundred dollars a day. Frank paid his assistants fifty dollars a day on long-term jobs, probably more for short-term contracts, but he did not guarantee a full year's work. By comparison, manual workers in Rhode Island were earning two dollars a day.[10]

Frank was back in the United States for a few weeks in March 1914, during which time he complicated Lillian's life enormously by abruptly whisking his three eldest children out of the Lincoln School and enrolling them in a nearby public school. Ernestine hated it. She was in the middle of third grade (like almost all the Gilbreths, she skipped grades) when her father moved them. She blamed herself: "I was becoming a little snob," she remembered, having announced that she did not want to sit next to the "common children" on the trolley. Moving to Slater Avenue School from the caring atmosphere and small classes at Lincoln was a shocking experience for Ernestine and still painful eighty years later. She remembers spending the first two weeks "just going down into the toilet in the basement at school and crying." She came home one lunchtime, terribly upset. "I cried and cried and cried and said please don't send me back to school," she recalled. Lillian and Frank were in the office, showing some of the micro-motion equipment to Mr. Remane of AEG—a vitally important client, if Frank's German consultancy work was to continue. Mr. Remane spoke little English and Frank spoke even less German, so Lillian's presence was vital. She left Frank with the client, however, had lunch with Ernestine, calmed her down, and took her back to school. After Lillian spent the afternoon with the principal, Ernestine had no problems for the rest of the semester. The following September the Gilbreth children transferred to the newly opened John Howland School. It had energetic, progressive teachers and the children became very happy there.[11]

Frank returned to Europe, leaving Lillian to mop up the problems caused by the change of school, but while he was away his relationship with Taylor and the scientific management mainstream, which had been strained for some time, finally collapsed. Frank had been working at Hermann, Aukum's handkerchief factory since August 1912; his contracts were renewed every four months. In March 1914 one of the owners approached Taylor to complain about Frank's work, and Taylor suggested that Horace Hathaway take over. Although Frank's latest contract was not due to expire until May, Hathaway visited the factory in March and told Taylor he found a state of confusion that he attributed to the Gilbreths' micro-motion experiments. He described Frank as "either raving crazy . . . or a fakir." Taylor forwarded this opinion to some of his followers and told them not to "lay too great a stress on the work that is being done by . . . Frank Gilbreth," because Gilbreth was interested solely in money and was "likely to do great harm to our cause." This exchange occurred as Frank was about to leave for Germany; he did not want AEG to suspect there was anything wrong so he did not respond. Nevertheless, Taylor's hostility was a serious blow. Hathaway and Barth urged Taylor to tell friends in Europe his misgivings about Gilbreth, but Taylor demurred, saying, "I agree with you that he might discredit the whole movement in Germany and yet it seems hard to write and point out his incompetence." Lillian disliked confrontation, but the quarrel affected her deeply and she could never speak kindly of Taylor again.[12]

Taylor's hostility combined with Frank's repeated absences inspired Lillian to think of better ways to organize their professional lives. She suggested the creation of their own management training school to teach the Gilbreth system. This endeavor would keep Frank at home more, thereby taking some of the domestic and organizational burden off her. Lillian decided to be businesslike and sent Frank a typed memo proposing "that FBG and LMG become consulting engineers on the science of management." She suggested that they should stress their scientific credentials, since management was scientific only insofar as work was measured accurately. Convinced that the best methods available were Frank's inventions, micro-motion and the cyclegraph, she felt that "it is the particular province of FBG to show those men who are installing scientific management how to use the methods of measurement." Noting that she was the best-qualified psychologist working in the field (though she politely included Frank as sharing in her expertise) and that they were ideally suited to "instruct those installing scientific management along those lines," Lillian maintained that the most profitable use of their talents was to train time and motion study experts, company by company, rather than do the work themselves. She further proposed that "FBG and LMG take no more jobs to install management in this country, but instead become real consulting engineers for management, in that they deal only with owners in plants, or with those actually installing management in plants, in other words, that they become of the expert type." She was careful to emphasize their departures from traditional Taylorism: "It is also advisable that we at once show the scope of application of our measurement to the human element as well as the handling of material."[13]

The Gilbreths needed to be seen as the "good exception" within the scientific management world. Their excommunication meant that they had to claim greater scientific precision to would-be clients while stressing their concentration on the "human factor" to reassure the workers. The importance of their partnership grew, as did the gendered division of work: Lillian's public image as nurturing and caring was as important as Frank's as the technical expert. As her children wrote in *Cheaper by the Dozen*, "It was Mother who spun the stories that made the things we studied unforgettable."[14]

In the short term they looked for work in Germany, as many Europeans agreed that the Gilbreths were the "good exception." One of the strange things about scientific management is that it appealed to people in all parts of the political spectrum. French socialists, who were bitterly opposed to Taylorism, made an exception for the Gilbreths' motion study methods. Lenin, the Russian revolutionary leader, was a keen student of the writings of Taylor and Gilbreth while he was in exile in Switzerland. He disliked Taylor's methods, but he wrote in the margin of one of Frank and Lillian's articles, "An excellent example of technical progress under capitalism toward socialism." He believed that motion study could smooth the transition to state socialism, which, he wrote, contained "important answers to the problem of capital accumulation in a non-exploitative fashion suitable to the workers' state."[15]

Even if Lenin approved, it is hard to see Frank's reliance on Lillian as anything less than exploitative. She was the academic member of the partnership, and Frank relied on her to build their public image. Her own reputation was starting to grow; 1914 saw her first individual entry in *Who's Who*. Meanwhile, Frank had become interested in the application of motion study to hospitals; he suggested, for example, standardization of the layout of surgical instruments and minimizing nurses' fatigue through more efficient bed-making techniques. "I haven't done a thing on the surgeons' paper," Frank wrote to Lillian. "I think that is our most important job. I wish you would go over our pictures and manuscript and see what you can suggest to make it a success." A few days later, however, he was off in another direction and asked Lillian "What do you think of your agreeing to furnish 26 articles with pictures of S.M. [scientific management] or motion study for the Sunday magazine during the next year?" In all these directives Frank was never sure whether the papers he wanted Lillian to write were simply publicity vehicles or contributions to scientific management, though her preference was for the latter.[16]

Frank was still in Germany when Lillian celebrated her thirty-sixth birthday in May 1914. She was eight and a half months pregnant, in the middle of her second Ph.D. program, planning the second Gilbreth Summer School, running the house, and coping with the intransigent man-of-all-work Tom

Grieves and a difficult mother-in-law, as well as running a business, and she could be excused for feeling a little tired. Yet Frank wrote complaining that he was exhausted and had slept until 2:30 in the afternoon, returned to bed after two hours, and got up again at 7:30 P.M. in order to go out to dinner. He instructed her to organize a house by the water for July, since he needed a rest as well as a chance to be "strenuous." He announced, "I want a place on the sea shore where the kids and I can live in our bathing suits. I want to get back to the Indian life once more. I also want a small sail boat with a sail twice too big for it so I can fight it."[17]

Lillian disliked Frank's summer plans. It always seemed so much easier to stay home and take the car for day trips to the seaside with "the comfort of supper at home and one's own bath and bed to finish the day." She was prepared to concede that a change was attractive and liked the idea of weekends at the shore with friends, but she recoiled at the disruption of moving everyone and everything. She thought that taking a summer place was hardly worth the effort since "so much furniture, equipment and clothing had to go along." She disliked the water, had never learned to swim, was terrified in small boats, and felt overwhelmed by the disruptions that moving the family to a rented seaside cottage caused. Nevertheless, she went to the shore and recalled that "many times she was so tired that it was all she could do to keep from boxing ears all around, or putting the small fry unceremoniously to bed until a good night's sleep could set everything to rights again." It took Lillian many years to divest herself of her girlhood training in "proper" behavior and abandon her efforts to run her household like her mother's Oakland mansion. "It was a much-needed and impressive lesson," she concluded, "that simple clothes, simple meals and a simple program took less time and effort and gave more real pleasure than complicated ones."[18]

Lillian's seventh baby was due on June 15, 1914. She planned to have it in the Providence Lying-In Hospital, whereas all her previous babies had been born at home. Frank insisted that he would be home in time for her "coming out party," but he proposed cutting it very close. He wanted to stay for the ASME meeting in Hamburg in early June, which he believed was vital if he was to win more European contracts and put his side of the Taylor conflict to his fellow engineers. To Lillian's relief Frank arrived in Providence on June 14, but the baby was in no hurry to be born. The Lying-In Hospital was notorious for its strictness; Lillian's pencils and notebook were confiscated and she was forbidden to read. When the labor pains proved to be a false alarm, she discharged herself and, according to her children, walked the couple of miles home, complaining that she had never had a more miserable day. Baby Lillian "arrived quietly" twelve days later, but Frank was not there. Tired of waiting, he had gone to a conference in Atlantic City.[19]

Despite her misgivings, Lillian had rented a waterfront cottage where the family lived for three months. By the beginning of August, however, she was back at work in Providence, where she and Frank were running their second Gilbreth Scientific Management Summer School, which she had spent much of the spring organizing. On August 31, 1914, Frank returned to Germany. It wasn't the best of times to be traveling; Britain had declared war on Germany less than a month earlier, and already the Germans had invaded Belgium, defeated a large Russian force, and launched an air attack on Paris. Nevertheless, Frank was in high spirits when Lillian saw him off from Providence station. He amused himself on the train to New York by writing a list of seventeen instructions for Lillian to plan her work "so you can do it with less fatigue and in less time." Most of the suggestions were detailed plans for running the business efficiently in his absence, though number sixteen did recognize that his wife had had a strenuous few months, running the summer school so soon after baby Lillian's birth. He instructed her to "take a *real* vacation before doing anything. You need it badly."[20]

Frank was away from home from late August 1914 until early January 1915, thus missing his second consecutive Christmas with the children. He was in Europe at an exciting time, and his letters and diaries are full of information about wartime Germany. After seeing trainloads of wounded soldiers, "a grewsome [*sic*] sight," Frank noted that "this war has but one good feature. I think it will be the last war for some time. Before it is finished there will be so many killed and such terrible hardships that all countries will be shocked at the thoughts of war, at least until this generation passes." He discovered when he reached AEG that "the war has absorbed their interests more than the installation of S.M." Nevertheless, he persevered with his micromotion studies, his training lectures, and his office systemization schemes. His German contracts were very profitable, or so it seemed, but as time went on it became more expensive and difficult to transfer money. He ended his three-month contract by sending home drafts totaling less than ten thousand dollars plus a fine collection of cameras.[21]

14   A Second Dissertation

*The house ran smoothly and the work at Brown
progressed in spite of many interruptions. The children
kept well and happy during Frank's trips. Lillian used every
available minute to complete her work for the degree
which she hoped for at the 1915 commencement.*

Lillian Moller Gilbreth, *As I Remember* (1998)

Although Frank's parting advice in late August
had been to take a vacation, Lillian wasted no time before starting her doctoral fieldwork. She planned to apply time and motion techniques to elementary and secondary education. She was not alone: a cult of efficiency was infiltrating the public schools, and professional administrators were starting to replace old-style head teachers. Lillian's purpose was a little different, however, as she wanted to make the teachers themselves more efficient, rather than impose layers of supervision upon them. During the fall and winter of 1914–15 she spent two and a half days each week observing classes in Providence schools, hoping to find similarities between school and industry and "to work out a method by which successful practice in the industries might be applied in the schools." Lillian wanted to reduce wasted materials, time, effort, and human potential, or as she put it, enable teachers and students to produce "the largest amount of work of high quality with the least expenditure of effort and with the least amount of fatigue possible."[1]

The Providence superintendent of schools granted Lillian permission to observe classrooms, but his restrictions made her research difficult. She was not allowed to take notes, visit any class more than twice, or tell the class teacher why she was there, since "if her purpose were known, she might be suspected of a critical attitude which might antagonize the teacher." As Lillian wryly remarked, some teachers were antagonized anyway, as "even the most broad-minded" of them "doubts the ability of any outsider to make an accurate and adequate record of his practice. Especially is this the case if the investigator has industrial rather than teaching experience." Lillian visited a wide variety of classrooms over the next five months. They included an evening class for Polish immigrants, whom she observed sitting uncomfortably in tiny chairs intended for fourth-grade students, a high school physics class where the girls' elaborate hair ribbons obstructed other students' view of the blackboard, and a mixed-grade grammar school class for the unruly. She prepared slips of paper with various headings such as "incentive," "socializing work" and "handling materials," which were the elements she wished to study. When she got home she described what she had seen, adding comments on the effectiveness of the practice.[2]

Her observations completed, in March 1915 Lillian dictated her dissertation into a Dictaphone, ready for her secretaries to type. At four hundred pages it is twice as long as any Brown doctoral thesis of that era. In her introduction Lillian stressed her credentials, tracing her knowledge of schools back to her undergraduate education courses eighteen years before and her knowledge of industry to her meeting Frank in 1903. She claimed that this double expertise enabled her to produce an accurate description of conditions in the schools and to suggest how teaching might be improved in future. She was equally forthright about the practice of scientific management; she described the Gilbreth version, rather than simple Taylorism, using three references to their own writings to every one of Taylor's.

Lillian's previous dissertation had also dealt with teaching and scientific management, but there the similarities end. The Berkeley piece was a theoretical effort to interweave the pragmatic and functionalist ideas of William James and John Dewey with classical Taylorism, while the Brown dissertation was more empirical; it included richly detailed field observations and made recommendations on applying the findings to secondary schooling. In the intervening three years, while the Gilbreths were modifying Taylorism by adding micro-motion, John B. Watson had revolutionized psychology by publishing an article in 1913 called "Psychology As the Behaviorist Views It." Impatient with "old-fashioned" introspective methods, he argued that psychology should be "a branch of natural science" that had no more use for introspection than "the sciences of chemistry and physics." According to Watson, the only valid subject for study should be behavior and the adaptations that animals and humans make to changes in their environment.[3]

In terms of that definition, Lillian's dissertation was purely behaviorist. She was interested only in behavior and its possible modification. Just as Watson wrote that the goal of psychology "is the prediction and control of behavior," Lillian, like all the scientific management experts, wanted a pre-

dictable and controllable labor force and was prepared to use her psychological expertise to get it. Just as she had at New England Butt, she used a combination of managerial and psychological methods to persuade teachers to
rearrange their classrooms, reorganize and systematize their teaching, and
delegate routine tasks such as handing out papers or organizing supplies to
"low paid workers"—in other words, the students. Although she nodded
toward progressive educational theorists such as Rousseau, Pestalozzi, and
Montessori, she endorsed none of them, saying a little vaguely, "The average
teacher has elements of all these different ideas of teaching in his own ideal
as to what teaching should be."[4]

Lillian's dissertation contained little experimental work. She did what she
could, however, within the superintendent's limitations, to determine how
the students' behavior was affected by different physical conditions. She
noted factors such as room arrangement, lighting, and clothing and observed
the reactions of pupils and teachers to changes in their environment. She witnessed approvingly some conditioned responses, such as the regimented mental arithmetic testing system she saw in a high school math class. The students
put pencil and paper in a predetermined place on the desk and when the
teacher barked out, "Write answer," Lillian noted that "the pen and pencil are
immediately drawn into position and the name of the pupil, date and answer
are recorded at top speed and the papers are collected by monitors in the back
seats, all this without [further] word of direction."[5]

Amy Wentworth, a Brown master's student who was practice-teaching a
sixth-grade class, enabled Lillian to circumvent some of the superintendent's
restrictions. She was interested in scientific management and offered to carry
out some experiments. She had twenty-one students ranging in age from
eleven to fifteen; the age range suggests that she had a number of immigrant
children. Lillian visited her classroom for several successive days but stopped
when the other teachers became curious. Lillian suggested some simple techniques then left Amy Wentworth to her own devices, realizing that she
"would take more interest in making the changes if it were left to her direct
supervision." Using a system of monitors to do everything from distributing
pencils to erasing the blackboard, Wentworth claimed she saved five to ten
minutes on every mental arithmetic test, which left more time for other subjects. Lillian included as an appendix Wentworth's account of her classroom
experiment, which was the only numerical part of the thesis.[6]

The first 100 or so pages of Lillian's dissertation involved a detailed description of the principles of scientific management; the next 150 applied scientific management techniques to schools. Lillian analyzed the efficiency of
the classrooms in terms of their physical amenities, their space, light, and
ventilation, and the types of desks and their placement around the room; she

even considered the location of clocks and wastepaper baskets, pens and pencils. There were also two long chapters on "the human element." One dealt with eliminating wasted physical motions, the other with planning work, to enable the students to learn most effectively.[7]

Lillian also included details of sixty classroom visits, each one followed by her evaluation of the technique being observed. She was careful to describe each of the public school cases in general terms, since she had been a guest (her word) in the classrooms "and must observe the obligations binding a guest." Her observations on private schools and her sister-in-law's music school were more specific—the superintendent's restrictions did not apply. Lillian bestowed both praise and criticism. She liked what she saw at a private girls' school, probably the Lincoln School. Despite Frank's removal of the children, Lillian was still friendly with Miss Lucas, the headmistress, who in turn was interested in scientific management and had been a panelist at one of the Gilbreths' Tuesday evening meetings in 1913. Lillian watched a seminar-style English lesson, where she saw animated seniors seated in a semicircle around their teacher. When she saw the same girls in a more conventional setting, she noted that "there was an immediate return to the stereotyped school room attitude"; she concluded, "The seating was an important influence." Similarly, she praised the seating arrangement in the mixed grade grammar school class, where the desks were also arranged in a semicircle around the teacher's desk. "This arrangement seems particularly fortunate here," she commented, "as the children are in the room because of ill adjustment of some sort."[8]

Lillian observed a less satisfactory situation at her children's school, John Howland Elementary. Her nine-year-old daughter, Anne, who had skipped a grade (as the other Gilbreth children would), was part of a restless and disgruntled group of fifth graders and came home complaining about the "baby" work. At this juncture the mother seems to have gotten the better of the disinterested observer, for Lillian found herself asking some questions. The teacher told her that many of the students "had very poor training in the fundamentals" and that they could not go on until this problem was rectified. Lillian urged her to explain this to the class and noted in her dissertation, "The report of the next day's work was brought home to the writer by one of the pupils, who said, 'Oh, mother, we had a wonderful time in arithmetic today. You know we have never learned to multiply and do those things as fast as we should, but we are going to practice on that a lot now and, as soon as we learn to do it fast, we can just race thru the whole term's work. I wish you could have heard us do it this morning.'" Lillian commented rather solemnly, "Here again we find an illustration of [Taylor's] eighth law, 'Secure cooperation.' The moment the pupils understood the situation they lined up with the teacher, instead of against her, to overcome the obstacle."[9]

Lillian's remarks on the effect of appropriate dress are typical of the personal tone of her dissertation, as well as her interest in "efficient" dress reform. She complained that the average schoolchild's clothing "defies every law of hygiene and beauty" and is "uncomfortable, glaring in color and extreme in style." She continued: "The question of clothing may seem unimportant, but its influence, economic, social and individual is enormous. It would certainly be a wonderful thing for this country, if school children, as a body, could be convinced that efficiency and appropriateness, the two being more often synonymous than is supposed, are the real tests of clothing." She went so far as to suggest that teachers wear a modified form of the pupil's clothing, an idea that was unlikely to be greeted with enthusiasm by the teachers: efficiency could be taken too far. Lillian reserved her strongest criticism for teachers who did not follow the Montessori notion of "doing nothing for the child that he can do for himself," believing that by handing out papers or even cleaning the blackboard, teachers were wasting their time and energy on nonproductive work. She praised "one of the most successful teachers [she] ever observed," who assigned a considerable amount of written work but avoided spending too much time on grading "by correcting the first few papers then allowing those with correct solutions to correct the papers of others."[10]

After her five months of observation Lillian concluded that "there was much waste in existing class room practice" and that "waste elimination methods that had proved successful in the industries might be used with profit in the schools." It is undoubtedly true that many of her proposals would have saved time and diverted energy to more productive learning experiences. But whereas her industrial proposals demanded hiring scientific management experts to show the workers what to do, she respected teachers as professionals and admitted that "actual application of such methods could best be left to the teaching force." Lillian proposed taking teachers into partnership rather than imposing ideas on them and suggested that the teachers should do the same with their classes. Amy Wentworth had told her that "she and the class are both much more interested in the work since the methods have been tried. This interest, she believes, has been a very real and valuable incentive." Lillian commented that she had found the same to be true in industry: "Not only does the individual become more interested in his work and accomplish more through the interest, but the class, as a whole, becomes stimulated to act as a group."[11]

Lillian Gilbreth was describing what was later known as the Hawthorne effect. She understood that participation in the experiment, as much as the new methods themselves, made Amy Wentworth's students more productive. A dozen years later, Elton Mayo and the other investigators at Western Electric's Hawthorne plant put a name to this phenomenon when they discovered that while the workers' productivity rose when the factory lights were brightened, their productivity also rose when the lights were dimmed. The most important factor was not the external conditions, but the attention paid to the workers and their belief that they were partners in an investigation. Lillian had found the Hawthorne effect in Wentworth's classroom.[12]

Meanwhile, Frank was in Germany, yet again. As usual, he fretted about Lillian working too hard, though he never worried enough to prevent her conceiving another baby or writing another article for him. She was, of course, pregnant again, with baby number eight due in September. "I suppose your thesis will nearly kill you," he wrote gloomily. "I hope you will take it as easy as possible anyway." She did not take it easy and completed the body of her dissertation by the end of April.[13]

Lillian's oral examination took place on a rainy afternoon in late May, on the eve of her thirty-seventh birthday. A "solemn faced" secretary led Lillian into a large lecture hall where her professors awaited her. Her first two questioners, Professors Colvin and Jacobs, asked her about the connection between scientific management and education, which was precisely the topic of Lillian's dissertation. "This part of the examination was, of course, a great joy," she wrote to her parents, "as I could have talked all night on any one of the topics." Dr. Jacobs had telephoned her a few days earlier, saying he planned to ask her about some of the parts of his course she had found most interesting, such as educational testing and the Montessori system. "The way in which he gave them made the questions very easy to answer . . . and gave me a chance to really do very well during this part of the examination."[14]

The third and final part of Lillian's oral exam was less comfortable. She faced Dr. Edmundo Burke Delabarre, whom she described as "a psychologist of the 'old school,'" who had "no sympathy with experimental psychology and is interested in the theoretical side." This statement is not quite accurate. Delabarre was a highly trained experimental psychologist who had studied under Hugo Münsterberg in Germany. His more recent work, however, involved a study of the effects of hashish on his own consciousness, so he represented a bridge between the old and new schools of psychology. He fired a series of questions at Lillian demanding precise definitions of terms such as the senses, perception, the imagination, emotion—all the concepts that both the functionalists and the behaviorists mistrusted. "Nothing but knowledge of the literature amounting to memory work was any use," she complained. Delabarre was clearly the most rigorous of her examiners; at one point she gave a definition of psychology that led him to "bark out," "So you have become a behaviorist, have you?" Finally, at 6:00 P.M. he leaned back in his chair and said, "Mr. Dean, I am satisfied."

Lillian was so exhausted that she was not sure "whether he meant satisfied with me, or satisfied that I did not know enough to be bothered with." The examiners filed out of the room and left her at her little table looking at her watch. After seven minutes, which seemed like seven years to Lillian, since she "felt sure that if they approved my work, it would only take them half a second to decide so, therefore they must be discussing how to break the news gently to me," they filed solemnly back and Dean Barus began, "It is my pleasure—" and she knew she had passed.

Lillian ran home through the pouring rain "the happiest person in Providence." As she went through the front door she was greeted by a mass of excited children pouring down the stairs and by a houseful of servants and relations. Her mother-in-law was there, as were Mrs. Cunningham the cook, Florence and Mary, the maids, Helen Douglas, who helped with the children, Tom Grieves the handyman, and her two secretaries—everyone but her husband, who was four thousand miles away in Germany, entertaining a group of Zeiss engineers. He was not due home for three more weeks, so Lillian had to make do with a congratulatory ode. As ever, there was a serious undertone to Frank's jaunty verses, which referred both to the money to be made in wartime Germany and to Lillian's highly placed relatives there. He wrote:

My dearest chum I wish you'd come to me without delay
(You'd be in touch with all that's Dutch and that would surely pay)
Your gorgeous key and Ph.D. and cousins in the army
Would put you high (and tho I'd try the mere thought does alarm me.)

Frank continued with an oblique reference to the importance of Lillian's Ph.D. to their position within the scientific management world and to the jockeying for positions by Henry Gantt and other revisionists after the recent death of Taylor:

Of course I know, it's soon to crow, when there are others older
And perhaps Gantt'll think the mantle should fall upon his shoulder
But in the race we'll set the pace and let them pass who can
(I just revel to think the devil has got the "foremost" man.)[15]

Lillian celebrated with a birthday dinner. The children chose the menu which included chicken and strawberry shortcake with lots of whipped cream, followed by an enormous birthday cake, beautifully iced and surrounded by lilies of the valley and pink flowers from their garden. Lillian looked at her presents, which included a mahogany writing table from Frank, a white dress from her parents, a pincushion in the shape of a doll from her sister Gertrude, a little green address book from three of her children, and a box of homemade fudge from her eldest daughter, Anne. She awoke the next morning with "the strangest feeling . . . of there being nothing to do, although I have heaps of work waiting to be attended to." Uncharacteristically, she awarded herself a holiday. "I think I will take the day off and start in working tomorrow."[16]

In spite of all the celebrations, Lillian's dissertation was not finally accepted until June 9, and she spent an anxious two weeks wondering whether her Berkeley experience was going to be repeated. Though her dissertation nominally contains 313 pages, it also includes almost one hundred extra pages with either Roman numerals, or addenda such as "160 a–o" or "178 a–x," which were typed in mid-May 1915, only two days before Lillian's doctoral defense. Since these sections contain an explanation of her research methods and detailed descriptions of her fieldwork observations, it is likely that one of her supervisors asked her to add this material to strengthen her dissertation, and the rest of the committee had not yet had time to read them. The preface came even later; it was added a week after her degree was conferred. When the dissertation was finally accepted, Lillian sent a cable to Frank telling him that all was fine and the degree was, at long last, assured.

On Wednesday, June 16, 1915, Lillian became the first of the scientific management pioneers to earn a doctorate. Although neither her husband nor her parents were there to witness the great occasion, she was determined to enjoy every minute of the celebrations surrounding commencement just as she had fifteen years earlier at Berkeley. On Monday evening there was an outdoor Promenade Concert on the main green. Lillian didn't need to go; her house was so near that she could hear the music and see the fireworks and the students dancing. Toward midnight she might have heard a band playing as the graduating seniors marched down the hill carrying torches, in "a haze of red and green-colored smoke, shot through with sparks, rockets and yells," as they went to their class supper, where they "made hilarious" until the early hours. Lillian probably felt a great deal better than the seniors next morning as she braved the rain to attend a Phi Beta Kappa meeting. Denial of the key in 1900 had been a bitter blow, but she had recently been elected as an alumna, thanks to Frank's cousin (and her ex-chaperone) Minnie Bunker, and membership was sweet. Before going to the Phi Beta Kappa society lecture later in the day, Lillian had a very pleasurable duty, namely, listening to Helen Douglas give an address at the Ivy Day celebrations. She took "Helen's Redheads," nine-year-old Anne and seven-year-old Ernestine, out of school to see their beloved Helen speak for the junior class.[17]

Commencement day dawned rather cloudy, but the sky soon cleared and it became a beautiful New England summer day. The children woke very early but were too excited to eat their breakfast. When Mildred Gray, one of Lillian's secretaries, arrived at 8:15, she found the house in an uproar, with the children helping their mother put on her black silk gown and admiring her from every angle. Eventually they were satisfied and lined up on the front porch with Grandma to watch their mother walk along Brown Street to join the procession. Five-year-old Martha was very envious of such sartorial splendor and resolved to find out what she would have to do to get a degree.[18]

Mildred Gray left Lillian on the green and walked with Anne down to the First Baptist Church, where Brown's commencement always takes place. They did not have long to wait; soon they heard a band playing and, along with everyone else, crowded to the windows to see the colorful procession coming down College Hill. Led by an eighty-eight-year-old veteran of the class of 1858, President Faunce and the fellows marched into the graceful eighteenth-century building. Anne and Miss Gray watched from the gallery as the box pews filled with graduates and faculty, the latter wearing a rainbow of colorful hoods. The seven doctoral candidates brought up the rear and sat in the front row to the right of the pulpit; Lillian was the only woman among them, though not Brown's first woman Ph.D.—two had gone before. After numerous speeches, the degrees were conferred. The new doctors of philosophy were given pride of place, and as faculty members placed their hoods around their necks, each was roundly applauded.

The procession back up the hill was much less formal, so both Anne and Miss Gray marched with Lillian all the way to the college grounds, to the delight of all of them. Ernestine, Martha, and Frank Jr. joined their mother on the green, where they were photographed, with Anne and Lillian, all looking uncharacteristically neat and tidy in their white summer clothes. Benjamin Ide Wheeler, president of the University of California, was at Brown for his fortieth class reunion. He was surprised to see Lillian but came up to congratulate her and said he was delighted, since she could not take her degree in California, that she was taking it at his old college. This was not much consolation for all the extra work she had done, but Lillian wanted to show him how well she was coping. "I think I was never prouder than when I introduced those four rosy, clean, little youngsters" to him, she wrote. He must have noticed she was pregnant again, though whether she admitted that there were two more babies at home is not recorded. Wheeler was not deceived and told her that "though I looked very well it was a great strain to bring up a family and take a Ph.D. and told me I ought to slow up and rest for a while."

Lillian was not one to rest, that day or later. She took the children home and then hurried to the Pembroke alumnae luncheon. Though her degree was from Brown, she was not comfortable being the only woman at the alumni lunch, so she joined the women, who ate separately, and then marched with them across the campus to join the men and hear the speeches, which went on for more than two hours. She decided to skip the ball game, though she did stay long enough to see the various classes of alumni march toward Andrews Field. Instead, she went home for a visit with Frank's dentist cousin Jane Bunker and a rest. Lillian's long day was far from over, however. At about nine o'clock she and Anne Cross went to the president's reception in Sayles Hall. Her friend Miss Lucas, the headmistress of Lincoln School, had sent her a beautiful corsage of roses and lilies, which she wore with her black silk dress. She had a wonderful time: "Everyone was so cordial and nice that it was a splendid ending to the day."

The following day was a bit of an anticlimax. Lillian carefully packed away her cap, gown, and hood and "buckled down" to all the small jobs that had accumulated over the last few days. When Frank finally returned, the whole family left for a rented cottage at Buttonwoods, a beach community about fifteen miles from Providence. The house had a spacious garden with a high hedge to provide shelter from the winds coming off Narragansett Bay. Ernestine and Frank fancied themselves Johnny Appleseeds; every time they had an apple they stuck the core into the lawn. The children were fascinated by the Indian peddlers who came around selling little scissors cases and sewing boxes made of sweet grass. Perhaps tensions were high, for while they were there, Frank and Lillian came the closest ever to a fight, at least in their daughter Ernestine's hearing. After a brush with fire in the New York apartment several years earlier, Frank was very nervous about fireworks and forbade the children to have even the most harmless of sparklers for the Fourth of July. Lillian was little fonder of fireworks, for she remembered her family's celebrations back in California, where she and her father had sat by the fire buckets instead of watching the displays. However, the children managed to wheedle so pathetically that she gave in, but when they proudly exhibited their new treasures to their father he turned purple, glared at Lillian, and slammed his straw hat onto his head as he strode off toward the beach without saying a word. The children never asked for fireworks again.[19]

Lillian's vacation was short. She spent much of August helping with the latest Gilbreth Summer School and in early September, less than a week before her eighth child was due, she visited two Boston hospitals with Frank. Their growing interest in surgical efficiency meant they visited hospitals whenever they could. On this occasion they watched operations carried out under very primitive conditions. There were pails holding refuse from several successive procedures in the operating room, which was far from sterile—the doctors also used it as a changing room and hung their outdoor coats on the wall.[20]

On September 13, 1915, a disaster happened. Somehow Lillian tripped and fell down the cellar stairs and went into labor. There was no time to get her to a hospital, so doctors and nurses were sent for and she was carried carefully to her bedroom. Usually on such occasions the children stayed in the house. Anne and later Ernestine slept next to their parents' room and, as Ernestine commented, "None of us had any illusions that having a baby hurt." This time, however, the children were hurriedly sent over to Aunt Anne's, and when they returned home they could not find the new baby. Frank and Ernestine wrote about this in *Cheaper by the Dozen* but made light of it, saying that their mother seemed so healthy that half a day in bed or the arrival of a doctor made them assume another baby had arrived. However, there was no baby on this occasion because she had been stillborn. Though Lillian's fall may have precipitated the labor, in itself it was not fatal; the baby's death certificate gives the cause of death as "knot in cord foot from umbilicus." The little body was handed over to a funeral director, and after a small, private ceremony the nameless daughter was buried in Grace Church cemetery, two blocks from the New England Butt plant. Her birth and death were not mentioned in Lillian's memoirs or Frank's diaries, and they never referred to the tragedy in public.[21]

Just as with the death of their daughter Mary some five years earlier, Frank and Lillian found this loss difficult to talk about, but there was another, very important reason for their reticence. They were afraid of the criticism they could face for the size of their family and the effects on Lillian's health of trying to do everything at once. Lillian was very conscious of this. Edna Yost, her friend and first biographer, wrote, with Lillian's tacit approval: "Theirs was not a marriage to find easy acceptance in its social environment. The world was critical, as one child followed another with their mother's appearance far from robust, more critical of him than of her. A woman as sensitive as she must have suffered greatly from implied, even if unspoken criticism." Not all criticism was unspoken; once, when Frank told a fellow engineer, "Lillie always feels better when she is pregnant," the colleague demanded to know, "How the hell can she tell?"[22]

Lillian left Providence as soon as she was able to travel and took the train to California. She vacationed with her parents at the Grand Canyon. Her mother had lost a child and was sympathetic, though privately she agreed that Lillian was trying to do too much. Nevertheless, Lillian was back in Rhode Island by the end of November and resumed her full schedule, traveling with Frank to meetings in Philadelphia and Chicago. Frank managed to spend Christmas with the family for once; and although he was planning to sail for Germany on December 27, wartime conditions forced him to stay in the Western Hemisphere, though not necessarily at home. By early 1916 Lillian knew she was pregnant yet again.[23]

15 Therbligs and Tonsils

The Gilbreths were not without their
critics; married women, especially mothers, were
not supposed to be professionally active. There was
an edge to the speaker's voice when Frank was
introduced to an audience as the man who earned
his living "by the sweat of his frau."

Edna Yost, *Frank and Lillian Gilbreth: Partners for Life* (1948)

AFTER HER RETURN from California in December 1915, Lillian tried to ignore all the criticisms, implied or spoken, of Frank; instead, she concentrated on writing about motion study for the disabled. At first glance this aspect of the Gilbreths' work contradicts their emphasis on efficiency and the "One Best Way," but it was part of their continuing effort to be seen as the "good exception" within the scientific management movement. Frank had seen many wounded servicemen in German hospitals and concentrated on physical adaptation, while Lillian recognized the psychological disabilities suffered by the "crippled soldier" and suggested ways to organize work to prevent him from becoming, in her words, "a discouraged and unhappy member of the community." Her voice is very apparent in the papers written over the next few years.[1]

Frank's work with the disabled led to his most important contribution to motion study, the isolation of the seventeen elements of movement, which he called "therbligs"—without pointing out that the word was almost Gilbreth spelled backwards.[2] He gave each element a color-coded symbol. For example, an eye with the pupil to one side represented "search." Not all elements had to be present for one action, but to write a note would involve searching, finding, selecting, grasping, positioning, and using a pencil, then inspecting, releasing the load, and resting. The therbligs, displayed graphically on Simultaneous Motion or Simo Charts for analysis of micro-motion films, told a researcher at a glance how often any one element of motion was used in a cycle and perhaps how to eliminate unnecessary movement.

Frank was trying to deduce the "One Best Way," a catchy slogan that got the Gilbreths into a great deal of trouble then and since. Psychologists rightly dispute whether "one best way" can be right for everyone; Lillian herself was always skeptical about the concept, stressing instead individual differences and preferences. Even Frank eventually backtracked a little, admitting that "it is useless to expect all to perform the same operations in precisely the same way."[3]

As a subject for their motion study, Frank and Lillian filmed the one-armed Mr. Casey, who was secretary to the mayor of Boston. Casey had adapted his typewriter with a month's supply of paper on a roll and two banks of keys. They also filmed one-armed men wrapping parcels, as well as dentists (including Frank's cousin Dr. Jane Bunker) working "to their satisfaction" despite the fact they had one hand behind their backs for the entire operation. Lillian wrote a series of papers with titles such as "Motion Study for the Crippled Soldier" and even "The Conservation of the World's Teeth: A New Occupation for Crippled Soldiers," which rather ingeniously suggested teaching one-armed veterans to be dental hygienists, thus solving two problems at once. The latter paper included a photograph of Martha having her teeth cleaned by her Aunt Jane.[4]

Lillian's ninth baby was born in Buttonwoods in August 1916, less than a week after the Gilbreths' fourth summer school ended and eleven months after their daughter was stillborn. Grandma was away for a few days, Frank was out of town, as usual, and Lillian was alone in the cottage with seven young children and only Mrs. Cunningham's young daughter Annie to help. There was a terrible thunderstorm, preventing the usual complement of doctors and nurses from reaching the cottage, and Frederick Moller Gilbreth was in a hurry to be born. One of the children ran for a neighbor, who, Lillian charitably recalled, was so scared that "she complicated the situation considerably." Mother and son coped well, however, and Lillian enjoyed the rest of the summer and managed to relax for a few weeks with "little to do except take care of and play with the new baby." Lillian was never one to neglect her professional duties, however; while nursing Fred she found time to check the galleys of her latest treatise, which dealt, appropriately, with fatigue.[5]

In *Fatigue Study* (1916) Lillian reiterated many of the ideas discussed in her doctoral dissertation. Her approach was pure behaviorism: "The observed man . . . may add introspections," she noted, "but this testimony, while interesting and worthy to be recorded . . . cannot be submitted to the accurate measurement of the observer." Frank's name still appeared prominently on all their writings, though they usually worked together on an outline, then Lillian took Frank's rough draft, added scientific and psychological references, and polished the prose. Sometimes he was in a hurry, wanting their work published even if the prose lacked refinement. Their book *Applied Motion Study,* for example, had "literary defects," which made Lillian very unhappy. She wrote the first draft of *Fatigue Study* on her own, however, as Frank was away in Germany. She recalled "his terse comment when he first read it,—'it certainly is gabby!'" adding defensively, "It certainly was, but at that time nothing more dignified and exact was possible and the book seemed to meet a certain need and be useful to a certain group." This statement would appear to be supported by the book's success; a second edition was published in December 1917, and it sold many more copies than their other books. For the first time the title page read, "By Frank B. Gilbreth and Lillian M. Gilbreth, Ph.D."[6]

Lillian recommended numerous ways to improve productivity by minimizing fatigue. She thought that as much as possible the work should be adjusted to the individual worker. Chairs, footrests, and armrests should be provided, as well as an adjustable workbench, improved lighting, and sensible clothes, "patterned after tennis or other athletic contests"; supplies should be laid out near the worker, and there should be vocational guidance so the worker is in the job that suits her best. Regular rest periods were important; Lillian was a strong proponent of the coffee break, which was far from routine in 1916. There should be, she wrote, time to rest and a seat to rest in: "It is your duty to rest when you need it" and "Let's go at the fatigue study all together." The Gilbreths' fatigue recommendations were somewhat dictatorial. The handkerchief folders at Hermann, Aukum were forced to rest for 21 percent of their time, whether they liked it or not, but according to Lillian these enforced rest periods led to a tripling of their productivity.[7]

The summer over, Lillian went back to work. Since Taylor's death the Gilbreths had won a series of remunerative contracts. Although Lillian often went with Frank for the first visit to get the feel of the business, she mostly stayed home writing while Martha Gilbreth ran the house, Tom continued to annoy Lillian and delight her children, and Frank continued to travel. Their clients including Cluett Peabody, U.S. Rubber, Eastman-Kodak, and the Remington Typewriter Company, where Frank and Lillian (and the children) worked out the best ways of teaching typing. The Remington experiments became part of the Gilbreths' scheme to train their children through real-life projects. Frank taught the children to touch type by coloring their fingers and the keys, while Lillian timed them with a stopwatch; after the younger children were in bed, the older ones took turns on a special white typewriter with blank keys. Ernestine at age eight became such a skillful typist that Frank wanted to enter her as a "child prodigy"—and as an advertisement for the

Gilbreth Method—in a national speed contest in Chicago, but Lillian talked him out of it, as the children recounted, by saying that "Ernestine is high strung and the children are conceited enough as it is." Frank compromised by filming the children touch-typing and released the film to a newsreel company, showing, according to the children, "everything except the pencil descending on our heads."[8]

In addition to their contribution to the children's education, the motion study films of typists' training provide an insight into the differing personalities and methods of Frank and Lillian. Like everything the Gilbreths did, the typing experiments were well documented, and photographs and fragments of a motion picture survive. They show an attractive young woman who resembled the movie star Mary Pickford, dressed in a black dress with sheer sleeves, blinking modestly into the camera as she was filmed touch-typing. The authors of a book on the psychology of typing borrowed the films from Lillian some twenty years later and included partial transcripts of the investigations. It is clear that Lillian was by far the better listener. She asked questions and responded thoughtfully to the answers, while Frank made pronouncements, many of which prompted a defensive or even antagonistic response from the person under investigation. When the speed coach was describing the correct wrist action and copy position to "avoid neuritis" (carpal tunnel syndrome?), Frank started to contradict:

> Mr. Gilbreth.   *Your copy ought to be squarely on the line of sight.*
> Typist.   *We incline the head so as to make it nearly square with the line of sight.*
> Mr. Gilbreth.   *You are mistaken. To be square that board would have to be like that.* (Readjusts copyholder).
> Typist.   *Then the top line and the bottom line are not in the right place for focus.*[9]

A little later Lillian again asked thoughtful, noninflammatory questions, suggesting that individual differences are valid, while Frank made dogmatic pronouncements. Lillian asked them "whether the reaction time to an eye stimulus or an ear stimulus is quicker. Some people do faster work from copy and others do faster work from dictation." But when the typists started to answer, Frank interrupted, saying, "The idea is this. The champion typist has got to get the copy from her eye up to the brain and then down to the fingers. We want the champion girl on the dictating machine to get the reaction from her ears to her fingers. The blind person gets information through the fingers. We are measuring all champions to see what champions are made of."[10]

Whatever their differences in approach, Frank and Lillian worked well as a team, and by early 1917 both their business and their family life were going very well. The feud with the Taylorites had been in abeyance since Taylor's death in 1915, and the Gilbreth management consultancy business was successful. Meanwhile, both Lillian and Frank were becoming well known in professional and academic circles. The four eldest children were settled in their new schools and the two toddlers and the latest baby were well supervised at home, so despite the almost annual additions to the family, the Gilbreth household system was working well enough for Lillian to resume some of the social activities she had given up thirteen years earlier when she married Frank. She was invited to join an exclusive women's debating society, the Wednesday Club, which met fortnightly. Members enjoyed a standing joke that the club had been founded by "youthful spinsters," but there had been a rash of resignations in 1915, and such women seemed to be in short supply. Eight married women were proposed as new members, their names reflecting Providence's "first families"—a Metcalf, a Gladding, and Mrs. Frank Gilbreth. Members were (and are) required to debate once a year, but though Lillian joined in December 1915 she took a year's leave of absence the following October. She did not, therefore, take part in the January 1917 debate, which was on a topic very close to her heart: "That scientific management is necessary to successful factory administration." Nevertheless, Lillian became a skilled debater. In her first debate she and her partner, speaking for the affirmative, carried the motion "That the manual arts are essential to a liberal education." A debate on woman suffrage in January 1918 was one the Wednesday Club found hard to live down; seven of the nineteen members present voted against the motion, though Lillian added "one wee thought" during the discussion period, suggesting that "it would be wise to pass it to get the indecision eliminated." Lillian very much enjoyed the Wednesday Club and continued to attend once a year even after she moved away from Rhode Island. Older members still remember her descending upon the club, asking, "Well, what's the topic?" and debating extemporaneously, unlike her partners and opponents, who had been studying in the Providence Athenaeum for the past month, condemning their husbands and children to cold suppers.[11]

Lillian became involved in the parent-teacher association at the children's school; she also joined the Collegiate Alumnae, which later became the American Association of University Women (AAUW), with whom she was involved for much of the rest of her life. She soon became the group's president, though she recalled with some amusement that when she "foolishly asked why she had been selected," they told her that "she was the only person in the club acceptable to everyone because she was the only member so new that she had not become affiliated with any small clique." Thus the Gilbreths' life was settling into a comfortable pattern. Unfortunately for Lillian, Woodrow Wilson declared war on Germany in April 1917 and Frank immediately volunteered for service. He was almost forty-nine years old, had seven children under the age of twelve and another due in September, and, at 240 pounds, was seriously overweight. The day war was declared Frank fired off a telegram to the War Department telling them how invaluable he would be to the war effort and dashed down to Washington on the next train. Frank's attitude to the war had changed; whereas in the early years he had been enthusiastically pro-German, he was now just as eager to help the Allies.[12]

Frank persisted despite the strong disapproval of his mother and sister, who told him in no uncertain terms that he was a fool to try to enlist. Lillian thought the same, insofar as she was able to think that anything Frank did was foolish, but she took the attitude that if he felt so strongly about it, then he should do it and she would cope with everything else. "He was so unhappy at the thought of staying or delaying," she wrote, "that his wife felt he must go at once if he felt so tremendously impelled to do this." The War Department was not, however, enthusiastic about this plump, middle-aged soldier; though Frank had contacts in high places, they listened politely and for several months did little.[13]

Lillian was relieved by this delay. "He was sorely needed in the household and could have found a useful place in an essential industry," she wrote. This was true, as there was more interest than ever in rationalizing production for the war effort and in training new workers to replace those who had enlisted. Firms needed higher productivity and were willing to institute change. Because many of the men were out of the way, new methods could more easily be imposed on the women who replaced them. Frank and Lillian's brand of expertise, which promoted the scientific determination of the "One Best Way" and the use of psychology to persuade workers and foremen to accept that method, was exactly the kind of labor force control that industry sought.

Patriotism and manliness were intertwined in many men's minds, however, and Frank wanted to go to France, "where I can do a man's bit." He was determined to serve his country in uniform, whatever economic sacrifices for Gilbreth, Inc. (or extra work for his wife), this might entail. His determination may have been reinforced by criticism of his work in wartime Germany and by the enlistment of many of his scientific management peers. Many of the Gilbreths' friends and acquaintances were involved in the war effort; Henry Gantt worked with the Emergency Fleet Corporation, and others were in uniform, such as Sanford Thompson and Hugo Diemer, who were commissioned to work in the Army Ordnance Department, but the only close colleague to see active service was Frank's old nemesis Horace King Hathaway.[14]

In the meantime, tensions rose in the Gilbreth household when many of the children became ill with sore throats and swollen glands. Frank was inclined to deny the existence of illness, while Lillian quietly coddled the afflicted children, read to them, and let them stay in bed. The family doctor suggested that all the older children except Martha have their tonsils removed, a common practice in those days. This gave Frank an idea for an experiment. His newfound interest in reorganizing surgery had met resistance from doctors, who did not want an ex-bricklayer telling them what to do: few surgeons were willing to be filmed, and most hospitals were afraid of lawsuits. Then Frank met a New York ear, nose, and throat specialist on one of his Atlantic voyages. This man, intrigued by Frank's ideas, was willing perform tonsillectomies on camera, so using his own children as subjects seemed entirely logical. Four procedures could be carried out on similar-size subjects all in one place and in one day; here was an ideal opportunity to discover the "One Best Way."[15]

A whole chapter of *Cheaper by the Dozen* deals with the tonsils episode, which is also one of the highlights of the movie, but Lillian's memoirs and the notes in Frank's diary tell an even more extraordinary story. The mass tonsillectomy took place on April 12, 1917. Frank had returned from his initial efforts to enlist and, as Lillian recalled, "Fortunately he could be at home the day of the 'Tonsil Party!'" The first-floor parlor of the Gilbreths' house was turned into an operating room. Klieg lights were installed, a camera was set up, and one of Frank's time clocks was placed in front of the operating table. Grandma Gilbreth's big bedroom on the second floor was turned into a ward where the children could be nursed. Martha ate a hearty breakfast before trotting round to Aunt Anne's for the day, but Lillian went without to keep Anne, Ernestine, Frank Jr., and Bill company. Two doctors and several nurses promptly set to work on Anne, watched by Frank, who was dressed in white scrubs and resembled, according to his children, "a large Alp," Lillian stayed in the next room with the other children, who were clad in pajamas and crying. As soon as Ernestine was on the table and anesthetized, the doctor realized that her tonsils were perfectly healthy, but reasoning that the anticipation was perhaps the worst part of the procedure, he removed them anyway. (They didn't break this news to Ernestine until her sore throat was completely better.) The specialist then said that Martha's should come out. A quick telephone call to Aunt Anne brought Martha protestingly home and, as Lillian later wrote, she was "subjected to the ether in spite of roars and kicks which almost subdued the entire operating group and lost not only the tonsils but the wonderful breakfast!"[16]

The motion study experiment was a flop. None of the films came out. In *Cheaper by the Dozen* the children claim the photographer forgot to take off the lens cap; however, Ernestine later admitted that "it wasn't as stupid as that, but he did something mechanically in the camera that went wrong." Ernestine believes, with eighty years' hindsight, that the tonsils incident was deeply distressing to her mother. "I think she felt that was a bad thing to do and it was an astonishing thing to do—if one of us, after Mary, if one of us had died from that thing . . ." It is also astonishing that Frank, after his heroic but futile effort to save Mary, was prepared to watch his other children on the operating table. In *Cheaper by the Dozen* the children portray Lillian as saying, "It seems rather heartless to use the children as guinea pigs," but they make no comment on Frank's original decision. Lillian's only published comment on the incident was characteristically mild: "Anyone who has tried the experiment of nursing several youngsters through the convalescent period after this particular operation has missed something." When they described the tonsil party in *Cheaper by the Dozen,* Ernestine and Frank Jr. used a little dramatic license, portraying Frank Sr. as feeling a little guilty and saying, "So, as a conscience balm, I'm going to let the old butcher take mine out as well." They suggest that this procedure took place a few days later (in the movie it is the same day) and that Frank was so confident that it was a minor operation that he declined the use of ether and had only a local anesthetic. In fact it happened two years later.[17]

As soon as sore throats were mended and school was out, Lillian took all seven of the children, aged eleven years to eleven months, to visit their grandparents in California. This meant she would miss the Gilbreth Summer School, but she was so tired and so upset with all the events of the last few months that she decided to go anyway. The cross-country train journey was a nightmare despite the assistance of the housekeeper, Mrs. Cunningham. Baby Fred was sick all the way from Niagara Falls to the Golden Gate, three-year-old Lill had broken a bone in her foot (apparently Anne had fallen on her—but not on purpose, Lill was eager to add many years later) and had to stay in her berth, and Lillian was seven months pregnant. In spite of her annoyance with Frank's military plans, Lillian wanted to prove to her parents that her marriage was a success. The children claimed that she had bought them a lot of new clothes in order to make a good impression in California, and so she economized on food, bringing along two suitcases of cereals and graham crackers. "We ate almost all our meals in the drawing room," Frank Jr. and Ernestine wrote, "journeying to the dining car only on those infrequent occasions when Mother yielded to our complaints that scurvy was threatening to set in." Lillian, on the other hand, said they experimented with the diner and also ate from a large lunch basket packed at home—though that cannot have fed nine people for very long![18]

Lillian had planned to get the children cleaned up and properly dressed before they arrived in Oakland, but her brother Fred surprised her by joining them on the train at Sacramento. According to the children, he found a scene of utter devastation. They were in the middle of a meal; there were suitcases full of food and a pile of diapers on the floor, and Lillian was holding a crying baby; young Lill, whose foot was hurting, was sobbing on a couch, and four-year-old Bill was doing acrobatics on the bed. On seeing her brother Lillian burst into tears; this was not the impression she had planned to give. She wanted to convince her parents that she had made the right choice in marrying her "strenuous" husband, that she could cope with the children, and that Gilbreth, Inc., was prospering. There are hints in Lillian's letters that her parents were less than enthusiastic about her frequent pregnancies; they were also (justifiably) concerned for her welfare if Frank succeeded in joining the army. Uncle Fred was sworn to secrecy, however, and by the time the rest of the Mollers met them at Oakland Station, the children were more or less presentable.[19]

A fleet of chauffeur-driven Packards took the Gilbreths to the house where Lillian had grown up and where her parents and her six unmarried brothers and sisters still lived. The house was spacious and the garden, where members of the family indulged their various hobbies, contained much to delight the Gilbreth children, including "a billiard hall, a radio shack, greenhouses, a pigeon roost and a place where prize-winning guinea pigs were raised." The Mollers had plenty of time for hobbies, since they lived very comfortably off rents and investments. Their peaceful life was about to change, however; their three sons, all in their twenties, were off to war, and the anti-German feeling prevalent in the United States led the Mollers to reject their heritage. They stopped speaking German at home, they burned all their German books, including some first editions of Goethe, and the young Gilbreths were instructed to call Annie "Grandmother" rather than "Grosie."[20]

The arrival of the rambunctious Gilbreths upset the Mollers' lives. Lillian recalled, somewhat ruefully, "It is awful to think what an upheaval that peaceful household had!" Her parents had forgotten how tiring young children could be—and the Gilbreths were more tiring than most. Bill and Frank got into all kinds of mischief, and Ernestine staged a sit-down strike, refusing to go in any car other than her grandmother's limousine. Lillian's children were not used to being "seen and not heard," although they _were_ accustomed to being put on show by their father. He, however, used them to demonstrate the effectiveness of his teaching rather than the prettiness of their outfits. And so they managed to get into trouble when their grandmother invited some friends to see "Lillie's little girls." Rather unwillingly, Ernestine and Martha donned their best white dresses and tied big satin bows in their hair, "only to follow Andie [Anne] under the sprinkler which was watering the lawn and to appear before the guests bedraggled and dripping." Lillian's description of this incident suggests that, at least in retrospect, she had some sympathy with her daughters' revolt against being "shown off."[21]

Lillian heard from Frank several times while she was in Oakland. Just as they had on her previous visits to her parents, his letters became increasingly agitated as he thought she might succumb to the easy life, or that the children would stop their lessons and become just like other children. He worried that Lillian would not want to leave "Fairyland," which he described as "the place of no strenuous life." He also fretted about what would happen if he died and she returned to California permanently. He wrote crossly: "You know what will happen—they just won't study. There is no excuse for not having two half hours per day *Maintenance*. We can't produce what we've aimed for on that basis. Talk German, French, Esperanto, Italian, Chinese, Japanese, anything you like but do something—Typing—well—Oh! What's the use—Yes, there is use—I would say either they study or come home and I'll make them study."[22]

It was still hot when Lillian got back to Providence, but it was good to be home. Before the month ended she produced her tenth child and her third book. "About ten days after Daniel's appearance, *Applied Motion Study* came from the press and became the second highlight of the month of September," she wrote. Frank was still waiting impatiently for his commission and spent much of the fall setting up management jobs so that Lillian could supervise them in his absence. His persistence finally prevailed; he was commissioned a Major of Engineers, though to his disappointment he was on the War College staff and was to serve at home, not in France. Frank's repeated visits to wartime Germany had not gone unnoticed, but soon after Frank was posted Lillian reported, "Our stock has certainly gone up since you went into active service. I am almost reconciled to missing you when I think how cheap some people must feel." This ignoble sentiment was, however, crossed out in 1941 when Lillian deposited her papers at Purdue.[23]

Frank left Providence on December 20, his trunks full of micro-motion data and equipment and some very expensive officer's uniforms. Lillian was not pleased that he was to miss yet another Christmas with his family, but the charming letter he sent to his mother and children might have compensated a little for his absence. It suggests why his family was able to overlook his many faults. He told them he would rather be home: "I'd much sooner look out at Laura Carr's, or watch the Brown Street Car's semaphore, or even hear the racket of the motor pumping air to release the brakes on the car that is waiting for the car to come up the Brown Street Hill. And oh, that Turkey that you will have and the fixings, to say nothing of the crambelly [*sic*] sauce. I'd let you eat with your knives, climb up on the table, chew with your mouths open, not wear your ear telephone, or anything if I was only home for Christmas."[24]

Instead of eating his "crambelly" sauce at home, Frank spent an irritating few days in Washington with nothing to do and joined his old friends the Bancrofts in Philadelphia for Christmas Day. Then he set off for Oklahoma to do his bit for the war.

Lillie Moller, September 1880, age two and a quarter, some four months after her sister Gertie was born. *Courtesy of Frank and Lillian Gilbreth Collection, Purdue University Libraries.*

Lillie Moller as a shy teenager, mid-1890s. *Courtesy of Frank and Lillian Gilbreth Collection, Purdue University Libraries.*

In 1900 Lillie Moller was the first woman to speak at the University of California's commencement. *Courtesy of Frank and Lillian Gilbreth Collection, Purdue University Libraries.*

Lillie Moller on Sutro Beach, California, December 26, 1903, the day she accepted Frank's proposal of marriage. *Courtesy of Frank and Lillian Gilbreth Collection, Purdue University Libraries.*

Lillian and Frank pose on their wedding day, October 19, 1904. From left: Annie Moller (Lillian's mother), Josephine Moller (Lillian's sister and maid of honor), Lillian, Frank, William Moller (Lillian's father), Everett Brown (Lillian's cousin and Frank's best man). Seated is Grandma Ernestine Delger. *Courtesy of Frank and Lillian Gilbreth Collection, Purdue University Libraries.*

Lillian in late 1909 with
(from left) Anne (age four), Mary (age three),
baby Martha, and one-and-a-half-year-old Ernestine.
Courtesy of Frank and Lillian Gilbreth Collection,
Purdue University Libraries.

```
                INSTRUCTION CARD.
                                                Continuous or
   Item          Detailed instructions         running time.

    1  Arise                                    7.00

    2  Breakfast                                7.30 - 8.00

    3

    4

    5  Begin the day of work                    10.00

    6  Work on book                             10-12

    7  With children                            12.-12.15

    8  Lunch                                     12.15-1.00

    9  With  children                           1.00-2.00

   10  Nap                                       2.00-2.30

   11  With baby                                 2.30-3.00

   12  Work on book                              3.00-4.00

   13  Callers                                   4.00-5.00

   14  With children                             5.00-6.00

   15  Miscellaneous                             6.00-6.30

   16  Dinner                                    6.30-7.30
```

An instruction card, suggesting how Lillian was to organize her day. Another copy of this list, dated 1912, has notes in Lillian's handwriting about starting the day off right, without rush or hurry. *Courtesy of Lillian Gilbreth Papers, Sophia Smith Collection, Smith College.*

Lillian photographed on April 1, 1913, writing at a grid-painted desk with an electric light on her finger, to demonstrate Frank's new methods of recording and measuring movement. *Courtesy of the Smithsonian Institution, National Museum of American History.*

Lillian in 1913 with Martha, Ernestine, Frank Jr., and Anne. *Photograph in the author's collection.*

The Gilbreth family on the beach, somewhere in Rhode Island, summer 1914. From left: Frank Bunker Gilbreth proudly holding Frank Jr., Anne, Ernestine in front of Lillian, Anne Cross holding the infant Bill, and Martha in front of her grandmother Martha Bunker Gilbreth, who is "standing ramrod straight." *Courtesy of the Smithsonian Institution, National Museum of American History.*

Brown commencement day, June 16, 1915. Anne, Ernestine, and Lillian's secretary, Mildred Gray (dressed in white) escort the new Dr. Gilbreth back up College Hill.

Courtesy of the Smithsonian Institution, National Museum of American History.

One of the typewrit-
ing experiments, c.
1916. Lillian, with a
Gilbreth clock behind
her, watches as a typ-
ist's fingers are fitted
with lights and the
angle of her arm is
measured. *Courtesy of
the Smithsonian
Institution, National
Museum of American
History.*

Lillian demonstrating typing techniques, c. 1916. *Courtesy of Frank and Lillian Gilbreth
Collection, Purdue University Libraries.*

Lillian and Frank c. 1916. *Courtesy of the Smithsonian Institution, National Museum of American History.*

Lillian working from home in her Providence office in September 1917, surrounded by seven children, including the infant Dan, just before Frank went off to join the army. Note the grid-painted desk and five-year-old Bill talking into his mother's Dictaphone. *Courtesy of Frank and Lillian Gilbreth Collection, Purdue University Libraries.*

The Gilbreth family in the Pierce Arrow car (known as the "Foolish Carriage") on Nantucket in 1919. The baby on Lillian's lap is Jack, and two more children, Bob and Jane, were to be born in the next three years. *Courtesy of the Smithsonian Institution, National Museum of American History.*

The whole family on a seesaw outside their Nantucket lighthouses and summer home in 1923. It is a very happy picture, showing the whole family. From left: Frank, Frank Jr., Bill, Fred, Dan, Jack, Bob, Jane, Lill, Martha, Ernestine, Anne, Lillian. *Copyright Bettman/Corbis.*

The Gilbreths at home in Montclair, New Jersey, 1923, listening to the radio. This image is from the period celebrated in *Cheaper by the Dozen*, when the Gilbreths were regularly featured in the press as a notable family. *Courtesy of Frank and Lillian Gilbreth Collection, Purdue University Libraries.*

Lillian dressed in widow's black with a group of engineers in Prague, 1924, shortly after Frank's death. *Courtesy of Frank and Lillian Gilbreth Collection, Purdue University Libraries.*

Eleven Children *and a* Career

DR. LILLIAN M. GILBRETH

By 1932 Lillian was a celebrity as a working mother and press coverage was frequent. The sketch of her family life, while taking a little poetic license, has a ring of truth. *Reprinted with permission of the* St. Louis Post-Dispatch, *copyright 1932.*

Lillian as a delegate to the Century of Progress exhibition in Chicago in 1933. She was active in numerous women's organizations, including the American Association of University Women. As national research chair of the Business and Professional Women Clubs she surveyed attitudes toward married women in the labor force. *Courtesy of Business and Professional Women/USA.*

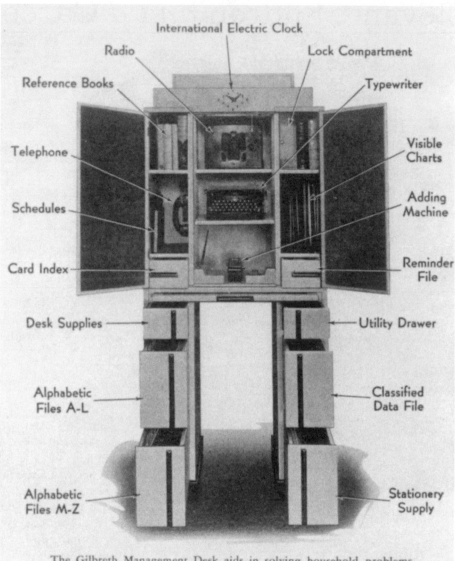

International Electric Clock

Radio

Lock Compartment

Reference Books

Typewriter

Telephone

Visible Charts

Schedules

Adding Machine

Card Index

Reminder File

Desk Supplies

Utility Drawer

Alphabetic Files A-L

Classified Data File

Alphabetic Files M-Z

Stationery Supply

The Gilbreth Management Desk aids in solving household problems concerning Children, Clothing, Education, Finance and Maintenance, Food, Health and Medical Care, House Cleaning, Laundry, Recreation and Culture, Servants, Social Affairs and many other subjects.

The Gilbreth Management Desk—"What a boon this desk is!" IBM's prototype was exhibited at the Century of Progress exhibition in Chicago in 1933. *Courtesy of Frank and Lillian Gilbreth Collection, Purdue University Libraries.*

Lillian in 1942, as she prepared to go to war. This photograph appeared above a heading "Dr. Lillian M. Gilbreth Battles Inertia and Fatigue to Increase Productivity of Nation's Industry." *Courtesy of Business and Professional Women/USA.*

Lillian was asked to join the Girl Scouts' national Board of Directors by Lou Henry Hoover in 1930, and she served until 1947. *Courtesy of Girl Scouts of the USA Archives.*

Lillian with a group of Girl Scouts in Kenosha, Wisconsin, in November 1949. Although she was no longer on the board, she continued her interest in Girl Scouting. *Courtesy of Girl Scouts of the USA Archives.*

The publication of *Cheaper by the Dozen* in late 1948 started a new chapter in Lillian's life. She is seen here with the book's coauthors, Frank B. Gilbreth Jr. and Ernestine Gilbreth Carey, in a photograph from the *Newark Sunday News*, March 6, 1949. *Courtesy of the Ernestine Gilbreth Carey Papers in the Sophia Smith Collection, Smith College, with permission from the Newark Public Library.*

Lillian Gilbreth was Honorary Member Number One of the Society of Women Engineers on its foundation in 1950. Here she takes tea with SWE president Katharine Stinson in 1952.
Courtesy of Society of Women Engineers Collection, Walter Reuther Library, Wayne State University.

Lillian, age eighty-three, in 1961.
The article quoted her as saying,
"'Just' housewives have big jobs."
Courtesy of Dayton, Ohio, Journal Herald,
copyright 1961.

Lillian was still a presence on the platform of a joint ASME-SWE conference in
Portland, Oregon, in 1966. She finally retired two years later at age ninety. *Courtesy of
Society of Women Engineers Collection, Walter Reuther Library, Wayne State University.*

The Gilbreth family in 1984. Back row, from left: William (Bill), Bob, Jack, Fred, Frank Jr., and Dan Gilbreth. Front row, from left: Ernestine Gilbreth Carey, Lillian Gilbreth Johnson, Anne Gilbreth Barney, and Jane Gilbreth Heppes. *Courtesy of Robert M. Gilbreth*

16 The Home Front

*Isn't it queer, how one can
always take on one more job?*

Lillian Gilbreth to Frank Gilbreth (February 2, 1918)

FRANK'S JOB at the School of Artillery at Fort Sill, Oklahoma, was to make training films on efficient ways to load a rifle or care for a horse. Lillian became his unofficial "Advisor on the Project," and she took her responsibilities very seriously: Frank relied on her for advice and sent films and papers home for her to analyze. Three years later, when Lillian was elected an honorary member of the Society of Industrial Engineers, the citation read, in part, that she had "acted as Consulting Psychologist in the field, working under the general Staff, standardizing the methods for teaching the 4,000,000 officers and men."[1]

Lillian's letters to Frank are full of suggestions on how to make the films more effective and, as a subtext, how to deal more tactfully with the officers and men. She suggested that movie stars be conscripted to appear in the training films. "If Douglas Fairbanks appeared three minutes in a film, it would wake them up," she wrote, adding that "it is actor's 'sob stuff' those films need. Nothing but that can make the boys want to copy them. You are trying to win them by hate, why not try emulation for a change?" She tried to limit Frank's passion for publicity, advising him to omit the Gilbreth clock from the training films as "it would look as though we expected to get fame out of the film."[2]

She was, meanwhile, busy writing. On January 17, 1918, she commented that she had four technical papers due by February 25, so "I sit at the Dictaphone . . ." She was a fast worker; within two weeks she had dictated three of the papers and outlined the fourth. Lillian coped with Frank's requests, the business, and the children with equanimity, which was fortunate, as Frank found the army bureaucracy extremely frustrating. During his first three weeks at Fort Sill his letters to Lillian were full of complaints. He was dieting so that his expensive new uniforms might fit a little less snugly; he was cold; he wanted his dress uniform; he wanted new visiting cards printed in a particular way; he wanted her to send photographic equipment.[3]

Lillian's replies were designed to reassure him that she and the children were all well and happy and that everything he wanted would soon be on its way. Her letters also show a growing confidence and delight as she juggled business and family responsibilities. In a long letter to Frank, Lillian describes "a busy day" when she found running Gilbreth, Inc., and simultaneously supervising her noisy children and the household "absorbing." Of course, Mrs. Cunningham and Tom Grieves were doing the actual cleaning, cooking and shopping, but as Martha Gilbreth was out of town, Lillian was household manager. She told Frank,

> I woke up very early, expecting a "Night Letter" from you, but have had no answer to my telegram as yet. Then I had my usual day's work to see to and it took longer than usual as Grieves is trying to get all the film up from the Laboratory before tomorrow night. In the midst of my busy morning a Mr. Lothrop came from Boston with an introduction from Prof. Johnson, to show me a wonderful new wheel with a spring that he is promoting. It seems a fine thing and I put the data in your trunk. He wants to sell stock to us. Then I had an interview with Clark [a photographer] who of course is praying for the Chicago job."[4]

Lillian still had the children's music and typing practice to supervise. She continued: "I went to Ernestine's violin lesson . . . then home in time to feed Dannie and put all the other little ones to bed. Now I am in the office with Frank Jr. at the other typewriter, Anne doing violin in the dining room, Martha at the piano in the library and Ernestine at my big desk. How's that for a day? Going some? And then they say housekeeping isn't absorbing. Nothing monotonous about it to me."[5]

Lillian's letters are full of news about the children. One cold Sunday they spent all day refurbishing their dolls' clothes. Lillian was very much amused when Ernestine came "trotting in" full of indignation; she was a good knitter and the others needed her skills, but she was also a rather bossy child, and as soon as her knitting was finished they asked her to leave. Later a deputation came to invite her back, and so it went on. Ernestine's great friend at this time was Louise Aldrich, a niece of Nelson Aldrich, who had been the most powerful man in the Senate for thirty years until his retirement in 1911. They had met at Lincoln School and remained close; Louise was an only child and much quieter than the boisterous Gilbreths, but, as Lillian remarked, "She is such a satisfactory playmate, always satisfied, no matter what happens." Later that evening the children decided to play charades, with their mother as audience. "What do you think the first one was?" she asked Frank. "It was 'Fatigue Survey.' How is that for breathing it in? I was really thunderstruck."[6]

Lillian disliked Sundays. She missed Frank terribly and found the distraction of work difficult to achieve because all the children were home demanding her attention. She insisted that they dress in their "Sunday Best" for dinner and tried to make the day as normal as she could, but though the children sang "Keep the Home Fires Burning," there was, as she wrote, "little zest in it." Lillian was proud of the children, however, despite their overwhelming energy. Another evening she told Frank:

> We have just finished supper. Toast, "Aunt Jemima's" and cut up fruit. Do you
> wish you had some? The children ate so much they can hardly walk. One is
> at the piano and Frank Jr. is at the typewriter with Martha waiting till he is
> done. Andie is getting out her violin. It surely won't be our fault if they're not
> educated, at least they have the opportunities. And I do believe it is beginning
> to show tho they are AWFULLY STRENUOUS, as well you know.[7]

Lillian typed her letters to Frank and often apologized for the mistakes, once adding, defensively, "I know I have made a million mistakes, but anyone would who typed against the clatter I do." Another day she forgot an enclosure, but "it isn't any wonder I do strange things for I work in the midst of confusion all the time . . . and the children rampaging all over the place and asking a hundred questions a minute." Somehow, in the middle of all this, Lillian found time to knit Frank a sweater. She mailed it to him on February 9, with a note saying, "I do hope you like it, I have so LOVED to make it. I only worked on it when I could do nothing else, or when I missed you so much that I had to work on something that could go to you, for a comfort. So every stitch has a message."[8]

Lillian filled several of Frank's speaking engagements while he was away. Her letters are full of delight in her achievements, which contradicts her children's view that she was terrified every time she gave a speech, becoming brave only after Frank died. In *Cheaper by the Dozen* they listed the things they thought their mother was afraid of, including fast driving, planes, walking alone at night, lightning, and lecturing: "She made public speeches, but she dreaded them," they wrote. Nevertheless, she had already spoken at several ASME meetings; at the first one, in 1914, Frank had written from Germany, reassuring her, "It will be even better than if I go. Say but you will have some questions to answer. And it is a great comfort to know that you can and will handle them properly." Her first solo appearance at a college was a lecture at the Massachusetts Institute of Technology on January 11, 1918, and her account suggests she enjoyed every minute of the experience. "Tomorrow I go to Tech.," Lillian wrote to Frank. "I have everything that I can do ahead done and I wish I could bathe and dress the children for the morning now. It is some job to start eight for the day." By the time she caught the ten o'clock train to Boston, Lillian had already put in several hours of work; the five eldest children were readied for school, the baby was fed (she was still breast-feeding four-month-old Dan at the time), and the two toddlers were settled down to play under the supervision of the housekeeper.[9]

Lillian took her secretary with her and the two women made quite a day of it. After a quick and fruitless visit to the Boston Public Library for material on surveys, they did a little shopping then lunched in Filene's Department Store before catching the subway to Cambridge. Lillian's lecture was part of a series; she was pleased to note that the only other management specialist to speak was Henry Kendall, an old acquaintance from the Dartmouth conference in 1911. As she wrote to Frank, "I know I can do as well as he can."[10]

Lillian had planned her talk carefully and spoke from an outline while her secretary took notes; she typed the speech later. Lillian's topic was "The Place of Motion Study and Fatigue Study in Industrial Development," and she talked about the aims, methods, applications, and results of the work she and Frank had done. She reported, "I talked for twenty minutes, then showed 36 slides, which took twenty minutes more, then answered a few questions and the time was up." This was the first time she had used slides in a talk; she found it very difficult, especially when the slides were "upside down, etc. and the fellow takes one holder out and leaves a bright disk on the lantern while he fixes the next one and you are expected to fill up the gap with improving conversation." Apart from her secretary, Lillian was the only woman in the room; she was very much conscious of her gender and of her all-male audience. Nevertheless, she felt the talk had gone well: "I tried to talk like a real worker at measurement and not like a 'Lady,'" she told Frank. After her lecture Lillian talked informally with a number of professors, including a Dr. Dewey, who wanted Lillian to meet his wife, a member of the Massachusetts Labor Commission. Lillian said she would be delighted, but as she had eight children, she would prefer to meet Mrs. Dewey in Providence. "That seemed to interest him a lot," she commented. She was home in time to give Dan his 6:30 feeding.[11]

Lillian was very proud of speaking at "Tech." and unwilling to keep her success to herself. A few days later, she was lunching at the Turk's Head, a club in downtown Providence, with some Wednesday Club friends when one remarked that her husband had been to MIT to hear Kendall's talk. Lillian replied, "Then I'm jealous that he didn't go to hear me." She commented to Frank, with some glee, "She nearly had a duckfit when I told her I had substituted for you there. You would have thought that to talk to Tech. was to talk to wonders. I shouldn't have told her, remembering your warnings that I'd lose all my women friends if I was too queer, but I figured she would hear it anyway and anyhow, I just couldn't help it."[12]

In late January 1918, soon after Lillian's lecture at MIT, the Providence School Department declared a long-rumored and indefinite "holiday" to conserve fuel. The weather was bitterly cold; a few days earlier Lillian had moved the piano into the office because the children had refused to practice in the cold parlor. "Now I can inspect typing and piano and work at my desk all at once," she wrote. The chilly parlor aside, the Gilbreths had little problem with keeping at least part of the house warm, for they had "connections" through Tom Grieves who "went to school with Fogarty, our coal dealer and has known the oil boy for ages, so we are sure to get by."[13]

During this holiday, the teachers, who were on full pay, were expected to do something for the war effort. Twelve-year-old Anne's Latin teacher volunteered to tutor her. Lillian reported to Frank that Miss Williams "considered fostering a bright and ambitious mind real war work. . . . Isn't it grand to have teachers ask for the privilege of teaching our kiddies during their vacation?" Anne, who was a year younger than most of her classmates at John Howland School, was at the top of the class, "with the rest nowhere near," according to her proud mother. During the enforced holiday Anne decided to start a morning school for five of her younger brothers and sisters. She taught Ernestine to do fractions and organized a calisthenics class, at which she counted in Latin. All the children spent time practicing either their music or typing, "and so far," Lillian told Frank, "I have not been called in once to settle a row," adding ruefully, "but that angelic state of affairs can't last." Two days later, Lillian gave Frank a longer description of the children's school. "It is real sob stuff," she wrote, "to hear the opening exercises, when all through Lillian salute the flag, sing all the War songs. Andie is a little too bossy, but better than she used to be. This morning she had to leave early to take her first Latin lesson, so Ernestine finished the session as teacher, much to her delight."[14]

Lillian was very proud of her children's vocabulary; when Anne had a nightmare one night, she called out, "Quick Mother, give me something else to think about." Lillian called back, "Think of Douglas Fairbanks in *Wild and Woolly*." A few minutes later Anne called again, "Say, Mother, that's artificial attention, isn't it?" Lillian commented, "Pretty good for 3 A.M." She played word games with them and told Frank they "have done wonders for their vocabulary." She suggested Frank use similar games to teach the recruits. She was also pleased when the children showed an interest in motion study; once Ernestine and Susie, Mrs. Cunningham's youngest daughter, asked if they might leave off the fork when laying the breakfast table, as "all you do is spill milk on it." She was also amused when seven-year-old Frank Jr. echoed the slogans of the Food Administration by announcing that since it was Mrs. Cunningham's day off, "This is my playless day."[15]

Lillian liked her children to have fun. On January 31 she took the four eldest to the movies to see a western. It starred William Hart as a solemn-faced defender of truth, justice, and the honor of good women. Frank Jr. kept shouting, "Go it, Buck!" which had members of the audience "in convulsions." It was the sixth anniversary of Mary's death, and Lillian agreed with Frank, in one of her very few references to their dead daughter, that "we should be thankful for those that are left" and "it always seems that to make them happy is the best memorial we can have."[16]

The next day, February 1, Lillian was unwell with "a case of dysentery" and told Frank, "I guess I got the life scared out of me. It is all gone now—the case, not the life." Lillian's appreciation for her children's noisy exuberance was diminished by her illness and as she told Frank, "it is a big responsibility to have eight little children and one old lady to be responsible for and sometimes I quake before it. . . . As usual I am writing in an awful clatter." By February 10, after a day when the plumbing was out of order, Lillian was feeling overwhelmed. "If I had really believed you were to be called into active service this winter, I think it would have been wise for the children and me to have taken a cottage in Berkeley for the winter," she wrote. "We have had enough of everything to be in comfort, but this heatless, sweetless, plumbingless, Dadless and now schoolless winter is no fun."[17]

Lillian was not, however, one to dwell on misfortune or inconvenience; she decided to take a more active part in the home school. She gave the children a talk on management, the first of several. She showed them how to draw Gantt charts, which they enjoyed and she told Frank that Susie Cunningham "thinks she is going to learn to be something and never wants to go back to 'real' school again." The rest of the school day sounds quite conventional: "I gave arithmetic drill, oral and written and heard Anne's Latin while the rest did written work. That, with the half-hour they all put in on the language [the whole family was learning French and German from cylinders played on Victrola machines] while I did baby and the music and the typing and a fine afternoon sliding and skating made up a fine day."[18]

By mid-February Lillian badly needed a respite from the children. She reported to Frank, with some relief, that an end to the school "holiday" was in sight, though frozen pipes delayed the planned reopening. Lillian went out occasionally, although she sounded somewhat defensive about leaving the children. She attended a series of lectures on a popular system of mnemon-ics, the Roth Memory system. She told Frank, "The children are hurrying through their work to have a play when I am gone. I hate to leave them even for a little while, but it is fun to learn something new to hand on and I find I must get away now and then." Lillian did not work all the time, however. She confessed to Frank she was planning to be "very giddy" and take her secre-tary to a "bargain matinee" of *Peter Ibbetson*, starring the heartthrob of the moment, John Barrymore: "Seats 50¢." Miss Bishop was feeling rather low: she was missing her fiancé, who was in the army, and was "tickled to death" by the plan. Lillian, however, felt a little guilty about taking the time off. "It seems like shirking to go off in the afternoon," she told Frank, but justified herself by saying, "I know we will both do better work tomorrow."[19]

While Lillian was coping heroically in Providence, Frank was starting to get used to army life in Oklahoma. On January 20 he rode a horse "for the first time since 1905" and felt much more cheerful, despite suffering from a cold and the army's losing his laundry. He had made a film, "The Care of the Horse and Mule," which, he enthusiastically remarked, was "so much better than anything ever done before [that] it is astounding." Lillian, however, thought that he was wasting his time on horses and mules and that he should concentrate on the crippled soldier work, which seemed to her "from every standpoint the thing that will be most profitable to us in the long run." By profitable she meant both financially advantageous and prestigious. Visiting plants where such men worked and teaching managers how to find the "One Best Way" to employ the handicapped would legitimize the Gilbreths and possibly lead to new contracts, and she asked Frank to persuade his superior officers to transfer him to this type of work. Unfortunately, her advice came too late. By the time Lillian's letter arrived, Frank was lying near death in the camp hospital; he was never to resume his army duties.[20]

On March 1, 1918, with the worst of the winter over and some of the chil-dren back at school, Lillian received a cable that turned her world upside down. It was a Saturday afternoon, the children were all playing, Grandma was talking to Mrs. Cunningham in the kitchen, and Tom Grieves was off on an errand somewhere when the telegraph boy knocked on her front door. Captain Ellis's cable said that Frank was very ill and that Lillian should come "at once." This was easier said than done. The banks were closed and there was little cash in the house, but Lillian telephoned a friend, who drove to her factory and opened the safe in order to lend Lillian money for the trip. Lillian hurriedly threw some clothes in a bag and set off for Fort Sill the next morn-ing, although it was "hard to leave the family and the work." Fortunately, she could leave the children in good hands. Tom, Mrs. Cunningham, Grandma, and Aunt Anne all rallied round.[21]

Fort Sill is in southwest Oklahoma, not far from the Texas border. During what seemed an interminable journey, Lillian wrote down exactly what she planned to do to help Frank pull through. She decided to keep a record of everything that happened, including the doctors' instructions, nurse him to the best of her ability, make sure he was comfortable, and above all, will him to live and provide "every moment, someone near him who would go on fighting and persuading him to fight, day and night, until the illness was over." When she finally arrived after two long days on the train, she found Frank slipping in and out of consciousness. Although she had been told he had uremic poisoning, Frank was in fact suffering from rheumatic fever, a terrible illness. Before the discovery of penicillin, recovery was a slow and painful process. Its side effects include kidney failure, pneumonia, and long-term damage to the heart. Lillian had visited many hospitals over the previous few years, and her lack of deference toward doctors was to serve her well. In what her son described as "perhaps the first real act of aggressiveness in her life," she insisted on staying by Frank's side, and a cot was set up for her next to his bed. It was a large ward; no private rooms were available, which meant privacy problems for Lillian, not to mention the possibility of infection. Fortunately, for once she was not pregnant.[22]

The two doctors assigned to the case could not agree on how to treat Frank, and by the time Lillian arrived at his bedside, he was dangerously ill. Because of a shortage of drugs, Lillian had to fight to get some adrenaline in case Frank's heart gave out. As she delicately put it, "High pressure [had to be] used on the hospital pharmacy and the doctors to get a reserve supply." The crisis came on March 11, a week after Lillian's arrival, when Frank was given four doses of adrenaline in twenty-four hours. Lillian held his hand, telling him over and over again how necessary he was to her and her children and, through his work, to the world. As she recalled, "The adrenaline doubtless kept the tired heart going until it could pick up again for itself and the friendly nurses, doctors and friends, all pulling together, were a large part of whatever pulled him through, but someone had to correlate everything and hold on!"[23]

Over the next seven weeks Lillian scarcely left Frank's bedside. Frank joked about it later, writing:

> Why at Fort Sill
> Her strength of will
> Makes all the doctors shudder still

(The principle reason why I resuscitated myself was because I wanted to see for myself with my own eyes just what she was going to do to them. Of course, when I came back, I didn't die—and so she didn't do as much to them.)[24]

In March and April 1918, however, Frank's illness was no laughing matter and Lillian had to be forceful to get anything done. There was a shortage of nurses—Lillian heard rumors that veterinary orderlies were being transferred to the wards—and Frank was not an easy patient. He refused to eat meals prepared in the hospital kitchens—"I've seen too much," he said—and insisted that his food be prepared where he could see it. He also insisted that his bedding and clothing be changed frequently, as he was acutely aware of the odor emanating from his failing kidneys. Lillian was eager to make Frank as comfortable as possible and not permit anything to irritate him. When he took a dislike to a trained nurse who had been brought in from a nearby town she told the nurse to leave.[25]

Lillian kept a detailed account of everything Frank did and said during his slow recovery. Although she later wrote that her notes "make amusing reading," she was earnestly applying observation methods acquired during her studies at Brown in order to distract herself from the painful reality of Frank's illness. After the crisis of March 11, he made very slow progress, as he had difficulty breathing and his rheumatism made any movement painful, but on Easter Sunday, March 31, Lillian noted the beginning of his recovery, for that day he sat up in bed for the first time. The next day he was carried to the porch, where he sat for a while in a rocking chair. He had been and was still hallucinating, however. Lillian wrote on Wednesday, April 3, thirty days after her arrival: "Patient has hallucinations which are more or less logical . . . all have to do with experiences at 'School of Fire.' . . . Prefers male attendants . . . hates to be argued with. Detects lies and insincerity at once, Much disturbed by not being able to locate himself in time and space. Wants continually to know points of the compass; which floor he is on; which side of the room; number of bed; et cetera. Allows no discrepancy in statements of others." On April 6 she recorded that he "conforms to treatments that appeal to him as reasonable. Is increasingly angry because doctors and nurses say he is better yet insist upon keeping him in bed." He didn't like the "typical 'medical man' attitude" but was responsive if they "talk to him as a colleague or a man of sense."[26]

Despite her note taking, the days were long for Lillian, who had little to do but watch Frank. The other patients had few visitors, though an occasional visit from a man from the local YMCA who distributed oranges and cigarettes to the men broke the monotony. The first day he was allowed out of bed Frank took a few painful steps supported by crutches; the next day he put on his clothes, though he was "rather fatigued from the effort." He had insisted throughout his illness on having a pair of his trousers hanging over the screen just in case he wanted to put them on. When he did so it felt like a major step toward his recovery. The specialist came onto the ward just then, and Frank asked when he could be discharged. The doctor replied, "When you can walk the length of the ward and back." Frank immediately took up his crutches and, despite excruciating pain, showed he could do it. As Lillian commented, "Whatever else he lacked, he did not lack determination."[27]

Lillian wanted to get Frank more specialized treatment at the Walter Reed Army Hospital in Washington, D.C., but army bureaucracy meant that she was unable to get his discharge papers properly signed and countersigned. After a little hurried and, as it turned out, botched paperwork, they set off without them. During the two-day train journey Frank started talking in his sleep about crippled soldiers, and Lillian made notes while he did so. She wrote that he "claims for the first time that he understands C.S. problems as he has had a cripple's experience. Advises all to at least go to the hospital to get in touch with the cripple's feelings." Frank was admitted to Walter Reed Hospital despite his lack of papers, and Lillian spent the next two weeks in a nearby lodging house; then, in late April, she decided to return to Providence. He was now well enough to be left and she was missing the children; she had been away from them for eight weeks. For the next three months Lillian commuted between the family in Providence and Frank's bedside in Washington, D.C., usually traveling back and forth on the night train, so as to waste no time—or money—on hotel rooms and so she could greet her children at breakfast. Lillian was glad to be home and back to work, which was a great deal less stressful than watching Frank's slow recovery. "I thought I was tired," she told him, "but I find that when I really get down to work I am as good as new." Everything had gone smoothly in her absence; Miss Bishop had kept the office work in good order and, far from missing her, the children seemed to have thrived. Grandma was "tickled to death" to be head of the household and had already taught four-year-old Lill to read. Lillian commented, "I imagine that in some respects our absence has been an incentive for them to go ahead with their work."[28]

The months from December 1917 to August 1918, when Frank was in the army, ill, or convalescing, were a turning point in Lillian's life. During these months she did everything, and because Frank's heart was permanently weakened by his illness, even after he returned to work Lillian continued to bear much of the burden. A new voice emerged in her letters. She sounded energetic and forceful as she tried to revive Frank's sagging spirits with messages from friends, suggestions for new papers, or ideas for new contracts. Frank was still in pain and feeling depressed. "I'm trying to work on the new Education book, but I don't take any real interest in it, or in anything else, I guess," he told his wife. Lillian, meanwhile, was widening her circle of contacts and continuing with the crippled soldier work. She spent a day in Cambridge attending a conference on occupational therapy and had a long conversation with the wife of Senator Wadsworth, who was in charge of the

Franklin Institute. Actually, Lillian listened while Mrs. Wadsworth talked. "I did not discuss our branch of the Crippled Soldier with her," Lillian told Frank, "finding I got along better by asking questions and listening to her expanding her side of the question." This was a technique Lillian was to employ with great success for the rest of her life.[29]

It had become clear to both of the Gilbreths that Frank's health was permanently damaged and that he could no longer serve in the army. He wanted an honorable discharge, but the lack of papers from Fort Sill proved problematic and one delay followed another. In the meantime, although he could not walk very well, he had himself wheeled about Walter Reed Hospital, where he studied the work of the occupational therapists who were helping the "crippled soldiers" to use their damaged limbs. The Gilbreths were facing financial problems, for while Frank was in the hospital he was on half pay. Several of his management consultancy projects were ongoing, however, so although he was far from well, when he was given a short leave in May he went back to work. He traveled to Utica, New York, to check on the micromotion films he had made at the Remington Typewriter Company. While he was there he consulted a doctor who told him that his blood pressure was too high and he should go off his medications, including, ironically, "Asperin," which he believed would damage Frank's heart. Frank's travels left little time for Providence; Lillian was distressed that he spent so little time at home and missed the children playing in a concert arranged by Aunt Anne. The four eldest played piano and violin solos, and six-year-old Billy was scheduled to sing *Joan of Arc,* "unless he gets too shy or it begins to rain." Frank told Lillian, "It can't be helped. I must dig up the money."[30]

Frank, however, never let cash flow problems stand in the way when he wanted to buy something, so before he went back to Washington he and Lillian traveled to the island of Nantucket looking for a summer cottage. Lillian remembered the journey as "no easy job," as Frank had such difficulty walking, but the sea air seemed to do him good, and they explored the island together by horse and buggy. (Nantucket did not, as yet, permit cars on the island.) They found a property comprising two small "bug" lighthouses dating back to 1838 and an old shack, formerly the lighthouse keeper's paint shop. Odd looking as the buildings were, the site could hardly have been better. It was a ten-minute walk from the town with nothing but sand dunes between it and the beach. The buildings were crammed with a conglomeration of mismatched, half-broken furniture, for the previous owner was an island doctor who had sometimes taken his payment in kind. The Gilbreths paid eighteen hundred dollars for the property, which was a bargain even for 1918, though one reason for the low price was rumors of German submarines in the waters off Nantucket.[31]

By June 1918 Lillian was showing the strain of caring for her husband. Frank had returned to the hospital and she was deeply concerned about him. He was still having tests; his doctors thought his rheumatism came "either from the teeth or the tonsils." They were not far off, as rheumatic fever invariably starts with a throat infection. This was no consolation to Lillian. She could not sleep, her hair was falling out, and she had lost a lot of weight. She weighed only 107 pounds, not a great deal for a woman five feet eight inches tall. One of Lillian's friends told Frank, who wrote a letter instructing his wife to eat "egg nogs, sweet chocolate, Page and Shaw's caramels, but eat all the time." Lillian replied defiantly, "I do not expect to weigh any more until you leave the hospital. I certainly cannot get any decent sleep until I can stop visualizing you in hospital surroundings. That is perfectly idiotic but absolutely true."[32]

Exhausted as she was, Lillian substituted for Frank at an ASME meeting in early June 1918, at which she presented a paper showing the use of motion study films to retrain disabled veterans. She prefaced her remarks by giving all the credit to her husband, but later, when Frank met a man who praised the presentation, he was quick to deny authorship. "I said it was really your paper and that I never saw it." As she had to combine her professional duties with motherhood, she missed the conference dinner and all the other socializing; she had to get back to Providence to attend another children's concert. "It seemed the least I could do in return for their year of faithful practicing," she told the absent Frank.[33]

On her return from the ASME meeting Lillian started to worry about spending the summer in Nantucket, especially if Frank was still confined to Washington. She wrote him an unusually forceful letter explaining why she wanted to stay in Rhode Island rather than travel to the island. "I am still very much upset about our summer plans," she wrote. She wanted the children to attend a summer school in Providence, so "going away as far as Nantucket would be impossible." She suggested that taking a cottage somewhere in Rhode Island "would simplify things greatly." The real problem was that Frank was still in the hospital. "I hate to invest even $100 in the Nantucket plan if it is not going thru and I simply cannot go so far away until you have left the hospital." It was relatively easy to get to Washington from Providence. "My one comfort is that I can leave by a night train and be with the children by breakfast," but "Nantucket seems the other side of the world to me."[34]

Somehow, Frank convinced Lillian to go to Nantucket (his letters are missing), and soon she conceded, "I am perfecting plans for going there and feel sure that I can adjust all domestic arrangements. The one thing I insist upon is that I do not want to go until I have some definite idea when you can join us." Lillian was not to get her way in this plan, either, for Frank's dis-

charge was delayed indefinitely. The children were in a Fourth of July pag-
eant, arranged by Aunt Anne; Lillian planned to leave for the island after
spending Frank's birthday, July 7, with him in Washington. She was thwarted
here, too, as Frank's mother was in Washington and Lillian did not want to
be there at the same time, "as it will spoil her visit there in more ways than
one." Lillian expressed her concern generously, telling Frank, "If we try to do
any business it will take you from entertaining her, which is of course what
you should devote yourself to this week."[35]

Lillian did not visit Frank on his birthday; instead, two days later she,
Mrs. Cunningham, six children, and a mountain of luggage went to Nantucket. Frank Jr. and Billy had gone on ahead with Tom Grieves with instructions to order milk and open up the house. Lillian worried a little about
the whole family being on a boat at the same time and "besides I think it will
teach the boys initiative . . . and they will be such a short time ahead of us
there will not be time for them to get into mischief." Frank finally joined them
in August, and Lillian wrote a little song for the children to greet him. Ernestine describes her mother as a "sentimental soul," and it was certainly a very
sentimental piece. It started, "Welcome dear Daddy, we greet you with joy."
Ernestine remembers how ill Frank looked when his boat docked—"like the
weary wounded soldier—he's got crutches, he's pale as a ghost, he doesn't
look like our father at all, but the ghost of our father." Frank was a shadow
of his former self, having lost about fifty pounds during his illness. The children burst into song and "everyone around us cried! He never expected us to
sing that song like idiots up there, but anyhow we did. Of course it touched
him, that sort of thing he thought was beautiful."[36]

The Gilbreths spent the first of many summers in "the Shoe," so called
with reference to the old woman who had so many children. Lillian commented that the cottage "seemed to expand in a wonderful manner and after
all, small girls and especially small boys, can be packed in like sardines!" Both
of the lighthouses were reserved for Frank; he used "Mic" (short for micro-
motion) as an office and the larger one, "Cyc" (short for cyclograph), to rest
in peace and quiet or spend the night if the children were too noisy. Frank's
mother and his cousin Jane came to stay for a while, but Lillian put them up
in a hotel "near enough to enjoy the children, yet far enough to retire when it
gets too confusing."[37]

Summer on Nantucket was a major source of Gilbreth family lore, at
least as presented by the children in *Cheaper by the Dozen*. Lillian was so delighted to have Frank back home that she temporarily got over her dislike for
the seaside; the summer of 1918 was probably the best and longest time the
Gilbreths spent together at the beach. Though Lillian described Frank as "so
lame" that he could not stand up without help, the children portray him as

spending his convalescence teaching them statistics, management theory, and astronomy, not to mention gambling. Frank was a gifted teacher. He taught the children statistics by telling them to collect shells and blades of grass from the beach and then arranging the items according to size and frequency. They learned Morse code after Frank painted the symbols on the lavatory wall and all over the ceilings of the children's bedrooms and then left messages for them to decode. Some of the messages were terrible puns, such as "Bee it never so bumble, there's no place like comb," while others were instructions about where to find a reward, like a Hershey bar or a note entitling the bearer to an ice-cream soda at the island drug store. Inscribed over the mantel in the dining room was the message "Eat, drink and be merry, for tomorrow you must diet." He also told them about the therbligs, and management symbols joined the dots and dashes on the cottage walls. Frank then taught the children about astronomy. First he aroused their curiosity by staring through a makeshift telescope on clear nights, ignoring the children, who of course begged to be allowed to look. He started a new series of wall paintings showing the planets, and he acquired a set of photographs that he mounted at the children's eye level. Frank also taught the children to play poker and other gambling games, to the less than enthusiastic approval of Lillian and his mother. He claimed that this was to teach the young Gilbreths that they could not beat the odds. They played every game of chance he could think of; Lillian's account of this suggests that like Theodore Roosevelt, whom he much resembled, Frank was six years old at heart. She wrote, "He pretended that it was an educational project and he only did it because of the lessons it taught the children. But even the youngest child knew that Dad loved every minute of it and loved it himself more because of that."[38]

The children swam and fished and hunted for clams; they also played on the sand dunes and learned to sail. The boys made a boat out of old planks and added a broomstick mast. It did not sail very well, but it kept them happy for hours. The children were in and out of the sea all the time, which made Lillian, who never learned to swim or like the water, very nervous. Frank made up a set of rules that can have done little to calm her fears: "No child may go in the ocean more than three times a day or stay in more than three hours at a time." Frank started to look and feel much better, the children were "happy and rosy," and the housekeeping was simplicity itself. "The sand or water which returning swimmers dripped everywhere did no harm and was easily brushed out," Lillian recalled. "The simplest food tasted delicious and everyone was content!"[39]

Even Lillian started to relax and meet other summer visitors. Miss Lucas, the head of Lincoln School, always vacationed on the island and introduced

Lillian to her friends. The most fascinating was the tall, slender, and utterly charming Margaret Harwood, the young Radcliffe astronomer who was in charge of the Maria Mitchell Observatory. Named for the famous nineteenth-century scientist who was born and worked on Nantucket, the observatory was a magnet for those summer visitors who preferred nature to the yacht club. Margaret Harwood held an open house every other Monday, and the Gilbreths were among the dozens of people who climbed up onto the observatory roof to look through the telescope and learn about the stars. She taught them how to use a sextant and navigate by the stars; she also ran a wildflower club. She was immensely popular on the island and is remembered as having "loads of charm—the way she greeted people she was just wonderful. She had loads of friends." Lillian became one of them. She joined the Maria Mitchell Association and gave a copy of *Applied Motion Study* to the library after she found out that Margaret Harwood spent part of the winter cooperating with the Red Cross on the rehabilitation of injured servicemen. There were not many opportunities for women astronomers in those days, but Margaret Harwood did what she could to help. Young women interns spent the summer on the island helping her run the observatory. Other Harvard astronomers summered on Nantucket, too, and Lillian got to know them and their families. She remembered Margaret Harwood as a "guide, philosopher and friend" and that she and "these fine young women" sometimes stopped by to go swimming with the Gilbreths and talk to the children. "Marnie," as they called her, was a great favorite of the girls and, Lillian recalled, "no one and nothing ever bored her."[40]

Lillian was in no hurry to leave and told Frank they could all stay in Nantucket as long as he wanted to be there. It was hard to go back to Providence, but by late September the nights were getting cooler and it was long past the time the children should have returned to school. Anne was due to start high school that fall, so Lillian invited her secretary, Miss Bishop, to spend a few days with them in late August and sent Anne back with her so that she could start at the beginning of the term. Anne stayed with her aunt on Cabot Street, which was only three or four blocks from the school.[41]

Anne started as a freshman at Hope High School, not as a sophomore, as her parents wanted. The Gilbreths found the public school bureaucracy very frustrating. As Frank Jr. and Ernestine remarked in *Cheaper by the Dozen*, "skipping grades in school was part of Dad's master plan," though in retrospect at least one of the children saw its disadvantages. Ernestine recalled, "I felt handicapped by my lack of knowledge of Math. I told myself this was the result still, of having skipped fifth grade in Providence R.I. at Dad's insistence." Anne did eventually complete high school in three years, but her acceleration happened in New Jersey, not Rhode Island. While several of the

Gilbreths did skip grades, one repeated a year lost through illness and several did postgraduate years at high school.[42]

Lillian had visited Hope High, at that time one of the best high schools in Providence, in June 1918. Her description of the interview with the principal demonstrates administrative resistance to overambitious parents and contrasts with the cheery way in which skipping grades is described in *Cheaper by the Dozen*. The fictional version, which is set in New Jersey, has the elementary school principal wanting to put eight-year-old Bill in the third grade while his father wanted him in the fifth. The principal capitulated easily on hearing that the baby, who was at home having his bottle, knew the population of Des Moines according to the 1910 census, so of course eight-year-old Bill knew even more, and into the fifth grade he went. The Rhode Island principal was less easily convinced. He was, Lillian told Frank with some exasperation, "the typical educator who asks for the child's age to start with and advises you against rushing her in any way." The principal was very much against Anne starting in the sophomore class; he told Lillian that they would have no idea what the child was capable of until she had been there a year. Lillian commented, with some asperity, "Seeing that she comes with a complete record from one of their own Grammar Schools under teachers they really know, this strikes me as very peculiar." She continued, "He advises that Anne does not look at a book all summer, goes into the regular work and then possibly if she finds it light takes up an extra subject in the fall. He says if she is going to try to do the course in three years it will be better to double up later on than now." Lillian was not prepared to force the issue and told Frank, "I believe if Anne is to fit in to the environment there at all happily it will be necessary for her to conform absolutely and to start the next term with her class."[43]

The Gilbreth children were not always easy to teach, for they had been encouraged at home to challenge authority. This led to "complications" when the children cited their father, claiming, "My Daddy says!" and ending with "My Daddy knows!" But, as Lillian later added, Frank "was never too busy to straighten this out." More often than not, however, Frank was out of town and Lillian was the parent available for teacher conferences when a problem arose. Her account of one such meeting suggests that although she took her son's side, she did it very tactfully. Lillian wrote:

> A certain mother was sent for one day by the teacher of one of her boys. She hastened down to the school with the sinking of the heart we all experience in such situations, to be told that the boy had broken school rules several consecutive days by keeping on with his geography when the class had been told to take out spellers. The teacher did not seem to realize that a youngster who

had developed a taste for any school subject strong enough to keep him absorbed in it, in spite of habitual commands, was far from hopeless. The mother went home, having made the peace, feeling that a new vista had been opened before her in grouping interests for that lively boy.[44]

Lillian thus avoided confrontation, encouraged the teacher to be more flexible, and "made the peace." It remained only for Woodrow Wilson to do the same so that their lives could resume a more normal routine.

17 The Gilbreth Family System

The fact that you will have nine or ten children by the time the book comes out will of itself sell the book.

Frank Gilbreth to Lillian Gilbreth (February 20, 1918)

To LILLIAN'S enormous relief, Frank finally received his honorable discharge from the army in September 1918. Now they could get back to work in earnest. Lillian was still concerned about Frank's health and didn't want him to overtax his damaged heart, so she spent more time than ever with the Gilbreth management consultancy business. She was ambivalent about leaving the children for any length of time, and her letters are full of schemes to include the children in business projects rather than leave them at home. For example, during the children's Christmas vacation she suggested combining a family trip to Boston with picking up their projector and visiting her sister Gertrude in the hospital. Frank had suggested sending Tom Grieves for the projector, but Lillian wrote: "Of course we can do this if we need it in a hurry but I hate the waste of money for him to take a trip to Boston when I enjoy them so much myself. Perhaps, you and I can take a trip next week and take the children and simply call for the projector on our way in a taxi." Lillian was less enthusiastic, however, about Frank's plan to take the older children to visit the Regal Shoe Factory. While eight-year-old Frank Jr. was "counting the minutes," she decided not to tell Bill, who was nearly six, about the outing and instead planned a treat for him at home. Bill was always the liveliest (or most difficult, depending on the point of view) of Lillian's children and as she pointed out to Frank, "He would be exhausted before the day was over and when he is tired he is always cross and unreasonable."[1]

The Gilbreths' work with the blind and the crippled gained them prestige rather than cold, hard cash; to provide the latter Lillian and Frank were building a healthy scientific management clientele. Frank's favorite client was Pierce Arrow, the automobile manufacturers, from whom he bought a secondhand car in May 1919. The car purchase coincided with the birth of a fifth Gilbreth son, John Moller, always known as Jack. (Wishing as ever to avoid unnecessary delays, Lillian spent her time in bed after the birth reviewing the galleys of their latest book, *Motion Study for the Handicapped*.) Frank paid three thousand dollars for the car, which had been little used by its former owner; he was convinced it was a great bargain, adding as a second thought, "I suppose the new boy #5 is some account too, but it is hard to visualize it, although every time I see a 'V' button on anyone's coat I think of it."[2]

Like "the Shoe," the Pierce Arrow was vital to the Gilbreths' image. It was a very large luxury car and could transport all the children, at a pinch, so they could display their prosperity and their large family simultaneously. The car also played a major role in Gilbreth family lore. Frank wanted to take Frank Jr. and Bill with him to pick up the car and make a slow journey via potential clients, filming along the way. He told Lillian to "buy them some good clothes and use an officer's trunk as a job-landing kit." Lillian vetoed the plan, which was perhaps fortunate, as the first journey was a fiasco. The leather lining came out of the clutch and Frank had to abandon the car at a garage and take the train to New York. He was not altogether sorry because he found driving very "strenuous" and after only a few miles his muscles were sore and his arms and legs were "lame" from the effort. Frank told Lillian not to tell anyone about the car's breaking down, but he remained confident that it was a good buy: "It made a fine impression that we bought it," he assured Lillian.[3]

As soon as the car was repaired, Frank got another publicity idea and instructed Lillian to get her dressmaker to sew a set of linen dusters for the children to wear in the car. "I'd have them made all alike," he suggested, "so as to show we have family enough to wear our own uniform." That was one of Frank's least popular ideas; in *Cheaper by the Dozen* Ernestine and Frank described the day a plump lady mistook them for inmates of an orphanage "Look at those poor, dear, adorable little children," they heard her say. "Don't they look sweet in their uniforms?" As his embarrassed daughters hid under the seat, Frank laughed: "That's the funniest thing I ever heard in my life. An orphanage on wheels. And me the superintendent. Gilbreth's Retreat for the Red-Haired Offspring of Unwed but Repentant Reprobates." Lillian was not amused and announced firmly, "No more dusters," and that was the last they saw of the hated garments. But it was far from the last time the children were embarrassed by their parents' schemes.[4]

As the postwar reorganization of industry progressed, Gilbreth, Inc., became increasingly busy, and Frank felt it was necessary to move nearer to New York. Although Lillian would have preferred to live in Cambridge, Massachusetts, where she had professional contacts, Frank decided that Montclair, New Jersey, had the best transportation, the best schools, and plenty of engineering neighbors. The real estate man drove Frank all over the town and impressed him with talk of all the "big men" and exclusive clubs in Montclair. It was not a cheap place to live. The houses Frank looked at ranged between $30,000 and $65,000, but in the end they took a three-year lease with an option to buy. Frank assured Lillian it was a bargain. She was not happy about it but let herself be persuaded, particularly when she remembered that several members of the Moller family lived nearby, including the Moller aunts. More important were the Gantts, with whom the Gilbreths were personally and professionally close. Knowing these people seemed a good way to start replacing the community Lillian had created around herself in Providence.[5]

The Gilbreths left Providence in November 1919, seven and a half eventful years after their arrival. Frank insisted on driving the older children to New Jersey in the Pierce Arrow. It is almost two hundred miles from Providence to Montclair and not an easy journey on 1919 roads. Frank's new car could, on a good day and a good road, "fly along" at forty-three miles per hour, but as it averaged only about twenty, the Gilbreth children must have had a very long day. Grandma was staying with Aunt Anne for a while; she wanted to avoid the upheaval of moving. Lillian and the babies, who were to follow by train, watched them start off, the car "overflowing with children, wraps, luggage and lunch!" She reflected that Frank did not seem to mind the chaos and the children always behaved better when "alone with Daddy." Anne, however, remembered that when they stopped for a meal she was "mortified, as I guess most of the older children were, that our table was at an outside window where all passersby could see us."[6]

Frank teased the children by stopping at several run-down houses and pretending that this was the place, but they finally arrived at their new house, 68 Eagle Rock Way, which the children recognized from his many descriptions. It was in Upper Montclair, a very exclusive neighborhood. Frank had told Lillian, hopefully, that it was as grand as her parents' house in Oakland, "tho not so well-maintained." Indeed it was similar; it was a very large house with bays and turrets and a steep-pitched roof with dormer windows. It was set back from the street and surrounded by tall trees. After Frank drove in through the circular driveway, the children swarmed out of the car and started to explore the house and its wonderful garden. The Japanese maples were just losing the last of their scarlet leaves and the oaks and elms were already bare-branched. To the side of the house was a lawn large enough for baseball and football games. At the back was a rose garden, a vegetable garden, greenhouses, and a barn, which Frank and Lillian planned to use as a photographic laboratory.[7]

The children entered the house by a wide hallway. To the right they could see a dining room with brown and gold damask wallpaper and a Tiffany glass light hanging over the table; the shade had a piece missing and it remained that way for the thirty years the Gilbreths lived in the house. Beyond the dining room was a big old-fashioned kitchen and a set of pantries, which were to be Tom Grieves's territory until he was too old and sick to work anymore. There were two large reception rooms, separated by pocket doors. Frank and Lillian transformed the drawing room into their office and installed their double-sided desk so that they could work together "shoving manuscripts across the table to one another for revision," as she recalled. There office contained banks of filing cabinets using the Gilbreths' idiosyncratic mnemonic filing system, the N-File, and shelves for their technical books. There was also a living room with a fireplace, two walls of bookcases, and built-in cupboards with cushions forming window seats. The six bedrooms on the second floor were "big enough to stow the family away comfortably," as Lillian remarked, and on the third floor were storerooms, rooms for Tom and Mrs. Cunningham, and a bedroom officially assigned to the "eldest boy." Ivy-clad porches circled two sides of the house. The one overlooking the lawn was screened and "well-stocked" with chairs and a swinging hammock where Lillian, in her rare leisure moments, could nurse the latest baby and watch the other children at play.[8]

By Thanksgiving the family was well settled into their new home, though not without one severe shock. Henry and Mary Gantt came by to help them unpack, but the Gilbreths' pleasure in their company was short-lived; Gantt collapsed and died less than a week later. Grandma's health also worried Lillian. She noticed that the old lady, who had celebrated her eighty-fifth birthday the previous August, was more tired than usual; whenever Frank was away she would make some excuse and doze in her rocking chair, or even lie down and share one of her grandchildren's naps. She was very irritable, as she hated being inactive and resented being unable to care for the children and cook the meals as she had for so many years. Like her sister before her, however, she did not want Frank to know she was unwell, and however ill she felt, she stubbornly insisted on joining in anything her son suggested.[9]

Eventually even Frank recognized that Martha was failing, but he was unwilling to lose the mother on whom he was so emotionally dependent. For weeks he stayed close to home, refusing to leave his mother for any length of time. He tried to prolong her life by experimenting with food and drink. The Gilbreths' usually rather simple household menu became, according to Lillian, "varied and elaborate" as Frank brought home every delicacy he could think of, as well as brandy and whiskey (and this during Prohibition, too). But his efforts were fruitless; as Lillian wrote, "The dear old lady could not respond to any of his attempts and it was evident that she was ready to go, if only he would reconcile himself to this." Lillian, who was seven months pregnant, nursed her mother-in-law until the last week, when Frank refused to leave Martha's bedside. During those last few days, Lillian had to deal with a major lawsuit. The case was settled out of court (in the Gilbreths' favor) just before the trial was to begin, but Lillian spent many hours conferring with lawyers and went to the courthouse and signed papers while Frank was at home frantically willing his mother to live. It was no use; Martha Gilbreth died in Montclair on May 2, 1920, in her eighty-sixth year. Frank's relationship with his mother was abnormally close and he felt her death as a major calamity. Lillian had to use all the psychological techniques she could muster to console him. She persuaded him that Martha would not have liked to live if she could not enjoy life and comforted him by suggesting that Martha's birthday should be celebrated as a joyful family holiday. He eventually became reconciled, but it was a hard struggle for Lillian to see him through the death of his mother.[10]

One event later that spring *did* serve to cheer Frank; his cousin Fred, who was on the Governor's Council in Maine, nominated him for an honorary degree from the state university. Frank was delighted; though he often expressed pride in Lillian's accomplishments, he could not help occasionally regretting his lack of a college degree. As he put it in his birthday ode to Lillian:

> But since my claws
> Grabbed D. of Laws
> I've given her a few Haw-Haws

(Lillie has never been the same to me since and I don't think she ever will be, until her Native State, at least finds the copy of her thesis sent to her in 1911.)[11]

Lillian was delighted, too, and in her memoirs recorded with some glee that the degree ceremony was one of the very few occasions when she publicly outwitted Frank. She had packed her black silk Ph.D. gown and ordered a mortarboard for Frank. At the last minute, however, he refused to wear "a woman's gown," and although she tried to argue there was no sex distinction in academic regalia, he was adamant that he would simply wear his "citizen's clothes" and then marched off with the other honorees. Lillian sat in a pew with cousin Fred and "mourned quietly" with the gown neatly folded on her lap. Another cousin noticed it and said, "Is that Frank's cap and gown?" Lillian later wondered, "Was it an angel or a devil that prompted her to say, 'Yes'?" The cousin passed the gown to Frank, who had no time to refuse it, "gave his wife one fierce glare, which she was careful not to see—then inspected the academic group, to discover to his intense and quite evident relief that he was dressed like everyone else. He never mentioned the matter again and neither did she, but they both knew who won that battle!"[12]

Soon after Lillian and Frank's return from Maine they took the whole family to Nantucket for the summer. Their arrival was noted in the local paper, which announced that "Major Frank B. Gilbreth and family" had arrived on July 2, bringing their Pierce Arrow car with them. Nantucket had finally succumbed to the automobile age and cars were now allowed on the island. Their caretaker, a local handyman called Bill Ray, had worked on the house during the winter so that "the Shoe" was a little larger and considerably more comfortable than when they left it ten months earlier. Lillian welcomed the improvements, for it had been a terrible squeeze the previous summer. Another baby was imminent, however, and she was exhausted. Caring for her mother-in-law and then comforting Frank had exacted a toll; she decided to have this baby in the Cottage Hospital, where she might be assured of a rest. She did not have time to get there, however, as Robert Moller Gilbreth was in a hurry and, rather to his mother's surprise, he was born in "the Shoe" on the Fourth of July, 1920, two days after her return to the island and only thirteen months after his elder brother Jack.[13]

Despite the improvements to "the Shoe," Lillian and Frank's bedroom was too dark and cramped for the birth, so they used a small room where, Lillian recalled, the children's clothes were efficiently stored in bins and on coathangers, all on "Motion Study principles"(!). Lillian commented that "she was always sorry afterward that she had not been able to register completely all the details of his coming," but she had fond memories of the next few weeks. The children welcomed a new baby and Bob became eleven-year-old Martha's special charge. Tom Grieves took the extra washing in stride. He already stripped each child's bed each morning and washed at least one outfit per child per day and said an extra baby was no problem. Mrs. Cunningham took over from the trained nurse and, Lillian remembered, proved "far more efficient and comfortable" than the hospital-trained nurses she had employed for her previous babies. Frank was in the middle of a contract with Lever Brothers and went back and forth to Cambridge. He told everyone about the new baby, of course, and the *Lever Standard* published a jaunty announcement welcoming the as yet nameless child: "Young Major Gilbreth arrived at the Nantucket home of Major and Mrs. Frank Gilbreth on July 4th. Besides notifying George M. Cohan that he is no longer the only 'Yankee Doodle boy born on July the 4th' we wish the young Major long life and prosperity."[14]

One of the ways Frank kept the children busy that summer was to use them as research assistants. They made motion study films of blueberry picking on the moors in the middle of the island, timing and analyzing different methods. They helped him on his Lever Brothers contract, experimenting with different ways of packing the boxes of soap. "It was fun to turn the whole 'Shoe' into a Motion Study Laboratory," Lillian later wrote. "The children felt they were making a real contribution."[15]

The Gilbreth children contributed to their parents' work in more ways than one. Their very existence was used by their father, and later by their mother, as a way of publicizing the Gilbreths' motion study business. Frank realized the possibilities in 1918, when he told Lillian that the size of her family would be a good publicity angle for selling her latest book. After that the Gilbreths lost no opportunity to display their children and their household system to journalists, supplying family photographs to the newspapers and allowing newsreel photographers to film them at play. Numerous press stories appeared in the early 1920s, with titles ranging from "Mother of Dozen Children Is International Authority As Industrial Engineer" to "Mrs. Gilbreth Gives Formula for Happy Home." These stories describe the Gilbreth family system with greater or lesser accuracy. The Gilbreths also tried to manage their own publicity; accounts written by Lillian in the late 1920s and by her children at various dates between the 1930s and 1970s reflect both the authors' personal situations and public attitudes toward working mothers.[16]

There were four distinct elements in the Gilbreths' home training scheme. In addition to supplementing regular school, they introduced group responsibility, trained the children in entrepreneurship and consumerism, and taught them about efficiency methods and motion study. Using John B. Watson's behaviorist psychology, John Dewey's progressive education, and Frederick Taylor's scientific management, they tried to develop the "One Best Way" of raising children. There was also a feminist and a eugenicist angle, as the Gilbreths were, in effect, creating their own laboratory where they would test the effects of both heredity and environment and prove to the world that a scientifically managed family could be successful and economical and permit the mother to be professionally active. In many ways it worked; all eleven surviving children graduated from college, and apart from the size of their family, their childhood differed little from those of other middle-class children; they had music lessons and dancing classes and joined the Girl Scouts; they learned to swim and sail; they played baseball. The children's later appreciation of their upbringing varied considerably, however, according to their position in the family.[17]

Lillian and Frank's educational ideas necessarily evolved over the thirty years there were children in the home. A fairly conventional early period, from 1905 to 1909, when they were dealing with preschool children, was followed by a more experimental middle phase, from 1909 to 1919, and finally, from 1919 until Frank's death in 1924, the elaborate system later celebrated in *Cheaper by the Dozen* held sway. After Frank died, Lillian modified, or simply abandoned, many of Frank's more regimented ideas while maintaining the work allocations necessary in a large family and the democratic experiment known as the Family Council. The Gilbreths were not unique; many Progressive Era parents introduced "real-life" projects and democratic ideas into their family life. What makes the Gilbreths different from their contemporaries, however, is their application of scientific management techniques to their children. When they lived in Plainfield they started a system of progress charts like the ones Gantt had designed for use in industry, but theirs involved personal tasks such as teeth cleaning and chores such as dusting chair legs. According to Lillian, the children enjoyed this from an early age; "the little girls seemed to enjoy Daddy's ideas and made out their worksheets and filled in their charts very happily."[18]

The system developed while they lived in Providence but reached its fullest operation after they moved to Montclair in 1919. Changes were inevitable, given the size of the family and the fact that the eldest children were old enough to take on more responsibility. Frank's mother was no longer available to act as manager, and Lillian's concerns about Frank's health contributed to her growing professional activity. Part of the children's work was simply necessary, given the size of the family, and was probably little different from other large families. Only the newest baby was Lillian's responsibility, while the older children each had a younger brother or sister to supervise. The Gilbreths got up early and did their chores before breakfast so that there was no last-minute rush before school. "When they are gone and the baby is bathed," Lillian wrote, "I then settle down to office work with the best of the day before me." She added, "It is an endless chain of responsibility. Every child has some chore to perform, besides taking care of his own personal things and thinks it grand to have the family responsibility." She suggested that if other mothers "trained their children to look upon home duties as a privilege instead of a hardship, there would be fewer children going wild—and mothers too." In this Lillian was echoing John Dewey, who believed that children should "learn through social discourse and constitution of the family." By participating in household occupations, the child "thereby gets habits of industry, order and regard for the rights of others and the fundamental habit of subordinating his activities to the general interest of the household."[19]

All the Gilbreth children old enough to speak were included in their Family Council. It usually met after Sunday dinner to decide on family policy, which included "the operating of the work plan and schedules . . . and the educating of the children to the responsibilities they were supposed to assume, the work they had to do and the records they were required to keep." The council was also a training ground in consumerism. A discussion on buying a new rug for the dining room might involve checking prices and quality and considering the kind of wear and tear the Gilbreths were likely to impose on it. The council evolved three principal committees, for purchasing, utilities, and special projects. The purchasing committee later found a department store that allowed them wholesale rates, while the utilities committee monitored waste of water and electricity and levied one-cent fines.[20]

As with many progressive ideas, the council was supposed to be democratic but often fell far short, and it sometimes more nearly resembled enlightened despotism. The children's account in *Cheaper by the Dozen* emphasizes the contrast between Father's bluster and Mother's use of psychology. After the children had declined to volunteer for household tasks, "Dad forced a smile and attempted to radiate good humor. 'Come, come, fellow members of the Council,' he said. 'This is a democracy. Everybody has an equal voice. How do you want to divide the work?'" It seemed that "no one wanted to divide the work or otherwise be associated with it in any way, shape or form. No one said anything." Frank was not pleased. "'In a democracy everybody speaks,' said Dad, 'so, by jingo, start speaking.'"[21]

Lillian's own account of the Family Council emphasizes the more democratic aspects of the system. She wrote, "It is a great temptation to parents, when the children are all together and in a listening mood, to seize the opportunity of pouring into them all the wisdom they can; but strong as the impulse is, it must be downed. . . . The parents must learn to take only their share in the meeting and unless especially invited, no more." The children's account stresses their mother's use of psychology to persuade them to accept her ideas. They quote her as saying quietly that of course the family *could* hire extra help. "But that would mean cutting the budget somewhere else. If we cut out all desserts and allowances, we could afford a maid. And if we cut out moving pictures, ice cream soda and new clothes for a whole year, we could afford a gardener, too." Lillian got her way, of course; the children gave in and cleaning the house and raking the leaves were added to their work schedules.[22]

The Family Council also organized the system of submitting bids for unusual jobs. A memorandum in Frank's handwriting survives in the Gilbreth Papers. It reads:

> Sealed proposals will be received by the undersigned for cutting down the dead tree in lawn, known as "dead pear tree on the croquet lawn," cutting the tree into lengths of 2 feet and putting it in the window of the wood room in

cellar. Also for removing the stump one foot below the ground and grass replaced properly and cleaning up all chips. The right to reject any and all bids is reserved. Bids will close at 1 P.M. Sunday. Five cents must accompany each bid as a guarantee of good faith and is to be forfeited to the undersigned if the bidder does not do the work after his bid is accepted. The money will be returned to all unsuccessful bidders at 2 o'clock, Sunday September 9 1923. Frank B. Gilbreth.[23]

The children did indeed submit bids, and the Gilbreths told the story in print on many occasions. The details vary but the message is essentially the same: children should be taught the value of work and of keeping to agreements they have made. The children were taught to be businesslike in their approach to life; if they made a mistake they had to live with the results. All the stories involve a child putting in a low bid for a garden task and the parents keeping him or her to the obligation, which the child meets, building his or her character—and business skills—in the process. Frank and Lillian were essentially small business people, and their home training schedule owed much to Horatio Alger and Huck Finn—there is even a fence-painting story. This is ironic, for the Gilbreths' work fostered the managerial revolution and indirectly the increasing scale and depersonalization of business. They were going against the spirit of the age and their own professional convictions in training the children to be entrepreneurs.[24]

Lillian believed that the Family Council trained the children to hold their own in conversation. She made notes and when the meeting was over took individual children to one side, "explaining [their] mistakes and helping to plan [their] presentation for the next meeting." The Gilbreths often entertained visiting engineers, and the children were encouraged to join in the conversation but only on topics deemed—usually by Frank—to be of "general interest." As Frank Jr. ruefully pointed out, "arithmetic, naturally, was deemed of general interest. . . . As for Motion Study, that was of such *especial* general interest that discussion often moved from the dining room to the living room after a meal." Encouraging the children to express themselves had some disadvantages, however, such as the time when Lill interrupted a long story from a distinguished French engineer, Charles de Freminville, who was Taylor's first French "convert." When she could stand it no longer Lill asked innocently, "Daddy, do you think what Mr. Freminville is saying is of general interest?"[25]

Frank filmed his children many times, and Lillian used their actions and words as illustrations in her lectures and books. Both parents caused their children enormous embarrassment, which is a key theme in the Gilbreth children's memoirs. The children understood their role in publicizing Gilbreth motion study projects, and when their father did the filming himself the results were more or less acceptable. Such films included the Remington pictures, in which the children used an all-white typewriter nicknamed Moby Dick, and a mock heroic burial of pencils on the beach at Nantucket at a time when Frank had a contract with an automatic pencil company. Less amusing and extremely embarrassing was the time a newsreel photographer filmed them eating dinner outside their Nantucket summer home. Opening with the caption "The family of Frank B. Gilbreth, time-saver, eats dinner," the film was speeded up so that "it gave the impression that we raced to the table, passed plates madly in all directions, wolfed our food and ran away from the table, all in about forty-five seconds." What made it worse was the fact that the Gilbreths saw the newsreel together in the local cinema on Nantucket, where almost everyone in the audience knew them and turned around to stare. The worst embarrassment of all came when their teachers read aloud newspaper or magazine articles that described the Gilbreths' child-rearing methods, such as the process charts they had to fill out in the bathrooms, the language lessons on the Victrola while they were in the bath, or the decisions of the Family Council. "We'd blush and squirm and wish Dad had a nice job selling shoes somewhere and that he only had one or two children, neither of whom was us."[26]

Given all the publicity, Frank was conscious of the potential for embarrassment—his embarrassment—if the children did not turn out well. In February 1920, when he saw Frank Jr.'s latest school report, he was furious that his son had been late for school on several occasions. "Twelve times tardy is bad for the Gilbreth name," he thundered, "*and I don't want to have any more of it.*" Frank installed phonographs with language rolls in the bathrooms, where the children were supposed to listen to them and practice their French and German daily, an ironic instruction from someone with no ear whatsoever for languages. Martha and Ernestine had to put in an hour a day, "and there is no excuse for Lillian, Fred, Bill and Frank not also putting in an hour each on the languages." The reason for Frank's anxiety on this score was apparent from his next remark: "I'm telling everyone how we teach the children by gramophone and it would be a terrible joke on me if our kids don't make good in languages."[27]

The relationship between the Gilbreth children and publicity is a complex one, as they knew that part of their parents' income derived from the human interest stories that their large family generated. The publicity was sometimes too much for them, however, and later some of the children refused to talk about their experiences as one of the dozen, while others tried to manage their own publicity. It also appears that some of the children had happier childhood memories than others. Jane, the youngest, remembers a very dislocated childhood with her mother absent for much of the time. Even Ernestine Gilbreth Carey, who has spent much of her life celebrating her parents' achievements, admits that there were essentially two families and that the older children had a very different childhood from their six younger siblings.[28]

The Gilbreth family system became much more regimented in 1923 when Frank decided that the family should be run on standing orders. He wanted to leave the children for two months while he and Lillian attended conferences in Europe the following year. He instructed Lillian, "Tell the kids you are going to Prague. . . . You do the Standing Orders and it will be the biggest thing for our business that we ever did. We will then have a household system—Something we never had before." The main burden would fall on sixteen-year-old Anne; Frank wrote,

> Dear Boss: I have got a *new* idea,—it consists of really doing our old ideas. Our office and our family must be run on standing orders. I suggest that Anne start in and make out standing orders for everything. She will need this experience if she is to be President of a college and it will be the best kind of training for all the boys. No work that she can ever do will be so valuable for her or for the boys or for you. I propose that you be relieved of your fool duties. There is no more fooling. *I shall attach.* DO IT. Frank.[29]

The tone of Frank's letters (Lillian's have not survived) suggests that she had misgivings; perhaps she remembered the responsibilities she had been asked to assume as the eldest child in the Moller family. At the same time, Lillian was not particularly eager to be relieved of all her household obligations. As Ernestine later wrote, "Her fool duties that he talked about were dusting and helping us daughters do the dishes which she loved to do because it was companionable & it kept her on her feet moving around & she liked to do it anyhow. He never liked this and would say you lazy girls why are you letting your mother do this?" Elements of the system did emerge, however, as older children took care of their younger siblings and a clear routine was established.[30]

Although Lillian admitted that "the idea of applying business forms to the routine of family life may appear startling at first," that was exactly what they started to do. Such a standing order form, she wrote, "tells *what* is to be done, *who* is to do it, *where, when, how.* It also tells who is to inspect the work when done and provides for over-inspection, or reinspecting exceptionally good or poor work, which gives the parents a chance to keep track automatically of how things get on. The work records are made on the output charts which show that the standing orders have been followed." Some of the tasks covered by forms were daily jobs, while others were much less frequently re-

quired. Lillian's list included setting the table, tidying the linen closet, putting new paper on the pantry shelves, washing the porch light, sorting and
putting away the clean laundry, distributing the mail, and mailing outgoing
letters. The children's tasks and their worksheets grew more elaborate until
they included a list of twenty-seven jobs, when they were to be done, by
whom, and who was to inspect them once they had been completed. There
was even an instruction sheet signed by Tom, the man-of-all-work, to "Bill
the sheepmover." Ten-year-old Bill had to "move sheep three times a day—by
moving lawn roller at least as far as the length of their ropes and at least as
far as 25 feet." This was written on an "official" standing order form; the
work was to be done "everywhere in lot"; it was to be inspected by Tom; and
Frank was to be informed "if work is not completed when and as called for
herein." The Gilbreths did indeed keep sheep for a while, as it was deemed an
efficient way of keeping the grass cut, so this order was no joke.[31]

Lillian and Frank both felt that standing orders had many practical and
educational advantages. The children agreed, at least in retrospect. They also
had Gantt process charts, which showed what was to be done and when.
Frank Jr. described his, which went (with a little exaggeration) something like
this:

7:00——Rise and shine. Mart will call you.

7:01——Your turn in the bathroom.

7:02——Play German records while brushing teeth, bathing and other unavoidable delay.

7:03——Did you remember to wash your ears?

7:07——Weigh self and post on weight charts.

7:08——Comb hair, wash ring out of tub, start bath for Bill, wind Grapho-
phone.

7:10——Wake Bill.

7:11——Play French records in bedroom while dressing.

7:16——Shine shoes.

7:18——Make bed.

7:21——Straighten room.

7:31——Eat breakfast.

And so forth.[32]

As they got older, the children were well aware that the charts, the stand-
ing orders, and the contracts were necessary in order to run a large family, but
Lillian and Frank somehow injected an element of fun into the proceedings.
As Frank Jr. remarked, his parents' methods "may sound about as gay and in-
formal as a concentration camp, but it seemed more like a game at the time."
The children found ways of beating the schedule so they could have a few

minutes to read the comic papers like *Krazy Kat* and *Happy Hooligan*. The only person who did not find the schedules amusing was Tom, who, in fact, did most of the work. Frank Gilbreth Jr. portrays him as saying, "Nobody but me never washed a Goddam tub around here in their whole lives, for Christ sake. . . . You little bastids can fool your Mother and you can fool your Father, but you can't fool me." And then Tom's clinching argument: "You know what Motion Study is, Frankie-boy? You study how to get someone else to make all your motions for you, for Christ sake."[33]

18   Indicting the Stopwatch

*Say Boss, you are some classy bear-cat and cave-woman
and I don't blame them for being scared.*

Frank Gilbreth to Lillian Gilbreth (March 7, 1920)

L ILLIAN'S FAMILY and friends saw her as a concilia-
tor who would back away from any argument, though she described herself
as hot-tempered. She usually had her emotions under tight control, but a confrontation with some of the orthodox Taylorites proves that she was sometimes prepared to fight in defense of her and Frank's motion study methods,
not to mention their livelihood. The problem started in December 1919 when
Horace Hathaway, the Gilbreths' nemesis at Hermann, Aukum, presented a
paper on standards at the annual meeting of the Taylor Society, in which he
described standardization at the New Jersey handkerchief factory without
acknowledging the Gilbreths' role there. They were furious and the dispute
with the Taylorites, which had been relatively quiet in the four years since
Taylor's death, flared up again. Part of the reason was undoubtedly economic. During the war there had been plenty of work for everyone, but in the
postwar recession management consultants were competing for contracts.

In early March 1920, while Frank was out of town, Lillian went to the
New York headquarters of the Taylor Society and asked to see Hathaway's
manuscript, which was to be published in the next edition of the Taylor Society's *Bulletin*. Ignoring the editor's remark that it was due at the printers, Lillian sat at a desk, took out pen and notebook, and proceeded to make detailed notes on the article. When her old friend Morris Llewellyn Cooke came
into the room, she told him that Hathaway was claiming credit for the

Gilbreths' work and that Frank was quite ready to "punch his head." She said she was advocating a less belligerent solution, namely that Hathaway revise the paper. At that point Harlow Person, the editor, returned; Lillian told him that she and Frank had photographs to prove what they did at Hermann, Aukum and that they would publish their own version of the "entire matter" unless Hathaway made major revisions to the article. She concluded by threatening bad publicity for scientific management, saying, "This is simply giving you an opportunity (which we do for the good of the Cause), to see that the matter is settled to our satisfaction without an open disagreement and without the publicity that would ensue." Lillian concluded her letter to Frank in which she related the affair by saying that she felt very satisfied with her day's work. "They know now that it was no bluff that we would read the paper and get ready to go for him." Frank replied by return mail: "I've just received the letter describing your interview with Person and I consider it a masterpiece. . . . I shall punch H.K. when I next see him. Leave that to me." Lillian's protest had some effect; Hathaway added a brief footnote acknowledging Frank's work.[1]

Later that year, however, the Gilbreth-Taylor dispute resurfaced when the New York chapter of the Taylor Society invited Frank and Lillian to present a paper, "Time Study and Motion Study As Fundamental Factors in Planning and Control." Frank added a subtitle: "An Indictment of Time Study." As Lillian later remarked, "Frank immediately saw an opportunity to present a full and even pugnacious exposition of the Micro-motion method." Presentation of the paper led to "many and heated discussions" and Person refused to publish it, claiming that the Gilbreths' assertions lacked proof. Frank and Lillian then arranged for its printing and distribution themselves.

In their original paper Lillian and Frank positioned themselves firmly as the "good" alternative to orthodox Taylorism, just as they had since 1914. Such a stance was even more necessary in the postwar period, as industry's readjustment to peacetime production was accompanied by labor unrest. The Gilbreths argued that their micro-motion methods were fairer than simple time study because they more accurately measured the time needed to perform standard operations (upon which wage rates were calculated). They described their calculation of the "One Best Way," which was based on a study of the best man available, and claimed that the films and the standardized methods derived from them made their training methods more effective. They charged the stopwatch proponents with being inaccurate and unscientific in rate setting and useless and misleading in the study of skills. They criticized "secret" time study whereby the investigator hid his stopwatch inside a specially designed notepad. They countered claims that their methods were too expensive by saying that it was cheaper to do it right the first time and that "scores of years of stopwatch time records have been totally abandoned because they were so inaccurate." They also asserted that the workers preferred their system, partly because they earned more money "and are *demanding* that they themselves should be allowed to take part in the investigations."[2]

The Taylor Society could not ignore the Gilbreths' challenge and held a symposium on the efficacy of filmed motion versus stopwatch time study. Five experts tried to refute the Gilbreths' charges point by point, and though they conceded that filmed micro-motion was more accurate, they suggested that it was not necessary for the determination of standard times for specific tasks or useful for retraining "workers with fixed habits," though it might be effective in teaching new workers. Carl Barth, who presented himself as a "direct disciple of Mr. Taylor" and a pragmatic engineer while portraying the Gilbreths as impractical scientists, said rather pointedly, "It did not take me long to learn to make allowances for their enthusiasm and not take it quite so seriously." Barth was followed by four further discussants of the Gilbreths' paper, all of whom conceded the usefulness of micro-motion under some circumstances while preferring the ease and economy of the stopwatch for calculating standard times.[3]

When the defenders of the stopwatch had finished damning the Gilbreths with faint praise, Frank and Lillian replied in an expanded statement published with the rest of the papers. Over the course of eighteen pages and 138 numbered paragraphs, they attempted to refute their critics. Quoting authorities from Frederick Taylor to John Watson, they claimed that "photographing of mental processes as indicated by behavior is the special work of the micromotion and cyclegraph methods." They also claimed that they could *modify* behavior and, so they claimed, avoid industrial accidents and produce better-trained, more productive, and better-paid workers.[4]

Although he published the Gilbreths' paper, Person remained skeptical and had the last word, remarking that the Gilbreths' arguments were essentially a priori and that the burden of proof lay with them. Twenty years later Lillian wrote that "from that time on, impartial evaluators could balance the pros and cons and ultimately an integration could result." And an integration of the two approaches is what eventually happened, partly through Lillian's conciliatory efforts after Frank's death.[5]

While some of Frank and Lillian's peers grudgingly acknowledged their contributions, others were more forthcoming in their praise. In April 1921, some two weeks after the stopwatch symposium, the Gilbreths traveled to the Society of Industrial Engineers' Spring Convention in Milwaukee, where Lillian was elected as the second honorary member of the society. Her predecessor was Herbert Hoover, the "Great Engineer," recently returned from his humanitarian work in war-torn Europe. Lillian's citation was long and glowing; the society believed that her principal claim to originality was the application of psychology to management. They praised her book *The Psychology of Management,* the demand for which, they claimed, "has continually increased and today it is recognized as authoritative." Finally, she was commended for "finding time and deriving a great deal of pleasure in bringing up a truly interesting family of ten children." The citation concluded, "We have added to our roster a remarkable woman."[6]

Lillian and Frank were delighted by the honor, which was a rebuff to their Taylor Society critics. Lillian was also a little embarrassed to be thus singled out and uncomfortable receiving an award separately from Frank, so she modestly asked him to thank the society on her behalf. Frank was speechless—an event the society's *Bulletin* noted under the heading "Strange To Believe, But True." Both Gilbreths relished Lillian's increased professional recognition, as they knew that Frank's heart was seriously weakened and that though he was only fifty-three, he was living on borrowed time. They reasoned that the better known Lillian was, the more likely it was that she could continue the Gilbreth work. Frank's heart problems grew less frequent over time, and his visit in August 1922 to the Life Extension Institute, an organization that acted as a clearinghouse for insurance company medical examinations, was somewhat reassuring. He reported to Lillian that they "seem to think I'll die of old age," though the list of provisos suggests a less than complete optimism: Frank was told to watch his diet, continue not to smoke, take some exercise, and wear wool next to the skin. In addition, he should carry digitalis, a heart stimulant prepared from dried foxglove leaves, with him at all times in case of emergencies.[7]

Meanwhile, the Gilbreths' international reputation was recovering, despite the unpopularity of Taylorism in some quarters. Many Germans were ambivalent about America and the values it seemed to promote: materialism, rationalization (the usual term for scientific management), and the mechanization of life. The Gilbreths were criticized in Britain, too, for some members of the Institute of Industrial Psychology were inclined to "disparage" American methods and took particular exception to the idea of the "One Best Way."[8] Frank was, however, more optimistic about Czechoslovakia. While in Prague in 1922 he lunched with the president, lectured at Charles University, and laid the groundwork for an international conference at the newly created Masaryk Academy of Work. Like many other Europeans, the Czech leaders believed that America's power derived from its technological expertise and that one way to harness this was by effective management. Frank sent pumps, typewriters, adding machines, and forges so that the Czechs could study the "One Best" product available.[9]

At the same time, the Gilbreth family continued to grow. Lillian gave birth to three children after Frank returned from the army: Jack in May 1919, Bob in July 1920, and Jane in June 1922. Although this may seem a little fool-hardy, Lillian justified the decision by telling an interviewer that she and Frank had prepared the family system and "standardized what he would want done if he went." Lillian was forty-four when her thirteenth and last child was born in the Nantucket Cottage Hospital in June 1922. Frank was "chief assistant" to the doctor and had, according to Lillian, "a marvelous time!" Although he had been out of town for most of the previous "coming out par-ties," he seems to have gone from one extreme to the other, as it was very un-usual for fathers to assist in childbirth in 1922. Lillian spent a week in the hos-pital before Jane arrived and stayed there for several days after. Frank visited her several times a day, strolling over from "the Shoe" clad in his white linen summer suit and bearing bouquets of Queen Anne's lace that he had picked by the roadside. Lillian enjoyed a good rest for the first time in many years, apart from a rather unsettling conversation. The nurse remarked as she brought Jane into Lillian's room that a woman who had murdered her ille-gitimate child had spent the night in the hospital "because of course you know we have no jail. She is going on trial this morning." Alarmed, Lillian asked, "Where did she sleep?" The nurse answered, "Oh, next door to the nursery." More alarmed, Lillian inquired, "And who was on duty to see that nothing happened?" only to be told, "Oh, she didn't make any trouble." Needless to say, Lillian was relieved to return to "the Shoe."[10]

Frank was in Nantucket for more time than usual that summer; most of his projects were well under control, including one with the Winchester laun-dry. He claimed that it was more efficient and economical to send clothes to the laundry rather than have underutilized equipment in every home. As a publicity stunt, he and the children, all clad in voluminous black bathing suits, buried the family wringer, washboards, and flat iron on the beach, watched by a press photographer. Tom Grieves grumbled in the background, and as soon as the photographer had gone he dug everything up.[11]

Lillian was very busy in early 1923. She now had eleven living children and a steadily growing professional reputation. She lectured at Columbia Univer-sity and Newark Women's Club in February and was planning a visit to En-gland in late March, where, as the official delegate of the American Society of Mechanical Engineers (and the first woman so designated, despite the fact that she was not a member of that almost entirely male organization), she was to give a keynote address to the British Society of Women Engineers. An elaborate itinerary survives, labeled in Lillian's handwriting, "The carefully planned schedule of the trip that couldn't be made." It was to be a two-month trip starting on March 31. She intended to spend four days at the conference in Birmingham, then travel to Prague to help Frank with detailed prepara-

tions for the Prague International Management Conference (PIMCO), stopping in Belgium and Holland on the way. She planned to return to the United
States via Paris. After one day in Montclair she then intended to travel to California to attend commencement and her parents' fiftieth anniversary celebrations, before arriving home on May 30 after a detour to a professional
meeting in Montreal.[12]

Lillian was unable to travel because she had an emergency hysterectomy
in March 1923. She was nearly forty-five years old and very nervous as she
went into the hospital. She wrote Frank a letter telling him what kind of funeral she would like if she did not survive the operation, which served to make
Frank even more nervous than she was. According to her daughter Ernestine,
many of her mother's later confinements were very difficult—but "my father
didn't seem to worry about that, but when she was in the hospital for her hysterectomy he was beside himself—he was convinced she was going to die. She
wrote him a letter to read if she didn't survive—I don't suppose that
helped."[13]

Lillian's letter began, "This is just in case anything should happen to me
in the hospital, the most unlikely thing in the world, but it does no harm to
be prepared." The letter combines a wish for efficiency with a belief in some
kind of afterlife, though not the conventional Christian kind. She also
wanted to be memorialized only as Frank's wife and partner. Her desire for
simplicity and economy was in stark contrast to her family's elaborate Gothic
mausoleum on Millionaires' Row back in Oakland and reflects how far she
had moved away from the values her California relatives espoused. She told
Frank that she wanted "the simplest, least expensive and most efficient of
funerals—AT ONCE—so that I could 'Return to the geology' with the least delay possible." She didn't want the ceremony of a wake or an open coffin, admitting, "I suppose I am foolish, but I do wish no one need see me, especially
the children, for I'd like to be remembered on the go, as I usually am. Can that
be done?" She asked to be cremated and her ashes thrown over Eagle Rock
near their house, "and no stone, tablet or inscription anywhere until it was
time to have one for you. Then I would like to have my name added to yours,
on yours, if you were willing." Finally she asked that he not grieve for her:
"Think of what a 'geological wink' it all is. Think of me when you look at the
star cluster—just a little star dust, waiting for you somewhere." She signed it
"Your Chum.[14]

Lillian went into the hospital in mid-March, so it was not surprising that
she had to cancel her European trip, which was due to start at the end of the
month. Frank was unable to say what was really the matter; when he wrote to
his English agent, he told him that she was "having her tonsils removed and
also a little repair work done." Lillian was very disappointed that she was

forced to cancel her speech. She and Frank had been conducting a quiet cam-paign to gain her membership in the ASME, and representing them, even if she was not yet a member, seemed to be a giant first step toward acceptance. Having to cancel because of "women's trouble" was particularly galling, as it would simply reinforce certain members' reservations about women engi-neers. Lillian sent her speech to Birmingham, where it was read on her behalf. Speaking more as an engineer than as a woman, she did not directly address women engineers' roles beyond acknowledging a "pressing need" for an or-ganization such as the Women's Engineering Society. She wrote more as a Gilbreth than as a mainstream engineer. She stressed the importance of stan-dardization and work simplification, which made it possible "to relieve high priced workers of all but their most interesting and profitable activities, con-signing the balance to less experienced workers, who are trained upward to undertake new duties which enlist their attention and interest." Whether or not the ASME liked it, she as their official representative closed with a refer-ence to Gilbreth methods: "We are anxious to co-operate in every way pos-sible to the advance of the science in which we are all interested and especially to more extensive interchange of data on the One Best Way to Do Work."[15]

Lillian convalesced through the spring and by mid-May felt fit enough to travel to California to help her parents celebrate their fiftieth wedding an-niversary. Though Lillian had recovered, Frank's heart problems returned; he had "sharp attacks" that frightened Lillian "so that she packed the stimulants for every trip." His doctor warned him that his heart had been permanently damaged and he should take every care of himself. By the spring of 1924 Frank's health seemed better, but just in case, Frank carried enough life in-surance to support the family for a while. In the event of Frank's death, Lil-lian knew as much as he did about motion study and how to run a consul-tancy business.[16]

Frank and Lillian's trip to Europe, for which the family had been planning over many months, was to take place in the summer of 1924. In the weeks be-fore they were due to leave, Frank was frantically busy; in May he lectured at Purdue, the University of Michigan, Harvard, Columbia, and Lehigh Uni-versity in Pennsylvania. While he was out of town lecturing, on scientific management contracts, or at planning meetings for PIMCO, Lillian dictated a short biography of her husband "and scrupulously paid for the time of the secretary who transcribed it by doing equivalent hours of work in the office herself." She called the book *The Quest of the One Best Way* and "was greatly tempted to give it to him," but she decided to surprise Frank with it on his fifty-sixth birthday, which they planned to celebrate in London that June. *The Quest* is Lillian's fullest contemporary account of their family experiment. Ostensibly a short biography of Frank, it also reveals a great deal about her own beliefs and contributions, especially the last chapter, which explains the connections between her family and her professional life, both being quests for the "One Best Way."[17]

In the summer of 1924 Frank and Lillian were asking the children to manage themselves and each other for two months. The standing orders were fully in place and the children's summer in Nantucket had been organized down to the smallest detail; they were to leave for the island shortly before Lillian and Frank sailed to Europe on June 19 and run everything until their parents returned on August 15. They did this, but not in quite the way Frank and Lillian intended.

PART V

"Successfully in Two Places at the Same Time"

A mother's place is in the home, without question, but if she can be successfully in two places at the same time, she is not only bringing up her children, but is leading them an example which will mean more and more to them as they get older.

Martha Gilbreth, "A Large Family Is Fun" (1936)

Man's place is in the home, says noted woman engineer. The answer to home problems, she says, is to teach men how to combine a career and a home.

"Man's Place Is in the Home," *Philadelphia Public Ledger* (January 31, 1937)

19   "Here I Stand, 'the Case!'"

> *Mother saw the beds were made and the house*
> *cleaned, supervised Ernestine's menus and Martha's*
> *budget program, kept an eye on Bob and Jane, sewed on*
> *buttons, wrote Anne every day and still found time to read*
> *to us at night, help us with our homework and go with*
> *us to Sunday school. And she worked ten hours*
> *every day in the office and laboratory.*

Frank Gilbreth Jr. and Ernestine Gilbreth Carey, *Belles on Their Toes* (1950)

In THE MONTHS after Frank's death Lillian created a pattern of activity that included management consulting, volunteer work, lecturing, travel, and an interest in women's issues that was to persist for the rest of her life. She also became a celebrity working mother as public interest in the Gilbreth family intensified and articles with titles such as "Who Washes the Dishes at Home When Ma Is Famous?" appeared in print. Lillian realized that allowing herself to be represented as both a scientist and a supermother had important economic ramifications. She knew, whether she could articulate it or not, that there were crucial gender contradictions between "scientist" and "mother" and between "engineer" and "woman." Being a representative of all these categories made her very unusual and allowed her to make a good living. She could speak to other engineers (or at least some of them) as well as be presumed to understand what women wanted. So despite her children's dislike of posing for group photos, Lillian used them to publicize her work, and as Laurel Graham has remarked, "The net result was that she was able to continue her quest to remove unnecessary fatigue from work without sacrificing the comforts of her own family life."[1]

Lillian knew what Frank wanted her to do. "He had always felt that the children should be brought up as strenuously as possible, given great responsibility and allowed to take over the direction of their own lives, as soon as they felt adequate to do this," she wrote. Several friends and relatives offered to adopt one or more of the young Gilbreths: Aunt Jane Bunker, the dentist, offered to take her namesake, two-year-old Janey. Lillian and the children were fiercely opposed to such an idea. Apart from strong personal ties of affection, their family experiment would be worthless if they allowed themselves to be split up and dispersed, but Lillian compromised a little and sent Lill back to California with her grandmother at the end of the summer. Although Lill was just ten, she was entering seventh grade, having skipped grades like most of her siblings. She was never quite sure why she was the chosen one, though being a girl in the middle of six boys may have had a lot to do with it. Lill recalled an extraordinary year when she lived in quiet luxury surrounded by solicitous aunts and uncles: Annie Moller and her five unmarried, middle-aged children had moved to an even larger house than the one where Lillian had grown up. It was a French-style chateau in Piedmont, a lush town in the Oakland hills, where they lived in luxury amid Oriental rugs, heavy drapes, and cabinet after cabinet full of Chinese ivories, Tiffany vases, and Limoges china. They were looked after by a housekeeper, a chauffeur, and two gardeners; their washing went to a French laundry, and meat, groceries, and vegetables were delivered every day. The chauffeur drove Lill to school, which she found most embarrassing—she insisted on being dropped off two blocks away.[2]

Despite her family obligations, Lillian put her work before her children immediately after Frank's death. She was away from home for half of June, all of July, most of August, most of November, and occasional weeks in between. Even when she was in Montclair her diaries show almost daily meetings. Lillian managed, however, even in these most difficult months, to make her children feel wanted; they recollect her spending a considerable amount of time with them. As Frank Jr. remarked, "Looking back it was the days she was there rather than the days she was away that one remembers"; Jane, however, recalled that her mother often disappeared to her room, particularly if the house was too noisy.[3]

When Lillian traveled to London in June 1924, she was not entirely sure if the engineering community would welcome her without Frank. She wrote to Colonel Sheehan, president of the Society of Industrial Engineers, asking him to "please express candidly whether a woman delegate would be acceptable," adding, "I want to live out [Frank's] plans if I can." The response was positive: Sheehan even offered to send his wife to Montclair to supervise the children in Lillian's absence. All the societies that Frank had been scheduled to represent appointed her in his stead, even those organizations such as the ASME to which she did not yet belong.[4]

Partly to prove herself in Frank's absence, partly to keep busy during the transatlantic voyage, and partly because she had been commissioned to report on the First World Power Conference for one of the engineering journals, Lillian read and annotated all the preprinted papers, making herself useful to the other delegates as she had for so many years to her husband. "She read and briefed them all," she later wrote, "and could hand over to her colleagues who were to discuss them material which saved them considerable effort." In London she stayed with friends, the Spooners, whose sympathy and "deep mourning" she found "difficult to endure," though it was a comfort to be able to talk about Frank with former colleagues.[5]

The First World Power Conference was a huge affair with more than four hundred papers presented between June 30 and July 12. Commerce Secretary Herbert Hoover, a hero to his fellow engineers, gave the keynote address on government energy policies; Lillian noted that he "depicts government not only as we wish it were, but what he feels it can be!" She later presented her paper "First Steps in Fatigue Study," which "went over well." Lillian then traveled to Germany to see Irene Witte, who had worked with Frank since 1914 and had translated most of the Gilbreth books into German. With other American engineers they took a train to Prague. After they crossed the Czech border the stationmaster put an entire car of the train at their disposal, decorating it with signs that read, "Reserved for the U.S. Delegation of the Prague International Congress." At this point, Witte remembered, "with a glass of Pilsner in one hand and in the other a pair of rather large hot dogs and a roll of bread and butter each member of the delegation took possession of a compartment for himself, stretched his legs and tried to look as proud and unapproachable as possible." Lillian and Irene Witte stayed where they were—it is hard, if not impossible, to imagine Lillian with a beer and a hot dog—and the splendid isolation enjoyed by the others soon began to pall. "Ten minutes later all were back in our cozy apartment glad to have company and full of good spirits!" Witte recalled.[6]

Lillian received a warm welcome from members of the Masaryk Academy in Prague. "To them," she wrote, "it was a personal tribute that Frank's widow had been willing to make the trip." The PIMCO conference was the first of a series of such meetings and has been described as being "of vast international importance in the development of scientific management." As an honorary fellow, Lillian was chair of the Society of Industrial Engineers' group. She took everything in stride and even found giving Frank's speech, being made a member of the Masaryk Academy, and presiding over the final session "no serious ordeal."[7]

On the other hand, Lillian found the memorial service for Frank, which preceded the conference, "a harrowing experience." She found it difficult to maintain her composure as a senior Czech official made a fulsome speech praising Frank's contributions to Czechoslovakia, to which Frank had "showed the way of the best progress in that time of storm and stress." Robert Kent, a longtime Gilbreth friend, spoke on behalf of the American delegation, stressing the character of "Frank Gilbreth, the man." He recalled that Frank had died just as his ideas were gaining acceptance, unlike earlier, when "his views were considered to be confused." Kent was grateful, however, that Frank had lived to "see those that scorned his views change their opposing views into agreement." Kent's references to the disputes within scientific management and the bitter irony of Frank's death just as his reputation was starting to recover made the memorial service particularly painful to Lillian. She also disliked the "black pall, mourning everywhere, eulogies—all of the things which could be avoided in Montclair had to be endured, now."[8]

Lillian sailed for the United States on August 6 and found Ernestine waiting at the dock in New York. After a couple of days in Montclair they traveled to Providence, where Lillian thanked her sister-in-law, Anne, "who had stood by so valiantly," and talked with her nephew John Cross, who had handled Frank's insurance policies in her absence. The money had been paid into the bank "and there was no immediate financial problem." Lillian was in no hurry to spend any extended time on Nantucket or even to see the rest of the children, so after seeing Ernestine onto the ferry she traveled to Fairfield, Maine, to arrange a memorial stone for Frank. The Crosses were there, too, for the burial of Grandma Gilbreth's ashes in the family plot. It was a very emotional moment for Lillian; Carol Cross remembered vividly what happened next. She told Ernestine, "Your Mother was exhausted from her travels and the terrific strain of keeping a stiff upper lip. Well, that night at the hotel I slept with her and I never felt so sorry for anyone in my life. She cried and sobbed and I was afraid she would sob her life away. When I tried to comfort her she held on to me so hard, I was astonished at the strength in her hands." Lillian got through the night somehow and went to Boston the next day, where she stayed with Myrtelle Canavan, the friend who had conducted the autopsy on Frank some two months earlier. After three days in Montclair she finally went to Nantucket for a week's vacation. Even then the elements were against her; a storm prevented her sailing on August 26 as she had planned. She finally arrived on August 27, almost eight weeks after she had left her chicken pox–smitten children and almost two weeks after her return to the United States.[9]

As soon as all the welcomes were over, the presents admired, and the sunburns examined, Lillian gathered her children around her and held a Family Council. She outlined their options, giving the children the choice between staying where they were, in the knowledge that she might be away from home for much of the time, or moving near to her mother in Oakland, where she could stay home and write. The children could attend the local schools and then the University of California. Little management consultancy work was available on the West Coast, however, and Lillian did not want to return home, which would be tantamount to admitting that her efforts to be a successful working mother were a mistake. The children gave her the answer she wanted, saying that they preferred to stay in New Jersey. This was fortunate, for Lillian had already accepted her niece Carol Cross's offer to take a leave of absence from her teaching job in Detroit. Carol was to live with them in Montclair and supervise the house and the children for the next three years.[10]

In the immediate aftermath of Frank's death, the question of money was important. Frank and Lillian had lived well on their consultancy fees, but with eleven children to feed, clothe, and educate, there was little spare cash. Much of the Gilbreths' profits were invested in new photographic equipment or mortgage payments on their expensive new house, which was, incidentally, in Lillian's name. After the children's "go-ahead," she told them she was prepared to "take a chance, financially" and use some of Frank's insurance money for day-to-day expenses until it became clear whether clients, old or new, would accept a female management consultant. The Gilbreths' beloved Pierce Arrow car was sold "out of town," for neither Lillian nor the children could bear the thought of seeing it in other hands. Mrs. Cunningham left; one of her daughters had married a car salesman and, feeling she had gone up in the world, asked her mother to come and help with her two young children— a much easier proposition than eleven Gilbreths. Henceforward they managed with only Tom Grieves, the man-of-all-work. College fees were reduced; Anne transferred from Smith to the University of Michigan, though this move had, apparently, been discussed before her father's death. Ernestine deferred her entry to Smith, having missed the entrance examination because of chicken pox, and stayed home to help her mother while taking a postgraduate year at Montclair High. Lillian's mother offered to lend her money, which Lillian insisted on paying back in full.[11]

As soon as the family returned to Montclair in September 1924, Lillian resumed her work. Although she had been well prepared for the possibility of Frank's death, she missed him badly and plunged into ten-hour days and six- and seven-day work weeks. In the short term she traveled and met people to take her mind off her loss: spending time with her children was not enough for Lillian, either financially or emotionally. In the longer term she worked because she loved to feel busy and involved. She believed that work "is in itself desirable and worthwhile" and that she was "adding in some way to the world's assets."[12]

Lillian was never entirely free of money worries, but she was careful not to let the children know how difficult her financial affairs had become. She sold almost all her jewelry back to Tiffany's, though she never parted with her engagement ring. She tried to deny the children as little as possible, even spoiling them somewhat. Carol Cross recalled an incident when she scolded Fred for playing in the fresh spring mud in his new knickers, telling him it cost money to have clothes cleaned, and Fred scolded her in return for making him conscious of their limited funds. This altercation was followed by a Family Council to decide whether the children should be "allowed to live as usual on a sort of 'Lord will provide' basis" or whether funds should be saved for college expenses. "It was decided that they should go along as always." Lillian wrote to her children frequently; one of many such letters is revealing. After sympathizing with Ernestine, who was feeling miserable, she told her that the family finances looked good, adding that she hoped to get a little car that Ernestine could share with Carol Cross. "I've told Carol you are to learn to run it at once as I shall too and have it for trips, holidays. She can have her outings in between. And she is glad to. Won't that be fun?"[13]

Lillian's first priority in 1924 was to prepare her biography of Frank, *The Quest of the One Best Way,* for the printers. The Society of Industrial Engineers helped finance its publication; half the printing of 1,500 copies went to its members, and Lillian distributed the rest to friends and colleagues. Her files are full of thank-you letters, including a telegram from a President Burdiansky of the Soviet Board of Trade, who found *The Quest* "very interesting for all admiriers of Jours [sic] husband too early deceased" and asked for permission to translate it into Russian. Even though Lenin was dead, Soviet interest in the Gilbreths' methods continued.[14]

Though Lillian later wrote, "It was of tremendous comfort to be able to send this to Frank's friends," *The Quest* was far more than a gesture of remembrance. It was, rather, the opening round of her campaign to present the Gilbreths' side of the conflict with Taylor and his followers. This dispute had ramifications beyond the personalities involved, since it would also affect her ability to gain professional acceptance and, by extension, her ability to support her family. Loyal Taylorites had revived the conflict in a demeaning five-sentence obituary notice, in which none of Frank's ideas or innovations was mentioned, other than his role in setting up the Taylor Society, which was "a monument to Mr. Gilbreth's vision and energy." A few months later, the society's *Bulletin* reprinted statements made by Taylor in 1910 in which he gave himself and Sanford Thompson full credit for motion study, which further undermined Frank Gilbreth's claim to originality. *The Quest* was Lillian's response to the Taylor Society. It was both romantic and quietly confrontational. In fewer than ninety pages she attempted to establish Frank's originality and prove that she and Frank were true followers of Taylor, while those who alleged otherwise were wrong.[15]

With *The Quest* safely dispatched to the printers, Lillian's second task was to generate some income. She was of two minds whether to pursue new contracts. She remembered how much time Frank had spent away from home, and she was acutely aware of her responsibilities to the children. Although she had moved in the male-dominated world of industrial engineering for many years, it remained to be seen whether clients would accept Lillian on her own. Her first solo experience had, however, been encouraging. In July, while she was still in Europe, she completed some consultancy work for Stork, a Dutch tobacco machinery manufacturer; this contract was renewed and she worked for them until 1927. America was to prove a more resistant market. Despite her excellent connections, in the short term she had some difficulties. Her other option was much more traditionally female, namely to teach. Shortly before Frank's death he and Lillian had decided to "set up a school, with the clients sending their men to be trained." They had accordingly taken no new contracts in the months before they were to leave for Europe, but as there were still loose ends to tie up, Lillian completed the remaining projects, letting staff go as soon as a job was finished. She decided to combine consultancy work and teaching, so she networked with friends, male and female, to obtain new contracts, while planning her first motion study course.[16]

Lillian discussed her plan with Robert Wood Johnson, vice president of Johnson & Johnson, during the fall. He was enthusiastic and offered to "send a man even if he's the only one and pay the entire cost of the course myself!" She planned to charge one thousand dollars per student for a four-month, nonresidential course. Attendance was limited to ten students, who, over the course of sixteen weeks, would learn how to equip and operate motion study laboratories. She would lecture each morning on scientific management, motion study, or applied psychology; students would spend the afternoons either visiting plants or in "practical instruction in the Motion Study Laboratory work in what Mr. Gilbreth called 'The One Best Way to do Work' considering the worker, surroundings, equipment and tools."[17]

Despite Lillian's own expertise in psychology and betterment work, she knew that motion study was likely to be more attractive to potential clients, since it seemed to promise more immediate savings. She trusted that once she started training the students, the interdependence of motion study and psychology would become obvious. She sent out her prospectuses in the fall and eventually had enough students enrolled to make the course viable. They included Eugenia (Jean) Lies, the research director of Macy's department store in New York, and William Dorman from Johnson & Johnson. Later students came from Borden Dairies, General Electric, and a tool company; the overseas students included a lieutenant engineer in the Imperial Japanese Navy, a cost accountant with a chain of Belgian department stores, and an employee of Cadbury, the English chocolate manufacturer.[18]

The course was scheduled to start in early January 1925. Given her fall schedule, it was not surprising that in mid-December Lillian collapsed with "the grippe"; she was suffering from a nervous rash as well. Matters were made even worse when her eldest daughter arrived home from college and announced her engagement to a young doctor. Anne was only nineteen. Lillian burst into tears when she heard the news, feeling "that her staunchest supporter would be taken from her." She was so tired and distressed that she stayed in bed for more than two weeks, including Christmas Day, getting up for the first time on December 29. "But flu or no flu, life must go on," she later wrote, "and the Course be started, even if the children did have to push her upstairs and the students pretend that they did not notice what a thin and shaky teacher they had."[19]

The course went well. Lillian lectured most mornings while Joe Piacitelli, whom the Gilbreths had met when he was an office boy at New England Butt, handled the filming. Lillian was never comfortable with the bulky film apparatus; the camera had to be hand cranked, lighting was always a problem, and there was so much equipment that Piacitelli sometimes had to hire two taxicabs to "haul the five or six cases containing arc lamps, the clock and the movie camera about the size of an ordinary suitcase." The class also had field trips to plants such as Tabor Manufacturing and Macy's. The children enjoyed the students more than they had expected and were pleasantly surprised to find them not old and cranky, but in their late twenties and early thirties. Ernestine was particularly impressed by two of the men who were "tall, husky and handsome" and by Jean Lies, who turned out to be "young, blonde, slim and stunning."[20]

Lillian was home for much of the next four months, at least during the weekdays, though she often went into New York for evening meetings and fitted in lectures and technical meetings on Saturdays. She even found time to travel to Providence in March to take part in a Wednesday Club debate, taking the affirmative on the motion "France should repay in full her war loans to the US."[21] Some of the children remember this period fondly; they recall taking tea or playing football with the students and interrupting their mother at regular intervals. They were not supposed to go into her office without knocking and then only if the problem was urgent, but they recalled that their definition of urgent did not always coincide with their mother's. Eventually she set up an "interruptions chart" and would ask the offender to make a check beside his or her name, while Lillian's secretary Miss Butler grinned into her typewriter. "'Thank you, dear,' Mother would say, without a trace of a smile. 'How many is that for you this week?' 'Eight.' 'Goodness, that's nothing like Tom's. He's up to thirty already.'" According to the children, Tom didn't think the chart applied to him, and Lillian was required to leave her work "to be shown a picture Bob had drawn, a mole that Mr. Chairman [the family dog] had dug from the front lawn, or a new trick that Tom had taught the cat."[22]

The carefully planned Gilbreth family system continued, but there was a discrepancy between how Lillian portrayed it for the public and how it worked in practice. Frank Jr. wrote that within months of his father's death, "the process charts in the bathroom and other strict matters of routine were slackened, because Lillie simply couldn't be strict herself and never had believed in regimentation, anyway. Instead there was an informal buddy system, under which each older child was assigned a younger one and made responsible for such things as seeing he did his homework and took his baths."[23]

Lillian was necessarily away from home and the children more than she had been when Frank was alive, so she had to find a satisfactory system of running the house and supervising the children in her absence. Lillian's niece Carol Cross was an enormous help. She had a car and met trains and ferried the children to and from school on rainy days, at least until the rear axle broke. She substituted for Lillian at school plays; Janey once told her kindergarten teacher that her mother couldn't come, but her "'Carol mummy' would." Carol picked up the mail so the secretaries could make an early start, did the shopping, supervised the chores, and sometimes broke up fights. She also helped nurse the children through illnesses; Fred had pneumonia and he, Dan, Jack, Bob, and Jane had whooping cough, which meant continuous bed-changing for five feverish children throughout the night. After Carol Cross returned to Detroit in 1927, Lillian set up a kind of apprenticeship system whereby a stream of young women who either worked for or were trained by her lived in the house and supervised the children while she was away. One such helper was Anne Shaw from Scotland, who was doing graduate work at Bryn Mawr; another was Margaret Hawley, an economics student from California; and a third was Saima Andrews, who came from Finland. After Martha Gilbreth graduated, she ran the household for several years until she married in 1940. She admitted that Lillian was away a great deal, but she said, "Our house runs itself. And I think it does because every member of the family has been trained to help."[24]

Lillian felt slightly guilty about being away so often and tried to be home on Sundays. Even then, however, she worked, as she preferred her children in small doses. She spent one morning, while the children were at Sunday school, dictating a report on Sears, Roebuck, and she "caught up at home" in the afternoon. That involved doing the mending and all the things that she knew parents were supposed to do. "I've bucked Lill up on Latin, talked football togs with Fred and Dan, helped Jack list forty precious stones and read 'THE WIND IN THE WILLOWS' to Jane and Bob," she wrote to Ernestine, adding, "So I have that virtuous feeling that comes too seldom." Lillian also liked to arrange outings. Once, after teaching all morning, "as usual," she took her niece and her two youngest daughters shopping in Newark. "I got them each an ice-cream and we went through all the top departments and the two little girls had a most gorgeous time!" she reported. Lillian particularly enjoyed her youngest daughter's company. She told Ernestine, "Janey is so cute! I suppose it is because I need her so and there is no tiny baby to demand attention that I am enjoying her so much."[25]

Lillian filled all of Frank's speaking engagements that fall, as well as her own. She talked to a wide variety of college audiences, including Purdue University, which had initially asked her to fill in for Frank and which now issued a standing invitation for annual lectures. Other audiences ranged from the National Retail Dry Goods Association to the New York Railway Club. She also kept up her contacts with women's groups, occasionally lecturing to fashionable New York City clubs such as Sorosis and Fortnightly Forum, though she was quick to add that "she had no time for the leisure-time-program as part of her day-by-day schedule." She did some volunteer work and was appointed to the Essex County (N.J.) Vocational Education board. She wrote articles on a wide range of topics, including vocational guidance, fatigue, skill development, and motion study. She even worked with others at the Bedford Hills women's prison, collaborating on a book entitled *Opportunities and Training for Women in Reformatories*, which, she recalled, "was to prove useful."[26]

These talks did not go far in supporting her family, as payment was often limited to traveling expenses. Her longtime secretary, Jane Callaghan, recalled, "Back in 1930 some group in New Jersey tried to beat her down when she asked $100. Of later years she didn't bother to quote. She simply said, 'First class airfare and other travel expenses plus whatever honorarium their budget was prepared to meet.' This ran all the way from nothing for student chapters to $600 for an appearance at a management conference." On the other hand, Lillian often combined lecture engagements with family visits to her parents or children away at college, thus saving considerable travel expenses.[27]

Despite the lack of immediate financial gain, such lectures were nevertheless important to keeping the Gilbreth name and methods in the public eye; they also helped generate new contracts. She varied her approach according to her audience. To engineering or business school groups she spoke about the use of scientific methods in industry, while to women audiences she spoke about the application of scientific management to the home. Increasingly the two approaches combined, such as when she addressed an audience of engineers' wives at an ASME "Ladies Night" on "Elimination of Unnecessary Fatigue in the Household."[28]

Within a few months of Frank's death, Lillian was becoming well known outside technical circles. She occasionally broadcast on the radio, getting her name and her message out to a national audience. According to the *Boston Herald,* "practically the entire United States and places in Canada and England" listened to her broadcast from Ford Hall in February 1925, and "messages were received saying that the speaker's statement came through clearly and distinctly." Lillian claimed that the six-hour day was an entirely realizable goal; if that was what people wanted, "Science can give it." Newspapers published photographs of the family with such headlines as, "Mrs. Frank Gilbreth Had Youngsters Brought Up on Industrial System So That She Might Work."[29]

A few months later, in December 1925, Lillian broadcast from Boston again, with the provocative title "Man's Place Is In the Home." The topic of men's domestic duties was clearly in the air; the same week Mrs. Sherman, the head of the General Federation of Women's Clubs, was quoted in the article "Husband's Turn As Dishwasher: Job Not Effeminate" as asking, "Why should a man have an eight hour day and a woman a fifteen hour day?"[30] Lillian's talk was covered in the local press, the *Boston Sunday Post* going so far as to send a reporter to Montclair to interview Lillian at home. The journalist, Kathleen Halliday, claimed she was nervous about meeting such a paragon and expected Lillian to be irritatingly grim and businesslike. Arriving an hour late for the interview and feeling flustered and inefficient, Halliday was favorably surprised when Lillian opened the door. "I expected Mrs. Gilbreth to be in orthopedic shoes and her family to be in white, because otherwise they might catch up with a microbe or something," but what she saw was "a charming and unaffectedly hospitable" woman, dressed simply "without being severe." Lillian apologized for the children. "This is the hour when we have to expect the children to be noisy and a bit troublesome," she explained, "after the quiet and confinement of school." She managed to stop three-year-old Janey clamoring for a cup of tea by explaining why she could not have one at that hour of the day; the impressed journalist recorded that Jane "subsided very gracefully" when told the reason. Lillian went on to discuss her views on engagements (preferably short), courtship ("ignore the emotional side long enough to decide that you want to live together as comrades all your life"), and the necessity for women to finish their education before they married. The reporter went away deeply impressed. Noting how youthful Lillian seemed, Halliday "was almost tempted to ask Mrs. Gilbreth if she would suggest any methods for other women to keep young looking when they are mothers of girls 20 years of age," but she had second thoughts about such a trivial question. "It was evident," she wrote, "that she has other and more worthwhile things to occupy herself with than worrying about signs of age. One feels that Mrs. Gilbreth would take her white hairs as philo-sophically as she takes the rearing of her family and the problems of man-size engineers and girls who want the seemingly impossible home-children-and-career." Such a story is an excellent example of Lillian's emerging publicity strategy, which was to disarm potentially hostile reporters and put a positive spin on herself and her ideas.[31]

Anne graduated with distinction from the University of Michigan in June 1926; Lillian went to the commencement ceremonies, where she "almost died of joy and pride." A few days later Lillian set off for Europe, taking Carol Cross with her as a reward for running the family and home for the previous two years. Anne was left in charge for the last time: she was due to marry Robert Barney on September 18, 1926, nine days after her twenty-first birth-day. Although, as she confided to a journalist, Lillian felt a little guilty about the children going to Nantucket without her, she believed that they "want to make it as easy for me as they can." She reported that fifteen-year-old Frank Jr. "always asks, 'But mother, won't it be good business for you to go?' And when I tell him that it will, his conclusion is at once, 'Then you must go.'"[32]

During her previous visit to Europe in the weeks after Frank's death in 1924, Lillian had spoken at engineering meetings, but by 1926 her interests and audience had widened. After meeting with medical researchers, indus-trial psychologists, and women engineers in England, she attended a Swiss conference on the use of scientific investigation in industry. Finally, Lillian took a train to Amsterdam where she addressed the International Federation of University Women; her topic was "The Reconciliation of Marriage and Profession." This issue resonated strongly among middle-class and college-educated women and was to dominate her public identity for many years. Claiming with some justification to embody the compatibility of marriage and career, Lillian presented herself as a role model to her female audience as she explained how scientific management techniques could enable the edu-cated woman to pursue a career.[33]

"Here I stand, 'the case!'" Lillian began, telling her audience that women should do what they were best at, whether this was paid work or domestic management, though her preference was that young women do both. Her reasons were both feminist and eugenicist: she noted, "Too often brilliant girls are advised to renounce marriage in favour of a career. People must be told that it is possible to combine both. We want intellectual women as moth-ers for the race, we want them in the home." She admitted that men needed educating to accept professional wives, but she also recognized that some men received good training from their mothers or grandmothers, who "made a boy feel that a 50/50 marriage, giving a fair chance to express the best of both partners, was the thing to look for." This remark was picked up by at least sixty-five American newspapers under titles such as "Man at the Cook Stove" and "Efficiency Expert Says Men Need 'Kitchen Duty' to Fit Them for Wedlock." The educated woman, Lillian continued, could "have it all" if she had the right attitude toward work. She should treat housework as a problem that could be solved scientifically, while seeing the home as more than housework; it should also incorporate "art and beauty and individuality." Unlike radical feminists such as Charlotte Perkins Gilman, who advocated collective living with shared kitchens and child care, Lillian accepted the single-family home but felt it needed "a new philosophy of work." Both family life and work should be organized around the twenty-four-hour day; children should contribute to the "family career" by performing certain chores, while other work could be delegated to "helpers" who should be treated as part of the family rather than simply employees.[34]

Lillian's message was popular throughout the 1920s. Women journalists were eager to emphasize her successful combination of career and motherhood, and she was willing to oblige by showing that traditional female roles were not abandoned. One of her earliest interviewers noted, "Following neither the conservative belief that woman's place is in the home, nor the radical one that 'the era of women's emancipation' has come—she has found a happy medium in the proof that woman can follow a career and yet have time for home duties." Another journalist painted a vivid picture of the career woman as mother. Zoe Beckley quoted Lillian, who had toddlers climbing all over her, as saying, "There's nothing wonderful about it. It's merely eliminating things that don't count and going after essentials. Dan, run, get mother a pair of Bob's rompers—So many women's lives are cluttered with useless doings that bring them nothing in the end." Lillian stressed the long-term satisfactions she gained from her work, claiming that "society women work just as hard as I do, or harder. And what do they get out of it that satisfies or lasts?"[35]

20 Am I a Lady or an Engineer?

Please tell me, am I a lady or an engineer?
Should I join in discussion of the papers—talk
to the wives—or merely charm in silence?

Margaret Partridge to Caroline Haslett (May 28, 1925)

Now that Lillian was a widow it was more important than ever that she should be seen as an engineer rather than a lady. In her efforts at assimilation she wrote optimistically, "It is surprising how few successful men or women in business ever give much thought to the sex of the people for whom or with whom they are working, unless it is especially called to their attention. . . . Successful people are too busy, too concentrated, too anxious to accomplish what they set out to do, to allow of their co-workers being anything but what they are, co-workers toward a desired goal."[1]

Despite her efforts to be gender blind, Lillian suffered from discrimination. In self-defense she used her status as a single mother of a large family to generate interest in women's issues and to publicize her own expertise. Her clever use of gender to market herself and her ability to get on well with many men meant that being female was not always an insurmountable problem in her dealings with the business and engineering community—and in some circles it was an advantage. She had to tread carefully, however, as she was entering a virtual minefield as far as women were concerned: engineering was a very male profession, even more so than science. Of 1,821 women listed in the 1938 edition of *American Men of Science*, only 5 were engineers. In addition to problems of training, there were problems within the work environment. Most professional engineers were also managers and many of those they managed were men. Unless they were connected to engineers by marriage or family, few women engineers could advance beyond a junior level. Even elite women had problems, as the career of Nora Blatch, an exact contemporary of Lillian's, illustrates. Blatch, daughter of the suffragist Harriot Stanton Blatch and granddaughter of Elizabeth Cady Stanton, graduated cum laude in engineering from Cornell and soon after married Lee de Forest, an inventor of radio. He used her family money and connections as well as her expertise to build up his business, then divorced her since she "persisted in following her career as a hydraulic engineer and an agitator [for woman suffrage] after the birth of her child." In 1916 she sued the American Society of Civil Engineers to gain full membership. She lost, but Blatch subsequently set up her own business.[2]

Much has been written about the issue of gender in engineering, but the example of Lillian Gilbreth complicates the issue, partly because her story was told in different ways for different audiences. Her own account of her activities after Frank's death emphasizes the help given by men, both in gaining membership to prestigious engineering societies and in finding new contracts. Her children stress their own contributions to the success of her plans, while feminist scholars emphasize her shift from work that coded male (in industry) to work that was coded female (in kitchens and department stores), as well as the influence of female networks. These three versions are not incompatible, for her children *did* help run the household, and in addition to her "women's" work, Lillian continued with her industrial contracts.[3]

Lillian was as eager to build male networks as she was to build female ones, perhaps especially the former, since men tended to control the budgets of companies that might employ her, though she also did some well-publicized consultancy work for women. She was realistic: she understood that men and women may see things differently, but as she worked mostly with men, she was able to adapt "what one may think may be done to their way of thinking." Most of the time she took a firmly nonessentialist stance, stating in 1928, for example, that "women who would succeed in business must realize that success will come to them not primarily because they are women or because they are not women but because they are trained, adequate, understanding human beings." Lillian's strategy was sensible in the 1920s, a paradoxical period when newly enfranchised women largely abandoned feminism, women's roles were being reexamined, and psychologists were reinventing femininity. Among the middle classes paid work was assumed to be a male prerogative; "real men" supported their wives and children. The opposite side to this assumption was that women who worked were somehow defeminized, or even repulsive. The sociologist Ernest Groves, to give just one example, wrote in 1929 that a woman who was "coarsened or hard-boiled" by business would "repel men," and he was not alone in this opinion.[4]

Lillian wished to present herself as feminine; an interview given while she was sewing her daughter's wedding dress shows the success of her strategy. The interviewer emphasized Lillian's "normality" and "motherliness" as Lillian and a woman friend sat together on a sofa, "in the tender and somewhat sad occupation of ripping up an old wedding dress." Lillian was transforming the voluminous skirt of her high-necked, tight-fitting Edwardian dress into a below-the-knee, waistless 1920s garment for Anne, who was built like the sturdy Bunkers rather than the slender Mollers. The journalist marveled over the old dress: "the countless stitches, the wealth of material and underslips, the exquisite small details." Carefully stored for twenty-two years, the creamy silk had "a lovely golden mellowness that only years can bring." There was a lot of fabric, too ("eight yards of it in the skirt alone"), and it had a "tiny waist, which to the observer seems incapable of ever having fitted a living girl." The journalist continued, "The mother looks up—a slight woman with blue eyes and light hair brushed simply and neatly back from her face. 'I like the sentiment of a girl's wearing her mother's wedding dress,' she says." Despite this archetypically feminine scene, the next paragraph suggests the journalist's ambivalence about women in business and science: "One would scarcely expect to find Mrs. Frank Gilbreth, or Dr. Lillian M. Gilbreth, to give her her official title, president of Gilbreth Inc. and internationally famous domestic engineer, looking so entirely feminine." Yet, so the article implies, a woman can have a career, run a family, *and* retain her femininity.[5]

Lillian's nonthreatening persona combined with her obvious competence helps explain why numerous men were willing to help her professionally. After Frank's death the editor of the *American Machinist* continued a series of articles on the Gilbreth methods exactly as planned. The first article, printed in 1923, had noted that Lillian's "influence on all her husband's work is very apparent," adding that it was probably why the Gilbreths were "successful where Taylor failed, in securing co-operation of the workmen in carrying out plans." One of the 1925 articles went further and demonstrated Lillian's contributions visually. Dressed in a neat print frock with a crisp white collar, Lillian was photographed peering into a stereoscopic device to analyze the elements of micro-motion, thus showing potential clients among the readership of the *American Machinist* that although she was a woman, she was also a scientist fully qualified to carry on the Gilbreth, Inc., consultancy business.[6] The newer disciplines of industrial psychology and vocational guidance were also welcoming. Douglas Laird of Colgate College was a friend and supporter who invited Lillian onto the directorial board of the journal *Industrial Psychology*.

Lillian knew that membership in professional societies was a prerequisite of peer recognition. She particularly wanted to join the ASME, which already had one female member, Lillian's old friend Kate Gleason, who had been elected in 1914. Gleason could be very abrasive and had offended some members, who apparently extended their animosity to other women engineers. Lillian wrote to the Membership Committee in 1925 asking whether they thought she, as a woman, could be elected. Reactions were mixed; one committee member told her that he would probably support her candidacy, while another said that there was "an impression on the part of the Membership Committee that the admission of lady members has not been an entire success and a disposition not to encourage it in the future." Other men were eager to help. Lillian was encouraged to apply by her friend John R. Freeman, a prominent engineer and former Providence neighbor and colleague, who told her she was "tenfold more worthy of membership than many in our list of members." She had friends in key positions in the society; Calvin Rice, its secretary, advised her as to the best way to fill out her application form and encouraged her to emphasize her practical experience, while her old friend Robert Kent, chair of the Professional Divisions Committee, also helped with her application.[7]

While her membership was pending, Lillian spoke at several ASME sessions. In December 1925 she read a paper, "The Present State of Industrial Psychology," noting that engineers and psychologists needed to work together, but tactfully suggesting a supporting role for psychology, because "engineering is a far more advanced science than is psychology. . . . It seems best, in this country at least, for the engineer to continue in charge of the investigations and correlations." The bulk of her presentation was a plea for the inclusion of industrial psychologists in management teams, with details of their three areas of expertise—vocational guidance, training, and securing group cooperation—the three areas in which she specialized.[8] Lillian's bridge-building approach and the careful coaching by her supporters were successful. The ASME admitted her as a member in July 1926, and nearly twenty years later they awarded her, jointly with Frank, one of their highest honors, the Gantt Medal.

Support from powerful men was vital to Lillian; the suggestion by scholars who have studied Lillian's career that her exclusion from male engineering circles led to her concentration on "women's work" needs modification. The real story is more complicated. In the two years following Frank's death, Lillian tried many types of work, hoping that some of them would pay off. She used her gender to advantage when it meant visibility as the only woman, or suggesting that her insight was somehow dependent on her sex, yet performing in other circumstances as a male industrial engineer might.

If Lillian's relationship with men was complex, her relationship with women was even more so. She first became involved in women's professional circles during World War I, when her letters to Frank described numerous contacts with well-connected women, a deliberate strategy on Lillian's part. "I am building up 'after the war' connections to the best of my ability," she told him. Up to this time Lillian had worked almost entirely with men, but her connection with the Boston Women's Educational and Industrial Union (WEIU) marked the beginning of her professional alliances with women's groups. In many ways it was a natural connection, the WEIU having been founded in 1879, the year after Lillian's birth. By the turn of the century, the organization's leadership had learned to "talk like a man" and to work with men, just as Lillian had, rather than settle for the female unity their mothers and aunts had favored. College-educated and progressive, the second generation of WEIU leaders was predisposed to like the ideas of efficiency and professionalism. This was problematic for some women, for it undermined the value placed on what they saw as special feminine qualities of compassion and empathy. However, the women of the WEIU believed that if they wanted to be heard they would have to speak a "masculine" language.[9]

Lillian was not, however, entirely comfortable rejecting femininity. During the war she had invited some members of the WEIU to her home for a "Hoover Lunch" to discuss the investigation one of them was carrying out on women in industry. Her old California acquaintance Herbert Hoover, who had been a Stanford classmate of her cousin, was heading the Food Administration. He had recently spoken at Brown University, and his publicity campaign for "Wheatless Mondays," "Meatless Tuesdays," and "Porkless Thursdays" was encouraging patriotic Americans to contribute to the war effort by reducing domestic consumption and thus feeding the Allies. Lillian's guests went without whatever was appropriate for the day of the week, but she told Frank that she planned to "have it nice, with good china, etc. Men never notice that, but women love it." Unlike the WEIU leaders, many of whom were unmarried or childless, Lillian was trying to straddle two worlds; she was exercising professional expertise while retaining her affection for "women's things" such as fine china and babies.[10]

Lillian's early efforts at cooperation with women's groups were not always successful, as she was impatient with what she perceived as the inefficiencies of many voluntary organizations. After one such experience with the American Collegiate Association she wrote to Frank in exasperation, "The meeting dragged terrible. . . . Or am I just unaccustomed to the way things are done?" With unconscious irony, given the Gilbreths' desire to teach the workers the "One Best Way," she continued, "I tried to not mix in too much for I think most people would rather do things their own way, even if it isn't very good, rather than take points from a stranger." But, she added, emphasizing Frank's unusual supportiveness, "it is hard for me to keep still, since you always let me talk and I have to tell myself all the time that YOU like to have me mix in, to keep out of things."[11]

Despite this shaky start, Lillian impressed women in senior positions. After Ellen Fitz Pendleton, president of Wellesley College, invited her to lunch, she "appointed" Lillian to carry out fatigue tests on women agricultural workers. The college psychologist, a Miss Gamble, was not at all happy about this and called Lillian's work on fatigue "very unacademic"; but the college president had spoken and Miss Gamble had to do as she was told. Lillian's position in relation to other professional women was, however, ambiguous. She was an upper-middle-class mother of a large family earning her living in industry—a largely male environment, at least at the managerial level. Many of her peers were single women working in social welfare, education, or health, professions that were largely staffed by women; upper-middle-class women's association with engineering tended to come through their husbands' work. When Lillian hosted a lunch in her house in September 1924 to honor Lady Parsons, the founder and former president of the (British) Women's Engineering Society, all but one of the other guests were wives of prominent engineers, as indeed was Lady Parsons. Lillian's lunch underlines the significance of the question "Am I a lady or an engineer?" and the continuing importance of her social class position. When Frank was alive she had felt the tension between being a wife and a professional in her own right. After Frank's death she tried to combine her roles as engineer, lady, and mother, basing her authority on the technics of science and the moral authority of widowhood.[12]

It was not always easy. Lillian still suffered from discrimination in an age when many organizations were closed to women, though she did not complain publicly. In her memoirs, the only example of discrimination was, at first glance, minor and possibly unintentional. In 1926 Lillian, another woman, and two men were invited to speak at a "Psychological Dinner." She noted that the chairman "gave both men their titles of 'Doctor' but carefully called Dr. Marston 'Miss' and Dr. Gilbreth 'Mrs.'!" Lillian's recorded reaction was small: fifteen years later she wrote, "The two women exchanged smiles, that even in this advanced group, the men had the preference." Frank Jr. wrote about a more embarrassing example, which occurred in 1927 and which his mother did not mention in her memoirs, though he must have heard the story from her; he perhaps exaggerated, in order to make a point. Lillian, who was giving a keynote address to the American Gas Association in Chicago, accepted a last-minute invitation to speak at a dinner in New York. The guest of honor was to be Baron Shiba, a Japanese nobleman and scientist, who was helping to plan the Tokyo World Engineering Congress scheduled for 1929. Lillian was flattered to be asked, so after delivering her Chicago lecture she took the sleeper to New York, changed into an evening dress on the train, and hailed a taxi to the University Club. It was a wet day; according to Frank Jr., Lillian dashed through the front door to get out of the rain and a uniformed attendant grabbed her by the elbow and said, "No you don't, lady." Although Lillian protested that she was the speaker, the doorman is said to have replied, "At the University Club? If you are, lady, I'm Fanny Brice. This club is for men only." Lillian was not one to make a scene, but rather to prove by sheer competence that such exclusion was outdated. It is not clear whether she gave the speech—the invitation, after all, had been sent to Mr. L. M. Gilbreth—but six months later she received an official invitation to the Tokyo Engineering Congress, where she represented the American Management Association, the Taylor Society, and Rutgers University and took a message from President Herbert Hoover.[13]

Although women of Lillian's generation were brought up not to show their anger, she certainly sometimes felt annoyed; Joseph Juran, a distinguished consultant engineer whose specialty was quality control, recalled an occasion as late as the 1950s when she had to wait for a male escort both into and out of a meeting in the Engineering Club; "she didn't say anything," he remembered, "but I could see she was seething—smoke was coming out!" She never, however, voiced her anger. Unheroic as her reticence might seem, it may have been realistic, given the business and engineering circles in which she moved. Lillian was not the only woman to react this way; a tacit acceptance of sexism was common among her peers. Ellen Swallow Richards, the MIT-trained chemist who applied her expertise to domestic science, explicitly disclaimed feminism. "Perhaps the fact that I am not a Radical or a believer in the all powerful ballot for women to right her wrongs," she wrote, "and that I do not scorn womanly duties, but claim it as a privilege to clean up and sort of supervise the room and sew things, etc., is winning me stronger allies than anything else." Lillian was a generation younger than Richards and did not need to be quite so explicit about her strategy; nevertheless, she, too, believed she won allies by appearing womanly and eschewing confrontation.[14]

This policy was not always successful. In the late 1920s Lillian seriously considered quitting the ASME, notwithstanding the trouble she had had in joining, after she was excluded from a breakfast meeting at the Engineering Club. Her fellow committee members were less than gallant; instead of moving the meeting to a nearby restaurant, they suggested that she "go out and get breakfast and return to meet with the Committee for a few moments in which they would relate for her approval what would be decided over their own ham and eggs." It took several more years and a generational shift for Lillian to be completely welcome in traditional engineering circles. In 1934, when the ASME held its first session on the psychology of management, Lillian was asked to chair a session after breakfasting with the speakers. The invitation added, "We have squared this with the Club and you are expected." When Lillian arrived at the Engineering Club, Clarence Davis, an assistant secretary of the ASME and a member of the younger generation of engineers, "took her hand, tucked it beneath his arm and with the friendliest kind of genuine welcome and acceptance of her in his whole attitude, escorted her through the sanctum where even Frank had never been able to take her." Lillian's patient, nonconfrontational approach eventually achieved results with the assistance of sympathetic men; other, less well connected women had to wait until the 1960s to be admitted to the Engineering Club.[15]

21   Counter Cultures for Women

*The customer must not only like the goods
she has bought, the surroundings in which she has
done the buying and the people from whom she has
done the buying, but she must also like herself
better at the end of the transaction.*

Lillian Gilbreth to the National Retail Dry Goods
Association (1927)

Aᴌᴛʜᴏᴜɢʜ ᴍᴜᴄʜ of Lillian's professional life was
spent with men, some of the women Lillian met were also in a position to give
her work, and some of her most lucrative contracts were with women and for
women. She was hired on the assumption that only another woman would
really understand what women wanted. Her solo career began just as the "culture of consumption" was widening the market for expertise such as hers.
The widespread availability of electricity meant that most urban Americans
wanted to buy new stoves, toasters, and refrigerators. There was a huge new
market for kitchen appliances, just as the feminization of the clerical labor
force created a niche for a woman management expert in planning and organizing "pink-collar" work.

Lillian's connection with Macy's, the New York department store, also
came through a woman. Eugenia Lies, director of Macy's research department, had been the only female student in the first motion study course and
became a family friend as well as a mentor to Ernestine. Lillian's relationship
with Macy's was not financially remunerative; as she delicately put it, she had
"no formal connections as far as pay was concerned," though it was extremely profitable professionally. The directors of the firm seem to have taken
advantage of the clause in Lillian's prospectus that offered "a certain amount
of subsequent teaching, inspection or consultation on the Motion Study
problems of the firm sending the student." Macy's paid their one-thousand-

dollar tuition for Lies, then used Lillian as a "free" adviser who would return to help her former trainee.[1]

Lillian advised Macy's from 1925 to 1928. As one student of her work has suggested, "At a time of intense interest in job testing and analysis, Gilbreth provided Macy's with a very cheap expert on both the physical and mental components of work." It seems likely that Lillian expected payment, but Lies was unable to persuade her superiors. Lillian continued as a "free" consultant, though she may have been paid for some of her later work. Lillian loaned cameras and other motion study equipment to Macy's, reorganized hiring and training procedures, and lectured to executives and managers on how to handle employees. Her main contribution to the firm, however, came in streamlining behind-the-scenes clerical work, applying both scientific management and psychology to routine tasks.[2]

The benefits were not all one-sided, however; Lillian made good friends and excellent contacts and learned a great deal about retailing. Just as at New England Butt, Lillian insisted that her techniques be applied to management as well as the workers, and she tried to persuade both groups that they were partners in an interesting experiment and that the worker's expertise was vital to the success of the enterprise. Her work at Macy's involved all three elements of department store culture: management, employees, and customers. The first part involved helping Jean Lies reorganize the tube rooms, where cashiers made change. The newly expanded Macy's store at Herald Square had eight hundred pneumatic tube lines. Thirty women sat at desks in front of a moving belt, twisted open cylinders containing sales checks and money, made change, and stamped the receipts. The best cashiers could do this two thousand times a day, which is roughly once every thirty seconds, while a relative beginner could process six hundred a day, or one every minute and a half. The tube room was incredibly noisy. Jean Lies wrote that it was "deafening"; even the cheery job description from the personnel department admitted that "at first the noise of the Tube Room may trouble you," adding optimistically, "Soon you will not even notice it." The noise came from the vibrating air drums operating the pneumatic tubes, the motors moving the belts, and the plop of the carriers dropping onto the belts. One of the first improvements Lillian suggested was noise insulation. The drums were covered with felt padding and the walls with a noise-reducing material. She also suggested improvements to the lighting, as she felt that eyestrain was making the cashiers tired and thus inefficient.[3]

The next step was to observe the cashiers and pick the five most accurate workers. Joe Piacitelli filmed them, then Lillian and Jean Lies analyzed the film frame by frame in order to eliminate unnecessary movements. Lillian had already taught Lies about therbligs; the younger woman classified the cashiers' movements and drew up process charts in order to discover which actions were unnecessary. She relocated the tubes, making them easier to reach, and the entrance of the tubes was reshaped so that the change carriers could simply be thrown in. Finally, the basic elements of motion were taught to the cashiers, "who experimented with the changes in the workplace layout and the motions, until finally the result was the 'One Best Way' of cashiering." Jean Lies and Lillian also administered psychological tests to these "best" workers to see what characteristics the hiring office should look out for, and they developed new training methods to teach the temporary staff hired for the Christmas rush. Previously it had taken a trainee four months to reach maximum speed, but now cashiers reached an acceptable level within two days. This obviously reduced the labor costs to Macy's.

Lillian and Jean Lies carried out similar motion studies among the typists in the correspondence department and developed a more efficient system of keeping employee records. Each of these studies helped consolidate managers' control over the workforce as well as reduce costs. Again, Joe Piacitelli got out his movie camera. Like the operatives at New England Butt a dozen years earlier, the typists were fascinated to see themselves on film. As Jean Lies put it, "the use of these motion pictures in making the analysis proved very interesting to the workers," who were more than ready to accept the new methods, as they realized that the changes would offer them "an opportunity to do more work and be paid accordingly." The workers were not, however, expected to show any initiative once the "one best way" was found.[4] The following verse, written by Betty Cohen, a member of the typing pool, suggests that some of the workers were not unhappy with this situation, if only for the pay bonuses involved:

> We started with less movements
> And we won in this campaign
> We got it down to such extent
> That no move was made in vain.
>
> The letters they just seemed to fly
> And the averages sure did soar
> The salaries, they were all quite high
> But yet we tried for more.
>
> This bonus system is just great;
> It makes you really love your work
> And puts such spirit into it
> You'll never again want to shirk.[5]

Lillian was never comfortable with the idea that pay was the only source of satisfaction for workers. She argued that the simpler methods would "free you from making unimportant decisions over and over again and teach you, when the precious time comes that is free to devote to really creative work, how to give most of yourself to it with the greatest effectiveness."[6] While Betty did not necessarily believe any of this, she was happy to receive a weekly bonus of twenty dollars.

Although she was not always successful, Lillian tried very hard to understand the psychology of women workers and the interactions between saleswomen and customers. She did not fully recognize the strength of the "counter culture" of the shop assistants, but she had a good insight into the psychology of the woman shopper and was well aware that the customer was the third element in the department store equation. As a psychologist and as a middle-class woman, albeit one who claimed she had never really learned to like shopping, she was uncomfortable with some managers' assumptions about female irrationality. She urged retailers not to treat the customer as "an 'Unclassified moron'" but as a "thoughtful, reasonable and reasoning person." She understood that shopping involved more than just the satisfaction of material needs and realized that department stores (as well as other retail outlets) provided a form of therapy for their customers, who could construct "a pleasing 'self' by purchasing consumer goods." In a speech entitled "The Psychologist Goes Shopping," Lillian made suggestions for profit maximization while simultaneously giving "full personal and economic satisfaction to the customer." She told a chamber of commerce group, "the customer does not come to a store to get goods alone. If she did, she would order her goods by telephone and never go near the store. She comes to get sociability, maybe to feel important and should be met by sales persons able to make her feel like a guest." This observation speaks to the central dilemma of department store managers: how to run an efficient, profitable business while appealing to and indulging their mainly female clientele.[7]

Lillian realized she needed to know more about working in a department store. She had spent numerous days in plants where she and Frank were planning motion studies, and she understood that if sales clerks were to be managed scientifically, she had to pay even more attention than usual to the "human element." She therefore spent part of the summer of 1925 selling on Macy's shop floor. She was interested in the application of psychology and motion study to retailing and decided "she must know more about customer and sales person's reactions and fatigue." She started work in late June, as soon as she had packed the children off to Nantucket. Percy Straus, vice president of the firm, told Lillian she could sell wherever she liked and had no need to report her findings to him. She later wrote, "It was a fine and courteous gesture and a splendid opportunity!" She spent a day on handkerchiefs and another selling hosiery from a table in the aisle. She also sold hats and shoes.[8]

The children decided in their Family Council that Lillian should not stay alone in Montclair, so seventeen-year-old Ernestine volunteered to keep her company; she did not care for Nantucket as much as her brothers and sisters did. Mother and daughter seem to have enjoyed a relatively carefree month: the house was very quiet and peaceful with the rest of the children away. Tom was in Nantucket, too, and since neither Lillian nor Ernestine was a good cook, they sustained themselves quite cheerfully out of cans. Ernestine took a paid job at Macy's and recalled selling on the bargain table and making all kinds of mistakes, which her mother somehow saw rectified.[9]

Lillian soon discovered that selling was hard work, and neither she nor Ernestine was sorry when they could stop commuting into New York and leave the hot city to join the rest of the family on Nantucket. Unlike her working-class colleagues, Lillian was only a temporary worker and she could escape to the beach; nevertheless, she had some sympathy for their tiredness and tried to distinguish between physical and mental fatigue. Although social class was never absent from her analysis, Lillian's emphasis was on the psychological aspects of fatigue. She was interested in the age and marital status of the saleswomen; as a middle-aged woman herself, she was especially interested in the efficiency of older workers. She wanted to find ways to avoid the "human waste" that resulted from age discrimination.[10]

In a speech later that year Lillian explained that though she had put in eight-hour days in industrial plants, as well as twenty-four-hour days at home, her experience at Macy's was a revelation. "This is what I found," she began.

> It is 4:30 in the afternoon and you look about you and who is sitting down? The older women who need it? Not at all. They are afraid, that if they do, the section manager will think they are getting a little bit old on the job. It is the girls that are sitting down. Turning to one of the older women you say, "Aren't you tired," and she says, "Tired, of course I am not tired." I say, "Oh well, it is not because you and I are perhaps older than some of the people here, but I am just wondering, that at this hour of the day after standing so long, you are not tired." "Tired, why should I be? Look at the customers coming in. This is our chance to work up on the bonus." Turning to one of the girls I asked "Are you tired?" "I am dead to the world." You say "what is the matter, with all these customers coming in?" "Customers, I don't care! It doesn't make any difference to me! My pay is plenty for what I need, I live at home, I am all right."
>
> Five-thirty in the cloakroom: The older women come dragging in. I say "Are you tired?" "Tired as a dog." "What are you going to do tonight?" "Oh, I don't know, I have darning to do, perhaps somebody may drop in." Then

the girls come along and I say "Aren't you tired?" "Tired, I am going to the movies, my best young man is outside and there is a fine dance on! Not tired at all!"[11]

Lillian's observations, however middle class her viewpoint, speak more to the psychology of saleswomen than to their scientific management. She was interested in the characteristics of those workers who became tired. She realized that workers' productivity was influenced by economic issues and that young women who lived at home and gave most of their paychecks to their mothers for their board were less interested in earning extra money than older women with dependents.

Lillian's Macy's experience was important to her. She helped Jean Lies and the favor was reciprocated. Lies became a member of the Gilbreth Motion Study Group and an active member of the Taylor Society. She also introduced her mentor to other retailers, and Lillian became a consultant to the National Retail Dry Goods Association. In 1928 she worked on personnel policies for Sears, Roebuck; in 1929 she did a series of talks on "Selling from the Motion Study Standpoint" for Dennison's, which had stores in New York, Boston, Chicago, and Washington. Also in 1929 she made a survey of the Green Line lunchrooms, a very early fast-food outlet, with a concentration on speeding up selling. She even helped the New York State Committee on the Blind with their merchandising problems, thus extending her interest in "crippled soldiers" to civilian issues.[12]

Lillian was starting to find a niche and by 1926–27 she was involved in two topics of keen interest to women, protective legislation for women workers and sanitary protection during menstruation. The proportion of married women in the labor force was rising rapidly. The 1920 census showed that almost a quarter of working women were married; most of the married women workers (nearly two-thirds) were between ages twenty-five and forty-four, when they might be expected to have children at home. In 1926 Lillian started a long-lasting relationship with the Women's Bureau of the U.S. Department of Labor. Mary Anderson, the bureau's director, was a firm proponent of protective legislation for women. A former factory worker, she believed that the best way to improve *all* workers' conditions was to start by protecting women, limiting the hours they could work, and regulating their working conditions. Legal sanction for protective legislation had followed *Muller v. Oregon,* a 1908 Supreme Court decision in which Louis Brandeis had convinced the Court to uphold a state law setting maximum working hours for women. Other states then passed similar legislation, to the delight of labor leaders and social workers. The issue was a complicated one and its supporters' motives were not always altruistic; male unionists were interested in protecting their own jobs by limiting female competition, as well as by favoring a "family wage" that would enable men to support their families, without women's financial help.

In January 1926 Mary Anderson called a four-day conference on women in industry. Her purpose was to examine the status and problems of women workers. Women from forty-five states attended; they included what the *Christian Science Monitor* dubbed "the soft hands and mellifluous tones of women whose knowledge of machinery is limited to shifting gears on an automobile," as well as labor leaders, businesswomen, and homemakers. More than 150 women's organizations were represented, ranging from the Amalgamated Clothing Workers to the National Women's Temperance Union. The 350 delegates also included several members of the National Woman's Party (NWP) who were campaigning for the Equal Rights Amendment (ERA). They believed that if women were seen as special cases requiring protection there would be no real equality. They wanted the legislation covering hours and working conditions to apply to women and men alike, an aim, given the prevailing attitudes of the courts, that was unlikely to succeed. NWP support came from well-educated career women who would benefit the most from the removal of restrictions on women's work, while most women's organizations, progressive women, and the Women's Bureau vigorously opposed the ERA, fearing that many years of effort would be lost.[13]

Lillian was present when the Women in Industry conference opened on January 18 and witnessed a remarkable confrontation. Mary Anderson had deliberately omitted from the agenda any discussion of protective legislation, but members of the NWP demonstrated noisily in favor of a change to the program, and eventually an extra session was added. The Women's Trade Union League's *Life and Labor Bulletin* printed a vivid—and disapproving—account of the scene. After Gail Laughlin, a lawyer, gained the floor, "other Woman's Party delegates, responding almost like puppets on a string, one after another and four at a time, obeyed the instructions of Mabel Vernon, their appointed floor leader, to 'get up and yell—you've got good lungs.'" While the other delegates hissed and booed and the chairman tried in vain to restore order, "the tumult, senseless, almost insane it seemed, raged for nearly an hour." Eventually, Anita Pollitzer of the NWP went over to the press table, "where, according to one of the reporters, she asked 'Have we done enough to get in the papers? If we have, we'll stop.'"[14]

What Lillian thought about this display of direct action is not recorded, but she became further involved in the debate about protective legislation when Mary Anderson created two groups, an advisory committee, on which all the political interests would be represented, and a technical committee, made up of her supporters, which would investigate the effects of labor legislation on women's work. Members of the advisory committee included three members of the NWP, including Alice Paul; two union representatives; and Maud Wood Park of the League of Women Voters and head of the splendidly named Women's Committee Opposing the So-Called "Equal Rights" Amendment. The technical committee comprised Lillian, Dr. Charles Neill, a former U.S. labor commissioner, and Mary Van Kleeck, the social investigator and reformer, who was committed to protective legislation and strongly opposed to the Equal Rights Amendment.[15]

The two committees had several meetings in early 1926, and the technical committee drew up a research agenda. The NWP representatives on the advisory committee persisted in calling for a public inquiry, while the proponents of protection objected, maintaining that it would subject women employees to intimidation. Matters had reached an impasse by May, when all the pro-protection advisory committee members resigned. Mary Anderson dissolved the committee and authorized the investigation to proceed on the lines recommended by the technical group. Lillian says little about her work for the Women's Bureau, apart from mentioning that she and Mary Van Kleeck were "designated as technical experts, without salary and consulted whenever this was useful." Mary Anderson's correspondence, however, suggests that Lillian was not as enthusiastic about this work as she might have been and that her colleagues were sometimes less than pleased with her. Anderson wrote to Mary Van Kleeck in November 1926, saying, "I feel personally that Mrs. Gilbreth is very much at sea in a technical discussion, particularly on industry. I am just saying this to you, however." The cause of Mary Anderson's irritation was a newspaper report that Lillian was to be a speaker at a conference on careers for women—a topic close to her heart—on the day she had just agreed to attend a Women's Bureau meeting. Mary Van Kleeck was also annoyed and wrote to Lillian, "We had, indeed, set the dates with the understanding you had accepted them. . . . I feel that you are so generous in giving your time to many causes that there is danger of the Women's Bureau not having its fair share. It is because of your generosity that I believe we must stand firmly for our rights. I do hope you can arrange to be present . . . so that we may be prepared to reach certain final decisions."[16]

It is not clear whether Lillian went to the meeting, but given her scheduling ability it is quite likely she was able to be in two Washington locations on the same day. Her name did appear on the bureau's report, which was published in 1928 as *The Effects of Labor Legislation on the Employment of Women*. The report found no harmful effects of protective legislation, but as the labor historian Alice Kessler-Harris suggests, "Politics masqueraded behind a facade of statistical data," and the Women's Bureau proved what it wanted to prove. Lillian's views on protective legislation have to be inferred from her very appointment by Mary Anderson. Like many of the women's organizations with which she was connected, however, Lillian's attitude to equal rights shifted over time. By the mid-1930s she was explicit in her support. In 1935 she told a journalist, "Sex divisions are idiotic anyway. The real cleavage is between workers and drones. We are judged as individuals if we prove we have something to contribute, rather than as men or women." The NWP journal *Equal Rights,* while noting that Lillian was not a member of the Women's Party, commented approvingly, "Dr. Gilbreth is obviously a Feminist."[17]

By 1926 Lillian's life, her family system, and her finances were in reasonable order. Her second and third motion study courses had attracted good students. Ernestine was doing well at Smith, where she was on a scholarship, and Martha was taking a postgraduate course at Montclair High. Anne had announced her engagement officially and made Phi Beta Kappa at much the same time; Lillian was delighted by the latter fact, though she remembered her own experiences with the honor society with mixed emotions. Anne sent her mother a telegram on hearing the news, and Carol Cross took it with her when she went to pick Lillian up at the station. A "tired and hungry" Lillian saw the telegram and heard Carol begin, "I have news for you . . ." and promptly sat down in the gutter and burst into tears; she was still nervous about "calamities that might come suddenly." Four-year-old Janey was alarmed and said indignantly, "What has Andie done to Mother? I am never going to do anything bad to her like that!"[18]

Lillian was by now marketing herself as a female expert, under which guise she carried out a pioneering study of the links between menstruation and fatigue for Johnson & Johnson. The sanitary napkin industry was in its infancy, as was market research, but as more women entered the labor force the need for a discreet, disposable product grew. Although several brands were available, most were highly unsatisfactory and many women continued to make (and wash) their own pads. The real breakthrough had occurred relatively recently, as a by-product of the carnage of World War I. After the Armistice, the paper manufacturer Kimberly-Clark found itself with a surplus of cellulose wadding intended for use as bandages. Learning that army nurses, who had no time to be "indisposed," had used the wadding to make themselves sanitary pads, the firm decided to sell this leftover stock to American women and call it Kotex. It was an enormous success. Johnson & Johnson had been producing a pad they called Lister's since 1890, but they had recently developed a new product, Modess, to compete with Kotex. Robert Wood Johnson, vice president of the company, asked Lillian to carry out a market research study. She insisted on adding a study of menstruation "with a hope of making a contribution to the health problem." Her motive was not purely scientific; as she noted in her conclusion, "It is easiest to arouse interest in a sanitary napkin when presenting it as a factor in a health campaign." The survey reveals a great deal about mid-1920s attitudes toward menstruation, as well as Lillian's own views. She clearly felt that no healthy woman should feel inconvenienced. She started with the assumption that everything currently on the market was inadequate, asked women about their needs and preferences, and then designed the "one best" sanitary napkin. Johnson & Johnson would then produce the nearest they could to this ideal for the price women were willing to pay. Kotex cost ten cents for each pad, a considerable sum in 1926.[19]

Lillian tried to find out what the consumer wanted, but sanitary protection was an embarrassing subject and very few women were willing to talk about it. She decided to target college students, surmising that they were trendsetters and trusting they might be more open. Lillian also wanted to involve health and hygiene experts and organizations involved with women workers and generated a long list of potential informants, ranging from the Women's Bureau through the American Federation of Labor to gynecologists, prison workers, and laundries.

Lillian had two assistants, Dorothy Miller, a college graduate with ten years' research experience, and Libby "Pos" Sanders, the neighbor who had accompanied Lillian to Europe in 1924, "who reflects the attitude of the undergraduate." She selected these younger women "in order to secure a divergent method of attack on the problem and widely distributed contacts." Lillian then devised a one-page questionnaire, which she sent to colleges, schools, and workplaces. Despite the potential for embarrassment, Lillian got a 54 percent return rate, which is remarkably good for a postal questionnaire. Lillian's high-level contacts did not always work, however. One of them was Ada Comstock, the president of Radcliffe, who had been a dean at Smith while Anne Gilbreth was there; despite Dr. Comstock's endorsement, Radcliffe's hygiene department was "too busy" to distribute the questionnaire. Lillian was equally frustrated at Vassar. She spoke to her friend Annie McLeod, head of the Department of Euthenics, who introduced her to the director of hygiene, "an older woman who finds such things as questionnaires burdensome." No questionnaires were distributed. Lillian had better luck at Smith, where Ernestine was a sophomore, and at the New Jersey College for Women, where Martha intended to start in the fall. She also used Carol Cross's contacts to advantage; two of Carol's former classmates at the Boston School of Physical Education were willing to cooperate. One of them worked at International House in New York and one in a Detroit public school, where she was head of physical education; she reported that because of opposition by parents and school boards, "The girls in Detroit have no sex education although the boys have." The girls received "no lecture on menstruation" but were advised not to do "violent exercises" during the first two days of their period and were "not allowed" to take part in athletic contests at those times. Completed questionnaires from those four sources made up a major part of the report.[20]

Lillian also interviewed or wrote to more than forty people, asking them their views on menstruation as a health problem. Most were adamant that the majority of women and girls suffered little or no discomfort and that they should continue with their normal routine. An unusual opinion came from Lillian's aunt, Lillian Powers, who explained "in typical Freudian vein" the solution for problem periods: "the remedy apparently being analysis and then education." Lillian continued, somewhat skeptically and without explaining what she meant, "She says that the psychiatrist finds the typical attitude of passivism indicative," adding, without comment, "As for a napkin,— she recommends a sausage-shaped German product filled with sawdust." Lillian was no Freudian and had not yet forgiven her Aunt Lillian's efforts to psychoanalyze her after Frank's death; she was "indignant at such an infringement of her privacy."[21]

Other correspondents included Lillian's former colleague on the Women's Bureau, Sara Conboy of the United Textile Workers, who said that her "girls" were very reticent about menstruation "and it is very, very difficult to get them to speak of it." Miss Rayne of the New York Bureau of Social Hygiene was interested "but up to the present they had dealt with general public hygiene problems only and . . . the work was all in charge of men," not a promising scenario. Lillian even wrote to the psychologist Elton Mayo, who believed that if women were fatigued during menstruation it was probably due to malnutrition.[22]

The final part of Lillian's report summarized the available literature on menstruation. She dismissed most of the volumes as "too old to be of much value," though she did praise Mary Putnam Jacobi's essay "The Question of Rest for Women," which had won the Boylston Prize at Harvard in 1876. Not surprisingly, in light of the "progressive" authorities she had consulted, Lillian concluded, "The normal woman can safely pursue her usual program and profit by so doing." She tied these findings in with Johnson & Johnson's marketing strategy when she said that "knowledge that the foremost health experts agree that a normal woman need make no change in her usual program . . . should increase the demand for a small inexpensive napkin which can be changed frequently." She suggested that a health campaign be conducted by a group other than Johnson & Johnson, who might be accused of commercial bias, to persuade women of this fact. She also noted that more research might be necessary and if so, "any further research should be made by people who have established contacts already,"—in other words, Gilbreth, Inc. She advised them to keep the name Modess—alternatives such as "Flush Down" were unappealing (and inaccurate—many of the interviewees' stories concerned the embarrassment caused by clogged plumbing), and "Lister's" sounded too clinical. Finally, she advocated that Johnson & Johnson appoint a woman to their staff and submit all products to women testers: "No laboratory devices for testing can take the place of actual wear."[23]

Johnson & Johnson incorporated many of her ideas, and before long Modess outsold every product other than Kotex. The firm used Lillian's gender in their marketing; a 1927 advertisement read, "Women designed Modess. Johnson & Johnson made it." This was, however, Lillian's first and last venture into market research. Although her contract was successful and profitable, she was never happy about commercial endorsements, and redesigning sanitary napkins must have seemed a long way from realizing Frank's dream of the "One Best Way."[24]

22 The Home-maker and Her Job

There was increasing interest also in the application of Motion Study in the household. This was encouraging, as that had always been a subject of tremendous interest to Frank.

Lillian Moller Gilbreth, *As I Remember* (1998)

BY 1926 IT WAS CLEAR to Lillian that she could have it all ways if she presented herself as an expert on women's work, so she straddled the femininity/engineering debate by developing an expertise in household management. She decided that her principal selling point, the way she could differentiate herself from all the other experts on the market, was her concentration on the minimization of fatigue and the application of psychology. She had important credentials in both areas, and her ability to combine a career with a large family was an excellent way of personalizing efficiency. On the boat back from her 1926 European trip she wrote the first draft of *The Home-maker and Her Job,* one of her "steamer books." Although she suspected that "Frank would have called it 'gabby' like *Fatigue Study,*" she felt "that it made easy reading of the material for the non-technical reader." What made *The Home-maker and Her Job* different from the works of her household efficiency contemporaries, such as Christine Frederick and Martha and Robert Bruère, was the public knowledge of Lillian's situation as a career woman and single parent.[1]

The book became part of the career versus marriage debate. Without explicitly endorsing one or the other, Lillian suggested that the middle-class woman should employ efficient housekeeping techniques so that she would be "the master" of right habits rather than "the slave" of wrong ones. Good habits would relieve her of the "unimportant routine things of everyday life" and leave her free for "the things worth consideration." What these "things" were Lillian left up to the individual woman, but she believed that a scientifically managed household resulted in the utilitarian promise of the greatest good to the greatest number. She wrote, "Efficiency is doing the thing in the best way to get the best results. And these, we must never forget, are the largest number of happiness minutes to the largest number of people."[2]

Lillian had been interested in domestic efficiency since at least 1912, when Frank presented "Scientific Management in the Household" at a home economics conference. Similar in tone to her recently completed Berkeley Ph.D. dissertation, it applied classic Taylor principles to the home and suggested ways of assigning household tasks and designing a scientific study of housework. The Gilbreths published a similar article in *Scientific American,* explaining that finding the "One Best Way" would permit housework to "become the skilled work that it deserves to be—a science and an art."[3]

The idea of a scientific kitchen was not, however, unique to Frank and Lillian. The same year Martha and Robert Bruère published *Increasing Home Efficiency,* which echoed Taylorite ideas to the extent of accusing the middle-class mother of "soldiering on the job." Like so many other experts of the Progressive Era and since, the Bruères believed that things were changing so fast that the traditional mother-daughter apprenticeship would no longer suffice; instead, the new homemaker needed "expert" advice. Frank was, however, the first of Taylor's inner circle to show an interest in providing such expertise for kitchens.[4]

Lillian had shown an occasional interest in applying motion study to the kitchen while Frank was alive. In 1917 she suggested painting grids on the kitchen work surfaces, as they had on the desks at New England Butt, and in 1922 she outlined a plan for "Efficiency in the Home," explaining the need for a survey and fitting the available jobs to the skills and age of the family members. Meanwhile, the journalist Christine Frederick emerged as the best-known exponent of kitchen efficiency. She was neither a home economist nor an engineer, though she had taken some courses in applied psychology from Walter Dill Scott at Northwestern University. She was, however, caught up in the Taylorism craze and popularized its application to the home through her job as household editor of the *Ladies' Home Journal* and her book *The New Housekeeping: Efficiency Studies in Home Management,* published in 1913. Lillian knew all about Frederick's work; indeed, she had written the foreword to her second book, *Household Engineering,* while Frank was in the army. Signing it "Frank B. Gilbreth, Consulting Engineer," Lillian emphasized the psychological benefits of household efficiency with a nod to equality in household responsibilities, saying, "Mrs. Frederick has rendered a real service to this country, in that she has eliminated from housework that monotony that comes from doing uninteresting and repetitive work without an incentive and in that she has seen the necessity for making the home a laboratory—a training school for the women and children in it and perhaps an example to the men." Lillian's heavily annotated copy of Christine Frederick's *The New Housekeeping* is in the Gilbreth Library at Purdue. Although Lillian approved of her description of motion study, her efforts to rearrange kitchen space, and her advocacy of better lighting and ventilation, she disapproved of Frederick's vagueness as to methods and her assumption that the housewife's labor was free. When Frederick claimed that heat was the most expensive item in cooking, Lillian wrote in the margin, "No—labor." She also believed that the other experts had missed a crucial element; by dwelling on efficiency they had failed to examine the psychological and physical pleasure that efficient work might bring.[5]

Lillian's aim in *The Home-maker and Her Job* was twofold. She wanted to professionalize housework and make the homemaker an executive engineer; she also wanted to democratize the household and teach children cooperation and citizenship. She cautioned women "that one must live more and not less with one's children," wanting them to find a parental middle way, neither too repressive nor too undisciplined. "We feel we are mid-Victorian if we impose the slightest restrictions of any kind or we swing to the opposite extreme and cut out too much freedom and turn them into little automatons or replicas of every other child on the block." Certainly, the Gilbreth children never became little automatons. Lillian tried to persuade the homemaker that an efficient home was vital to the community and that she was contributing to society by teaching her children good working habits by giving them meaningful tasks.[6]

Lillian was a firm advocate of delegating routine work to lower-paid workers, just as she and Frank had done with their bricklayers' tenders, their machinists' helpers at New England Butt, and even their children, as she explained in a rather chilling speech to a group of businesswomen:

> We considered our time too valuable to be devoted to actual labor in the home. We were executives. So we worked out a plan for the running of our house, adopting charts and a maintenance and follow-up system as is used in factories. When one of the children took a bath or brushed his teeth he made a cross on a chart. Household tasks were divided between the children. We had three rows of hooks, one marked "Jobs to be done," one marked "Jobs being done" and a third marked "Jobs completed" with tags which were moved from hook to hook to indicate the progress of the task. These are just examples of the kind of systematization we used in our household and the result was that I was able to bring up a family of 11 children and give plenty of time to my business besides.[7]

Lillian tried to apply industrial practices to the home, describing the standard tools of motion study analysis, including a functional chart "to make the housekeeper realize her affiliation with those in industry," as well as a domestic adaptation of the complex movement models derived from filming workers. She suggested supplying a child with a ball of string and a handful of pins and telling him or her to unroll the string while following mother as she clears the table and gets the dishes ready for stacking. "A sketch of the dining room and pantry is then made and her path traced by the string, pins being inserted, as suggested, at the turns." Lillian added, a shade defensively, "No one who has not made such a pin plan can know how interesting the process is." She explained that the purpose of such analysis in industry was to find the "One Best Way" and when that was derived, an instruction sheet was prepared and pinned up at the workplace. She admitted that this might sound a little "ridiculous" at home, but she justified it by saying that it minimizes children's questioning, especially if the "why" of the procedure is included on the sheet. She was not as wedded to the "One Best Way" as Frank had been; as a psychologist she was aware that "some natures" found being told exactly what to do unpleasant and restrictive; in such cases it "should never be forced if it offends an aesthetic taste or a feeling of individuality." She added that in some areas standardization might be inoffensive: "kitchen utensils, dishes, buttons for underwear, notepaper, soap, dozens of such articles can be standardized without any danger of seriously offending individual taste."[8]

Lillian was not always consistent in her advice, as she also tried to desystematize the home, arguing that schedules were there to be ignored. "Break the schedule and do the thing when it seems attractive to do it," she declared. "Or let someone else break it, just for the fun of the breaking, now and then." She also argued against rigidity in the use of space: "The way we have always done things is probably wrong." She criticized those who slept only in beds or who believed that beds had to be upstairs, and those who ate only in dining rooms instead of "on porches or out under the trees or off on motor trips."[9]

Lillian was careful not to align herself with any particular school of psychology. She told her readers that they need not accept everything psychologists said: "After all one individual is the subject of all the studies no matter what the training or the viewpoint of the students." Lillian's recommendations are usually well laced with anecdotes about her family. She demonstrated the principle of skill transference with a delightful description of teaching Janey to bathe herself. A child's first independent bath should, Lillian wrote, be "a real occasion." The child should be given "her own small cake of guest soap and her own small bath towel and the whole family should be impressed with the importance of the event and take an interest in its progress." The child cannot and should not be simply told what to do and left to do it. "She must be watched, not only through the first successful performance, but until the habit with all its motions exactly right has been well established." Lillian was well aware of individual differences, whether they were based on character or gender. She remarked, "Small girls are usually docile and satisfactory pupils but there is something about a small boy that makes the teaching process doubly interesting." She added ruefully, "As every mother knows, there is only one problem more difficult than getting a small boy into the tub and that is getting him out."[10]

Lillian constantly emphasized the importance of relaxation and play. One family anecdote leaves the reader a little breathless, but it nevertheless illustrates the kind of strenuous family life that she advocated and all the different elements that made up relaxation. Lillian explained their evening routine when Frank was alive. Dinner was often interrupted by "animated discussions" that were settled by consulting dictionaries and encyclopedias, which were kept in the dining room for just such an eventuality. Then there was dancing until the children were "exhausted enough to attack the more quiet job of dishwashing." This was followed by "a boxing match in the big old hall, cooling off at an astronomy lesson on the porch, then returning to the dining room for study with perhaps another dance to finish up the evening." More restful is Lillian's advice to the homemaker to take regular naps. "This requires a couch with a dark cover placed where it is easy to reach from the work place—and with a favorite magazine tucked under the flat pillow. Woe to him who takes Mother's book!"[11]

Lillian believed that "home-making is housekeeping plus." She defines the "plus" as "the art, the individual variation, the creative work," while "the housekeeping is the science, the universal likenesses, the necessary activities that must be carried out in order that we may have more time and energy for the rest." She offered her readers "a philosophy that will make her work satisfying, a technic that will make it easy and a method of approach that will make it interesting." The industrialization of the home had, unfortunately, precisely the opposite effect; while new technologies reduced dirt and made some tasks easier, in the absence of servants the housewife had to operate the machines herself. Encouraging higher standards of hygiene, housekeeping, and child care meant, in effect, "more work for mother."[12]

Lillian was *not* in favor of more work for mother; on the contrary, she advocated delegation and wanted to build in free time for the housewife. She warned women not to be too tidy and house-proud, since the space belonged to the whole family. "After all, a man's pipe on the living room table, the boat that Johnny made in his manual training class proudly displayed on the bookcase and the small girl's clay model over the fireplace in the living room mean to a discriminating visitor not a careless housewife, but a home-maker who makes her home the possession of the entire family." She argued that by involving the family in household decisions, "if Father helps select the material for the new pillows, if Johnny finds the best china is being used for his birthday party and Mary takes over the arrangement of the flowers for a while," they were far more likely to notice and appreciate what the homemaker did. Lillian assured her readers that "the best engineering mind in the family . . . need not be lodged in a masculine body." She also suggested that the process of studying the tasks done in the home would make men more aware of the work involved in running a household: "For the first time, perhaps, every member of the household will realize it *is* a problem and *his* problem as well as the home-maker's."[13]

Lillian presented herself as a prime example of household efficiency without domestic perfection, arguing that time could be better spent on things other than ironing shirts. If scruffy little brothers made her daughters embarrassed, she wrote, then the causes of discomfort must be investigated, attitudes adjusted, and all would be well (and efficient). It seems that "in a certain household" the older sisters were troubled by the appearance of their brothers' shirts. Lillian continued: "Mother started to investigate! Did her boys have a sense of inferiority? On the contrary, they reveled in the fact that no one warned them to keep their shirts clean. Were the teachers impressed by the hand-ironed products? No, for different as the shirts looked after they left the homes, all looked about alike after the three or four blocks' walk, varied by wrestling, marbles, tops or other contests. Mother trailed the gang to school and proved this!" She concluded that the problem was psychological— "the feelings of the older sisters—and these adjusted themselves to a satisfaction in the status quo, when it was once thoroughly understood!"[14]

Ernestine, one of the older sisters concerned, told this story rather differently. She described Lillian sitting in her room surrounded by a huge pile of linen waiting to be mended. She recalled marching in and saying, "The boys' shirts, Mother, they're so rumpled it's a disgrace. We're embarrassed that Tom does such a grade B. job." Ernestine portrayed a much more irritable Lillian than appears elsewhere: "She began to jerk her needle back and forth. 'When I think of the time I waste doing this every week, I could have a cat-fit. I wouldn't mind if it were necessary, or if I could get the mending done before one of the children comes shouting for it. But it's a never-ending, hopeless job. Nothing in the world exhausts me as much as sewing a squirming boy together while the rest of you threaten to go off without him.'" At this point, Ernestine describes herself as "round-eyed"—amazed that her mother had any problems or difficulties of her own. However, Lillian promised to look into the issue of the crumpled shirts and report back to her. It was this investigation that Lillian described in her book, the solution being to abandon the ironing altogether.[15]

Lillian believed in making housework a group responsibility and thus more enjoyable. She used dishwashing as an example, noting that everyone in her family disliked washing dishes and that each child gave a different excuse to escape the chore. The job was disliked, she eventually decided, because the family rotation system meant it was left to one person at a time. That discovery led to a collective solution: "The whole group was assigned to the job and the work was socialized." After dinner "everyone clears off and stacks, meanwhile talking over the news of the day. It is amusing to see that putting away the food and emptying the refuse are still rated the most distasteful phases of the work, because they are isolated." Lillian recognized that machines would soon take over many routine household tasks, but if dishwashing were mechanized, "some other group activity must be supplied," she said. "We can't afford to lose opportunities to work as well as play together." Carol Cross painted a less rosy picture of cooperative dishwashing. One day when Lillian was out of town, "the fight of all fights" broke out. Frank Jr. was supposed to wash the dishes and Bill was supposed to clear the table. Bill delayed starting, so Frank hit him, "and the battle was on." Bill found an "oversized" grapefruit and "quietly opening the door to the pantry where the dishes were being washed—heaved it—hitting Frank on the back of the neck—knocking him out and causing him to fall head-first into the dishwater—where I found him and pulled him out." Bill ran away and locked himself in the boys' bathroom, where he stayed for the rest of the evening.[16]

Fights notwithstanding, Lillian believed that parents underestimated the ability of children to take responsibility. Children should be trained to take over when necessary. Perhaps reflecting on the summer when Frank died, she wrote, "No household is efficient which cannot run smoothly even though several members who are ranked as heads are removed permanently or temporarily. It is only when we see a fourteen year old or a twelve year old handle things in an emergency that we realize how little we really use the capabilities around us." She also saw the home as an economic unit and each family member as both a contributor of money or services to the home and a consumer of the benefits of the home. Even the baby contributed, giving "everyone a chance to wait on her and admire her."[17]

Lillian thought technology should be used if it made life simpler. She felt that it was unfortunate that "many women seem forced by conditions beyond their control to cook, sew and wash in their home," but that they should investigate "electricity, automobile service, parcel post and rural free delivery," which were "increasingly available" to eliminate other jobs. She also believed that equipment should be placed where it was most convenient, though with her belief in individual differences and preferences she did not specify a list of "efficient" appliances. Like other American domestic writers, she blamed male architects for faulty design, echoing many irritated housewives when she told an interviewer, "When you go into your man-designed kitchen in the dark and fan the air wildly as you hunt vainly for the chain to pull the electric light on, only to have it eventually hit you in the face, you have a simple enough problem in the elimination of unnecessary fatigue in the household. Get rid of the waste motion by having a push button at a convenient place in the wall." She also noted that "if those who supply the soap, the water, the sinks, the dishes etc." actually washed some dishes, "we would have much better equipment in a short time."[18]

Lillian shared with contemporary radical feminists a desire to delegate some housework, though her solution was commercial rather than collective. She accepted the single-family home with a full range of appliances but drew the line at washing machines. She believed that laundries were more economical than home washing, though given her reservations about Tom Grieves's skills in the laundry department, this may have been a very personal preference. She told of an experiment wherein "a New Jersey family" used parcel post to send its flatwork to a laundry in Massachusetts. The family was, of course, the Gilbreths, who installed a scientific management scheme at the Winchester laundries in the early 1920s. They had to buy extra sheets, but Lillian claimed that great savings in time and effort resulted, since "not only the laundering but the repairing was eliminated from the home work budget, the time of a valuable utility worker was freed for other work, the laundry looked better . . . and there was no more wear and tear and no increased cost."[19]

Scientific management was not the only element in the emergence of the modern kitchen. The rise of the consumer economy, the expansion of the suburban middle class, and the contraction in the supply of servants, together with the increased availability of gas and electricity, led to a market for new appliances. Lillian was interested in the housewife as consumer, but as she had in her recommendations to department store managers, she treated the female consumer as a rational being, rather than as a subject to be manipulated by the inculcation of guilt. Lillian's interventions into domestic consumption were aimed at minimizing routine household activities rather than encouraging a desire to spend. As she told an interviewer in 1926,

> Whether we like it or not, the machine age is upon us and it is a distinct advantage for the woman who wants to save time for other things outside her home. Don't insist upon buying and darning expensive stockings. Buy them cheap and give them away when they require darning. Hand-smocked dresses

for the children are charming, but simple bought frocks are quite as effective. It seems to me that to bake bread and do the laundry at home these days smacks not a little of medievalism.

Lillian was, however, pragmatic about the value of hand work, "If grandmother's pie or mother's bread or sister's fudge have a special meaning they must stay." She equated housework with service, giving as examples ironing a shirt and doing a college-age son's laundry. "But make sure," she warned, "that your husband would not rather have you spend the shirt-ironing time with him and that Bobby would not prefer a daily letter."[20]

Lillian's gender politics were ambiguous. She sometimes emphasized traditional divisions of labor: "Father turns in money, the boys cut the lawn, the girls wait on table," but she also told women not to ignore their own needs. "If the children have seen the Saturday matinee," she wrote, "and Dad is tired from his afternoon at golf and prefers to read a book, it is natural for her to stay in when she should get out, even though she has been at home all day and knows that restful sleep is impossible without a breath of air, a walk and a change of thought." Lillian's solution is to let the family "have the pleasure of reconstructing their own programs to give her the things she needs," concluding that "it is really selfish to be too unselfish in the matter of giving up to others." Her example is relentlessly middle class but was nevertheless designed to tell her readers that their desire for personal fulfillment was legitimate.[21]

In *The Home-maker and Her Job* Lillian attempted to defeminize housework; tasks should be performed by the person best suited for the job, be it man, woman, or child. She backpedaled a little on the fifty-fifty marriage idea that had led to such an outcry after her Amsterdam speech, claiming that she "made no appeal for 'kitchen husbands' or 'kitchen sons'" unless the breadwinner was a woman, in which case she "should not be expected, except in an emergency, to be a member of the working force within the home." Lillian did not recant entirely, however; she recognized that some men liked to cook: "Camp cooking is a joy to many men and cooking a chafing dish supper on a Sunday evening, a pleasure to many a boy." She added, "Each of us doubtless knows several men who spend the happiest hour of the day in the kitchen concocting wonderful surprises for an admiring family." If that was the case, they should be encouraged to do so, without fear of "losing caste or authority." She pointed out to an interviewer that "many husbands, it happens, have a furtive love of cooking or some other domestic streak that a tactful wife can cultivate to her great advantage. The wife who laughs at her husband's waffles is frightening off what might have become a valuable and interested assistant."[22]

Lillian ended *The Home-maker and Her Job* as she started it, with a family anecdote designed to show that her methods encouraged the children to become thoroughly involved in family life. "A certain small boy" (actually Dan, then eight years old) wanted to hear a talk on eliminating waste that she was giving to the junior high division of his school. He asked the principal if he might attend and the latter agreed, saying, "Any boy who has heard his mother talk for eight years and still wants to hear her talk, may!" Lillian must have mentioned Commerce Secretary Herbert Hoover's efforts to limit waste in industry. A few days later, when she returned from a trip, she was met by Dan, who informed her "in high glee" that he had awakened at three o'clock and gone into the bathroom for a drink; discovering that the hot tap had been left on and the tub was full, "I went back to my room and got my pillow and beat Jackie over the head and woke him up and we went in and took a bath!" Lillian asked him, "But didn't you take one last night?" to which Dan answered, "Of course we did. We don't always if you're home—just to see you get mad. But we always do if you're away. Look at the chart if you don't believe me." After Lillian wondered why in the world he took another bath at 3:00 A.M., Dan proudly replied, "Use the water, Hoover!" Lillian concluded, "To share the problems and joys of home-making with every member of the family! To let them be part not only of the results but the process! To make it interesting! That's our job!" Despite the abundance of exclamation marks, it is a laudable aim.[23]

23 The Kitchen and the Office

MY ALL-ELECTRIC KITCHEN
With power at my finger tips
I work whene'er I please
With shortest motions, space and time,
Efficiency and Ease.

Lillian Moller Gilbreth, "My All-Electric Kitchen" (1930)

LILLIAN'S REINVENTION of herself as a homemaking expert was marked by a conference she organized and directed at Teachers College, Columbia University, in the spring of 1927. Working with Professor Emma Gunther, she persuaded experts from the fields of industrial engineering, psychology, and sociology to address the approximately two hundred students, faculty, and wives who attended the lectures. Many of the speakers were her former students, either from the Providence summer schools or from her motion study courses. Some were experts in other fields, such as the psychologist Elton Mayo, already well known for his work at General Electric's Hawthorne plant, and Helen Lynd of Sarah Lawrence College, soon to be famous as coauthor with her husband of the study of small-town America, *Middletown*.[1]

This conference at Teachers College was the first concerted, organized effort to explain scientific management to home economists. In sixteen three-hour sessions spread over eight weeks, the lecturers addressed the application of scientific management techniques and psychological methods to the home. The home economists in the audience were impressed; articles in the *Journal of Home Economics* over the next few years stressed motion study, standardization, and home experimentation. They were equally impressed by the inclusion of psychology and were pleased to note that "in no way was the emphasis put on the mechanical so-called efficiency methods alone. . . . The personnel work and all the aspects of better relationships among workers is of course the accepted interpretation today rather than the mechanizing of an office or a home."[2]

Lillian wanted to emphasize that efficiency should never get in the way of family relationships. She lectured on interruptions, using family anecdotes to get her point across. Having got up early to write an important letter, she was constantly interrupted by one of her daughters. Twelve-year-old Lill had an important day ahead—she was chairman of the committee for the class candy sale and needed her mother's advice on what to wear. Lillian recalled thinking that she had been trying to teach this child to make up her own mind for twelve years and then "suddenly remembered that this was a very important event in this young person's life," so Lillian advised her to wear a middy blouse. The interruptions went on as Lill prepared her lunch, hunted for the paper to wrap it in, and tried to wake her brothers. Lillian attempted in vain to write her letter. She told the assembled teachers that it is not always possible to be efficient at home. "What can you do when somebody needs you?" she asked. "If we analyze our interruptions of the day we will find that an awful lot of them are not really legitimate excuses for leaving something that we have decided to do. And on the other hand," she concluded, "others stand for something that we would not give up for the world."[3]

Lillian put on this conference without receiving any fees; nevertheless, she was pleased with the outcome, concluding that it was "highly satisfactory."[4] As part of a strategy for converting her expertise into a usable form it certainly was, though her path to celebrated kitchen designer was not straightforward. Her most lucrative contracts were still at least two years in the future.

In the meantime, Lillian was increasingly involved in international management circles, though her European audiences were far more critical of scientific management ideas than were groups she encountered in the United States. In the summer of 1927, after packing the children off to Nantucket, she again sailed for Europe. Over the next five weeks she attended four conferences in three countries and visited plants in Italy and Switzerland and department stores in France and Belgium. In Italy she chaired a summer school dealing with personnel issues, then she visited factories and colleges. Although she made no reference to political conditions under Mussolini, she was clearly impressed by the efficiency she saw in plants in Milan and the interest in welfare and training she saw in two colleges in the city. The fifty or so participants in the summer school impressed her less. They included engineers and economists, physiologists and psychologists, factory managers, foremen and workers, factory inspectors, and welfare workers. They were, however, "not easy to confine to formal procedure," as she wrote with impressive understatement, "seeming at times rather to resent necessary routine and time schedules." Lecturers (one of whom was Joe Piacitelli) covered the history and application of fatigue study, the causes of fatigue, and the effects of temperament. Lillian was surprised by the critical response of some of the audience, writing that the speakers "were submitted to perhaps too rigid an ordeal" during the question sessions, as the usual requests for clarification "were supplemented by criticisms and the frankest personal reactions." In Zurich she lectured at an "International Course of Instruction on the Rationalization of Labour" in front of an audience of more than two hundred academics and industrialists. Here, too, there was heated debate, which was "on the whole, highly stimulating." Her final meeting was with the newly merged French scientific management group who had suffered divisions similar to the breach between the Taylorites and the Gilbreths, but after the deaths of the principal antagonists they agreed to differ.[5]

This summer demonstrates the breadth of Lillian's contacts and influence, but while it increased her expertise, her networking did not go far toward supporting her family, at least in the short term, and her expenses were mounting. Late spring of 1928 saw two graduations. Frank Jr. finished at Montclair High School and was preparing (a little unwillingly) to attend St. John's College in Annapolis. All three of his elder sisters had done a postgraduate year at the local high school; St. John's was a more expensive substitute, but Lillian had sold the back lot of her house and decided to invest some of the money in her children's education. Frank wanted to be an engineer and thought that a year in a small liberal arts college would be a waste of time. Lillian thought otherwise; she felt that seventeen-year-old Frank was "too young and inadequately prepared" to go straight into an engineering degree program. She wanted him to "have all the general foundation and culture possible." The president of St. John's was an old friend, Colonel Garey, who had worked with Frank Sr. at Fort Sill and was "so cordial and insistent" that it seemed "ungracious" not to send Frank Jr. there for at least a year. Lillian turned out to be right; Frank enjoyed his time at St. John's so much that the following summer he asked her, "Do you know where I'd go, if I didn't go to Michigan?" And when that turned out to be Oxford University, "she was sure that the year in the literary atmosphere had been no mistake!" After his transfer to Michigan, Frank became editor of the college newspaper and went on to a successful career in journalism.[6]

Within a few days of Frank's high school graduation, Ernestine graduated from Smith. Lillian was a familiar figure on the Northampton campus, having addressed chapel and guest lectured in psychology classes while her two eldest daughters were students there. President Neilson introduced her as the chapel speaker with no reference to her family, but rather as a shining example of higher education for women. Ernestine remembers feeling very proud of her mother, who spoke on the theme "Rejoice in being women. Rejoice in being Smith College women" for exactly the prescribed ten minutes.[7]

Lillian was remarkably unpossessive toward her children. She once criticized James Henry Breasted, the founder of American Egyptology, whose biography she was reading. Every time he needed help he called his son away from his own work and life. She asked, "How can a parent do that to a child? How *can* they make demands like that? What is it, in some people, that permits them to treat children as something they own?"[8] Most of Lillian's children were to marry and leave home soon after they finished college, rather than share her household responsibilities. Some years later, Anne wrote a poem of thanks to her mother. After describing her as the "old woman who lived in a shoe" and acknowledging that she had many worries "of shelter and clothing and food" in order to bring up her "big brood," the last stanza reads:

> But who, since the stories that Mother Goose told,
> Had each of eleven in college enrolled!
> Then freed them to build their own lives with no thought
> Of the Debt that they owed her, or how she had fought
> To let each of them carry the torch to another
> And none stay at home being grateful to Mother![9]

Ernestine did not marry immediately after graduating, but neither did she return home, moving instead into an apartment in Greenwich Village with three college friends. Lillian may have needed her help, but despite the criticism of some of her friends, who felt that "girls should fit back into their homes when they left college," she encouraged her daughter's independence. "Ernestine was so eager for the experience," she wrote, "that it seemed cruel to deny it to her." By the fall of 1928 Martha was at New Jersey State College for Women, where her aptitude for budgeting made her "a sort of perennial treasurer of every project that came along." Bill and Lill were both seniors at Montclair High and would be going to Purdue and Smith, respectively, in the fall. Although Bill was eighteen months older than Lill, he had lost time because of illness and had repeated a year. The five youngest children were all at local schools.[10]

By the fall of 1928 Lillian's networking was really starting to pay off and she won some very lucrative consultancy jobs. She was hired because her motion study expertise, combined with her tactful approach, was thought to achieve significant improvements to the firm hiring her. She also interacted socially with some of her employers; for example, when she advised Sears, Roebuck on personnel policies, she worked with the vice president, Lessing

Rosenwald, who "always seemed to have plenty of time not only for business . . . but for showing and talking over his beloved etchings."[11]

Working for Mrs. Katharine Gibbs, the founder of a small chain of secretarial colleges that bore her name, was less enjoyable, though Lillian was paid handsomely. In one of her very rare critical remarks she described Mrs. Gibbs as difficult to work with, noting that she "did not prove the satisfactory 'boss' that later women clients were to be and Lillian was relieved when the year's work was accomplished!"[12]

Katharine Gibbs had set up her first school in Providence in 1911, two years after her husband, vice commodore of the Edgewood Yacht Club, was killed by a falling ship's mast. Forced to support herself and her two small sons, Mrs. Gibbs moved into a profitable field with the rapidly increasing feminization of office work. Her empire expanded rapidly; she opened schools in Boston and New York during World War I and employed part-time faculty from prestigious universities such as Brown, MIT, and Columbia to supplement her full-time staff. Lillian was an obvious choice of consultant; Mrs. Gibbs may have known Lillian when the Gilbreths lived in Providence, for her secretarial school was then situated on Angell Street less than a hundred yards from the Gilbreths' house. Lillian had been associated with office efficiency for more than a dozen years, starting with the Remington typewriter studies and continuing through her recent office reorganization for Macy's. Most office consultants were men, but Mrs. Gibbs had strong views about working women, announcing in 1924 that "a woman's career is blocked by lack of openings, by unjust male competition, by prejudice and, not least, by inadequate salary and recognition."[13]

Mrs. Gibbs certainly paid generously. Lillian asked for and received $250 a day plus expenses, which totaled $10,000 for forty days' work, spread over ten months. Lillian laid out her terms very firmly, stating, "As for the cost, I get $250.00 a day, $1000.00 a month payable monthly and expenses if the work is out of New York." She added, "It has not seemed wise in the past to arrange for less than ten months work. We do better work when we only undertake a few projects and I should want to give this my best." This remark suggests that others were also paying her $250 a day; as Lillian's concurrent projects included a motion study course for five or six students at one thousand dollars per student and work for a sandwich shop and for Sears, Roebuck, her income in 1928 could have been as much as $25,000, an extraordinary amount compared with most married women's earnings in the 1920s. When the American Association of University Women surveyed its married members in 1926–27, it found the median income of those with Ph.D.'s and full-time jobs to be three thousand dollars.[14]

Lillian visited the Gibbs colleges in May 1928 and started work in September. She planned to start just as she would in a factory, by surveying existing practice, drawing up organization and functional charts, and writing job descriptions of both management and faculty. Then she hoped to conduct a micro-motion study of the various office skills taught at the school, to see if they could be made more efficient. She wanted to conduct market research to find out what industry and commerce wanted in a secretary, as well as study the use of space and time within the schools. Mrs. Gibbs agreed to all these proposals, adding that she and her sons "will co-operate with you in every way." Very little of this ambitious scheme was achieved, however, partly because none of the Gibbses seems to have been available when Lillian wanted to talk to them and partly because Mrs. Gibbs had Lillian spend much of her time lecturing, which was not part of the initial agreement. Her courses were called "personal efficiency" and topics included the heredity versus environment debates, motion study, fatigue study, and the use of leisure. She reported that the students listened "with apparent interest" and was gratified that their attitude to efficiency, which began "with resistance and sometimes dislike," ended with "open-mindedness and I feel in many cases actual liking."[15]

In March 1929 problems between Lillian and the administration came to a head. Mrs. Gibbs seems to have demanded to know when she was going to start the systems work she had promised. Katharine Gibbs's letter does not survive, but an unusually brisk letter in Lillian's files suggests how angry she was. "My dear Mrs. Gibbs," Lillian wrote on March 11, 1929, "I have been thinking over very carefully and at length our talk on Wednesday afternoon and planning how to make the rest of my time with you most serviceable." She said she planned to be at the New York school the following week, when they could discuss what could be done, adding, "I do hope that you and Mr. Gibbs may be able to hold the time when I am not lecturing . . . so that we may cover as much material as possible in the time that remains to me." She went on to explain that she had wanted to start the systems work sooner, "but as I told you I felt that you had not found it possible to save the time for participating in it or feasible to assign others to this function."[16]

It would seem that Lillian's efforts to salvage something of her original plan were not altogether successful. Her final report hints at Mrs. Gibbs's unwillingness to delegate and her idiosyncratic management style. "As for my comments on the running of the school," she wrote, "I am especially anxious that these be received exactly in the way in which they were meant," an ambiguous remark if there ever was one. Lillian continued, "It seems to me that the schools are extremely successful, but at a tremendous expenditure of energy on the part of the executives." Her solution: delegation. "I should like to see Mrs. Gibbs relieved of everything except the minimum of decisions that nobody else can make," she wrote, adding, "A functional chart delegating duties and responsibilities . . . and the various other devices of Scientific Management should be useful." Lillian tried to be constructive in her report and suggested that the secretarial training be more practical and that students be placed in part-time positions before they graduated. She added, sounding a little exasperated, "I realize that I am asking a great deal but I do wish that the schools could be set up more nearly approximating business offices. I should like to see appropriate desks, chairs, working conditions, etc. I greatly fear that it is difficult to establish right habits of work under present conditions and that there must be much adaptation of habits to actual working conditions out in the offices."[17]

During the same period Lillian was laying some of the foundations of the fast-food industry. She worked for Mildred and Rowland Johnson, owners of the Green Line lunchrooms, who were "so interested, so cooperative and so ready to accept the findings and carry them on through the years that followed"—the very antithesis of Katharine Gibbs. Lillian streamlined sandwich preparation by making a motion study of a woman who did a particularly good job. There was music playing in the background of the sandwich shop, so Lillian conducted a little experiment, putting "two or three different records on the mechanical piano" and noticing that the woman speeded up with one and slowed down with another. Finally, Lillian asked her what her special favorite was. "She looked at me as if to say, 'Are you putting up something on me?' And I looked back as much to say, 'No, I am making a scientific investigation.' So she said, 'I can't give you anything but love, baby.'" Lillian did *not* conclude, however, that there was one best rhythm for everyone to work by; she had abandoned her belief that there was only one best way.[18]

Lillian described her Green Line work to a group of engineers in a speech entitled "Skills and Satisfactions" that shows how and why she appealed to these practical men. She criticized the "high-brow" magazines and referred to Fritz Lang's 1926 movie *Metropolis,* where most of the population is reduced to slavery: "if you believed them, you would think that [the average machine operator] would come in and say 'here am I, your slave. Come to you for my day's work.'" She said that she knew and they knew that this was not the case and that some people were actually happier at work than anywhere else. "They may come from home with inadequate breakfasts. They may come from home after settling all kinds of family disputes. He sits down and thinks, 'here is something that belongs to me.' And he says, 'Come over and listen to it. Doesn't she run pretty?'" She told her audience to create conditions where the worker would get satisfaction from his machine and from his surroundings: "That is what I am here to appeal for, gentlemen—that you give these men in our industries a chance to get all the Skills they can; that you show them where the Satisfactions lie so that they really are getting them. There are a good many there."

It is easy to see why Lillian was in demand as a speaker. She did not disturb the status quo, but she nudged her audience gently in the direction of human awareness. And she always ended on a light note with an anecdote about her family. On this occasion she told a story about Frank Jr. and a car. Describing a factory visit one day at breakfast, she announced that a machine should be an extension of personality. Frank Jr. tackled her later, asking if she really meant that. 'Yes,' said I. 'Well,' said he, 'there is a nice Ford down town that I can buy for twenty dollars. How about extending mine?' So," Lillian reported, "we bought the Ford and the boy and the automobile extended themselves literally over a good part of the community."

Lillian's family story (and stories), combined with her technical competence, added to her popularity as a speaker. Her name recognition increased each time the press ran a piece about her family, and despite the onset of the Depression, her consulting work increased rapidly and became very lucrative. Firms were searching for techniques to make their workers more productive, while utility companies sought ways to encourage housewives to invest in new gas- and electricity-powered products.

Mary Dillon, head of the Brooklyn Borough Gas Company and one of a small but growing number of female executives, recognized Lillian's potential. This was an astute move, for Lillian's celebrity as mother and engineer could be associated with the products she endorsed, thus, according to an authority on Lillian's work, "uniting gas, modernity, motion savings and what we would call today *superwomanhood*." Dillon asked Lillian to design an efficient kitchen, known as the Kitchen Practical; it was unveiled at the Women's Exposition in September 1929, before being moved to the company's sales offices on Coney Island.[19]

In Mary Dillon's foreword to the promotional booklet for "The Kitchen Practical: The Story of an Experiment," she tried to suggest that as a businesswoman and cook she had realized the need for kitchens to be engineered as well as decorated. She described making a cake and realizing that modern decor was not enough, as she was taking "an unconscionable number of steps to get ready" and her utensils were awkward to use. So she called in Dr. Gilbreth to redesign her kitchen. Lillian was not only an engineer but also a psychologist; as such, she had two aims. She wanted to show the homemaker how to minimize the time and effort spent on routine tasks while demonstrating how the kitchen might be made so attractive that she would want to spend more time in it doing some of the really enjoyable tasks a good kitchen makes possible.[20]

Lillian did not, however, always practice what she preached, and she was not a competent cook. She had grown up with servants and, though she had memorized the recipe for Frank's favorite apple cake, the children claimed, "Lillie and kitchens were natural enemies. She hated them and they retaliated. Stoves burned her, ice picks stabbed her, graters skinned her and paring knives cut her." She also had a very inefficient and old-fashioned kitchen, though she was careful not to publicize the resistance of her cook-handyman to innovations in *his* kitchen. Tom Grieves's objection to Lillian's efforts at modernization captures in microcosm the problem of the isolated housewife with machines instead of company. The gregarious Tom entertained many tradesmen in his kitchen. According to Frank Jr., writing many years later, "The iceman, milkman, garbage man, ash man, coal man, mail man and express man were all bosom cronies of his" who regularly stopped by for a coffee ("occasionally laced with a 'smile'") and a chat. When Lillian bought an electric refrigerator, Tom saw it as a device aimed at separating him from one of his friends. A compromise was reached: they kept both the refrigerator and the icebox, and the iceman continued to take what Tom called "a little demmy tassy, for Christ's sake," in the kitchen.[21]

Perhaps with Tom in mind, Lillian did not attempt to standardize kitchens. She emphasized that the homemaker should not take her suggestions as an unchangeable blueprint, but adapt them to her own family's needs and circumstances—"physical, mental and emotional." She devised a circular work plan based on her investigations of baking, yet she was honest enough to admit that she had not tested any other kitchen procedures and suggested that "every housewife study her stove to see what exactly she does on it, the time involved and the delay periods when she could do something else and try to utilize those periods." She also included a "service table" on wheels, designed to minimize walking, and a planning desk, elements that were to recur in her later work.[22]

She believed that if the homemaker "can be led to feel that it is for her to determine *what* is to be done in the kitchen, *who* is to do it, *where, when* and *why*—then this kitchen can suggest the *how!*" Lillian's phrase "led to feel" suggests, however, a role for the expert such as herself in persuading the homemaker to be experimental. As ever, Lillian seemed at first sight not particularly interested in disturbing conventional gender arrangements. She insisted that homemaking could be a fulfilling activity for women. Pictures may, however, speak louder than words. A careful look at the pamphlet shows a more subversive notion; there is a photograph of a man in an apron working alongside his wife and daughter in the Kitchen Practical. Perhaps a house husband was a tempting idea to the Brooklyn Gas Company's many women customers.

Lillian took the idea of male cooperation a step further in her Teamwork

Kitchen. When Ernestine married Charles Carey in 1930, she asked her mother to design a kitchen for her as a wedding gift. "I said, well there's one thing I want which I think you could combine with your business and it would be good publicity. . . . She said that's a wonderful idea . . . so she worked it all out and she insisted on an apron for Chuck, a butcher's apron. . . . It was the team work kitchen."[23]

Lillian saw her daughter and her new husband as exponents of the fifty-fifty marriage that she so often advocated: Ernestine was an assistant buyer at Macy's and her husband was an engineer. As Lillian pointed out to an interviewer, "They have the same business hours. Why shouldn't they share the housework?" Lillian adjusted the work surfaces and supplied a stool on wheels so that Ernestine could sit while she worked. Lillian's domestic engineering was highly individualized when it came to planning this kitchen. Ernestine remembers that someone from the *Herald Tribune* Institute came to see it and said, "There was only one problem, 'The husband had to be six foot one or two to reach up to these shelves and he'd have to be left handed.' Mother said, 'well that's what my son-in-law is, he's tall and left-handed.'"[24]

Lillian's Teamwork Kitchen became part of a much bigger project when Marie Brown Meloney, the new editor of the *New York Herald Tribune Magazine*, asked her to design three model kitchens and set up a kitchen laboratory for the newspaper's institute. "Missy" Meloney, energetic and a brilliant organizer, was the same age as Lillian. The two women had become friendly shortly before Frank died, and when Lillian fled from Nantucket later that summer, Missy had comforted her; they became even closer the following year, when Missy's husband died. The youngest of twenty-one children (by three wives) of a Kentucky physician, Missy started work at the *Washington Post* when she was only sixteen, though she was soon fired after forgetting an appointment for an interview with a senator because she was absorbed in a collection of rare music in the Library of Congress and did not notice the time. A little later, while singing in a choir at St. Paul's, Washington, she chanced on the unannounced wedding of Admiral Dewey, a scoop that regained her the job at the *Post*.[25]

She married the same year as Lillian, 1904, and then spent ten years rearing her only child before returning to journalism. She was interested in using her publications to promote women and reform. In the *Delineator*, which she edited from 1921 to 1926, she serialized the autobiographies of prominent women such as Marie Curie and Ethel Barrymore; she also printed articles on better teaching, improving child health, and the rebuilding of war-torn Europe. She raised $100,000 to give Madame Curie a gram of radium for use in cancer research and brought her to America to receive it. Missy Meloney's characterization of Marie Curie as an impoverished, brilliant, yet motherly woman coincided nicely with the antifeminism of the early 1920s. Curie, who worked very long hours and left her children for long periods of time, was portrayed as anguished at having to do so. When Missy came to promote Lillian's career, she also stressed her motherliness, though with less of the anguish, as Lillian's family system was assumed to have minimized her missing them.[26]

Like many of her women contemporaries, Missy Meloney admired Herbert Hoover, and when he, as secretary of commerce, urged the country to build a million new homes, she created the Better Homes in America Movement. Three years later, in 1924, it was incorporated as a public service organization with Hoover as its president and Meloney as its vice president. It became part of what has been called Hoover's "adhocracy" in that, despite being closely tied to the U.S. Department of Commerce, it was designed to stimulate and work through private groups. It had 3,600 local committees and aimed to provide exhibits of model homes, promote better "household management," and encourage the building of decent housing for low-income families.[27]

Soon after her appointment at the *Herald Tribune,* Missy Meloney created the *Herald Tribune* Institute, where home economists tested food and equipment and prepared information on nutrition, child care, entertaining—anything that might be assumed to interest women readers and that manufacturers could link to advertisements for their products. Lillian became a member of its Advisory Council. Other members included distinguished women (and Lillian's old friends) Martha Van Rensselaer, the Cornell home economist; Louise Stanley, now director of the Bureau of Home Economics in the U.S. Department of Agriculture; Grace Abbott, director of the Children's Bureau in the Labor Department; and Emily Post, the etiquette writer. In 1930 Meloney set up the *Herald Tribune* Forum on Current Problems, which became international in its scope; Lillian spoke at it on several occasions.[28]

In 1928 Lillian planned three kitchens and a laboratory for the *Herald Tribune.* The largest kitchen, designed for a ten-by-twelve-foot room, was very similar to the Kitchen Practical. Lillian reiterated her circular workspace, which was the forerunner of today's accepted triangular work pattern for kitchens. In an experiment involving a strawberry shortcake, she claimed to reduce the number of movements required from 97 to 64 and the number of steps from 281 to 45. "The Institute is not opposed to walking and exercise for the woman of the family—far from it!" exclaimed the author of the pamphlet describing Lillian's work. "But we do maintain that she should take that exercise in the open air, rather than in a tread-mill round of refrigerator to sink, to stove and back again." Lillian advocated adapting the work surfaces to the height of the kitchen's principal worker to minimize back strain. As a free service, the Institute measured visitors to the exhibit against a very Gilbrethian gridded wall, in order to tell the housewife exactly how high her work surfaces should be. Two of the kitchens were tiny; in addition to the one based on Ernestine's kitchen, Lillian designed one for a studio apartment where the whole kitchen practically fitted into a closet. The motions involved in cooking and cleaning up were similar whether the appliances were gas or electric, so Lillian easily adapted her designs to whichever utility company was paying the bills. These commercial model kitchens ignored many of the ideas Lillian had put forward in *The Home-maker and Her Job*. There was no effort to teach women how to do their own motion study, or any notion of involving the children in a democratic household.[29]

Perhaps Lillian's favorite element in these model kitchens, and the part that best matched her notions of homemaker as household manager, was the planning desk, which, as she explained, was necessary as "the business of running a house demands a well-planned little 'office' just as surely as does any business run by a man." The desk had a shelf for recipe and nutrition books, drawers for paid and unpaid bills, and a "housewife's tool drawer" containing hammer, nails, screws, "and other implements necessary for quick repair work." A radio would connect the homemaker to the outside world and since a telephone was "a necessity for the modern housewife," one was included in the desk.[30]

Lillian's work with Mary Dillon and Missy Meloney was the basis of much of her later career, and her friendship with the two women was to continue for the rest of their lives. Before she became more involved in kitchen work, however, she made an interesting excursion into politics and public policy.

PART VI

"One of America's Foremost Women"

*I have been asked to name the fifty
living women who in my judgment have done
the most for the welfare of the United States. . . .
The list includes . . . Lillian Gilbreth, internationally
known popularizer of scientific management. Has
published valuable time, fatigue and motion studies.
Consulting engineer with large European
following. Mother of thirteen children.*

Ida Tarbell, "Ida Tarbell Lists Fifty Foremost Women"
(September 13, 1930)

24 This Home Is for Hoover

*We started it in this house with Bobby showing
me a "This Home is for Hoover" sign he had put on
the goldfish bowl and Janey bringing up a doll's
carriage with a Hoover sign on it.*

Lillian Moller Gilbreth, *As I Remember* (1998)

Although she had dabbled in politics during her time as a technical consultant to the Women's Bureau, Lillian's political life began in earnest during the presidential election of 1928, when she became president of the Women's Branch and the only woman among the twenty-two honorary vice presidents of the Engineers' Hoover for President campaign. She was in distinguished company; her fellow vice presidents included Thomas Edison and Henry Ford, though in keeping with the domestic tone of her memoirs, she downplayed her role and claimed that the most important event of the year was the arrival of her first grandchild. Nevertheless, her first foray into electoral politics was to have far-reaching consequences. It led to her appointment as head of the women's division of one of Hoover's Depression-fighting agencies, which was to be the first of Lillian's many presidential advisory roles.[1]

Lillian had known Herbert Hoover and his wife, Lou Henry Hoover, since the 1890s. After the Hoovers returned from China and Europe, her contacts were renewed through her Berkeley classmate Alice Marchebout Dickson, who had been at high school with Mrs. Hoover and worked with Herbert Hoover on the Commission for Relief in Belgium during World War I. Lillian was not alone in her support for Hoover, who was viewed as exceptionally well qualified for the White House. Many prominent and progressive women, including Jane Addams and Alice Paul, were enthusiastic about his candidacy, and the National Women's Committee for Hoover included women's college presidents M. Carey Thomas of Bryn Mawr, Ada Comstock of Radcliffe, and Ellen Fitz Pendleton of Wellesley. Leaders of practically every middle-class women's club from the National Parent-Teacher Association to the League of Women Voters backed him; he even attracted women who called themselves Democrats, such as the prolific novelist Kathleen Norris. She was a leading prohibitionist, and the Democratic candidate Al Smith's support of the "Wets" drove her and many other women to the Republicans. Supporters cited Hoover's humanitarian work both in Europe and the United States and his championing of the Better Homes in America Movement (Missy Meloney's brainchild) and the Child Health Association. Asserting that "Hoover's cause is the cause of the home," they urged every woman to vote for him and feel "the deepest pride that her vote can make this great man the leader of our country." Articles appeared in women's and mainstream publications with such titles as "Herbert Hoover As Women See Him." Several recalled Hoover's appeal to housewives during World War I, when he had made even pacifist women feel part of the war effort since, as Kathleen Norris wrote, "Men or women can reveal as much greatness in the amelioration of war's results as in the conduct of war itself." They supported him because he was "the only executive . . . who ever took the women of the United States into his confidence and who, over his personal signature, enlisted their aid in a national crisis." As Charlotte Kellogg asserted, "He made it possible for the most isolated woman suffering from her conviction of the futility of her apparently petty and unrelated task, to feel her shoulder against that planetary wheel that was grinding the grain of the world's bread."[2]

Although the chair of the National Engineering Committee saw the women's group as the supportive wives, sisters, and mothers of engineers, Lillian envisaged a more active role for herself. She talked to groups of industrialists on issues of technological unemployment, not unexpectedly arguing that scientific management had created new jobs, instead of causing unemployment, and she had occasional meetings with candidate Hoover. Lillian did not forget the women's angle, however, and organized a breakfast for Lou Henry Hoover, herself a graduate engineer, at the Waldorf-Astoria Hotel in New York. Press photographs show Lillian wearing a fetching hat and standing behind Mrs. Hoover, who was seated between Mrs. Henry Ford and Mrs. Thomas Edison. Ready to present a large bouquet of chrysanthemums to the guest of honor was Lillian's six-year-old daughter, Jane.[3]

The 1928 election demonstrated yet again Lillian's ability to involve her children in her projects and combine her professional and family interests. The day after Hoover's victory she wrote two letters. She told the president-elect that her group planned to continue and was ready to work in support of the Kellogg Peace Plan as soon as he gave them his endorsement. "We must not lose our work habits, so please give us a job," she wrote. In her letter to the candidate's wife Lillian struck a more familial note, with a long description of her children's enthusiastic support for the campaign. Telling "My dear Mrs. Hoover" that the Gilbreths all sent their congratulations to the "First Lady of the Land," Lillian described spending the evening with friends "with everyone chalking up the returns and the men making progress charts in real engineering fashion." She felt a sense of anticlimax, however, and despite talk of organizing an Engineering Women's Club, felt the need to work, as "it is even more fun to work than to play together."[4]

Lillian's friendship with the Hoovers flourished during their years in the White House and continued until Herbert Hoover's death in 1964. Lillian attended his inauguration and stayed in the White House on many occasions. Her first night at the White House was memorable, since it turned into a weekend at Camp Rapidan, the presidential retreat in Virginia. It happened in late September 1929, just as Lillian was about to leave for Japan. She was a member (the only female member, it almost goes without saying) of the U.S. delegation to the World Engineering Congress in Tokyo. Hoover, as an engineer, was quite interested in the meeting, having been the keynote speaker at the previous congress in London. The half-hour meeting between Lillian and Hoover was scheduled for 6:30 on a Friday evening, and Lillian's business was swiftly concluded. "However," she continued, writing in the third person, as usual, "he said he had set aside that half hour for her and she was going to have every minute of it," so he showed her his "Chamber of Horrors," a small room that his son "had filled with all the cartoons and caricatures which have been made of the President."[5]

Lillian dined with the Hoovers and about twenty guests. The Hoovers loved entertaining and were said to dine alone only once a year, on their wedding anniversary. These White House dinner parties were elegant affairs; in the center of the table was a bowl of pink roses surrounded by little Japanese ivories, and the guests ate off the best silver and china. Mrs. Hoover was an efficient hostess; guests were given a card telling them whom they would be seated next to and what interests they might have in common. Breakfast was less formal. Lillian joined the Hoover family on a little porch at the back of the White House, and when the meal was half over the Hoovers' dogs "were admitted to receive tidbits from the hands of the President." As Lillian was preparing to leave, Hoover asked her if she couldn't come to their camp and spend the weekend. Her first reaction was surprise. It was "like a bolt out of the blue" and, as she was leaving the following Monday for Japan, seemed impossible. Lillian's next problem was the lack of suitable clothes, but Mrs. Hoover was insistent and found her a white silk damask dress "and even shoes which fortunately fit perfectly." They then started out with Mrs. Hoover driving her Cadillac, Lillian sitting beside her in the front seat and the Secret Service men following at a discreet distance, though they caught up and were "right on hand" when it was time to stop for a picnic lunch. Camp Rapidan, the predecessor of Camp David, was some hundred miles from Washington in the foothills of the Blue Mountains. It was new, having been completed only six weeks before Lillian's visit, and it became Herbert Hoover's favorite place to relax, fish, and entertain friends and important official visitors. The previous weekend Charles and Anne Lindbergh had been there to help Hoover celebrate his fifty-fifth birthday, and the weekend after Lillian's stay, British prime minister Ramsay MacDonald and his daughter paid an equally impromptu visit, and again the Hoovers had to dig into their closets to lend them appropriate clothes.[6]

When Lillian and the Hoovers arrived at the camp, Lou Henry Hoover suggested going for a horseback ride. Unlike her husband, who liked to fish alone, Lou Henry liked company on her excursions, so with some misgivings, as she had not been on a horse for many years, Lillian went with her. She was very sore the next day. Dinner was informal, and Lillian had an early night. The next day they all returned to Washington, stopping midway for tea in the woods, "the President and Mrs. Hoover entering into the picnic spirit perfectly." Mrs. Hoover had an ulterior motive for inviting Lillian to Camp Rapidan. The two women spent much of the journey "discussing educational and youth problems, a great deal of it pertaining to Girl and Boy Scouting," according to Mrs. Hoover, who added that "our ideas are very similar along these lines." Mrs. Hoover wanted to recruit Lillian as a consultant to the Girl Scouts. Lillian demurred, saying she was not sure she had the time, but Mrs. Hoover was not one to take no for an answer. A few months later she invited Lillian to tea at the White House with a group of Girl Scout leaders and announced that she would enroll her guest in the Scouts then and there. Realizing that refusal was impossible Lillian rose and took the oath.[7]

Lillian's Camp Rapidan stay in 1929 was the first of numerous visits with the Hoovers. Lillian stayed with them when she was in Washington working on the President's Emergency Committee on Employment in 1930–31; she also took her children to receptions from time to time. Lou Henry Hoover sent her a letter after one such visit, when Janey Gilbreth, who was then age nine, had been one of three hundred or so children "waiting to say 'how do you do'" after a White House egg-rolling party. She added, "Don't forget that we are expecting the eleven and their attachés either here or at camp! I am sure we will have room for them,—because I have just learned that once the five Roosevelt boys and their friends slept crosswise on the Lincoln bed!"[8]

Lillian took Frank Jr. with her to Hoover's inauguration. In *Belles on Their Toes* the children give an amusing account of the "March on Washington," when all six boys attended a formal White House reception for the cabinet, the Supreme Court, and the diplomatic corps. After numerous adventures in their decrepit Model T, the vehicle Frank Jr. had bought for twenty dollars, they arrived in Washington wet through. Lillian "accidentally" managed to burn a hole in the pants of the mustard-yellow suit that was her eldest son's pride and joy and replaced it with a sober blue serge, and the reception went without a hitch. The Gilbreths did not stay the night, however; the Lincoln bed had to wait and they drove back to Montclair, taking their mother with them.[9]

In late September 1929, after thanking the Hoovers for her unexpected weekend at Camp Rapidan, Lillian boarded a train for the West Coast. She traveled with the rest of the American delegation to the Tokyo conference, which included her old friend John R. Freeman, who had brought his family along with him. His daughter Mary Elizabeth, recently graduated from Smith College, shared a cabin with Lillian and always remembered that when she crept into bed in the early hours after a night's dancing, she would find Lillian ready to get up and start her day's work.[10]

Lillian's attendance at the World Engineering Congress was extremely important to her, for she could spread information on the Gilbreth system to an international audience and network with the world's leading engineers. She arrived in Japan at an inauspicious time, three days after the infamous "Black Thursday," October 24, 1929, when the U.S. stock market began its collapse. Though most analysts assumed it was simply a market correction, stock prices were to decline by around 40 percent over the next month, rendering the livelihoods of many engineers precarious as building contracts were canceled and industrial projects postponed. This was in the future, however, and as the liner drew into Yokohama harbor, many of the passengers were on deck craning their necks for their first glimpse of Japan. Beyond Mount Fuji and the welcoming committee on the dock was, however, a scene of chaos. A typhoon had washed away part of the railroad track to Tokyo, and flooding had left seventeen thousand people homeless.[11]

Nevertheless, the delegates found their way to Tokyo and the conference proceeded as planned. Lillian was in the front row of the vast Municipal Auditorium as dozens of men filed onto the platform for the opening ceremony. The Japanese government was taking this conference very seriously; Prince Chichibu, brother of the Japanese emperor, was the patron and the first speaker, and the prime minister also spoke. There was a packed agenda for the three thousand delegates, but as most of the papers were in Japanese and interpreters were scarce, the six hundred Westerners were often a little lost. In characteristic utilitarian mode Lillian wrote, "We were all anxious that the greatest good for the greatest number should result from the sessions and were content to piece out our information with abstracts and blackboard illustrations."[12]

Scientific management was clearly a hot topic in Japan, and the Westerners were a tiny minority, generally less than a half dozen in a packed meeting room. Lillian played a very public role, entering discussions and chairing a session, which, she said, was "an easy job" since her translator was calm and unflappable. She was very much in control; the local newspaper reported that she gave the session "a vitality and speed which was unique among sectional meetings so far observed." Prince Chichibu, who was conscientious in his attendance at the conference, chose to visit Lillian's session. When he arrived all the Japanese stood and bowed until he had taken his seat in a special armchair on the platform next to Lillian. The prince showed "a lively interest" in a heated discussion between European and American delegates over the effects of scientific management on unemployment. An old friend of Frank's from the Technische Hochschule in Berlin, Dr. Georg Schlesinger, was very critical of Japanese industrial practice. He described seeing "labor cheaper than machine tools . . . too many workers for the jobs done. . . . Apparently the surplus workers could not be dismissed." He argued that scientific management was necessary to increase productivity, even if it meant short-term unemployment. Lillian was on the side of the optimists in the vigorous debate that followed. She argued that technological unemployment was probably inevitable, but that the scientific manager should and must find ways of redeploying labor. She also felt that unemployment might be much worse "if it were not for the better industrial management which has been introduced since the war." The Europeans argued that if this was so, it was due to special industrial conditions in the United States.[13]

The discussion had a powerful effect on Lillian, who became increasingly interested in the issue of unemployment. Some months later she asked the liberal historian Charles Beard for his perspective, writing, "I know of nobody who thinks so clearly on this as you do." It is a complicated problem. Lillian knew from her work with the Women's Bureau that women often benefited from technological rationalization. When "men's" jobs, so called because of the heavy labor or the training involved were reorganized, women sometimes stepped in. Female unemployment rates in the United States, after 1932 at least, were lower than rates for males. On the other hand, women earned less than men; thus, such technological innovations were often a device to decrease labor costs. In Japan Lillian argued vigorously that better industrial management was helping to minimize unemployment. Later, when she learned more about the pay differentials involved and the reality of low wages for women workers, she advocated equal pay for equal work and criticized employers she designated as "unprogressive."[14]

The scientific management sessions met four times in all. Lillian spent much of her spare time lecturing up to three times a day to audiences "that numbered as high as three thousand." Lillian's reputation had preceded her to Japan, and there was great curiosity about this woman who could combine an engineering career with raising a large family. She made nearly thirty speeches, many arranged by her former student Mr. Yoiti Ueno, who had been busily introducing the Gilbreth system of motion study in Japan since his return from Montclair in 1925.[15]

The conference closed on November 7, and over the next nineteen days Lillian visited plants, stores, and colleges all over Japan. She wanted to learn all she could about the country and, thanks to Mr. Ueno, was able to visit Japanese homes, a privilege rarely granted to foreigners. Lillian did not learn as much as she had hoped, however, for most of her hosts wished to display how Western they were. Instead of sipping green tea, she was given black tea with milk and sugar; Japanese delicacies were replaced by dainty sandwiches; and instead of sitting on a tatami mat, she perched on chairs in "foreign style rooms." The experience was less than satisfying.[16]

Many of the industrial and commercial sites Lillian visited were also partially Westernized. She toured a shipyard and a steel mill, which she found in a "surprising state of tidiness." She paid a brief visit to a factory where they made tabi, the Japanese socks with separated toes, and gave a short speech to the firm's three thousand women employees. She was impressed by management's involvement. "The intimate acquaintance" of the chief men with the problems of their industry, she wrote, "proved that they spent much time in it." Lillian realized that she was shown only what the managers wanted her to see and that it was impossible to see "the full swing of the working day of the workers, much less of the 24-hr day," but she supplemented her visits by talking to everyone she could find with detailed knowledge of Japan.[17]

Lillian found some of the plants modern and efficient. "They are making rapid progress in their efforts to copy the achievements of the great world powers," she wrote, without conscious irony, on the eve of the Japanese invasion of Manchuria. Others were, however, very old-fashioned and poorly run, which supported Dr. Schlesinger's criticisms. Lillian's insights into the Japanese psyche did not transcend mainstream cultural assumptions; nevertheless, she returned to Japan at least twice in the next thirty years, and her work influenced W. Edwards Deming, who was instrumental to the postwar Japanese economic miracle. In December 1968, when she was ninety years old, the Japanese government awarded her the interestingly named Third Class of the Order of the Precious Crown for her "outstanding contribution to the guidance and diffusion of scientific management and industrial development."[18]

25 A Dollar-a-Year Woman in Washington

We are depending on you to work out a technic of cooperation for the club women of your State.

Lillian Moller Gilbreth to the General Federation of Women's Clubs (1931)

THE YEAR 1930 was a very busy one for Lillian, though she was slowed down somewhat by a motoring accident in the spring. Margaret Hawley, the young economist from California, who had recently written a master's thesis on Frank's contributions to scientific management, was staying with Lillian for several months. One evening in March, as Hawley was driving Lillian back from an ASME meeting, a drunk driver in a Pierce Arrow sideswiped a truck and collided head-on with the Gilbreths' 1928 Plymouth. Lillian's knee was injured and her nose broken. She claimed to have never liked her nose, thinking it too thin, so she decided to have it reshaped by a New York plastic surgeon.[1]

On hearing of Lillian's accident, the Hoovers sent her flowers with a note saying, "We're thinking of you, Lou and Herbert," which, according to Frank Jr., led to a profound change in the surgeon's attitude. He had asked for payment in advance on hearing that his patient was a widow with eleven children, but as soon as he discovered who Lillian's friends were, he claimed that it was all a mistake. "Has my secretary been . . . ? Yes, I'll wager she has! She thinks she has to take care of me—we do so much charity work and our expenses are so high." He thereupon refused to take Lillian's check, saying that later would do, "at your convenience, my dear lady."[2]

Lillian's accident happened at an inconvenient time where the Girl Scouts were concerned. The director was planning to leave and they were searching for a replacement. Lou Henry Hoover was sufficiently impressed with Lillian's expertise to suggest her for the job of national director, "if the salary stays *very* good." Lillian was not appointed, but instead she became a consultant and a member of the board of directors and was active in Girl Scouting for more than twenty years. President Hoover also used Lillian's expertise, and although he did not follow the advice of a Vermont woman who suggested he appoint Lillian to his cabinet, he put her on a subcommittee of the National Conference on Home Building and Home Ownership in August 1930 and wrote letters of introduction when she traveled to Europe. "Of course," she remarked, "such letters open all doors."[3]

Lillian spent the summer of 1930 in Europe, following her usual energetic schedule of conferences and business meetings. She also visited two former students, Anne Shaw, who now worked for Metropolitan Vickers, the British equivalent of General Electric, and Bill Sanderson, who worked for Cadbury, the chocolate manufacturer. Though she intended only to have lunch with Bill, he insisted she visit the factory and see how he was applying the motion study analysis she had taught him in Montclair. It was a Saturday afternoon, so no one was working, but Lillian saw "dozens" of Cadbury teams playing cricket and tennis in the playing fields surrounding the factory. She was much impressed by the facilities the paternalistic Cadbury family provided: the model village, with its "miles and miles" of substantial houses, each with its own garden; schools, colleges, hospitals, "everything a big industrial project can use." The one omission was public houses, or pubs: the Cadburys were Quakers, as were most of the other British chocolate manufacturers, and like other industrialists, Quaker or not, they believed that drink was the scourge of the working classes. Cadbury's workers had to travel to adjoining suburbs to enjoy a pint of beer.[4]

Lillian had good connections with the Cadbury family, having met Dorothy Cadbury at a conference in Switzerland in 1926 and again the following year in Italy. Dorothy was one of the few female directors of a major company in England; in her late thirties by the time Lillian visited Birmingham, she had begun work at Cadbury as an ordinary pieceworker earning twenty-five shillings a week. Partly because of this and partly because of her Quaker beliefs, Dorothy Cadbury became interested in welfare work and in promoting the position of women in industry; sending Bill Sanderson to Montclair was part of this interest.[5]

Early next morning Dorothy Cadbury came to pick Lillian up in her brand-new Austin car. She had the roof down and drove fast, and Lillian had to hang on to her hat as they "howled along the lanes" to the Cadburys' home, where she met Dorothy's mother. Geraldine Cadbury served milky coffee while Dorothy "jumped up" to serve oatmeal, fish, and bacon from covered dishes on a hot plate. "No maids," Lillian commented. The three women discussed unemployment and a new book, *Robots or Men?* until it was time for family prayers. Dorothy rang a bell and in filed the housekeeper, dressed in brown, three or four housemaids in pink, and a "tweeny" in white, accompanied by a little dog who sat next to Dorothy, "still as could be."[6] Mrs. Cadbury read a chapter from St. Paul, then after silent Quaker prayer the maids filed out, the dog "scampering after." Then, "oh rare favor," Lillian was taken to see the Cadburys' kitchen. It was enormous: "The help walk miles, love it, wouldn't have it otherwise for worlds!" she commented. Mrs. Cadbury told the housekeeper that Lillian was a famous kitchen designer and that she put in service tables on wheels. "The housekeeper looked polite scorn. I could see she was thinking, 'what would the maids do?'" When it was time for Lillian to leave, Dorothy Cadbury drove her to Birmingham station. Anne Shaw met her in Manchester in what seemed an incredibly tiny car: "It only holds four gallons of petrol [gas] and makes forty miles to the gallon."

After visiting more students and trade shows and taking her first ever plane ride—"I felt part of the machine age," she told her children; "It was grand!"—Lillian returned from Nantucket in late August and resumed her routine. The first event of the fall was Ernestine's wedding on September 13, but Ernestine herself was too busy working as an assistant buyer at Macy's to do anything but turn up the evening before. She left Lillian to make all the arrangements, though Lillian in her turn delegated much of the planning to her friend Mrs. Roy Wright. Like Anne's wedding five years earlier, the ceremony was held in the Gilbreths' Montclair home, and the Hoovers sent flowers. Afterward, while the newlyweds spent their honeymoon fishing in New Hampshire, Frank Jr. returned to college, and the seven youngest children, now aged from seventeen to eight years old, went back to school. Twenty-year-old Martha, who had graduated the previous spring, was working at the New York Telephone Company, though she went on living at home and continued to run the house.[7]

When Lillian wrote to thank Mrs. Hoover for the flowers, she said, "We are trying to calm down and settle things," but she could never stay still for long. She was planning to go to Washington for a meeting of the President's Housing Committee later in the month before traveling to Indianapolis on Girl Scout business. These were both volunteer activities, and Lillian had to keep up her paying consultancies. It had become clear to her that the motion study courses were no longer as necessary as they had been. This was partly because colleges were starting to offer similar courses and partly because Lillian now had enough other contracts to render them less financially important. Ending the courses would mean less time spent at home; nevertheless, she tried to keep a delicate balance between her family's emotional and economic needs and her public service.

On October 9, 1930, Lillian's mother died. She was seventy-five. Although she claimed to have been unwell since the birth of her first daughter in 1874 and had been waited on hand and foot by her children for decades, Annie Moller outlived her husband by seven years. Her estate was valued at just over a million dollars. The bulk of the property was in real estate and property values and rents were depressed in Oakland in 1930, but in theory each of the nine Moller children was to receive $82,920.21 if and when the properties were sold. In the meantime Lillian and her sisters shared their mother's jewelry, and she and her eight siblings each received two hundred dollars a month from rents. Annie Moller's luxurious house with all its contents, the largest single asset, was given in trust to her unmarried children. Relations with the Mollers seem to have been strained, however, for seven months later the widowed Lillian, sole supporter of eleven children, signed a document waiving "any construction of said will whereby I would be considered as one of the unmarried children given the rights and privileges to use and occupy said home."[8]

Less than two weeks after her mother's death, Lillian received a telegram from Arthur Woods, the chairman of President Hoover's Emergency Committee for Employment (PECE), telling her that the president had suggested that she head the women's section of PECE. She immediately canceled most of her engagements, postponed her consultancy work, and set off for Washington as a "dollar-a-year woman." Arthur Woods was an old friend of Hoover's who had used his wealth—he was the son of a Massachusetts textile family and had married a cousin of J. P. Morgan— to support himself in a series of public-spirited but less than well-paid jobs. After the war he had helped Hoover organize President Harding's Conference on Unemployment and then directed the Rockefeller Foundation, where he oversaw part of the Colonial Williamsburg restoration project. He was familiar with many of Hoover's ideas about the limited role of government and believed, like Hoover, that an organization such as PECE was simply a "booster engine" that was necessary to help the system up "a stiff grade," namely the winter (about which there was much concern), though there was no need to replace the engine itself. Like Hoover, he firmly believed that economic depression could "not be cured by legislative action or executive pronouncement" and that a solution could only come from "producers and consumers themselves."[9]

PECE was an integral part of Hoover's strategy for dealing with unemployment by using voluntary organizations. He envisaged the role of government as mobilizing "the intelligence of the country, that the entire community may be instructed as to the part they must play in the effecting of [employment relief]." When the stock market crashed in October 1929,

Hoover consulted with bankers, businessmen, and labor and farmers' leaders, asking for their cooperation in maintaining confidence and keeping up production. When the stock market collapsed again the following April, however, Hoover realized that exhortation might not be enough. After creating a number of fact-finding committees, he set up the PECE with the aim of preventing "hunger and cold to those of our people who are in honest difficulties" and formulating plans for "continuing and strengthening the organization of Federal activities for employment during the winter."[10]

Lillian went to Washington with high hopes that she might be useful. She started work in late October and a few weeks later her old friend Alice Marchebout Dickson joined her, on temporary leave from Doubleday, the publishers. It is worth noting that Lillian was chosen to head the women's division of PECE, although the Hoovers knew Alice Dickson much better. This can only be due to the Hoover administration's desire to use Lillian's fame as a mother and as a domestic efficiency expert to demonstrate to other women what they could do to combat unemployment. Lillian was very much a celebrity in 1930, appearing on the journalist and former muckraker Ida Tarbell's list of the "Fifty Foremost Women of the United States," women defined as having done the most to advance the country's welfare. Lillian was in distinguished company. The list included Jane Addams, the founder of Hull House in Chicago and an indefatigable reformer; Carrie Chapman Catt, the suffragist and peace worker; Helen Keller, the deaf and blind woman who had become a campaigner for the handicapped; Mary McLeod Bethune, the black educator and civil rights worker; Margaret Sanger, the birth control pioneer; and Amelia Earhart, the aviator. Between the wars there were many such lists, and Lillian appeared on several of them. In December 1930 she was one of twenty-two women featured in a *Good Housekeeping* readership poll to discover America's twelve greatest living women, though she did not make the final cut: the "winners," who were listed alphabetically, ranged from Grace Abbott to Mary Woolley. As the magazine's editor noted, only four of them had ever been married: "Again the old controversy of home vs. career." Lillian was also starting to receive honorary degrees. In 1929 Rutgers gave her an honorary doctorate of engineering, the first such degree ever awarded to a woman.[11]

When the call to Washington arrived, Lillian received a lot of publicity, most of it stressing the size of her family. A report distributed by the Associated Press to newspapers all over the country shows Lillian eager to serve, eager to engage the cooperation of her family and immediately set up a women's network within government. She told Colonel Wood that she would be on the job within twenty-four hours and cabled Grace Abbott, Dr. Louise Stanley, and Mary Anderson, three women who headed government bureaus, asking their cooperation. The Associated Press article went on to explain how the family would cope in her absence, stressing Lillian's organizational skills: "Every one of the 11 children, aided by Tom, the family helper who has been with the Gilbreths 18 years, will swing into action to keep the home fires burning while 'Mother' is in Washington." Martha was to be in charge; everyone down to eight-year-old Janey had chores, and Tom, "who can plan a meal or bind up a cut finger with equal ease," was to do the rest.[12]

Lillian saw her work for the Hoover administration as "a real opportunity for service." Her aims combined Hoover's preferences for an "associative state" and her desire to professionalize middle-class homemakers. Taking Hoover's ideas on American individualism and limited government, she applied them to middle-class women. She appealed to science and community, just as Hoover did, by advocating a "technic of cooperation" between women's groups and government. Women's clubs had long served as a vehicle of entry into the mainstream of public affairs, but Lillian's work at PECE marked one of the first times that organized women were *invited* into partnership with government, rather than being obliged to act as an extragovernmental pressure group.[13]

Lillian was extraordinarily active and energetic during her months in Washington. While she dealt with a voluminous mailbag, she saw her main role as fact finder and cajoler and traveled extensively. In early December, for example, she spent three days in New York meeting with women's organizations and engineers; she was increasingly comfortable moving between the two worlds. One Tuesday morning in December she met with leaders of three national women's organizations, followed by a luncheon given by Mrs. Alexander Haddon of the Girls Service League of America. She told Edward Hunt, secretary of PECE, that

> all the established agencies resent the extent and the wastefulness of unregulated relief. They feel that anyone willing to take relief and stand in a bread line can get limitless meals, opportunities to sell apples and such things, but that the "white collar" group is as yet neglected because of the difficulty of establishing adequate agencies and a psychology of persuading to accept what is now offered. The representative of the school department says that New York will train any that come to her for training. An excellent suggestion was that no employer maintain a waiting room but that all out of jobs be sent to schools and all employing be done from schools or through clearing agencies.[14]

Later that day she spoke to the Women's Auxiliary of the American Society of Mechanical Engineers and did some administrative work, preparing publicity materials, before boarding a train back home to Montclair and the fam-

ily. After the arrival of Alice Dickson, some of the day-to-day pressure was removed and Lillian concentrated on meetings and lectures, though she had to
make a little money, too. Her seventh and final motion study course, which
started in January 1931, concentrated on the effects of unemployment on fatigue. The students made new micro-motion films and used statistics and
case studies from PECE to study "the effect of insecurity in general and insecurity of employment in particular on the worker, his work methods and his
skills and satisfactions."[15]

Lillian's most important contribution to the work of PECE was her mo-
bilization of nearly three million middle-class women to generate both data
and jobs. Women had run numerous "municipal housekeeping schemes" during the Progressive Era, and some of these had developed into broad-based
social justice campaigns under such leaders as Jane Addams and Florence
Kelley. Many earlier women's campaigns were predicated on notions of
women's moral superiority and resultant "domestic feminism"; Lillian occasionally appealed to essentialist ideas, such as the idea that middle-class club
women spoke the same language as underprivileged women "because they
were mothers." Most of the time, however, she operated on the assumption
that as postsuffrage American women they were equal to men and that they
should go about their fact-finding and job creation in an efficient, well-
organized manner. She contacted the heads of two hundred women's organizations asking for their cooperation and soon received "enthusiastic" replies
from the General Federation of Women's Clubs, the National Parent-Teacher
Association, and the YWCA, each willing to take responsibility for a particular group of women. Lillian reported that she also received "a thrilling
amount of cooperation of women . . . of every race [illegible] and religious,
political and other affiliation" and that "the response of the women of the
country is extraordinary. They are not only working most actively, but are delighted to be called upon and to assume responsibility."[16]

Lillian's role at PECE included coordinating research, speaking to
women's organizations, and dealing tactfully with a mountain of correspondence. She had to operate in something of an information vacuum, however,
since no national data on unemployment were available, nor was there any
central collecting system for information on relief efforts. She used women's
organizations, particularly the General Federation of Women's Clubs, to
gather the information she needed, though she was under no illusion that the
women's surveys would be scientifically valid. "There has been no idea of getting accurate statistical information," she wrote in a December 1930 report.
"The purpose has been to arouse the interest of the women who are cooperating."[17]

She tried to obtain more reliable information from trade groups such as the National Retail Dry Goods Association, asking for data on prices to help with her Wise Buying campaign. "We are advising our women to buy wisely, but I need to know, in order to be able to tell them, just what wisely means," she wrote. She also appealed to charitable organizations to "send data on minimum budgets for health and decency [sic] levels of living" and to home economics groups for "any information on extent of unemployment, agencies, coordination of activities, wise buying and give a job programs [which] will be immediately useful here."[18]

Publicity was an important part of PECE's work. With the active assistance of Sigmund Freud's nephew Edward Bernays, known as the "father of public relations," PECE worked through the advertising industry to publicize its recommendations. Bernays issued "A Challenge to Women's Clubs" in Missy Meloney's magazine The Delineator giving detailed strategic advice to women's organizations, including gathering data, appealing to the emotions, handling practical matters such as staging demonstrations and parades, and cultivating local newspaper editors and providing them with good copy. Missy Meloney accompanied his words with a dramatic image of a female knight on horseback ready to slay the dragon and reach the city on a hill. Lillian did not stage parades or talk about slaying dragons; instead, she used the radio to reach as many women as possible. Broadcasting in November 1930, some three weeks after her appointment to PECE, she demonstrated the difference between her approach and that of her chairman. It was the difference between talking to members of the existing power structure and appealing to the grass roots. "Last week," she began, "Colonel Woods, talking over the radio, questioned the Mayors and City Managers of the country as to what was being done to solve the employment problem. Tonight I am questioning the women of this country. There are about sixty million females in these United States and we do approximately 85 per cent of the buying, and there is not one of us who cannot help in some way."[19]

Lillian liked to involve the children in her projects whenever she could. She and Alice Dickson went to prepare a radio broadcast at the recently opened Chrysler Building; "it is ultra-modern, very interesting, but doesn't seem to me comfortable," she wrote Ernestine. They met a "rather hard-boiled" New York World reporter by the name of Violet Oaks, who explained the system; she would interview Lillian and have their conversation transcribed, Lillian would then review the script and read the "accepted result" onto a record, "and that record does the broadcasting when the time comes." Lillian planned to "snatch" Janey out of school, "take her to town to see me make the record . . . then out to Scout Headquarters to buy her a Brownie uniform, then to Macy's to see Santa Claus and Tony Sarg window displays. Won't that be a treat for us both!"[20]

Lillian cajoled other prominent women into broadcasting. She was very persistent; as she told Alice Dickson, "I phoned Mrs. Roosevelt several times and finally got her." Amelia Earhart broadcast in February 1931, and other speakers included leaders of the YWCA, the Girl Scouts, the Jewish Welfare Board, and the National Council of Catholic Women. Lillian also used print media to get her message across. She wrote editorials and newspaper articles and submitted to numerous interviews with journalists, few of whom neglected to include the human interest angle on her large family. One story included a photograph of some men working in heavy industry, with the memorable caption "A therblig, in case you hadn't heard, is a unit of motion by which the efficiency of a job is measured. . . . So whether one is washing dishes, running a machine or dancing the rumba, all God's chillun got therbligs."[21]

Lillian received many letters urging the firing of married women as the obvious solution to the unemployment problem. She was adamant, however, that competence and need rather than gender should be the criteria for hiring during the Depression. Press reports, memos, and letters repeat the same theme: "I feel very strongly that the proper measuring sticks are efficiency and then need and that no sex lines or other discrimination should be made." Lillian knew that this was a very sensitive issue, but she had strong views on the topic herself and understood the depth of the National Woman's Party's opposition to any discussion of limiting the employment of married women. Nevertheless, behaving very much like a politician, Lillian persuaded the NWP not to picket the White House, fearing that it would inflame public opinion further; she meanwhile warned Edward Hunt that a government spokesman should make an "authoritative statement to stabilize their thinking," since "the discharge of efficient women would arouse great unrest" and "these groups would immediately cease cooperating and may seriously hinder constructive activity."[22]

The response, as devised by Hunt and sent out to hundreds of correspondents, was one of PECE's finer moments. It read:

> Under the law the President's Emergency Committee for Employment sees no way in which the Government can discriminate against married women now employed, assuming that such discrimination is desirable. The proposal has been made in letters to us that in a period of depression such as the present, married women whose husbands are employed should be discharged. This does not commend itself to us as sound from a business point of view or desirable from a social point of view.[23]

Though this response sounded stiff and legalistic, its effect was fair; it remained official policy under the Hoover administration, at least until 1932, when Congress passed the Federal Economy Act, Section 213 of which stated that in the event of personnel reductions, persons with a spouse also in government employment should be fired first. Although the wording of the act was gender-neutral, within a year more than 1,600 women had been dismissed.[24]

An important element of Lillian's work at PECE was the "Spruce Up Your Home" campaign, which was an effort to find work for the unemployed through voluntary means. It was Colonel Woods's idea; he had been part of a similar campaign after Hoover's unemployment conference in 1921. Although Lillian loyally promoted the scheme, she realized that it would do little for unemployed women, since most of the jobs listed required skilled workers such as plumbers, painters, or electricians. Nevertheless, she supplied a list of home improvement projects and urged housewives to defer maintenance no longer. Lillian spoke directly to the club women of America, urging them to create jobs for women, and women in every state responded. In Rhode Island, for example, club women organized a Women's Central Employment Committee, in which eighteen women's organizations cooperated. They tried to find work "that otherwise would not be done" such as "cleaning and sewing and putting files in organizations up to date." They had some success. Between January 2 and February 16, 1931, they registered 828 "girls" and filled 143 jobs. Their president reported, however, "It has been particularly difficult to find places where many women can be put to work. Many of the women in R.I. who need employment are factory and jewelry workers and can do nothing else. Sewing and cleaning seems to be the only thing open to them." Even cleaning, however, posed problems since "some of the women are unable to do the strenuous work of the cleaning of the large buildings. Many of them have been on such small rations for such a long period that discretion is necessary in placing them when an opening comes."[25]

Lillian also tried to educate women consumers. She cooperated with the Bureau of Home Economics in the distribution of the "Market Basket," a weekly booklet of menus and recipes. She urged women to spend responsibly. She asked them to "Follow Your Dollar" back to the department store and factory to ensure that purchases made for their homes created more jobs. In a rather extreme example, Lillian declared, "If eighty million sheets and pillow cases were bought by the women of the United States in the next three months, that would give employment to sixty-four thousand workers for a year." She suggested that women talk to union representatives as well as store owners and make a "white list" of firms who were keeping their employees in work. The white list was a key tactic of the National Consumers' League (NCL), which printed a list of those employers who met minimum standards of hygiene and fairness. Lillian suggested applying the same idea to combat the Depression; though she was not part of the inner circle of NCL activists, she was acquainted with some of them, notably Josephine Goldmark, whose scientific management work overlapped Lillian's.[26]

Lillian worked hard for PECE. In the six months between late October 1930 and April 1931 she gave dozens of speeches, attended hundreds of meetings, and got organizations with millions of middle-class women members involved in combating the Depression. It soon became clear, however, that palliative measures were not enough to combat the triple problems of unemployment, drought, and Hoover's ideological opposition to large-scale governmental intervention in the economy. On several occasions Hoover was unwilling to support measures that PECE members recommended. Lillian endorsed Senator Robert Wagner's bill to create a system of federally financed employment bureaus, only to find it rejected by Hoover's pocket veto. In the face of Hoover's unwillingness to support major public works spending, Colonel Woods and many of his committee members, including Lillian, resigned and PECE was reduced to "Advisory Status." It was replaced by the President's Organization on Unemployment Relief (POUR), headed by Walter S. Gifford, president of the American Telephone and Telegraph Company. Lillian was one of the sixty "prominent persons" on the advisory committee, though she no longer had a women's division to head. As Hoover's relations with Congress deteriorated, even the small ($120,000) appropriation needed to keep POUR going was denied in July 1932. POUR died quietly "and its passing went unlamented except by Hoover."[27]

In April 1931 Lillian cleared her desk in Washington and prepared to return to Montclair. She turned various aspects of her work over to other branches of government and some to the voluntary sector. The General Federation of Women's Clubs would continue to oversee local employment bureaus, while the "Market Basket" and "Spruce Up Your Home" schemes would go to the Bureau of Home Economics. The Better Homes in America group within the Commerce Department would supervise construction projects, and she hoped that the industrial and retail pamphlets would also be distributed by the Commerce Department. Thanking Lillian for her work, Arthur Woods wrote, "What you did was unprecedented and of the greatest possible value to the sufferers from unemployment. You conceived a new method to apply to an old evil." He went on, "It was a brilliant conception and you carried it through with speed and skill." Woods's appreciation was personal as well as professional; he ended, "Besides this, you added greatly to our councils and to my personal grasp of the situation, such as it was and it was grand fun to have you around." To Alice Dickson he reiterated his admiration for Lillian and her work. "What an extraordinary record it is and what an amazing lot she is able to accomplish both in quantity and quality!"

Arthur Woods was being polite; the Depression was too serious for middle-class women to solve alone. However, Lillian's effort to mobilize and professionalize club women was an important step toward involving them in public policy.[28]

Lillian's last official act was to be an address to the General Federation of Women's Clubs meeting in Phoenix in late April, and she intended to fly there. Bad weather prevented this, however, and her attempts to transmit her speech over the radio were frustrated by technological problems. Finally, Lillian had to rely on older technology: she telegraphed her speech and the vice president, Grace Morrison Poole, read it to the assembled delegates. This incident serves as a metaphor for all the high hopes and urgent activity of the Women's Division of PECE, which were dashed by a combination of natural and man-made problems. Lillian's efforts to involve women in a "technic of cooperation" had faltered because of circumstances beyond her control. The club women still wanted to be involved, however, and a few months later the new first lady, Eleanor Roosevelt, took up the idea with enthusiasm. As an admirer wrote, while failing to mention that the idea was not new, "Mrs. Roosevelt's special interest in the emergency needs of unemployed women has served to coordinate the interests of numerous women's organizations dealing with the needs of jobless women."[29]

Eleanor Roosevelt's efforts were little more successful than Lillian's; the severity of the Depression required the resources of the federal government and the threat of world war to create jobs and restore the economy. During Lillian's six months in Washington she had tried and failed to use women's cooperation to solve the problem of unemployment. For the rest of her life she set herself more attainable goals.

26 Woman Power

*An older person, unless extremely happy away
from work, with well-established avocations, is
more apt to prefer work to leisure. If his family life
has been changed by deaths or marriages, he often
finds his work habits his greatest consolation and
his working comrades his truest friends.*

Lillian Moller Gilbreth, "Work and Leisure" (1930)

WHEN LILLIAN wrote these words for Charles
Beard's *Toward Civilization* she was, of course, writing about herself.[1] When
she returned from Washington in April 1931 she was nearing her fifty-third
birthday and very much in her prime; she had no intention of slowing down.
Her six months in Washington had a marked effect on her thinking, as well
as on her involvement with women and their organizations. She became increasingly active in a number of women's groups, serving as research chair for
the Business and Professional Women's Club (BPW); she was also on the advisory committee of the General Federation of Women's Clubs' Division of
Problems of Industry and active in the American Association of University
Women.

By the early 1930s Lillian was very well known both inside and outside engineering and academic circles. In the spring of 1931 Brown gave her an honorary doctorate of science and Russell Sage College awarded her a doctorate
of laws, and in October 1931 she was the first recipient of the Society of Industrial Engineers' Gilbreth Medal, created to honor the couple's work. The
SIE dubbed their annual meeting "Gilbreth Day," and one after another old
friends and colleagues got up and told stories about Frank and the children
and about Lillian's influence on her husband's thinking. Fortunately, Lillian
was a modest woman, for the tributes to Frank far outweighed those to her.
She could not resist pointing out, however, that she had "extended" Frank's

work, which had been mostly in production, into "distribution and selling—thruout business and industry and in other lines of work and of leisure." Lillian was, as usual, putting her point across in a nonconfrontational way.[2]

Although she still occasionally claimed she was not a feminist—it was not a label many women aspired to in the early 1930s, whatever their private beliefs—Lillian's actions suggest the opposite, as she started to criticize employers who discriminated against women. Lillian was particularly concerned about the practice of firing older women workers (those over forty) to make way for younger, cheaper labor. The worst sin to Lillian was wasting human potential; discarding older workers would, in her view, "not only increase the number of non-productive, unhappy people in the community, but commit what is surely the greatest of industrial wastes—human waste."[3]

Lillian initiated a research project on age discrimination, using her networking skills to the fullest. Her old friend Professor Susan Kingsbury of Bryn Mawr headed the project. They had been graduate students together at Columbia, had met again while Kingsbury headed the Boston WEIU's research department, and after Frank's death, when Lillian was exploring alternative ways to make a living, Kingsbury had hired her as a part-time lecturer at Bryn Mawr. The two women set out to discover what factors affected older women employees in their search for work, whether there seemed to be age discrimination, "and whether there are any clues pointing toward a remedial attack." Bryn Mawr graduate students conducted more than three hundred one-on-one interviews and a further sixty thousand questionnaires were mailed to BPW members. Lillian also probed attitudes toward women working after marriage "even if [their] earnings are not needed" and ended with questions about whether the respondent had ever been discriminated against or knew any woman who had.[4]

The twenty-thousand-odd returned questionnaires were tabulated and analyzed by the Women's Bureau of the Department of Labor, headed by Lillian's former colleague Mary Anderson. They discovered discrimination against white-collar women who, of course, made up the membership of the BPW. The findings were far from conclusive, however; some women complained of discrimination due to age, some due to youth, and some due to marital status, though almost all received lower pay than male workers in equivalent jobs. Lillian reacted cautiously and wrote that the findings could be "a starting point for a discussion as to whether the situation of older women is better or worse and as to whether she had made her age an asset or a liability."[5]

Although Lillian had always been sympathetic to the needs of women workers, her knowledge of the effects of low wages and limited skills on women's lives made her more proactive about vocational training and women's self-assertiveness. She also became more outspoken about the need for men's contributions to the home and the "twenty-four hour day." Lillian's views on working women reflected those of the Women's Trade Union League and also of Mary Anderson, who was tireless in her efforts to dispel the myth that married women worked for "pin money."[6]

Lillian analyzed the reasons for women's low pay. Stating firmly, "As myself a woman worker, I am speaking to you from that point of view," Lillian sketched a brief history of women's employment, tracing the movement of manufacturing from the home. She suggested that women found themselves in the lowest-paying jobs because traditional women's responsibilities, such as housework and child rearing, were seen "either as an unpaid benefit to humanity, as free as air—or as being paid for in appreciation, love for service or some other intangible coin." Women, not knowing the value of their labor in the home, "had no idea of its value in industry and sold [their] labor cheap." The solution, according to Lillian, was for women to recognize their own value and for men to make adjustments at home. "A shared industrial burden must mean a shared home burden—if there was to be 'equality of opportunity' and efficiency," she declared. Whereas in 1926 her endorsement of fifty-fifty marriages had caused an uproar, by 1932 Lillian was able to say, "The answer to home problems is to teach men how to combine a career and a home," and get away with it.[7]

Lillian's official duties did not end when she returned from Washington. She had already been one of the delegates to the White House Conference on Child Health in 1930; she incorporated many of its findings into her speeches on nutrition, and in 1932 she conducted a survey of the American Child Health Association's administration. Here, as elsewhere, she tempered sensible advice about efficiency measures with warnings to avoid the very thought of reducing salaries, as "the effect upon morale of even plans for salary cuts should be recognized." Despite this advice, the organization did decide to cut salaries, but Lillian suggested ways of easing the burden by exempting the lowest paid. Lillian was also a member of the executive committee that coordinated Hoover's Conference on Home Building and Home Ownership. Her faith in Hoover was undimmed; in 1932 she again worked with the Women's Engineering Committee in the fruitless task of trying to re-elect him.[8]

Lillian traveled to Paris in the summer of 1932 for a board meeting of the International Federation of Business and Professional Women's Clubs. She also "had the honor" of being received by Marie Curie, probably because of their joint connection with Missy Meloney: both women had benefited (and perhaps suffered) from Meloney's "spin" on their lives. Lillian also visited Mrs. Nicholas Brady, whom she knew through her Girl Scout work, in her luxurious apartment in Paris. Lillian did consultancy work for Mrs. Brady for a number of years, noting that the arrangement was "never formal enough for records to be kept on file," though she was very well paid. Genevieve Garvin Brady's late husband had amassed a fortune in utilities. He bought the old Cosmopolitan Club on Madison Avenue for his wife, who created a club similar to the YWCA to serve Catholic women. She asked Lillian to look into ways of "enriching" the program, so Lillian interviewed the staff and the "girls" and attended classes before making some suggestions about new courses. The girls were "enamored" with her and asked her to speak at club meetings, which she did on topics such as preparing for work and dressing for the job. Lillian also persuaded Mrs. Brady, who was clearly used to having her own way, to relinquish some day-to-day control and remarked that working for her "was a fascinating combination of volunteer work with the necessity of persuading a generous donor that it must become more and more democratic in every way."[9]

During her time in Europe Lillian became convinced that America had "made rather a mess of things." The Depression had hit harder and was lasting longer than in other countries, and Lillian placed part of the blame on engineers whom she accused of seeing themselves simply as technicians unconcerned with the human implications of their work. Echoing her late friend Henry Gantt, Lillian concluded that the engineer should think more holistically; instead of simply making things cheaply and well, he should think carefully about the consumer and the more equitable distribution of goods and jobs. Lillian's concern for social justice was tempered with caution; that fall, soon after Hoover lost the presidential election, she wrote an article entitled "How Can Federal Expenditures Be Reduced?" in which she applied scientific management principles to government. It is clear that she was alarmed by some of Franklin Roosevelt's promises about using government to solve the unemployment problem, though she was not against public works, which she saw as a "stabilizing force," nor was she unequivocally in favor of a balanced budget, which she believed could be overspent in "extraordinary" times.[10]

Lillian's new emphasis on social justice may have been one of the reasons she was invited to serve on the advisory committee of an ambitious project, the Congress of Women, which was to be part of the Chicago Century of Progress Exposition in 1933. She joined a group of prominent women that included Jane Addams, Carrie Chapman Catt, Judge Florence Allen, the suffragist Harriot Stanton Blatch, Congresswoman Ruth Bryan Owen, Labor Secretary Frances Perkins, and Eleanor Roosevelt. As chair of the economics committee, Lillian played a more active role than most of these celebrities. Lena Madesin Phillips, a feminist lawyer who had founded the Business and Professional Women's Clubs in 1918, was also president of the National Council of Women; it was she who did most of the organizing, while the historian Mary Ritter Beard was responsible for the six-day Congress of Women. Beard found nearly a hundred men and women willing to speak on the congress's theme, "Our Common Cause—Civilization." It was a timely topic, with Franklin Roosevelt's "Hundred Days" (the flurry of activity as his administration attempted to combat the Depression during his first three months in the White House) in full swing. The dislocations of the Depression were fresh in everyone's mind and, as Mussolini and Hitler consolidated their power, so was the frightening specter of the rise of fascism.[11]

Lillian was in the audience on July 16, 1933, when Lena Madesin Phillips used Susan B. Anthony's gavel to bring the congress to order. The Congress of Women had aroused serious interest, though it must be admitted that the average visitor to the exposition was more likely to be interested in the antics of Sally Rand, the striptease artist. Nevertheless, among the speakers were politicians, educators, and suffragists from around the world, plus the usual stalwarts from the advisory committee and Lillian Gilbreth, "celebrated consulting engineer." It was a left-of-center group: Lillian was moving in progressive circles. Over the next six days delegates from thirty-two countries (including Germany and Italy) discussed employment, war, disease, education, and the role of women in a changing world. Lillian was one of three speakers in the first session of the congress. The topic was "The World As It Is." After Mary Beard recommended the study of history for understanding the rise of fascism (which she termed "banditry"), Paul Douglas, a University of Chicago professor and one of the most influential economists of the era, gave a talk titled "The Economic Collapse." He suggested listening to "my friend, Mr. J. M. Keynes of England" and extolled many of Franklin Roosevelt's efforts to stem the Depression.[12]

Lillian's lecture was entitled "Can the Machine Pull Us Out?" The short answer was, "Yes—if we design and use it properly." It was an optimistic view of the future. After tracing the evolution of the worker to the "hand" and blaming industrialists' shortsightedness and their concentration on profitability at the expense of the "human element" for the hatred of the "machine age," she gave her listeners a brief history of the Gilbreth system of scientific management, which, she claimed, put the worker rather than the machine at the center of the picture. Warming to her theme, she concluded that "wrongly used the machine can be a peril," while "rightly used, it can help pull us out of our depression and it can help keep us out of another," but only if attitudes were changed: "the shift from materialism to humanitarianism is imperative."[13]

While she was at the congress, Lillian attended the IBM exhibit to see what they had made of her planning desk; characteristically, she had become friendly with Thomas J. Watson, the company president, and IBM had paid her traveling expenses to Chicago. IBM manufactured a prototype desk as part of their Depression-era diversification strategy. Lillian's desk epitomized her simultaneously radical yet conservative response to the woman question. She encouraged the professionalization of middle-class women while encouraging them to stay home. When the Art Deco–style tallboy desk was opened, it revealed all the tools of the home office, including a radio, a typewriter, an adding machine ("What a boon to housekeeping that little device is!"), and a telephone. There were shelves for reference books, schedules, and budget charts; large drawers to keep household files in alphabetical order; and a reminder file in a smaller drawer. The promotional brochure tried to combine the consumer's desire to avoid embarrassment, a staple of advertisers, with managerial efficiency. "When is Grandma's birthday . . . I wonder when the taxes are due . . . Goodness, haven't I paid that bill . . . These and many other important questions are brought to your attention before they can become embarrassing, by the Management Desk Reminder File." The brochure proclaimed, "Order is Heaven's first law," then suggested that the "artistically designed desk brings home a little nearer to Heaven by establishing and maintaining *order* in household planning."[14] IBM never put the management desk into production, however, so heaven had to wait a little longer.

27　Professor Gilbreth

One of her small boys came to her not long
ago and said he wanted to keep threaded needles
in his pincushion for shirt buttons . . . [which] kept
coming off. . . . When she suggested that he go to her
housekeeping assistant in these emergencies, he
informed her that he "didn't want to be dependent
on a woman every time it happened."

"Man's Place Is in the Home" (1932)

DESPITE LILLIAN's IBM contract and her public prominence, and almost certainly because of the Depression, her finances hit a low ebb in 1933. She had three children in college: Bill was at Purdue and Lill was at Smith, where she made the dean's list, and although Frank Jr. had graduated from the University of Michigan that summer, Fred was due to start at Brown in the fall. Frank Jr. had become a Big Man on Campus through his role as managing editor of the student newspaper. Nevertheless, 1933 was not a good time to be graduating and Frank returned home feeling "like something less than a hero" as he searched for a job.[1]

Lillian did what parents always do and helped Frank out financially. Over his protests she gave him an allowance—"she'd tiptoe into my room after I had gone to bed and put money in my wallet. She knew and so did I, that I had to have some cash to get in and out of New York while I was looking for work." Then she started networking on her son's behalf. Lillian had a very useful contact in the newspaper world, Missy Meloney, who spoke to the city editor of the *New York Herald Tribune,* and a month after graduation Frank Jr. started work at the princely salary of eighteen dollars a week.[2]

Lillian's friendship with Missy Meloney was one of the brighter spots of this period: it was through Missy that Lillian had repeated contracts for Better Homes of America, and in 1934 she designed three of the rooms in "America's Little House," a three-bedroom model home on Fifth Avenue. It was designed as a "maidless" house, and Lillian was in charge of the homemaker's "work centers." She saw the four main tasks as "the food problem, the clothing problem, the care of the child problem and the problem of keeping the house clean and in order." In order to solve these "problems" Lillian designed three rooms: a kitchen, a clothery, and a nursery. There were special cabinets on both floors to house two sets of cleaning materials, which she believed should be placed near to where they were to be used. She was given a budget of $1,500 and spent the grand total of $1,347.22. She cheated a little, as she badly wanted her management desk to be part of the setup. It could not, however, be procured from the list of suppliers and stores who were helping to finance the "Little House." Lillian explained that the desk was "not yet on the market but can be made by a skilled carpenter"—clearly she was still hoping IBM might put it into production. Working on the assumption that "the average housewife would have a certain number of gifts," she included one of IBM's prototypes anyway.[3]

Lillian made a gesture toward the disposable society by urging homemakers to buy several mixing cups and spoons, so that a set might be placed in each of the areas where they were to be used; she also said that such items could be bought "at a five-and-ten-cent store to be replaced by more durable accessories when that becomes possible." The nursery was a new departure for Lillian: all her previous domestic advice had concerned the kitchen, but here again she emphasized minimizing effort. In addition to "adequate care of the child," she wanted to promote "saving of the strength of the mother."[4]

The Columbia Broadcasting System was a co-sponsor of "America's Little House," and Lillian broadcast from the house in February 1935. In her talk on home safety (titled "Is Your Home a Hazard?"), she dutifully relayed statistics from the National Safety Council and the Bureau of Standards and explained how her plans for the work centers kept safety in mind. There were special places for knives; cleaning supplies were out of small children's reach; and the use of white paint created reflected light and minimized accidents. It was in the last few minutes of the talk, however, that Lillian's characteristic voice emerged, as she gave family anecdotes to illustrate what she meant. "I am wondering," she began, "if you are saying, as my husband used to say, 'But we must train the children so that they can meet a dangerous situation safely.'" She went on, "I can see him yet, taking each youngster as he learned to creep and showing him how to go to the stairs, turn around and crawl down carefully, step by step. It took time and patience. It was a serious business, in spite of the fact that the onlookers found it very funny and it did mean of course, that if the safety gate was open, the baby knew how to meet the situation comfortably and happily." Perhaps aware that she was undermining her own argument about all the safety features in the "Little House," she turned to the role of fatigue in accidents and the need for careful planning to avoid excessive tiredness. "Our records in industry, of course, show this, for the tired worker is the one who gets into trouble." She went on,

> I remember learning this when I was a bride. I had put in a very strenuous day and when my husband came home that night he came to the rescue and offered to do a little repair work that I felt could not wait until morning. It was in a rather dark place, for I had not had much experience in planning then and he asked me to hold a lighted match so that he could see better. Well, I burned his ear. Naturally he gave a yell, but while I stood there expecting the well-deserved scolding, he gave one look at me and said "You poor tired thing." That was all. Perhaps it was because of this experience I was so eager to put every possible fatigue eliminating device into our Little House.[5]

As part of her work for the "Little House," Lillian made further investigations of the correct height for kitchen equipment, which were described in a somewhat hostile piece in the *American Magazine*. Under a full-page close-up of Lillian the caption read: "Dr. Lillian Moller Gilbreth does a man's job in a woman's sphere—the home. She has put more U.S. kitchens on an efficiency basis than French cooks have fried potatoes. Mother of eleven, she has almost as many major degrees as she has children." Warming to her subject, the journalist described a recent project in which Lillian "stopped 4,000 busy housewives shelling peas, baking cake, stirring little Willie's cereal, so that she could measure the distance from their elbows to the floor—Gilbreth's step No. 1 to get the dope on the shape and height of stove and sink." Lillian "divides the house like a factory—into work centers, work surfaces, work motions," with the result that "housewives of the country have more time for bridge."[6]

Neither the "Little House" nor the *Herald Tribune* Institute was an altruistic operation, of course; both were vehicles for manufacturers eager to showcase their products or to advertise them in the *Herald Tribune Magazine*. Nevertheless, Lillian believed in the educated, rational consumer, and the remodeled *Herald Tribune* kitchen reflects both that view and the commercial interests of its sponsors. Lillian described the elements of the kitchen, which included her home management desk, a circular work space, and a table on wheels, but nowhere did she prescribe equipment. That was left to one of the Institute's home economists. Rampant consumerism made Lillian uncomfortable, despite the fact that much of her income depended on it. She told a journalist in 1935 that trying to keep up with the Joneses caused enormous and unnecessary distress. "Women especially," she declared, "are inclined to try and possess things and they must spare themselves the sheer, sheer agony of wanting curtains like those of Mrs. Jones, or clothes like those of Mrs. Smith." She was never willing to lend her name for product endorsement. When Janey was three or four years old, Lillian turned down a "very attractive" offer from Cream of Wheat, which was running a celebrity endorsement campaign for its breakfast cereal. The company wanted "a dignified picture" of mother and daughter but Lillian refused (although this was a product the Gilbreths actually used), saying, "I don't believe in found money. It's much better to depend on one's money earned from hard work." Eleanor Roosevelt had no such qualms and extolled the virtues of Cream of Wheat accompanied by one of her grandchildren. Lillian could have made an easier living had she agreed to endorse the products and appliances she incorporated into her kitchen designs, but over her long career her name appeared in only two advertising campaigns, one for the Gilbreth management desk and one for a laundry owners' trade organization.[7]

Meanwhile, Franklin Roosevelt's New Deal was not having the hoped-for effect on the economy. Lillian's consultancy income was erratic, to say the least, so in 1935 she took a salaried job for the first time in her life. She became a full professor of management in the School of Mechanical Engineering at Purdue, the first woman in the United States to hold such a title. Both Frank and Lillian had a long-standing relationship with Purdue; Lillian had taken Frank's place as a visiting lecturer starting in the fall of 1924, and by 1935 she was a familiar figure on campus. Purdue University was and is a large state university in West Lafayette, Indiana, with a heavy concentration on engineering, agriculture, and the sciences. The university's president, Edward C. Elliott, was concerned about the imbalance in the number of female to male students—they were outnumbered almost six to one—and after hearing both Lillian and Amelia Earhart speak at one of Missy Meloney's conferences, he decided to hire both of them as an inspiration to the coeds. Earhart became a counselor on careers for women and was paid two thousand dollars a year for a part-time appointment.[8]

Lillian and Amelia Earhart formed a mutual admiration society. Lillian told a reporter (who noted that she bore "a marked resemblance to the aviatrix") before she started the job that she would be working with Miss Earhart, "and I'm so glad, because I'm one of her ardent admirers." For her part, Amelia Earhart, who had pasted a photograph of the Gilbreths into her scrapbook in 1924, long before she herself became famous, told a friend, "The most rewarding part of my time at the University is my association with Lillian Gilbreth."[9]

Lillian talked to the remaining children about moving to West Lafayette, but as they were unwilling to leave Montclair, where they had many friends, she went without them. For the next two years she spent three weeks of every month of the school year at Purdue. While Martha ran the family on a day-to-day basis, Lillian supervised and networked on their behalf from a distance. Some of her networking was at a very high level; for example, she wrote Eleanor Roosevelt a letter on Purdue notepaper asking if Janey's middle-school class could drop by the White House during a school trip to Washington. Mrs. Roosevelt instructed her secretary to invite them all to tea.[10]

Lillian combined her time at Purdue with local consultancy work for the Duncan Electric Company in Lafayette, as well as a similar project in Michigan. Lillian lectured on management engineering in all the schools of engineering—civil, mechanical, electrical, and chemical. She was also instrumental in creating a motion study laboratory where students majoring in management were trained and engineers in other disciplines visited. She helped set up an honors course in which the students worked in local industries, many of which were tied in with her electric company research project.[11]

Although Lillian was not closely involved with the women students at first, since there were none in the School of Engineering, like Earhart she lived in the women's residence hall, and the students learned that if they got up very early they could join her for breakfast. Lillian worked very hard during her first two years at Purdue, reaching out to the female undergraduates by offering courses to students in home economics, education, and agriculture. Also, for a while after Amelia Earhart's disappearance in July 1937, she took over some of her responsibilities as a career counselor for women. Later in 1937, however, she reduced her commitments, though she remained a part-time professor of management until 1948, when Purdue insisted she retire.[12]

Lillian's friend and biographer Edna Yost believed that her years at Purdue were "an altogether happy experience," though she hints at some problems. Being the only woman in a very male environment, the School of Engineering, was not always easy. Lillian collaborated with a younger professor, Marvin Mundel, who was, apparently, a very abrasive character ("a well-known SOB," according to one of his former graduate students) who repeatedly embarrassed the unmathematical Lillian in front of other engineers at Purdue. She would have to admit that Frank had always done the calculations. There may have been more personal reasons, as she had liked Mundel's first wife and was deeply offended by his divorce, so much so that many years later, in 1961, when she was staying with friends in Tokyo, she absolutely refused to see her former colleague, which resulted in a loss of face for Mundel.[13] Other Purdue colleagues were less abrasive, however, and the university provided a secure base for Lillian for more than a dozen years.

28 A Superannuated Bachelor Girl Goes to War

"Of course I liked it!" But then, with a perfectly straight face she added mildly, "But let's just say, dear, that it occasionally had its disadvantages."

Frank Gilbreth Jr., *Time Out for Happiness* (1970), on his mother's attitude toward living with eleven children

IN THE FALL OF 1939 Lillian was alone in her big old house in Montclair, New Jersey. It seemed unnaturally quiet. The big double desk that she and Frank had shared was still there, as were the filing cabinets crammed with papers, all classified in the Gilbreths' own idiosyncratic N-File, but it seemed very big just for her. The old-fashioned kitchen was quiet; she had never been fond of cooking and now that Tom, the handyman-cook and the bane of her life for a quarter of a century, was gone, very little cooking ever got done. The lawns around the house were quiet; there was no baseball or touch football game, nor were there young men in cars scrunching up the gravel drive and blowing their horns, impatient to take one of her daughters to a dance. Upstairs was quiet, too; the bedrooms were unnaturally tidy, and there were no lines for the bathroom and no Victrola machines playing French or German records while the children cleaned their teeth. Her two youngest children, Bob and Jane, had just started college and now she had the house to herself. She had time to think about what to do with the rest of her life. She was sixty-one years old and had no thoughts of retirement. She loved work: she felt incomplete without it, though her definition of what constituted work was a broad one. It involved what she always called the "twenty-four hour" day and included her partnership with Frank, mothering and organizing her children, and her engineering activities. Now that only one of these elements remained, she decided to fill all the empty spaces in the day with professional work and travel.[1]

As a first step she simplified her domestic arrangements by moving into an apartment in the center of Montclair. There was no one to look after the house since Tom retired; he spent his last few years in a nursing home. It was very expensive to maintain and was starting to show the effects of eleven children and nearly twenty years of deferred maintenance. For the short term she just closed it up, but she felt, and the rest of the family reluctantly agreed, that it was too big and too decrepit for anyone to want to buy, and as they did not have the money to renovate it, she decided to have it demolished. The barn, which had once housed Frank's photographic laboratory and where later the children had kept a flock of Plymouth Rock hens, was left standing and converted into a house.[2]

Lillian had never learned to drive, so she chose an apartment within walking distance of all the places she wanted to be: the First Congregational Church, the Montclair Public Library, and the train station. After Jane married, Lillian converted the back bedroom into an office, adding a studio couch for any out-of-town children who might want to spend the night, without making it so comfortable that they would stay too long. She gave away most of her furniture, pictures, and china, though she kept one of the two rocking chairs that had been in Martha's apartment in Boston the first time she met her formidable mother-in-law-to-be. She kept her books and a few items with sentimental value: presents from Frank, awards from engineering organizations, and some of her very best china, which had been put away all the years her strenuous children were growing up. Visitors to her apartment saw stacks of papers everywhere. Files from the office overflowed into the hallway, and almost every flat surface was piled with magazines, technical journals, and letters. Lillian was a compulsive correspondent; she traveled with ready-stamped postcards in her pocketbook and often wrote thirty or more short notes a day. Her friends joked that she was so prompt in writing thank-you notes that they expected to see them in the mailbox when they returned from taking her to the airport.[3]

Lillian did not pressure any of her children to follow in her footsteps; the Gilbreth children were all encouraged go their own ways. Martha Gilbreth, the third daughter, wrote, "Individuality has always been as highly developed as possible in our family. There was always the element of the survival of the fittest and it was natural to develop either a good right arm or a sharp tongue, or both, for use when necessary."[4]

Bill was the most difficult of the children, but he became a successful engineer. One of the stories the family tells of his misdeeds reflects very favorably on Lillian and her childrearing methods. It seems that when he was a student at Purdue he overslept one day and cut class. The professor introduced a guest lecturer, namely Lillian, then called the roll. There was a silence when he came to Gilbreth, until a number of Bill's friends simultaneously decided to come to the rescue and "Here" rang out in a dozen voices from all over the room. According to Frank Jr.'s account, the professor glared and said sarcastically that there seemed to be a great many Gilbreths here today, to which Lillian replied sweetly, "The whole family. That's nice." She met Bill later in the day and talked to him at some length about the work she was currently engaged in, namely motion study for the disabled. The next morning, the professor announced a quiz, asking the class to summarize what yesterday's speaker had said. Bill whispered to a friend, "Who did the old fool drag over here yesterday? I overslept." "You overslept! It was your own mother, you stupid jackass," was the reply. Everyone started writing. Bill nudged his neighbor again and said, "Would you mind telling this stupid jackass what my mother talked about?" "Motion study of the disabled." Bill grinned and started writing.[5]

Jane was the baby; only two years old when her father died, she was always the center of attention and a little spoiled. When Janey was very small Lillian used to sing:

> We love Anne and Ernie, away off in Smith—
> We love Frank and Martha, though they're inclined to tiff!
> Bill, Lill, Fred, Dan, Jack, Bobby—we love them one and all—
> But Janey! She's the baby!
> And we love her best of all![6]

Jane graduated from Montclair High like all the others, though she spent grades six through eight at Brookside, a progressive private school where, to her mother's delight, she "avoided the strenuous junior high days of the public school." Lillian tried to keep Jane out of circulation as long as possible, for her youngest daughter became "a social butterfly" in high school; like several of her siblings she was involved in sororities, and as her mother put it, with commendable understatement, her "unduly busy social life made keeping high standards of scholarship difficult." Nevertheless, she skipped grades and was only just seventeen when she graduated. Her family remembers her as a "free spirit" and none of them was much surprised when she was asked not to return to Sweet Briar College, in Lynchburg, Virginia, at the end of her freshman year, allegedly for drinking while out on a date. Lillian swept down to Virginia in her daughter's support and transferred her to the University of Michigan.[7]

Lillian had a great capacity for concentrating on one thing at a time and seemed able to switch seamlessly from the role of mother to the role of busi-

nesswoman. She would come home after a long day advising factory managers or designing efficient kitchens and listen patiently while a daughter
thought aloud as to whether her new summer shoes should have high or low
heels, or while one of her sons tried to decide whether to get a crew cut or a
regular haircut. Martha wrote, "To see your own mother able to work all day
and then come home and suddenly snap from a 'business man' into a most
understanding and sympathetic mother, makes one wish it were possible for
more people to do the same." Lillian's example was not enough, however, to
convince her daughters to follow in her footsteps. Most of them, having
helped bring up their younger brothers and sisters, married young and had
small families. Only Ernestine had a career. Lill, who was only nineteen when
she graduated "creditably" from Smith in 1934, worked for a few months at
Macy's, then married and stopped working. According to her mother, "Lill
asked for no career except for a home and a family!"[8]

Martha was an exception to the family rule of early marriage; she lived at
home, running the house until the two youngest went to college. In the mid-
1930s she published a breezy article in *Colliers* under the heading "A Large
Family Is Fun!" claiming that the house ran itself. She admitted, however, that
although the family was supposed to run on a cooperative basis, with the
younger children expected to help, none of them were "model citizens" and
coping with them was not always simple. Martha also emphasized the fact
that Lillian, despite her frequent absences, was a very real presence in the
household. While she admitted that the younger children were envious of
friends whose mothers supplied "the proverbial ginger-ale and cake" after
school, she suggested that Lillian's ability to be "successfully in two places at
the same time" meant that "she is not only bringing up her children, she is
leading them an example which will mean more and more to them as they
grow older." Jane, many years later, was less rosy about her childhood,
lamenting her mother's physical and emotional distance. Most of the
Gilbreth children, however, seem determined to put a positive spin on their
upbringing. A family anecdote suggests that Lillian may have also thought
she was doing a good job. According to Frank Jr., Jane's third-grade teacher
once said to her, "Now Janey, we know that your father isn't alive, so suppose
you tell us what your mother does." Jane is said to have replied, "Well, anything I ask her to. Sometimes she irons my party dresses and she reads to
me and helps with home work." The teacher persisted, asking, "But Janey,
doesn't she have a career?" only to be told, "I don't know. If she does, it never
bothered me." Lillian always claimed this was the best compliment she ever
received.[9]

Lillian quickly settled into her apartment, but some of her children worried that she might be lonely. She kept in close touch with them, however; she

either saw or wrote to all of them at least once a week and found time to visit all those who lived far away two or three times a year, frugally getting her fares paid by combining her visits with lecture engagements. Most of the children lived nearby: Dan and Jack lived in Montclair, relieved they no longer had to mow two acres of grass up at the old house, and Ernestine, Bill, Lill, Fred, and Bob were not far away. Martha and Jane both moved to the West Coast after their marriages, Anne was in the Midwest, and Frank Jr. lived in the South. Lillian went out of her way to assure them all that she enjoyed being a "superannuated bachelor girl." She told Frank Jr. how much she liked living on her own and what a comfort it was to be able to put something down "and know that, when you come back, it won't have been lost, moved, broken, smeared with jam, painted, or colored with crayons." She also reveled in the luxury of having a bath without worrying that she'd used the last of the hot water, or that someone would barge in.[10]

The disadvantages of having eleven children were insignificant, however, compared with the problem of disposing of a third of a century's accumulation of films, photographs, and business records, as well as more private materials, such as letters between her and Frank. Lillian felt that they should all be preserved as a record of both the Gilbreth work in motion study and their family experiment. She shipped carton after carton of Frank's motion study films—almost three hundred thousand feet of it—from her basement, where it must have created a significant fire hazard, to a motion study laboratory in Illinois. Engineers there, headed by James Perkins, made selections from the films designed to show the highlights of the Gilbreths' work in the 1910s and 1920s. The compilation was to have its premiere at an engineering meeting in 1945, with a commentary spoken by Lillian.[11]

The film is a mixture of family and work: to the Gilbreths there was no division between the public and private parts of their life. It starts with Frank and Lillian walking up a Providence street before World War I and contains footage of Frank speaking into a Dictaphone, his bricklaying work, and several scenes of the innovations they introduced at New England Butt in 1912 and 1913. There are also soap-packing experiments, typewriting by both the able-bodied and the disabled, and film of the Giants versus the Phillies in 1913. The Gilbreths' hospital work is represented, too; a patient is shown having a stomach tumor removed. The movie ends with family scenes shot at Nantucket with Lillian surrounded by children, holding the latest baby; some of the children on a seesaw outside "the Shoe"; and Frank playing leapfrog, followed by numerous small children, all of them, including Frank, clad in old-fashioned black bathing suits.[12]

Lillian donated her papers to Purdue and in 1940 dozens of cartons of papers and books were shipped to West Lafayette. The Purdue trustees were delighted with the gift and offered her an assistant funded by the Works Progress Administration to help her get them into order.

Her children settled, her living arrangements simplified, her papers sorted, it was time for Lillian to get back to work. She had extraordinary stamina. Freed from most of her domestic responsibilities, she started a pattern of intense work and extensive travel that was to characterize the rest of her long working life. She still served as a consultant, though that income was sporadic and occasionally her finances were straitened. She also did a great deal of volunteer work. Though she spent a lot of time at Purdue during the 1940–41 academic year working on her papers and her memoirs, she also traveled on special assignments for President Elliott. On one such trip, over an eight-day period between February 22 and March 1, 1941, Lillian visited four colleges, gave ten lectures or speeches, and attended two daylong meetings as well as several shorter ones. Most of her activities were connected with the war effort in one way or another, though as usual she combined business with pleasure with a stop at Princeton, where her son Jack was now a senior. She spent two days in Washington with the Housing Committee of the Twentieth Century Fund discussing the defense housing program and visiting housing projects. The fund was the brainchild of Edward Filene, head of the Boston department store and an old acquaintance of Lillian's. Like many Progressives, he believed that if the "facts" were brought to light, then most of society's problems could be solved. During World War II the fund's attention turned to the economic problems of peace; it was feared that the returning servicemen would put an immense strain on the economy; one of their recommendations, among a package of governmental measures to stimulate demand, was housing, and Lillian was working on a low-cost housing scheme. Lillian's other meetings during this packed week included a whole day with the AAUW planning a forthcoming conference on the economic and legal status of women and an evening with the Society of Industrial Engineers discussing defense issues, where she spoke, giving a "short closure" to the meeting. She found time to hear the anthropologist Ruth Benedict's lecture "Individual Behavior and the Social Order," which she found "excellent."[13]

In the spring of 1941 it was becoming clear to Lillian as well as many others that American entry into World War II could not be delayed indefinitely. Manufacturers were starting to convert to war production; Franklin D. Roosevelt had already asked Congress to authorize production of fifty thousand planes per year. Agencies such as the Office of Price Administration, the War Production Board, and the War Labor Board were created to organize the defense program, thereby expanding the role of government further and faster than any of Roosevelt's New Deal agencies ever did. By 1945 twelve million Americans had joined the armed forces, most of them men, and their jobs were filled either by women or by men who had been deemed unfit for service. Lillian's expertise in work simplification and fatigue elimination covered both women and "crippled soldiers," and as plants needed to operate as efficiently as possible, less skilled or less experienced workers had to be trained to fill the jobs. Accordingly, she reduced her commitments at Purdue, though she retained her professorial title, and became professor of industrial relations and chair of the department of personnel relations at the Newark College of Engineering, "nearer to the defense industries where I hope to be a little help," as she told an inquiring journalist. Yet again, she was the first woman to hold such a position.[14]

Lillian did three types of war work: she was a government adviser, a role model to other women, and an ergonomics expert. For some of these roles she was paid and paid handsomely; in other cases she worked for expenses only, doing her "bit" for the war effort. Lillian was a member of the advisory group on the formation of the Women's Reserve of the Navy, which became known as the WAVES—Women Appointed for Volunteer Service. The WAVES filled noncombatant jobs and released men for active duty. Their work was voluntary in that the women had not been conscripted, but they wore a naval uniform, were posted to naval bases all over the country, and were paid a good salary. Lillian encouraged others to help with the WAVES. Dean Dorothy Stratton of Purdue recalled that even before the legislation was passed, "Dr. G. insisted that I should volunteer and do it early," and accordingly she went to the officers' training course at Smith that fall.[15]

Lillian realized that the defense program offered "exceptional" opportunities to professional women, noting that firms that had always refused to hire women engineers "are glad to get them now." But she was cautious about the future: "whether this will apply to the same degree after the emergency is ended remains to be seen." She presented a paper on the topic at the ASME's fall 1942 meeting, applying "the engineering method" to the issue of what, who, when, how, and why women could be engineers, while acknowledging that the "many emotional factors involved" made dispassionate analysis difficult. Lillian suggested that much more research was needed to establish how and why women's career choices differed from men's. She also advocated research into women's capabilities. "Are there any areas of engineering work that women cannot do, should not do, do not so well as men, do as well as men, do better than men?" she asked. Lillian was addressing the fundamental issue of equality versus difference. Women were already being hired in the defense industries, and management was trying to cope without the luxury of time to ponder the issues Lillian raised. She suggested that many problems could be resolved as they went along, but only if employers made up their minds whether women were simply substitutes for men, or whether they reorganized the work, on the assumption that women had different skills and capabilities. "The first problem implies making over women," she declared; "the second problem implies making over jobs." If the work remained the same, then the personnel department was responsible for choosing the right women and keeping them reasonably content; if the jobs were adapted to women, then industrial engineers such as herself needed to analyze what needed to be done and devise more woman-friendly ways to do it. Lillian's own views became clear when she suggested that most of the questions she posed also applied to men, whose skills and native abilities varied widely. "In fact," she wrote, "it becomes increasingly evident that we have paid too much attention to sex differences and too little to the difference between efficiency and inefficiency."[16]

Lillian's expertise was in demand; though she had never cared much for FDR, being too much of a Republican and a voluntarist to appreciate his New Deal, she responded to a call to join the educational advisory committee of the Office of War Information. She was also on the education subcommittee of the War Manpower Commission. Missy Meloney kept in touch and included Lillian in a group of "outstanding women in industry" featured in a little booklet issued by the National Industrial Information Committee in 1942. The booklet, American Women at War, was written by a group of "crack newspaperwomen" who "trudged miles and miles" through "humming factories" to see what women were doing for the war effort. Lillian also continued her association with the Women's Bureau. From early 1942 she was involved with the efforts of Mary Anderson, the durable head of the bureau, to organize and monitor women's war work. The Women's Bureau issued numerous pamphlets during the war; one that clearly shows Lillian's mark is bulletin no. 190, "Recreation and Housing for Women War Workers," issued in 1942. It included as appendix B the "Code of Ethics for Volunteers" that Lillian's committee of the AAUW had labored long and hard to produce. It is a document very characteristic of Lillian; the second paragraph reads: "I believe that all work should be carefully analyzed in order that work methods may be standardized. I believe that people should be studied in order to determine what jobs they can do and like to do and that, as far as possible, they should be assigned to jobs they can do well and enjoy."[17]

Part of Lillian's income came from her consultancy work, the most important of which was for the Arma plant in the Brooklyn Navy Yard, where she spent Mondays and Thursdays each week. She always arrived at eight o'clock sharp, but one Monday when she was not there by ten her colleagues were starting to worry. She arrived a few minutes later, with her left arm in a splint. Explaining that she had slipped while hanging out some washing, she claimed her inquiry was only a hairline fracture, and according to her son, said, "And I thought we already had enough Monday morning absenteeism here at Arma. . . . I'm sorry I'm late." Absenteeism was one of the many issues that plants such as Arma had to deal with as they expanded to meet war needs. Working conditions for women left something to be desired. Lillian's first reaction on being asked by a panicky Arma executive for advice on how to prepare for women workers is said to have become "something of a byword in the War Manpower Commission." She is reported to have said, "If that's all my job is, I can finish it with this one sentence: 'Build separate restrooms.'"[18]

Rosie the Riveter and Winnie the Welder have become iconic figures of World War II, but the integration of women into the male culture of the yards was not easy. In early 1942 there were practically no women engaged in production work in shipyards, but by January 1944 almost 10 percent of the greatly expanded labor force was female. Shipyard work was strenuous and by December 1943 women were leaving faster than they could be hired: simple exhaustion was one of many reasons for the women's unhappiness. Arma created an exercise program, which reduced absenteeism. Sometimes the sixty-five-year-old Lillian went to the gymnasium and joined in, according to Edna Yost, with "a suppleness and verve that put some twenty-year-olds to shame."[19]

The Women's Bureau issued a pamphlet on "Employing Women in Shipyards" in April 1944, noting that "just a little over two years ago the subject and purpose of this bulletin would have been considered as fanciful as a tale from the Arabian Nights." Lillian's influence is clear from the table of contents: "Select and place women carefully"; "schedule rest periods"; "set up an effective woman counselor system." The woman counselor was an innovation. Somewhere between a foreman, a personnel officer, and a social worker, her role was to select, test, and supervise the women and provide for their welfare beyond the eight-hour workday. In conjunction with local women's organizations like the YWCA, she also helped provide recreational facilities. At the Arma plant Lillian helped train such counselors.[20]

The introduction of new workers, who also included older men and less fit men, none of whom had been through a traditional apprenticeship, required many changes. Lillian helped plants modify working systems and training schemes and reported that industrial accidents decreased. The new methods were "better not only for the workers but for production records as well." She also helped the Arma Corporation and the U.S. Navy to organize work assembling naval ordnance equipment for disabled seamen, some of whom were still confined to their hospital beds. The program combined physical therapy with "the emotional satisfaction of a pay envelope." She worked with the War Manpower Commission and the New York Heart Association on ways of simplifying work so that men with cardiovascular disease could be utilized in industry. Lillian was returning to the "crippled soldier" work she and Frank had started during World War I, and in 1944 she collaborated with Edna Yost on *Normal Lives for the Disabled,* which they dedicated "To the Memory of Frank B. Gilbreth and His Work for the Disabled." She lectured on the topic all over the United States, speaking as a psychologist as well as an engineer. "The mental state of the disabled is all-important," she declared. "If a person has the normal American outlook, the optimism, the belief in God, man and the future, it is a beginning."[21]

Lillian was still involved in a number of projects at Purdue, including the National Work Simplification Project: just as her man-of-all-work Tom Grieves had charged, she was trying to "make it easy for folks to work hard." It was a logical continuation of her lifetime work in motion study and fatigue study. She organized two leadership training sessions in 1942, one at Purdue and one at the New Jersey College of Engineering in Newark, both funded by General Electric. She helped Purdue acquire a fifty-thousand-dollar grant from the Rockefeller Foundation to apply motion study to agriculture, but like her work with model kitchens, many of the changes affected women in unforeseen ways. A more efficient layout of farm buildings and equipment often meant that barns were bigger and farther away from the farmhouse, which in turn led to a separation between women's work and men's; farm specialization meant less autonomy for women, as cheese making and egg production were transferred to agribusiness. With rural electrification farm women's lives became easier in some ways, but they became, like their city cousins, consumers rather than producers.[22]

Lillian was also involved with Purdue home economists in researching low-cost, efficient housing. This was part of the war effort, as accommodations had to be available near the defense plants. They were trying to build a house for two thousand dollars; it had to be inexpensive to run and, rather alarmingly, they wanted to include windows that would not open to avoid heat loss. That there was a window at all was a concession to those people "who feel they must have some window," for a completely windowless house would be more energy efficient! The furniture was to be built-in and the kitchen was to be even more efficient than the ones Lillian had designed in the mid-1930s, for this time she did not have manufacturers wishing to promote their new appliances. Accordingly, she was willing to question everything. She claimed, "From the beginning I have felt that refrigerators and stoves have kept their shape because of the original design for ice and coal and wood. But now there is no longer any such necessity." She was willing to abandon the traditional stove and replace it with an oven and a cooktop placed separately; she speculated that one day all appliances could be fitted into a table, around which the whole family could sit so that meal preparation would become truly communal. This idea appealed to Lillian, as she thought about the advantages to her own household and perhaps to others where there were working mothers. At that time, early 1942, two of her unmarried sons were living at home, in her apartment. "We live together and we are all out working," she explained. "We could all get around one table and one boy could prepare the salad and one broil the chops and we would all be together."[23]

Lillian was prepared, however, to allow for individual tastes and differences. "A system is there only to simplify things," she explained. "If it makes you happy to junk it, then you should junk it." She was obviously not in favor of having the family sitting in the dining room while the mother runs in and out of the kitchen bearing food; she even suggested disposable plates, citing a hospital that was planning to abandon the use of china in favor of "fiber dishes that might be tossed away after using." She acknowledged that perhaps some families liked more traditional ways, conceding that "on holidays, I, myself, enjoy taking all morning to gather the china and the silver," but that as a working woman she had to find quicker and more efficient ways.[24]

Lillian worked hard during the war. As ever, her work was an effective way to keep her mind off other worries, as eventually five of her six sons served in the armed forces. She helped management solve technical problems and was often effective as a troubleshooter. She was able to sit down "with a group of men who were tense and knotted about their differences, to invite free expression successfully from representatives of groups whose whole industrial background make them feel in opposition to each other and skillfully direct their discovery of means within their power to achieve their common purpose with satisfactory fairness to all." Lillian was not, however, tough enough or cynical enough to stand up to some of the less scrupulous employers; she always believed in industrial democracy, but as corporations grew in size some of them developed autocratic management systems. There was little she could do about it by simple persuasion, but she went on trying.[25]

29 As Resilient As a Good Rubber Band

Lillian Gilbreth was in tip-top condition
when the war made its heavier demands on her.
She had always loved work and had worked hard
all her life. At sixty-five she had the resilience
of a good rubber band.

Edna Yost, *Frank and Lillian Gilbreth: Partners for Life* (1948)

WHEN THE WAR ended in 1945, Lillian was sixty-seven years old and far from ready to retire. The Gilbreth name was well known and increasingly respected; the previous year the engineering profession had given Lillian one of its highest honors, the Gantt Gold Medal. There was still some resistance to honoring a woman in this way, but Joseph Juran, a young engineer who was on the committee, broke the logjam by suggesting that Frank be included in the citation. The medal was presented at a joint meeting of the American Society of Mechanical Engineers, which Lillian had fought so hard to join, and the American Management Association. The citation read, "To Dr. Lillian Moller Gilbreth and to Dr. Frank B. Gilbreth, posthumously . . . the 1944 Gantt Medal, in recognition of their pioneer work in management and their development of the principles and techniques of motion study." This was a major triumph for Lillian.[1]

Medals do not pay bills, however, and in the immediate aftermath of the war, Lillian found profitable consulting jobs scarce and was reduced to calling in past favors. Missy Meloney had died three years earlier and with her had gone Lillian's best contacts at the *Herald Tribune,* with the exception of Eloise Davidson, who had been a home economist at the *Herald Tribune* Institute and had since become its director. Lillian had worked with her before and had been one of the consultants on *America's Housekeeping Book,* a six-hundred-page tome that Davidson published in 1941.[2]

One raw, cold day in April 1946 with a late snow in the air, Lillian took Ernestine out for a birthday lunch, but she decided to first call on Davidson, to see if there were any consultancy jobs going. Mother and daughter went together to the *Herald Tribune* offices on Forty-second Street. Ernestine had met Davidson in the late 1920s, had admired her tremendously, and had even invited her to her wedding as a "special friend." Sixteen years later, it was a different story. Davidson made them wait; she "let us cool our heels there without explanation for half an hour." Ernestine was indignant. "I had been with mother on many occasions. . . . Unfailingly I had seen her treated like a Queen. And now this!" She went on: "Eventually '*Miss Davidson*,' all the executive in an English tailored suit, swept toward us. After shaking hands with mother and ignoring me she said crisply, 'I'm sorry, Dr. Gilbreth, but I've combed our need here. And I see no possibility of your being useful to us right now. Or we to you.' Ernestine was furious, but Lillian reacted mildly, admitting over lunch that Davidson had been "difficult," adding, "But of course her job can't be easy." She and Davidson remained friends—it would, of course, have been pointless to do otherwise with a woman in such an influential position.[3]

Meanwhile, Lillian continued her work for the government. She advised the Women's Army Corps (the WACS) and the WAVES for a number of years; she was one of only two women on the Chemical Warfare Board in the late 1940s, and in the early 1950s she served on Truman's Civil Defense Advisory Council. She was also active in volunteer work with women and girls, especially the Girl Scouts, for whom she chaired an advisory committee on the integration of handicapped Scouts into regular troops.[4] Her Girl Scout colleagues had fond memories of Lillian's technique at board meetings. One recalled seeing her sitting quietly at the back of the room with her crocheting while the board members argued until "Dr. Gilbreth would speak a well-thought-out resolution of the situation and settle the question." Another Scouting friend paid tribute to Lillian's extraordinary memory, one of the traits that must have endeared her to many. Martha Coe Davis was a trainee manager at the Green Line lunchrooms in New York when Lillian carried out a motion study there in 1927. In 1949 Davis was working for the Girl Scouts in Milwaukee, where Lillian was to give a speech. The recently published *Cheaper by the Dozen* had made Lillian more famous than ever; "adoring fans" eager to get her autograph were blocking her way to the auditorium, so Davis decided to rescue her and give her a chance to rest a little—Lillian was, after all, over seventy years old. She recalled that Lillian "turned and looked at me and she said 'Martha, how nice to see you. Have you heard from Roland since Mildred died?' I practically fell through the floor . . . it was 22 or 23 years since she had laid eyes on me or probably even thought of me."[5]

When the postwar recession ended, Lillian's expertise in women's issues and work simplification led to numerous contracts, both in the United States and overseas. She was also well known in academic circles as a scientific researcher, though her technique was often to ask the right questions and leave others to do the actual work. Jane Callaghan, formerly a kitchen consultant at the Brooklyn Gas Company who did secretarial work for Lillian after she retired, explained how her friend worked.

> The pattern is always the same: first, Dr. Gilbreth has a helpful idea; next she inspires someone to start a pilot project to explore the idea. She herself stands by to help if needed. She offers few suggestions but asks many, many penetrating questions. As the pilot project develops she spreads the news, mentions it in her talks, discusses it with people who have something helpful to offer, particularly management people and generally stimulates an exchange of ideas, until finally the baby project is "born" into a welcoming climate where it can grow and prosper and expand.[6]

Lillian applied this technique to the application of industrial engineering to hospitals. Harold Smalley, who had a distinguished career in this field, acknowledged that most of his inspiration came from her. Like many of her colleagues and former students, he revered Lillian, whom he described as "my inspiration, my motivator, my mentor, my colleague and collaborator and my friend." In 1966 Smalley wrote a textbook on hospital management, stating firmly that "one of the most significant developments in the methods improvement movement occurred in 1945 when Dr. Lillian M. Gilbreth . . . began to urge that hospitals take advantage of the tools and techniques of industrial engineering." From 1954 to 1958 she collaborated with Smalley in research on nursing, organizing hospital supplies, and the best types of hospital beds. When Smalley moved to Georgia Tech in 1958, Lillian transferred her consultancy work there. During one of her hospital visits, in the early 1960s, the driver got lost on the way back to her hotel. As one of her traveling companions recalled, Lillian said nothing but hummed a tune, her way of showing disapproval and containing her anger. Later, after they eventually reached the hotel and met for dinner, Lillian ordered scrod; the southern waiter, unable to understand her rather clipped accent, thought she had asked for squab and the whole party waited and waited while a squab was located and cooked. Notwithstanding such misadventures, Lillian persuaded Smalley to write his textbook and in 1966, at the age of eighty-eight, she wrote the foreword.[7]

Lillian's second important postwar project was her work with the "handicapped homemakers," a logical continuation of the "crippled soldier" work she and Frank had started during World War I. This occupied her for the next ten years or so, until she was nearing eighty years of age, and she regarded it as her most important contribution to motion study. The first part of the project, the Heart Kitchen, was sponsored by the New York Heart Association and opened in the Rehabilitation Center of New York University, based at Bellevue Hospital, in 1948. The Heart Kitchen was a direct descendant of the 1929 Kitchen Practical, where Lillian had tried to fit kitchens to the height of their occupants, as well as of her more recent research into work simplification and her wartime consultancy work on cardiovascular diseases in industry. Eva Hansl, a journalist, attended one of Lillian's courses at Rutgers and recalled her telling the class to take all the equipment out of an old-style kitchen, dump it in bushel baskets, and then put everything back where they found it. "We couldn't do it. There was no logic in it . . . and we had learned to be logical—the things requiring water near the sink, those for cooking near the stove. Simple as that!" Later Lillian demonstrated how to set up a kitchen for a wheelchair-bound woman and arrange it to eliminate unnecessary bending or reaching.[8]

Lillian could not, of course, do all this alone. Instead, she acted as a catalyst, bringing a group of people together and encouraging them to work as a team. She headed a committee made up of industrial engineers, home economists, and rehabilitation experts, as well as psychologists and architects, and together they designed a model kitchen. They hoped to inspire women with low energy and impaired mobility to apply the same principles of saving time and energy to their own homes. She and her team were pleased with their handiwork and felt that they had designed "a rather attractive kitchen" for women with certain disabilities, but Lillian also felt "there wasn't a single thing in it which wouldn't be equally good for a person who had nothing in the world the matter with her except overweight."[9]

Lillian told a story about the Heart Kitchen that illustrates her notion of family teamwork. Relations between husband and wife should be complementary, each having his or her own expertise and area of responsibility and assisting the other as necessary. When the Heart Kitchen was opened to the public, she noticed that "innumerable women with nothing the matter with them and with very nice husbands came to look at it." She went on:

> Almost every one of these women, I regret to say, said to her husband, "Do I have to have a heart condition to have a kitchen like this?" And he would turn to us and he would say, "Does she?" And we said, "No, all she has to have is a willingness to remodel her kitchen. You, undoubtedly, have had experience in this work of simplification and could help a great deal." Whereupon he would usually nod and modestly say, Yes, he had, but his wife had always told him to attend to his work and she would attend to hers. He had failed to re-

member that when he wanted to institute reforms in a factory he had to secure the approval of "top management." Finally I said, "Did you ever stop to
think who was top management in the home?" "So she is," he replied. And
so we hoped that after we had been through the thing in a friendly fashion we
had set up a good type of team.[10]

Not only "nice husbands" adapted the Heart Kitchen, which was widely
copied by state heart associations. In Detroit, Wayne State University helped
pioneer "Take It Easy" classes, movies, and television programs. Lillian's files
contain information on a filmstrip titled *The Heart of the Home,* based on a
booklet that had accompanied the first Heart Kitchen. Its heroine, "Catherine Landis," described as "a typical housewife," has been advised to take it
easy by her doctor because of a heart defect. With a family of four to care for,
she wonders how she will manage. Her doctor urges her to enroll in the local
Heart Association course in work simplification, where she and her husband
learn how to adapt their kitchen. "They learn too that housework is a family
affair, so Ray Landis and son Don pitch in to revamp her kitchen." When the
rehabilitation expert has "helped" Catherine analyze and simplify her work,
she "finds she has more time than ever to relax and enjoy her family."[11]

The Detroit projects were even featured in the mass media. The glossy
magazine *Better Homes and Gardens* printed an article by Lillian entitled
"You Can Be a Time Saving Expert, Too!" It featured a photograph of Lillian,
resplendent in a flowery hat and an elaborate corsage, folding a towel with
lights attached to her fingers. The text of the article applied work simplification techniques to the "average" family, and Lillian explained her philosophy
of family and work before giving timesaving tips. She advised each family to
plan its time and money budgets carefully and then decide what they were
saving time and money for. She quoted Rudyard Kipling, as she had for many
years:

> I keep six honest serving men
> They taught me all I know,
> Their names are What and Why and When
> And How and Where and Who.

The rest of the article consisted of pictures of "Who" was to do the work and
"How" and "When" it was to be done. Gender roles were usually, but not always, conventional: "Mother assumes responsibility for serving good nour-
ishing meals" while "Father takes care of the man-sized jobs around the
house." Roles were based on contemporary assumptions about abilities and
aptitudes; father's "strength and handyman experience make him undisputed
choice among 'personnel' to tackle awnings, screens, storm windows, do the

heavy lifting." On the other hand, jobs were also allocated to those who like to do them irrespective of gender: Dad was pictured with a supermarket cart, carefully reading labels. "Dad has 'job appetite' for marketing, does it the same day every week. He looks over food bargains before he sets out. Mother gives him a list, but he has fun of impulse buying, too." Dad's job didn't stop there, as he had to unpack the shopping. "Don't dillydally," admonishes the next caption. "Get the job out of the way. With such convenient storage right inside back door, Dad won't postpone put-away." It is easy to see this article and the *Heart of the Home* filmstrip as part of the oft-described back-to-the-kitchen ethos of the postwar era, yet Lillian's position was a little more complicated than that, for she firmly believed in the cooperative household where every member had a role to play, though the woman had the most important, "managerial" job.[12]

Lillian worked as a consultant at the University of Connecticut for nearly twelve years, from 1953 through 1964. It started with a conference she organized on work simplification for the handicapped. The timing was auspicious, for Lillian's friend Mary Switzer, then Commissioner of Vocational Rehabilitation, was working on landmark legislation that would direct funds toward *all* the disabled and permit schools of home economics to apply for the first time. This act passed in 1954; Lillian helped the UConn home economics department become the first in the country to win a vocational rehabilitation grant to study work simplification for handicapped homemakers. This study led to the movie *Where There's a Will*, made in 1955. Lillian was one of the advisers and appeared on camera at the start and end of the film. Four women were featured: Mrs. Albright, partially paralyzed in a road accident; Mrs. Smith, in a wheelchair after polio; Mrs. White, born with only one arm, and Mrs. Greer, in a wheelchair for an undisclosed reason. They were all shown struggling with household tasks, peeling potatoes, making a bed, or bathing a baby with one hand, making Jell-O, or teaching a 4-H sewing class from a wheelchair. Mr. Albright had offered to help peel the vegetables but was told it would be more helpful if he made it possible for his wife to do the job herself. Accordingly, he had hammered nails into a board to pinion the vegetables while his wife peeled them. The narration emphasized the satisfaction each of these women found in being independent and in discovering her own best way of doing things. "Her way may not be the best way," the narrator said, "but it makes her happy." Lillian appeared at the end of the film to explain that there were ten million handicapped homemakers in the United States and that among them, if they had the will, they would find *many* ways of adjusting to their handicaps and "finding it is still possible to lead a useful, happy life." Lillian had come a long way from the quest of the "One Best Way."[13]

Her experiences with work simplification led Lillian to write a new household management book. It was called *Management in the Home,* with the significant subtitle of *Happier Living Through Saving Time and Energy,* and it continued where Lillian's *The Home-maker and Her Job* left off in 1927. The introduction, subtitled "Scientific Management in the Home," starts with the firm statement "Homemaking is a job . . . it's a good job and an important one and it ought to be an enjoyable one." She added, "The woman who likes her job of homemaking, who does it with skill and zest, whose home is well managed and whose family is contented, is a happy woman." Lest this sound too traditional, the next paragraph acknowledges that women are not confined to the housework. "We no longer say 'Women's place is in the home,' because many women have their places outside the home." Women, however, have the primary responsibility for the family, which is "a privilege and a trust, whether she has an outside job or not."[14]

Lillian and her coauthors listed the functions of the home: shelter, comfort, training, consumption, and education. They emphasized the old adage "The hand that rocks the cradle rules the world" but added, "Yet sometimes the hand gets tired of 'rocking the cradle.'" They went on to list middle-class women's complaints about housework: its monotony, their loneliness, its status as unpaid labor. Lillian's solution was to apply principles of scientific management, thus simplifying housework so it takes less of the homemaker's time and energy and leaves her free for other activities. Another solution was to regard housework as an interesting engineering problem so that the rest of the family will cease to regard running the home as "just 'mother's work.'" Lillian cautioned against perfectionism, against using "sterling silver standards where stainless steel would be more appropriate." In a paragraph that would have appalled her fellow *Better Homes in America* board member Emily Post, Lillian announced that this was a problem that "young married people often have to deal with quite firmly" if they are given silver flatware as a wedding gift, as it requires china, linen, and fine furniture,

> So before you knew it you would have your whole house furnished according to a sterling silver standard, requiring quantities of time and energy to keep in order, when what you really should have started with was a set of stainless steel. It never needs polishing, it doesn't scratch, you can dump it into the dishpan, it goes with all informal furnishings and it sets a standard that leaves you free to paint, wash diapers, hold a job, or fill whatever other role life has cast you for.

Lillian concluded that "the homemaker who holds a job has to be especially careful not to cling too hard to a set of standards that dates back to the time when the lady of the house was always at home and moreover had servants to help her."[15]

Lillian took this last thought a stage further in early 1957 when she encouraged Eva Hansl to call a conference of home economists and psychologists to discuss the feasibility and contents of a course on work simplification for working women. Their discussion led to the book *Management Problems for Homemakers*, which was issued by the U.S. Office of Education. As Hansl remarked, "Little did Mr. and Mrs. Gilbreth imagine—far-sighted as they were—that some day their time and motion studies would be the greatest help to the woman with the dual job—one inside and one outside her home."[16]

PART VII

"Only a Thermometer Has More Degrees"

Mother found it very embarrassing . . . though she was very proud of us all . . . but she must have thought why don't they recognize my life time work?

Ernestine Gilbreth Carey on *Cheaper by the Dozen* (1998)

30 Cheaper by the Dozen

*I always had the feeling she was just slightly em-
barrassed. . . . On one occasion when she presented
me the gift of* The Quest *she said half-apologetically that
it was sort of an antidote to the presentation in* Cheaper
by the Dozen *which she felt didn't give quite a fair
picture of her husband.*

E. M. Chervenik, "Reminiscences of Lillian M. Gilbreth" (1978)

THE BOOK *Cheaper by the Dozen* was originally
Ernestine's idea. She and her husband moved to the New York suburbs in
1944 after their second child was born. She gave up working and spent the
next three years as a full-time and rather frustrated wife and mother. She
missed her job at Macy's when her husband came home and talked about the
events of the day. "Like an old fire horse, I'd itch to be back in this world of
his," she wrote. Unlike her mother, Ernestine did all the things that suburban
mothers were supposed to do; she cooked and sewed, taught a Sunday school
class, and occasionally entertained the neighbors for supper. Meanwhile, Lillian was rushing from meeting to meeting, receiving honorary degrees, and
being active and useful. Ernestine's heart was not, however, in the "feminine
mystique"—and she spent her spare time writing. Her father's death had
been particularly stressful for her; his heart attack and her high school graduation were inextricably linked, and in focusing on Frank she was working
out her own feelings toward him. She once said she had only been alone with
her father twice in her life. She also wrote that going for a drive, even with her
father's erratic driving, was a great treat, for sometimes she got to sit in the
front between her parents. "There were so many of us and so few of them that
we never could see as much of them as we wanted."[1]

Ernestine finished the first draft of her book as the war ended, but on ap-
proaching an agent she was told, "No one wanted to read about large fami-

lies nowadays." Lillian suggested she talk to her brother Frank. "Mother said," recalled Ernestine, "'Frank's coming back from the service, he has adjustments coming up in his family life, I think he needs this.'" To Lillian's great relief all five of her sons had returned safely from the war. Frank Jr. was demobilized in 1945 and went back to work for the Associated Press, this time based in their New York office. He, his wife, Elizabeth, and their eight-year-old daughter took an apartment in Montclair. The next two years were miserable, however, as Liz missed the South and hated the cold; their marriage was fragile.[2]

Frank agreed to "whip" Ernestine's manuscript "into shape," though he moved to the *Charleston Post and Courier* that fall. Drafts of the manuscript flew back and forth between Long Island and South Carolina. He made it considerably shorter and added many humorous touches and a little poetic license and, in Jack's words, "it became a little less of a biography and more of a fact-based story." *Cheaper by the Dozen* was a family project; Ernestine used copies of the Gilbreth magazine *Ambidextrous,* a new edition of which appeared each Christmas, and asked her brothers and sisters for stories she could use in the book. As Jack recalled, "All of us contributed one thing, one idea, or another." They were, nevertheless, alarmed about what Ernestine and Frank would write. They had long memories of public embarrassment. Anne hoped that the family would "keep their sense of humor and realize that sometimes the truth isn't flattering and besides one can't write an entertaining book without a certain amount of 'fictionalizing.'" When she read the book she said, with a touch of relief, "I agree with Frank who wrote us that if it isn't all the way it happened, it is the way it should have happened, and I think Dad would have liked the book."[3]

After Lillian read the manuscript and suggested one or two small changes, *Cheaper by the Dozen* was finally published late in 1948, just in time for the holiday season. Lillian sent Ernestine a note the moment she received her first copy. "I *love* the book," she wrote, "and I am so proud of the dedication and know that Dad would have been, too." The dedication read: "To DAD who only reared twelve children and to MOTHER who reared twelve only children." Ernestine and Frank also included a Foreword that explained the "serious" facts behind the story, adding that after their father died in 1924, "Mother carried the load by herself and became perhaps the foremost woman industrial engineer. She is still active today after rearing twelve children. But that's another story. This book is about the Gilbreth family before Dad died."[4]

Cheaper by the Dozen was an immediate success and by March 1949 it was near the top of the national best-seller list. It has been in print continuously since its first publication and has sold more than three million copies.

Described by its publishers as "heartwarming" and "hilarious," it is a set of anecdotes about the life in the early 1920s of a family with twelve children. It presents Lillian Gilbreth through the lens of the late 1940s: it downplays her professional activities in favor of warmth, nurturance, and domesticity. The death of Mary and the existence of the stillborn daughter are ignored in the interest of simplicity.[5]

Cheaper became a best-seller at a time when American tastes in reading were eclectic. It shared bookshop space with George Orwell's *1984* and Simone de Beauvoir's feminist classic *The Second Sex*, but the top-selling novels were the now forgotten *The Egyptian* by Mike Waltari and the vaguely remembered but seldom read *Dinner at Antoine's* by Frances Parkinson Keyes. Among the top ten nonfiction books, four had religious or inspirational themes; three were manuals on how to play canasta; two were picture books in which dogs and other animals were dressed in suits and aprons and "worked" in offices and kitchens; and one was *Cheaper by the Dozen*. In perhaps one of the oddest occasions connected with its publication, Ernestine and Frank shared a platform at a literary lunch with Arthur Miller, whose play *Death of a Salesman* was a major Broadway hit. Miller lectured on the meaning and purpose of tragedy, then the Gilbreths took the rostrum in what they described as "a song-and-dance man fashion." Like Arthur Miller, the Gilbreths struck a nerve in postwar America, though theirs was a much more comforting vision than Miller's angry and alienated Willie Loman. Their portrayal of caring parents and strong American family values was reassuring as the Soviet Union detonated its first atomic bomb and China "fell" to the Communists. Contemporary reviewers were impressed; as one pointed out, "At times such as this, when parent delinquency is so rightly being screamed at us from our radios and newspapers, it is a breath of fresh air to read of at least two undelinquent parents."[6]

Cheaper by the Dozen was published the same year as the Kinsey Report on sexual behavior but portrays a world where father insisted on chaperoning his daughter at a high school dance. It celebrated large families during the height of the baby boom and it *apparently* celebrated female domesticity at a time when there was widespread public concern over the ever increasing participation of married women in the labor force. *Cheaper by the Dozen* continued to sell steadily through the 1950s, during a time of national nervousness about teenage alienation and male anxiety, the era of James Dean in *Rebel Without a Cause*, which his ineffectual father underlines his inadequacies by appearing in a frilly apron, and of the conformity of *The Man in the Gray Flannel Suit*.

It is not surprising, then, that a Hollywood producer approached Ernestine and Frank Jr. Nor is it surprising that many of their siblings, not to mention Lillian, were alarmed. Ernestine recalled that her brothers and sisters liked their privacy and thought a film was a bad idea. "Then Frank and I said we want to share very generously, as we have with the book, because if you were doing any of this and our characters were used we'd expect you to do that for us." Lamarr Trotti offered one hundred thousand dollars for the screen rights, but the other Gilbreths were not convinced. Next, Trotti called on Lillian and thoroughly charmed her, but the answer was still no. She finally succumbed, more for her children's sake than her own. Ernestine explained that her mother's feelings were very mixed, but "she could see the financial blessings of it and it would help sell books."[7]

The Gilbreths regarded the film contract as a "calculated risk" and decided to cooperate with the movie studios as far as possible and try to prevent them from changing the story around and making them all look foolish. Frank Jr. said they got on well with most of the studio people and that his mother met—and liked—Myrna Loy, who was to play her. He told the story of an unpleasant Hollywood official who decided to pay a call on Lillian before the casting decisions were made. One trusts that this story was exaggerated, but nevertheless it suggests the risks they were running in selling their story to Hollywood. The Gilbreths hoped that once the visitor had met Lillian he would be less likely to depict her as either a "*femme fatale* or, worse still, a screwball." Arriving by limousine in Montclair, "Mr. Ward" took one look around Lillian's apartment, with its piles of books and papers and its furniture, much of which had seen better days, and said, "I guess that the family can use the money, eh Missus? Well can't we all." He proceeded to offer to fly her to Hollywood for a *Queen for a Day* makeover. "Think of it, Missus," he went on, "your dreams come true. A dress by Edith Head. Maybe a dance with Fred Astaire. And a candlelit dinner complete with pheasant under glass and wine, with someone like Cary Grant or Spencer Tracy or . . ."[8]

This was one of the very few occasions when Frank Jr. had seen Lillian angry: "She was so furious that her hands trembled and her voice shook." He decided not to mention it, however, when he was on a morning television show. The host, Richard Kollmar, complained that Frank and Ernestine had made Lillian "so terribly saccharine" that he had felt "almost literally, sick" and tried to get Frank Jr. to admit that his mother was less saintly than he had portrayed her. "Do you mean to tell us that you never saw her lose her temper, or slap one of the kids, or take a sip of wine, or stand in front of a mirror and admire herself, or swear when she cut her finger?" Frank's answer was no and if she ever did get mad, "she was mighty good at covering up her wrath."[9]

The movie version of *Cheaper by the Dozen* was released in April 1950. Lillian left before the end of the first screening, pleading an urgent appointment, but she later returned alone and watched the film through. Clifton Webb made an unconvincing Frank; he had made his reputation playing waspish, irritable, self-centered men and was not good at projecting family warmth. Myrna Loy as Lillian won better notices: one critic said she was the only actor "who comes off with full credit." The film did not please all reviewers; one remarked that it was "an innocuous diversion" but that it "lacked outstanding originality" and was "derivative of films which Hollywood makes by the dozen, not because it is cheaper, but because it is safer." *Cheaper by the Dozen* became, nevertheless, the fourth-highest grossing film of the year, competing with *All about Eve*, *Sunset Boulevard*, and *The Winslow Boy*. Most viewers of *Cheaper* recall one or more of the scenes featuring Dad; his demonstration to a horrified middle-school principal of efficient ways to wash oneself is the most memorable to many people. The mass tonsil removal scene is also remembered, but the one vision of Lillian that occasionally surfaces is her inability to swim and her unwillingness to go into the water at Nantucket— not the most positive of images.[10]

Long before the movie version of *Cheaper* came, out Ernestine and Frank Jr. started writing a sequel. They sketched it out during a vacation on Nantucket during the summer of 1949. They called it *Belles on Their Toes* and it concerned the girls' efforts to get rings on their fingers while Lillian labored alone after Frank's death. It, too, was widely reviewed and appreciated amid the rising tensions of the cold war, Korea, and McCarthyism. One critic noted that "gentle, rollicking humor is a tonic to be welcomed at any time. . . . In a period of general tension and insecurity 'Belles on Their Toes' offers special refreshment. For underlying its high comedy lies the moving story of one family's brave, united stand against adversity." Another reviewer noted that it was "the story of Mrs. Gilbreth and you will find it—in more than one sense—the better half."[11]

Belles on Their Toes was filmed in 1952, though with considerably less commercial or artistic success than its predecessor. Myrna Loy again played Lillian, who was trying to keep her family together, economically and emotionally. The screenwriters Phoebe and Henry Ephron could not allow her to do this alone; instead they invented the wholly imaginary Sam Harper—not a character in the children's book—a client who works to further Lillian's career, while carrying on a small romance with her.

Frank Jr. later admitted that his mother was not "too crazy" about either of the books because they stressed the "comical" aspects of motion study and opened it up to ridicule. However, Lillian agreed to help publicize the books by appearing on radio and television shows with him and Ernestine. Frank also reported, "She laughed out loud at the movie [*Cheaper*] and, while I don't think it was exactly the way she would have staged it, she conceded when it was over that it might have been infinitely worse." Doubtless it could have been much worse; "Mr. Ward" was ousted in a studio upheaval and the Gilbreths' fears that he would cast "Marjorie Main and Andy Devine as Ma and Pa Gilbreth, or even worse, Frank Sinatra and Lana Turner as Frankie and Lillie" were not realized.[12]

Lillian, however, became known as "the mother in *Cheaper by the Dozen*" for the rest of her days, and her very real achievements in ergonomics and industrial psychology were subsumed under her identity as "Mother." It was an odd kind of celebrity, as though the press, the public and the engineering profession were unsure how to categorize her. The 1950s was a contradictory era as far as women were concerned. It was the time when what Betty Friedan has described as "the feminine mystique" was emerging, yet domesticity was not the only option for women. Career women displaying individual excellence and success were celebrated, while the joy of motherhood was extolled. Nowhere did these two approaches coincide more often than in press treatment of Lillian Gilbreth. The way newspapers presented her and her career vividly illustrates the complexity of gender roles in postwar America. In the early 1950s Lillian was celebrated in the media both for her family and her career—often in the same sentence. Lillian's achievement in combining a remarkable public and professional life with the raising of eleven successful children made her an icon for those who wanted to show that middle-class women could work without destroying their families. Despite her virtual invisibility in her children's book, many of its readers knew that the quiet, supportive woman in the background had a distinguished career.

Cheaper by the Dozen was in many ways an antifeminist book, minimizing Lillian's achievements as it did. It was, however, very mild compared with other works of the 1940s, notably Philip Wylie's *Generation of Vipers,* published in 1942, and Marynia Farnham and Ferdinand Lundberg's 1947 bestseller, *Modern Woman: The Lost Sex.* While Wylie blamed American women for emasculating their husbands and sons, Farnham, a psychiatrist and mother of two, and Lundberg, a well-known Progressive journalist, went a step further and said that the pursuit of careers had led to the masculinization of women and in the process made them extremely unhappy. "What is wrong with modern woman?" they asked rhetorically. "What has happened to her that she is, today, in overwhelming numbers, restless, dissatisfied, unhappy?" Their answer was both Freudian and essentialist. They urged women not to be "poor imitators of men" who were "imbued by penis-envy," but to practice and enjoy the skills and qualities that made women different. Women, according to Farnham and Lundberg, should be discouraged from entering "male" fields such as law, mathematics, physics, business, industry, and technology: "The emphasis of prestige, honor, subsidy and public respect should be shifted emphatically to those women recognized as serving society most fully as women." Such views make public confusion about Lillian Gilbreth a little more understandable. Here was a businesswoman and scientist who had spent a long career in a very masculine field as a consultant engineer. Yet one of the criteria for true womanhood was heterosexual marriage and the production of children; Lillian had done all that and in *Cheaper* was portrayed almost exclusively as Mother. Even heads of women's colleges were unsure how to categorize her. When she received an honorary degree at Mills College in Oakland in 1952, Lyn White, Mills's president, introduced the engineer Ruth Pollock as "the feminine intruder of the masculine realm" and Lillian as "the biological phenomenon of this century."[13]

The engineering profession decided to honor Lillian. During the 1950s and 1960s Lillian won many engineering awards; in every case she was the first woman to do so. The ultimate honor was her appointment to the National Academy of Engineering in 1965; Lillian was the first woman member in the academy's history. The engineers usually tried to disassociate themselves from the *Cheaper by the Dozen* bandwagon; they were serious men and could not be concerned with such fripperies, though on at least one occasion an engineering society gave copies of *Cheaper* as a "party favor" at a "Ladies Evening" banquet at which Lillian spoke. In February 1954 she flew to São Paulo, Brazil, to receive the gold medal of the Comité Internationale de l'Organisation Scientifique (CIOS), whose international meetings she never failed to attend. In the case of the CIOS medal, a writer in a management journal pointed out that the award had nothing to do with being married to Frank or to her celebrity through *Cheaper by the Dozen*. Instead, "management leaders of twenty-two nations . . . an international group of hard-headed business men" were showing their "ungrudging and sincere recognition" and honoring her "solely on her own performance."[14]

Later in 1954 the Western Society of Engineers gave Lillian their Washington Award "for accomplishments which pre-eminently promote the happiness, comfort and well-being of humanity" and for her "unselfish devotion to the problems of the handicapped." The committee of engineers described her career and her achievements in eleven paragraphs; only one was devoted to *Cheaper by the Dozen,* which was described as giving "the entire world a needed 'lift.'" The popular press treated her in exactly the opposite way. When *Newsweek* picked up the story, under the heading "At 75, 'The Greatest,'" they decided that Lillian's medal was newsworthy *because* of her connection with *Cheaper by the Dozen,* though they failed to say what exactly she had done to deserve the honor. They wrote:

The mother of the *Cheaper by the Dozen* family, 75 year old Dr. Lillian
Moller Gilbreth has been acclaimed "the greatest woman engineer in the
world"—and by the professionals best qualified to appraise her, five top engineering societies of the U.S. . . . As the first woman to receive the award, Dr.
Gilbreth whose career as a mother became world-renowned through the
best-selling biography and movie *Cheaper by the Dozen* (written by two of
her twelve children) joins a distinguished list of previous winners including
Herbert Hoover, Orville Wright, Charles Kettering and Henry Ford.[15]

The desire to praise Lillian did not stop there. Two years later she was in
Berlin to receive an award from the Verein Deutscher Ingenieure, and the
American Institute of Industrial Engineers (AIIE) celebrated her eightieth
birthday in 1958 with a special banquet. The AIIE devoted the whole of its
May 1962 conference to the work of the Gilbreths, and in 1966 the four
biggest engineering societies representing American chemical, civil, mining,
and electrical engineers joined together to award her their top honor, the
Hoover Medal. The citation included her public and private activities. It read:

> Renowned engineer, internationally respected for contributions to motion
> study and to recognition of the principle that management engineering and
> human relations are intertwined; courageous wife and mother; outstanding
> teacher, author, lecturer and member of professional committees under Her-
> bert Hoover and four successors. Additionally, her unselfish application of
> energy and creative efforts in modifying industrial and home environments
> for the handicapped has resulted in full employment of their capabilities and
> elevation of their self esteem.[16]

Universities and engineers did not have Lillian to themselves, however;
she was also claimed by numerous organizations. Many of them gave her
honorary membership as a way of reflecting glory on themselves; in addition
to most of the relevant engineering societies, groups ranging from the American Society of Hospital Administrators to the American Home Economics
Association wanted to call Lillian their own. The University of California—
which had refused to award her a doctorate in 1912—named her their Outstanding Alumnus in 1954, when again she was the first woman to win the
award.

Other groups wanted to name Lillian "Mother of the Year" or sometimes, a little less restrictively, "Woman of the Year." The first such accolade
was awarded in late 1948, a few weeks before the publication of *Cheaper by
the Dozen,* when Lillian received the American Woman's Association (AWA)
Award as Woman of the Year. She was familiar with the AWA and had
worked with one of its founders, Anne Morgan, back in the early 1930s.

Though Morgan, daughter of the financier J. P. Morgan, was immensely wealthy, she had put much of her formidable organizing ability into creating facilities for working women of moderate means. Thus, it is not surprising that the AWA emphasized Lillian's professional work and her resourcefulness in organizing her family so that she might work; starting with a standard reference to her career, they said, "Dr. Gilbreth is . . . one of the few women who are top-ranking engineers in the U.S. . . . To her and her husband and associates is due the credit for discovering, recognizing and formulating the laws of human motion which in industry are accepted today as fundamental." They went on to praise her ability to combine career and family, stating, "She was so resourceful as an engineer—and I would say as an economist, too, that she was able to rear this big family and still go on with her professional career."[17]

In 1957 New Jersey made her its "Mother of the Year," though they had to go through some contortions to mold her to the American Mothers' Inc. criteria, which did not quite fit a professionally active woman. According to those rules, the most important qualifications were the character and achievements of her children, and the mother herself should exhibit "courage, cheerfulness, patience, affection, kindness, understanding and a homemaking ability." Some involvement in civic or community affairs was also a good thing. Lillian's long career and her choice to continue working after Frank's death were cautiously praised. The decision of "our intrepid heroine" to sail for Europe five days after Frank's death was passed over without comment, though she was congratulated for giving her children "the same sufficiency and independence that she herself possessed." In 1959 the Industrial Management Society went one better and named Lillian the "Mother of the Century"![18]

Similar stories continued throughout the 1950s. Lillian's achievements were celebrated in the same sentence as her family. Her femininity was frequently stressed; one journalist wrote: "I won't invoke the trite phrase 'she thinks like a man.' Heaven forbid! She thinks like a woman . . . a warm, sympathetic, fulfilled woman. A woman whose love has brimmed over the top of a full heart and into the steel blue limbo of wheelchairs and braces. A woman whose life is so full she does not hesitate to dedicate a great portion of it to civic needs and the needs of education and humanity. But above all, a woman."[19] Despite such hyperbole, the treatment of Lillian Gilbreth in the media suggests that it was difficult to read her as "only" a mother in the 1940s and 1950s. In many cases she was presented as a woman who had successfully combined work and motherhood. As such, she was an antidote to writers such as Farnham and Lundberg, who feared the masculinization of career women, and an encouragement to those for whom changing gender roles were not necessarily alarming.

31 Work, for the Night Is Coming

"I suppose I have a 'Work, for the Night Is Coming' complex. I've felt that way ever since your father went."

Lillian Moller Gilbreth, quoted in *Time Out for Happiness* (1970)

Iₙ THE 1950S AND EARLY 1960s Lillian was busier than ever. Although she officially retired from Purdue in 1948 at the age of seventy, she continued working for the next twenty years, until 1968, when her doctor forced her to rest. Lillian had always dreaded inaction; years earlier she had written a poem about being forced to stop work:

> How do you dare to say I may not work
> Because I am forty, forty-five or more?
> What can youth offer that I cannot give?
> What waste could equal that of forcing me
> Out of the Industry I know so well
> Am keen to serve, live in, spend myself
> Into that idleness that can alone
> Bring me old age, inaction, even death
> For while I work life, youth, remain to me.[1]

If Lillian dreaded inaction in her forties, how much worse it seemed in her seventies and eighties. Lillian knew herself well; she knew that her work was her life. In addition to her handicapped homemaker projects in the United States, she continued traveling into advanced old age, as well as encouraging and mentoring young engineers, particularly women. Lillian was always wary of women engineers isolating themselves into groups. She was uncomfortable with organizations that stressed gender rather than qualifications; nevertheless, she became a stalwart supporter of the Society of Women Engineers, which was founded in 1950, and spoke to them many times. In turn, they made her Honorary Member Number One.[2]

A student engineer remembered chancing upon Lillian in the ladies' room during a convention in Chicago in 1952. It was an important meeting for the women engineers, as their very new organization had been invited to participate in the "Centennial of Engineering" to celebrate the founding of the ASME in 1852. The famous Dr. Gilbreth was sitting in a chair in the lounge area, unpacking a neatly folded evening gown and pulling a thread out of her underskirt. To the amazement of the younger woman, when Lillian stood up "her underskirt slipped down to her ankle—from short to long in a moment! She laughed when she looked up and caught me staring. 'I had an afternoon meeting to attend,' she smiles, 'Now I'm giving a speech tonight at the banquet. I just basted the skirt up—saves changing!'"[3]

Another of the women engineers present recalled the banquet, to which the male engineers came to hear Lillian speak and then stayed for dinner. "We had ordered lobster tails. And all those men ate the lobster tails, so we of the committee, the last to reach the buffet table, ate the leftovers from lunch. But we didn't mind. When Lillian spoke, the audience was enthralled. We were a great success!" The man who was to introduce her made a very long speech but forgot to mention her name. "For a moment there was utter silence," recalled one of the guests. "I saw the flush of pleasure drain from his face." An engineer, Dot Merrill, saved the day; she rose and said that since the speaker was known to every engineer in the country she needed no introduction, "so instead of introducing Dr. Gilbreth to you, I introduce all of you to Dr. Gilbreth." Merrill came to know Lillian well and recalled that she seemed to enjoy quiet meetings with women engineers where "one could have conversation instead of the usual blare." She added, "I think it irked her mildly to have a bunch of non-professional women gush all over her about 'Oh Mrs. Gilbreth, you're the mother in CHEAPER BY THE DOZEN aren't you?' when she was in the midst of a professional situation or discussion."[4]

Dot Merrill and Lillian attended several ASME management conferences in the Pocono Mountains in Pennsylvania; they were usually the only women there and Lillian "was always in the middle of everything going on." In 1956 she drove Lillian back home to Montclair, only to find the apartment full of packing cases; Lillian was about to move to a small apartment near Washington Square in New York. Unperturbed, she asked everyone in for tea. "We had a lovely time sitting on the packing cases."[5]

Margaret Hyndman, a Canadian attorney, also became friendly with Lillian, who stayed with her in Toronto several times. Hyndman had fond memories of Lillian as a houseguest, recalling that she was always up very early and "would be sitting and reading, as she knitted, a French book or a German book." Lillian also had a way with her hosts' children. John Schwab recalled that one morning Lillian was still in bed at 9:00 A.M., an unusually late time for her, the reason being that his four-year-old daughter had wandered into her room in the middle of the night and snuggled up in Lillian's bed. "Later we found out that neither knew the other was awake and did not want to disturb each other." Jerry Nadler, another colleague, recalled that whenever she visited his house, his young children were very noisy. "She turned off her hearing aids and continually smiled at the children. They still remember her."[6]

Lillian hated to turn down an invitation and was always ready for new experiences. In 1954 she arrived in Guadalajara, Mexico, to participate in a series of seminars. There was a grand reception committee with a mariachi band to welcome her and the other overseas delegates. She rejected the proffered limousine and begged a ride in a little red sports car, telling the surprised driver that she had always wondered what it was like to travel "in one of *those*." So while the welcoming committee and the other delegates proceeded in a stately fashion to the conference hall, the seventy-six-year-old Lillian "streaked down the pike with her beautiful white hair flowing in the wind as the flaming red 300SL proved its capacity for cornering, down-shifting and jackknife starts."[7]

Although Lillian had resumed her regular visits to Europe soon after World War II, it was not until 1953 that she started on truly heroic travel with the first of three world tours. She began in Manila, where she spent three months helping to create a management training program. She witnessed firsthand the problems of modernization, which were perhaps more noticeable in a foreign environment. She became interested in an anthropological approach to work at this time, approvingly citing Margaret Mead's work on technology and culture. The farmers were still using wooden implements; the American team decided to import metal scythes and sickles, reasoning that this was a good intermediate step because to introduce mechanized farming all at once would disturb the equilibrium. To Lillian's surprise, the farmers did not want the metal tools, although they acknowledged they were sharper and worked better. Lillian discovered that other family members and village neighbors made their living out of making and repairing wooden tools; the culture of the community would be altered if one part was changed. This was a useful insight and one that she later shared with other engineers.[8]

Lillian was busy in the Philippines. She described a typical day as follows: "I made two talks this morning and in the afternoon I did a taping for a broadcast that will close Girl Scout Week. Then on to the Post to have a yellow fever shot. I needed this and two for cholera. I was warned to expect a bad reaction, but I found the technique of giving the shot so excellent that it was worth experiencing. In the evening I spoke at the annual meeting of Unity Church. The women had all brought chicken, rolls and dessert." She then confessed a little economy: "I brought the big cake I had received the day before from the Filipino Nurses Association, after carefully removing the inscription which said 'Welcome Dr. Gilbreth.'"[9]

Lillian's next stop was a two-week lecture tour of Australia. Her host, an Australian engineer, Sir Walter Scott, had sent her a copy of the schedule, remembering that she was in her seventies "and we did not want to over tire her." Lillian wrote that they could put more into it if they wished, for she was, she said, "durable and resilient." The resulting schedule was "heavy," but Lillian took it all in stride, to the amazement of her more laid-back Australian hosts. Although her plane was delayed for twenty-four hours, as soon as she landed she talked to local reporters for half an hour, went to a welcoming cocktail party, and insisted on being driven around Sydney for two hours to see the sights. The next morning she was up at seven with a dozen postcards written and ready for posting. Over breakfast she discussed economics with the elder Scott child, English literature with the younger, home management with Lady Scott, and Australian flora and fauna with Sir Walter, then started her official duties—she attended three meetings, gave a press conference, lunched at the zoo, spent half an hour with the lord mayor, and held a three-hour question-and-answer program with the Australian Institute of Management. And all that before dinner.[10]

Australia was followed by a week in Hong Kong and six weeks, which included Christmas 1953, at the Tainan Engineering College in southern Taiwan. She was with a team from Purdue University who were studying how to set up management studies in the school. Among her other duties, she gave fifteen lectures.[11]

Lillian then spent an extraordinary two weeks in India, where Mary Cushing Niles, a management engineer, traveled with her and wrote a very detailed account of her guest's packed schedule. Lillian arrived in Calcutta in early January, perhaps the best time of year to be in Bengal, as the daytime temperatures seldom rose above the low eighties. It was late on a Saturday night when Mrs. Niles met her at the airport; nevertheless, Lillian was "full of vitality," though her ears were bothering her: she was increasingly deaf and air travel seems to have made things worse. She spent only twenty-four hours in Calcutta, during which time she visited a temple, saw refugees crowded into the town, and lunched in quiet luxury with a group of dignitaries. After a short rest she flew to Delhi, where January nights can be cold. When Mrs. Niles looked in on her the next morning, she found Lillian writing a few lines of poetry in tribute to the fire in her bedroom hearth. By midday it was delightfully warm and they lunched on the lawn with a group of distinguished Indians: bankers, an MIT-trained industrialist, and one of Gandhi's close supporters, now chairman of the Backward Classes Commission. This was followed by a press conference and a big reception—a relatively quiet day.[12]

The next day Lillian (age seventy-four and a half) got into her stride. She visited a cotton mill, lunched with a group of prominent Indian women, and then spoke to the All India Organization of Industrial Employers, the main reason for her visit. According to Mrs. Niles, she "gave a splendid talk on management and charmed the industrial and business people at tea." The following day she visited a "typical" Indian village, where she walked through the dusty streets, went into some houses, and had a cup of tea with "the leading family." Back in Delhi by 11:00 A.M., she visited the Rajghat, the memorial at the site of Gandhi's cremation, then spoke to the assembled home economists at the Lady Irwin College before lunch with a U.S. embassy official and the secretary of the Indian Ministry of Education. After a call on the minister of commerce, she found she had three hours to spare before the final engagement of the day, a reception in Lillian's honor, so she went shopping. She wandered among the handicraft stores sniffing the sandalwood boxes and admiring the carved elephants and the alabaster vases. Lillian stopped in the Kashmir store, where she bought wool scarves, dress material, and silk for a blouse.[13]

Over the next two weeks this kind of schedule was repeated in Madras and Bangalore. Lillian lectured, visited hospitals, factories, and cottage industries, and took tea with local women and men, with barely any time off. It was Republic Day, January 25, when Lillian arrived in Bombay; though she said she planned to relax on her hotel balcony, she in fact had a most extraordinary time, full of activity and contrasts. It started at 8:30 A.M., when two Indian women came for breakfast and took Lillian and Mrs. Niles to a potters' cooperative. They walked through the colony, stepping around the holes in the ground, where the clay pits competed for space with the latrines. They were admiring of the prize-winning pots, but appalled by the dirt and squalor of most of the houses.

Lillian was then taken on a tour of Bombay, but not to the usual tourist sites. The first stop was what Mrs. Niles described as the "amazing" dhobitown, where most of the laundering for the city was performed. It was a hive of activity. Lillian saw water heating in giant cauldrons. The clothes were soaked in the hot, soapy water, then beaten on cement platforms with sticks. Later Lillian was driven through Bombay's notorious red-light district, where she saw prostitutes sitting in their drab little cages in front of dingy houses.

This depressing vision was replaced later that day with drinks on the balcony of the Bombay Club and watching the fireworks on Malabar Hill.

Lillian left India the next day and arrived in London in the midst of a severe snowstorm. A week later she flew to Brazil. She was a day early for the conference she was attending, so she decided to explore São Paulo on her own. "I got a map of the city and started off. . . . Of course I got lost at every crossing, but everyone was kind and I got pats of approval for trying." She then stopped by a bookstore and bought a biography of Gandhi: "You know me," she wrote to her children, "I must have a lot of reading ahead or I starve. And I wanted to finish my studies on India before I started on Brazil." The next day Lillian, wearing the silk dress made for her by a Bangalore tailor, received the CIOS medal.[14]

When she got back from this six-month world tour, one of her children asked her, "Now won't you be glad to settle down?" To which she replied, "Good heavens, no, I'm just beginning." Lillian spoke the truth. Though she was in the Western Hemisphere from March to August, this period included excursions to Canada and Mexico, and then she returned to Europe for nearly three months in the fall of 1954. Following two weeks in Spain and a week in London, she attended a meeting in Torquay, England, before traveling on to Holland, Geneva, Germany and Paris —"and I hope to fly home in time for Thanksgiving."[15]

Lillian managed to stay in one place for several months in 1955, though the place was not her apartment in Montclair. The University of Wisconsin appointed her as Knapp Visiting Professor in the School of Engineering, so she moved to Madison, subletting an English professor's apartment. She later complained, "Books lining the wall solidly and not a thing to read." Not all visiting professors hold a press conference on their arrival; Lillian did, and at least one local journalist went away thinking, "Mrs. Lillian Moller Gilbreth, made famous by the book and movie *Cheaper by the Dozen,* is a greater woman than she was portrayed in that book or movie." After the press conference Emily Chervenick, the university's director of career advising, took Lillian shopping, stepping gingerly on the icy sidewalk on their way to the A & P. They met again a few days later; Lillian had taught her first class and told Chervenick that she thought "the boys" were surprised when she walked in: "I think they expected to see Myrna Loy in the classroom and there seemed to be a bit of disappointment." During her four months in Madison, Lillian gave nearly a hundred talks to groups all around the state and helped organize a women students' careers conference, in addition to teaching two courses. She also worked with the home economists on the Madison Heart Kitchen.[16]

In spite of Lillian's legendary stamina, by the time she was in her late seventies her robust health started to show occasional cracks. Her hearing was not good, but eventually, after experimenting with several types of hearing aid, she found one that worked satisfactorily, and she discovered the delights of switching it off during particularly long and tedious meetings or when surrounded by noisy children. In Germany in 1956 she fell and broke her arm; a few weeks later, the offending limb still in a cast, she told a management audience that breaking her right arm had given her two fine opportunities:

> One, to say to yourself, "This is a project. Think of the people who have to get along with one arm all the time and try to work out that experience." And two, to see how kind and thoughtful people are. I could very nicely have asked the waiter to cut up my meat every day, instead of which the gentleman next to me did; and I could give you quite a detailed report as to how a French gentleman, an Italian gentleman, a Swiss gentleman, a British gentleman and an American gentleman will cut up your meat for you.[17]

Gentlemen—and gentlewomen—from all over the world came together in 1962 when the Institute of Industrial Engineers honored both Gilbreths by designating their annual meeting "The Frank and Lillian Gilbreth Conference and Convention." Friends and colleagues were invited to reminisce about the Gilbreths. Many of them told stories about how Lillian and Frank had inspired them in their life's work; Joe Piacitelli, the consultant engineer who had been an office boy at New England Butt fifty years earlier, recalled that Frank "increased my appetite for a better education." Erwin Schell, a young management consultant, recalled that his life was changed the moment he met Lillian: "I instinctively knew she was . . . ready or even eager to encourage me to reach for a fuller realization of any talents I possessed, someone who cared and would leave me hopelessly hooked to a new and higher set of standards for myself. For me it was love at first sight!" A Dutchman, B. W. Berenschott, detailed Lillian's contributions to the rebuilding of the Netherlands after World War II; a Swede, Bo Casten Carlberg, recalled her many visits to Scandinavia and her emphasis on holistic approaches to engineering problems; Sir Walter Scott, the Australian, praised her youthfulness and the freshness of her ideas, while Lillian's old friend and student Anne Shaw said she suspected that without Lillian to carry on the partnership, "the writings of Frank Gilbreth would have lapsed into relative obscurity." Celebrants at a special conference are hardly likely to inject a note of criticism into the proceedings; nevertheless, the tributes to Lillian Gilbreth are remarkably consistent. Erwin Schell of MIT saw her as a woman of "true and unalloyed greatness"; Andrey Potter of Purdue described her "innate urge for the best and the first rate"; Walter Scott described her as simply "the most unforgettable character I have ever met." Jerome Barnum noted that every group she worked with, including the home economists, the handicapped, nurses, librarians, and Girl Scouts, "each claim her for their very own."[18]

Anne Shaw summed up what all the rest were trying to say. She described Lillian as having "a genius for human relations," adding wryly that her friend's "charming" way of handling people was not shared by any other psychologist of her acquaintance. It was only appropriate that Shaw should illustrate her point with a family anecdote. She recalled: "It was in 1948, by which time all the Gilbreth daughters were married with children of their own and each one, when I visited her, told me 'Mother is wonderful. She has no favorites among her grandchildren, but I know she loves my little Johnny (or whatever the name might be) the best.'"[19]

At much the same time Lillian was practicing similar skills at the Newark College of Engineering. A colleague recalled, "Each week, no matter how busy, she would sit down with every member of the department, discover the disturbing problems, if any, and offer mutual understanding and solutions. In the personnel field she was almost unique; she practiced what she preached." Perhaps that was the secret of Lillian's success.[20]

32 "It Doesn't Take Long to Get Back from Rangoon"

*You know, if I ever have to go into a home and I
wouldn't want to be a burden to my children, if I get
to the place where I can't do for myself I would like to go
into a home where I would be kept clean and cared for. But
I would hope that the home would be near a school . . .
because I think there would be nothing lovelier than to
hear the voices of children in one's old age.*

Lillian Moller Gilbreth to Margaret Hyndman (c. 1960)

LILLIAN WAS in great form during the 1962 Gilbreth Conference. She contributed an essay, on "Frank the teacher," to the conference proceedings, and she also gave a long after-dinner speech titled "Management's Place in the World Today." The organizers were already looking forward six years to Frank's centennial; they anticipated more papers on the importance of Frank's work but added, "This is certain: none will have more importance to the engineer, to the citizen and to the human being than that to be presented by Dr. Lillian Gilbreth at that time."[1]

Those words were published when Lillian was eighty-four years old; her fellow industrial engineers were obviously expecting—or at least hoping—that she would continue her current pattern of activity into her nineties. If the present was anything to go by, their expectations were not unreasonable. Her secretary and friend Jane Callaghan described Lillian's activities after her eightieth birthday; as Callaghan admitted, "It does not seem humanly possible for any one person to go all the places and do all the things that Dr. Gilbreth manages to cover, but she does them and, furthermore, she does them with the exuberant zest of one who is forever young." The Internal Revenue Service had doubts about her travel expenses, but "they were easily convinced when they saw her airplane ticket records."[2]

Between 1962 and 1967 Lillian did, indeed, look as though she was indestructible. She embarked on her third world tour in 1964, speaking in Hawaii,

New Zealand, Australia, the Philippines, India, Egypt, Greece, and France. After a few weeks in America (though she was scarcely "at home"—she attended thirty-four conferences in the United States that year) she was off to Europe for more meetings. In the first twenty-five days of June 1965 she gave twenty lectures, including five in different parts of California, one in Madison, Wisconsin, five in three different German cities, three in different Canadian cities, and one in New Jersey. By now an expert, she traveled light. In her briefcase she carried a raincoat, slipper socks to wear on the plane, a book to read, "a sandwich in case I get hungry before we start . . . and the last *Saturday Evening Post* in the pocket." In her small suitcase she had a pair of shoes, a wool scarf, a sweater, a simple evening dress, five day dresses, a cotton dress for picnics, her nightclothes and toiletries, and the papers she needed for the ergonomics conference, as well as a gift for her host's daughter's hope chest. "In an emergency I could carry it all," she wrote, "and I am quite proud of myself."[3]

Lillian had started lecturing on lifelong learning; her "Need to Be Needed" lectures gave rise to an organization of retired executives who offered their assistance to people starting up in business. She frequently said that retirement was particularly hard on suburban men, since women had their volunteer work but there was little for the men to do. Her interest in the handicapped continued; she worked with the American Institute of Architects on a project to survey wheelchair accessibility in existing buildings and to incorporate handicap-friendly bathrooms and elevators and provide ramps in new buildings. She still did some consultancy work and continued to serve on presidential commissions, including Lyndon Johnson's Committee on the Employment of the Handicapped.

A reporter who caught up with her in Chicago in early November 1966 was clearly entranced by Lillian, whom he called a "real swinger at 88." She was in the city to address the Society of Industrial Management before embarking on a nationwide campus tour as part of a group investigating engineering education. He asked her how she kept in touch with her family during her travels and she told him that she had told them to phone her immediately "in case any of them is ill, or anything." The reporter persisted, "But what if you're in Rangoon at the time?" and reported Lillian's response: "'It doesn't take long,' said this lively lady, 'to get back from Rangoon.'"[4]

Lillian's children, however, were less than convinced by such an answer and started to ask her whether it wasn't time to slow down. She always told them that there were still many things she wanted to accomplish. To stop their fussing, she started giving them an edited version of her schedule. As her secretary pointed out, "She was really having the time of her life." Jane Callaghan added, "she looked frail but her health was extraordinarily good—no sign of heart trouble, no stiffness in her bones and incidentally her legs were still slim and beautiful."[5]

Lillian was, however, well aware that she could not go on indefinitely. There had already been embarrassing incidents; there were, for example, times when she had not been able to hear herself being introduced to speak and thus remained seated when she should have been talking or had started to get up before the introduction was finished. She even told a story about the time in Mexico City when she had not realized that she was being praised and so had joined everyone else in a standing ovation. She nevertheless continued to resist her children's attempts to get her to slow down, and some of her domestic activities suggest that she was planning—or at least hoping—to live a long time yet. She had never been particularly fussy about her furniture; she had lived with Martha Gilbreth's tables and chairs for more than sixty years, but in 1967 she sent a marble-top table to be repaired and had an antique sofa and armchair reupholstered.

Such efforts to deny the inevitable were forestalled in April 1967 when her doctor started to talk about her retirement. Lillian was visiting her daughter Anne, who now lived in northern California, and went to the nearby Palo Alto Medical Clinic for a routine checkup. The doctor found cancerous lesions on one of her eyelids and recommended immediate surgery. Lillian sailed through a three-hour operation with only a local anesthetic. Everything went well and her progress "astonished" her doctors; nevertheless, she was told to cancel all her engagements for the next six weeks. After a few days in the hospital she convalesced at Anne's house and they enjoyed an unexpected opportunity to "catch something more than a fleeting glimpse of each other." Whether this was an unalloyed pleasure was unclear; for whatever reason Lillian flew back to New York well before the six weeks were up. She was a delightful houseguest, as her many friends attested, but she could be tiring. As Frank Jr. once put it after one of her regular family visits, "some twenty-four or forty-eight hours later, she would depart, still as fresh as a daisy, flying blithely to her next overnight stop and leaving in her wake an assortment of limply pooped descendants and their spouses."[6]

When the six weeks' enforced rest were up, Lillian went back to work. Her first stop was in upstate New York. She had not missed one of the annual Lake Placid Work Simplification conferences for more than a quarter century and did not intend to start now. There were, however, problems; Jane Callaghan recalled that she was "physically shaky" and when she tried to quote Rudyard Kipling's *Serving Men,* which she had been quoting for sixty years or more, Lillian "fumbled" the words and was very upset about her mistake. Nevertheless, she continued with her schedule. In mid-June she spent ten days in Montreal, attending conferences and visiting Expo 67, then went straight to a conference of women engineers in Cambridge, England. Her Australian friend Dorothy Scott was alarmed by her appearance, but Jane Callaghan tried to explain it away, saying that Lillian had just had "a particularly aggravating flight from Montreal and she must have been tired."[7]

Lillian returned to California for another checkup in August. Her doctor was delighted with her recovery, so, "feeling on top of the world," according to her secretary, she resumed her lectures and travels, trying to include the missed six weeks' engagements in an already packed schedule. She was back in England in September, attending an ergonomics conference in Birmingham. In her diary-letters from England Lillian did not, however, seem her normal enthusiastic self, in marked contrast to similar letters the previous year. She was grumbling about everything: she had had a bad flight; it was hard to find a bus ticket; the food in the university cafeteria was "not well-selected or well-prepared"; the "endless papers" were not "important or interesting"; and all in all she was not having a good time. Lillian had spent a lifetime finding even the most unlikely events interesting, so she was obviously very tired. Matters improved, however, on the third day of the conference, when Lillian turned from a passive member of the audience to the center of attention. She was on television in the morning and then gave a speech to a thousand production engineers, "The Expanding Field of Management." This was not just an after-dinner speech; she also fielded questions and received honorary membership in their institute. "All went well," she reported.[8]

Lillian, now feeling much more cheerful, spent a weekend in London with Walter and Dorothy Scott and her Nantucket astrologer friend, Margaret Harwood. "Swinging London" did not impress her very much, she commented on the young people she saw with the "ugly 'new' long hair cuts and odd-looking clothes." Then it was on to Dublin, for lunch with the U.S. ambassador, "where he and a few of his friends asked innumerable questions," before she lectured to and received honorary membership in the Irish Work Study Institute. There were reporters everywhere she went; a "mob" of them met her plane, and attended her talk. Lillian was becoming more and more of a celebrity.[9]

After five days of meetings in Germany, she returned to the United States, and Lillian started rushing around the country to fulfill the engagements she had canceled in the spring. There were also family events; her granddaughter Julie, who had followed her mother Lill and her Aunt Ernestine to Smith, was married in October. In December Lillian paid what turned out to be her last visit to the White House, to attend Lynda Bird Johnson's wedding to Chuck Robb, who was the son of family friends. Eventually even Lillian realized she could not keep up this pace, and in her 1967 Christmas letter she announced that she was reserving her energy for the events surrounding Frank's centennial. "I want to be able to attend them all," she told her friends, "so am suspending my usual activities during 1968." Lillian had told the engineering profession of her impending retirement a few days earlier at the Marshall Space Flight Center near Huntsville, Alabama. She met there the famed rocket scientist Dr. Wernher von Braun and told a group of engineers, "This will be my last talk for maybe—ever."[10]

Lillian spent Christmas in Montclair with her son Jack and his family and then in early March 1968 she paid another visit to Anne in California on her way to the first of the year's Gilbreth Centennial celebrations. She was much frailer than when Anne had last seen her, and she visited the doctor, hoping for some kind of pick-me-up. To Lillian's dismay, she was admitted to the Palo Alto Clinic for tests, after which the doctor ordered total rest. The doctor "grounded" her, saying she must reserve her strength.[11]

On March 28, 1968, Lillian wrote to a friend, apologizing because she could not attend a meeting. "The M.D. said that my eye is fine but that I am completely exhausted and must give up travel and speaking and rest the remainder of this year. I suppose that he is right," she added, "but I am so disappointed. The meetings include a number on management given in honor of my husband—and I had looked forward to them so eagerly." That letter was handwritten; Lillian's large scrawly writing was not much different from the way it had been for half a century, not yet the wavering script of the elderly and infirm. Lillian also had Jane Callaghan type a number of letters, the most painful of which was undoubtedly to the chairman of the Frank Gilbreth Centennial Committee explaining that her doctor had ordered her to cancel all her engagements, "including all the meetings designed to celebrate the Centennial of Frank's birth." She added, "As you can imagine, I am not at all happy over such severe restrictions, but I realize that 'Doctor's orders' are something that must be obeyed."[12]

Lillian was not telling the whole story when she described herself simply as "exhausted." She spent much of 1968 in and out of hospitals and doctor's offices as surgeons removed skin cancers from her forehead and left cheek. After another battery of tests in July, she was diagnosed as suffering from arteriosclerotic heart disease. To make matters worse, her daughter Martha was dying of cancer; she passed away in mid-November at the age of fifty-nine. Martha was the last to marry and the first to die. Her death was a blow to the family, particularly to her own five children, but after the funeral Lillian knew there was one last thing she had to do.

On December 3, 1968, she insisted on attending a conference in the New York Hilton, as part of the Gilbreth Centennial celebrations. Most of the family was there and listened as speaker after speaker praised Frank and Lil-

lian's contributions to motion study. Specialists working with the reha
tion of the handicapped, doctors and hospital administrators, librarians
dustrialists, even a space engineer explained how Gilbreth techniques w
used in their fields. During a short break before lunch, Lillian gathered he
children around her and told them that she was, finally, retiring. "I'm grounding myself," she said. An hour and a half later, after lunch and more speeches
praising Lillian, it was her turn to speak. She got up slowly, wearing one of
the little hats she had adopted to disguise her thinning hair. Everyone applauded. Her back was still straight, though she was a little shaky as she held
up a hand for silence. When the hall was finally quiet she said something in
German, then added in English, "My mother used to say that. It means 'The
heart speaks loudest when the lips speak not.'" And then she sat down.[13]

Lillian's work was her life and retirement meant relinquishing everything
that gave meaning to her existence. If this was fiction, she could have lain
down and died happy, her work done. But life seldom has tidy endings. Immediately after the Gilbreth Conference Lillian traveled to Paradise Valley,
Arizona, where Ernestine and her husband, Chuck Carey, now lived. Lillian
intended to stay only until the end of January 1969 and then go to Anne in
Palo Alto for a while before returning to her apartment and her friends.
Ernestine soon discovered, however, that her mother was in a lot of pain; she
was suffering badly with infected teeth and deep fissures in her feet. Trips to
a dentist and a dermatologist got both problems under control by Christmas;
but Ernestine knew, and Lillian conceded, that she was too frail to go back to
New York and live alone. Jane Callaghan offered her a room, but the family
felt that Jane's Long Island home had too many stairs and was altogether unsuitable and so, as Ernestine had offered to have her, in Arizona she stayed.
Ernestine and her husband lived in a long, low house in an exclusive, country-
club neighborhood; Lillian moved into the small spare bedroom overlooking
the swimming pool. Ernestine reported that her mother was "blooming": she
had put on a little weight and things seemed to be going well. It is hard to
imagine, however, that Lillian was content doing nothing, but nevertheless in
March she was still with Ernestine while some of the Montclair family were
clearing out her New York apartment, sending materials to libraries and stor-
ing other items in Dan's basement.

By April 1969 Lillian's health was declining rapidly; she had fallen and
broken a hip and suffered a series of small strokes. She could not feed herself
or write, though apparently there was nothing physically wrong with her
arms. It was as if she had given up. She had to be lifted in and out of bed and
needed more nursing than Ernestine was able to give, so the family placed her
in the Beatitudes, a nearby nursing home. They reassured themselves that it
was a nice, clean place, with kindly nurses, but to conserve her financial re-

...es they put her in a double room, doubting whether she knew where she ... Lillian probably knew more than her children thought; even if the ...okes had robbed her of mobility and some of her memory, she could still speak and sometimes showed glimmers of recognition. Ernestine visited her almost every day and Lillian came to depend on these visits.

Bill visited her in late April and reported that she was very thin and confined to a wheelchair. She was also a little confused; the first day he visited she was not sure which son he was, though a day later she sent greetings to Jean, his wife. He concluded that, although her organs were working well, physically there was nothing but a shell.[14] Two years later she was still in the Beatitudes. Family members continued to visit; her youngest brother, Frank Moller, stopped by and reported that she was doing very well physically and seemed to be enjoying life, though her memory seemed to have gone. Her son Frank Jr. visited and reported that she often thought she was on the campus of a university and that the nurses were coeds.[15]

Lillian lingered on. As she continued to decline, she was blithely unaware of events around her. In 1960 she had told a journalist "she saw no reason why a woman should not be a pioneer space traveler to the moon." And so it was sad that she missed the first moon landing, especially as Neil Armstrong had traveled in a space module designed on Gilbrethian motion study principles to make his "small step" in 1969. Lillian had spent the last four decades traveling. While she was in the Beatitudes, the Concorde and the Boeing 747 jumbo jets went into service; how those two planes would have made her life easier! Changes connected with her lifetime's work included the rapid movement of married women into the labor force: by 1969, 41 percent of U.S. married women were working outside the home, up from 31 percent a decade earlier. Lillian had spent many years trying to make the workplace more hospitable to the "human element": in 1970 President Nixon signed the Occupational Safety and Health Act, authorizing an office designed to minimize hazards in industry. Lillian knew none of this; she was quietly slipping away. By Christmas 1971 she was bedridden, and finally she suffered a massive stroke. She died at two o'clock in the morning on January 2, 1972, in her ninety-fourth year.

Just as she had in 1923 when she entered the hospital for her hysterectomy, Lillian had left detailed instructions about her funeral arrangements. She wanted to be cremated right away, though Arizona state law required a delay of forty-eight hours. She wanted to donate her eyes for transplant or research. She emphatically wanted no viewing, no embalming, no displayed coffin, no funeral directors, and no flowers. She wanted a memorial service at Scottsdale Congregational Church, with "only a few passages from the Bible and a short prayer." She added, "Only family and a few friends that it would help any member of the family to have there. No out of town family to feel it necessary to come." She wanted her ashes scattered and her name to be added to Frank's stone in Fairfield, Maine.[16]

Some, but not all, of Lillian's wishes were carried out. She was cremated, her name was added to Frank's gravestone, and her ashes were scattered in the waters off Nantucket. Though her body, as arranged, was taken to the Good Samaritan Hospital, no surgeon was available and thus, according to Ernestine, "the eyes were not used after all. Such a waste and needless situation!" Two services were in fact held, both on January 9, 1972. Ernestine followed her mother's wishes and held one in Scottsdale, while the rest of the family organized another at the First Congregational Church in Montclair, where Lillian had been a member for more than half a century. It is unnecessary to read too much into this; the family felt they had to have an East Coast memorial service as so many people wanted to pay their respects. Although the Montclair service was private, there were several hundred people in the large, neo-Gothic church, and despite Lillian's instructions, there was a large bouquet of white flowers in the chancel.[17]

It was a gloomy, rainy Sunday, as promptly at two o'clock members of the Gilbreth family filed in; they filled three rows of the Montclair church. When Lillian died, she left ten children, thirty grandchildren, and twenty-two great-grandchildren. There were a few Bible readings and some of Lillian's favorite hymns, but the minister, N. Wesley Haynes, also talked about Lillian's work and read from her writings, a departure she would not have approved. He stressed her modesty and her simplicity and pointed out that while Lillian belonged to each member of the congregation "in particular and unique ways," she "also belongs to a larger world of men and women who have never met her, yet have had their lives more meaningful because she lived." He listed those who had benefited: "the factory worker, the handicapped, the blind, the housewife, the executive, the space pilot," as well as "hosts" of people all over the world, though they had never heard her name. "But that is always the lot of creative people," he continued. "They always serve in ways they cannot see. But because she did live and work their homes will be happier, their work more productive and their lives made richer. For this we thank God." Many years later, the Reverend Haynes recalled Lillian as "the wisest person he had ever known."[18]

Since her death Lillian has been much talked about, no doubt more than she would have liked. In 1984 the U.S. Post Office issued a Lillian Gilbreth stamp as part of its "Great Americans" series; and in 1995 she was inducted into the National Women's Hall of Fame at Seneca Falls, New York. A nomination in 1978 for the National Medal of Science by all twenty living past presidents of the American Society of Mechanical Engineers was not, however, successful. Nonetheless, she is well remembered within the Society of Women Engineers and amongst the older members of numerous engineering societies. Women in their seventies, eighties, and nineties remember her speaking at their college graduations or descending on their hospital, factory, or organization and trying to make it more efficient. Since the 1980s, some women's history scholars have started to look at Lillian's work; to date there have been three doctoral dissertations on Lillian and there are several more in progress. A new version of the movie *Cheaper by the Dozen* was released in late 2003, and there's the rub.

The vast majority of people who recognize Lillian's name do so only after being prompted by the words "Cheaper by the Dozen." This was true of the obituaries, which appeared in newspapers all over the world. Most of them included anecdotes from *Cheaper by the Dozen* or *Belles on Their Toes*. The article in the *New York Times* was headed "Dr. Gilbreth, Engineer, Mother of Dozen" and though it dealt very fairly and thoroughly with her career, in its first sentence it said that she "was better known as the real-life mother in the book and movie 'Cheaper by the Dozen.'" Meanwhile, Philippine television played the movie over and over for a week.[19]

The book and the film, as this account of her life has tried to demonstrate, do not do Lillian justice. They were not meant to; they were intended as entertainment and as such they succeed, but as a portrayal of the life of a complex and talented woman, they leave much to be desired. Lillian was well aware that one day someone would write her biography: why else would she so carefully preserve so many materials? Her son Frank once asked her if she would object to his writing it; she replied, "The longer you postpone that, the better it will suit me."[20]

Lillian's friend and secretary once wrote, "Some day somewhere some one will no doubt do a complete 'Zelda' job telling all about it." Jane Callaghan was referring to a biography of F. Scott Fitzgerald's wife, in which Zelda's unfulfilled ambitions, her drinking, and her mental instability were displayed for all to read. It would seem that there were no such scandals to uncover in Lillian's life, which was filled to the brim with work and family. She was also deeply in love with her husband and continued to love him to the end of her life. She told her son, "That I should have married the one who was, to me, the most interesting, is one of those miracles one hopes for—and is eternally grateful for."[21]

Lillian's life, both public and private, speaks to many of the issues that face women and men, able-bodied or otherwise, in both the developed and the developing world today. How can women find work that satisfies them, while raising a family and having time for their own interests? How can work—whether it is in industry, in offices, in hospitals, on farms, or in the home—be made more productive without dehumanizing the worker? How can children be brought up to be both individuals and responsible members of the larger community? How can people with differences of skill or of physical ability be helped to be useful members of society?

Lillian did not have all the answers, but she spent a lifetime looking for them.

Archives and Libraries Consulted

I either visited or corresponded with more than forty libraries and archives.
The ones I quote from are as follows:

Bancroft Library, University of California

Brown University Library, Wednesday Club Papers

Business and Professional Women's Association, USA

Green-Wood Cemetery, Brooklyn

Herbert Hoover Presidential Library

Massachusetts Institute of Technology, Special Collections

Menninger Archives, Topeka, Kansas

National Archives: Women's Bureau papers, PECE and POUR Papers

Newark Public Library

Purdue University, Frank B. and Lillian M. Gilbreth Collection

Rhode Island Historical Society, Wanscuck Company Records and YWCA
Records

Schlesinger Library, Radcliffe Institute, Amelia Mary Earhart Papers

Smithsonian Institution, National Museum of American History, Gilbreth
Collection

Sophia Smith Library, Smith College, Lillian Moller Gilbreth Papers and
Ernestine Gilbreth Carey Papers

Tainon College, Taiwan.

Other archives and libraries consulted include:

Alameda County (Calif.) Superior Court records

American Association of University Women

Birmingham (Eng.) City Reference Library

Cadbury Archives, Birmingham (Eng.)

Columbia University Library, Special Collections

Ebell Society, Oakland

General Federation of Women's Clubs

Katharine Gibbs College Archives

Johnson & Johnson Archives

Library of Congress, League of Women Voters Papers
Maria Mitchell Observatory, Nantucket
Montclair High School, Montclaire, N.J.
Montclair (N.J.) Public Library
Nantucket Historical Society
New Jersey Institute of Technology
New York Athletic Club
Oakland Public Library, Special Collections
Providence Public Library, Reference Division
Franklin D. Roosevelt Presidential Library
San Francisco Public Library
Stanford University, Cecil H. Green Library
Teachers College, Milbank Memorial Library, Special Collections
Harry S. Truman Library
University of Birmingham (Eng.), Special Collections
University of Connecticut, Special Collections
University of Wellington Library, New Zealand

NOTES

Abbreviations

    In the notes, short titles have generally been used after the first full reference. People, works, manuscript collections, and organizations frequently cited have been identified by the following abbreviations:

AF	Lillian Moller Gilbreth, unpublished "Autobiographical Fragment" [1941?] in the Gilbreth Collection, Purdue University, West Lafayette, Ind.
AGC	Anne Gilbreth Cross
AIR	Lillian Moller Gilbreth, *As I Remember* (Norcross, Ga.: Engineering and Management Press, 1998)
AM	Annie Moller (Lillian's mother)
Ancestors	Frank B. Gilbreth Jr., *Ancestors of the Dozen* (Columbia, S.C.: privately printed in cooperation with the [Charleston, S.C.] *Post and Courier,* 1994)
ASME	American Society of Mechanical Engineers
Belles	Frank B. Gilbreth Jr. and Ernestine Gilbreth Carey, *Belles on Their Toes* (New York: Thomas Crowell, 1950)
Carey Papers	Ernestine Gilbreth Carey Papers, Sophia Smith Collection at Smith College, Northampton, Mass.
Cheaper	Frank B. Gilbreth Jr. and Ernestine Gilbreth Carey, *Cheaper by the Dozen* (New York: Thomas Crowell, 1948)
DAB	*Dictionary of American Biography*
DBG	Daniel Bunker Gilbreth (Lillian's son)
EG	Ernestine Gilbreth (Lillian's daughter)
EGC	Ernestine Gilbreth Carey (Lillian's daughter after her marriage)
FBG	Frank Bunker Gilbreth (Lillian's husband)
FBG Jr	Frank Bunker Gilbreth Jr. (Lillian's son)
GC	Frank and Lillian Gilbreth Collection at Purdue University, West Lafayette, Ind.
HH	Herbert Hoover, president of the United States
HI	Hoover Institution on War, Revolution, and Peace, Stanford University, Stanford, Calif.
HHPL	Herbert Hoover Presidential Library, West Branch, Iowa
Home-maker	Lillian M. Gilbreth, *The Home-maker and Her Job* (New York: Appleton, 1927)
JGH	Jane Gilbreth Heppes (Lillian's youngest child)
KG	Katharine Gibbs
LD	Lillie Delger (Lillian's aunt, later Dr. Lillian Powers)

LEM   Lillie Evelyn Moller (name before marriage in 1904)
LGJ   Lillian Gilbreth Johnson (Lillian's daughter)
LHH   Lou Henry Hoover
Living   Lillian M. Gilbreth, *Living with Our Children* (New York: W. W. Norton,
               1928)
LMG   Lillian Moller Gilbreth
LMG Papers   Lillian Moller Gilbreth Papers at Smith College, Northampton, Mass.
MBG   Martha Bunker Gilbreth (Lillian's mother-in-law)
NAW   Edward T. James et al., *Notable American Women 1607–1950: A Biographical
               Dictionary,* 3 vols. (Cambridge, Mass.: Belknap Press of Harvard University
               Press, 1971)
NAWMP   Barbara Sicherman and Carol Hurd Green, eds., *Notable American Women:
               The Modern Period.* (Cambridge, Mass.: Belknap Press of Harvard University
               Press, 1980)
NEB   New England Butt
Partners   Edna M. Yost, *Frank and Lillian Gilbreth: Partners for Life* (New Brunswick,
               N.J.: Rutgers University Press, 1948)
PECE   National Archives, President's Emergency Committee for Employment
POUR   National Archives, records relating to activities of officials of the Women's
               Division of the President's Organization for Unemployment Relief
Psychology   L. M. Gilbreth, *The Psychology of Management: The Function of the Mind
               in Determining, Teaching and Installing Methods of Least Waste* (New York:
               Sturgis and Walton, 1914)
Quest   Lillian Moller Gilbreth, *The Quest of the One Best Way* (New York: Society
               of Industrial Engineers, 1925; reprint, New York: Society of Women
               Engineers, 1990)
SEW   S. Edgar Whitaker (Gilbreth employee at New England Butt)
SIE   Society of Industrial Engineers
SWE   Society of Women Engineers
Time Out   Frank B. Gilbreth Jr., *Time Out for Happiness* (New York: Thomas Crowell,
               1970)
"Waste in   Lillian M. Gilbreth, "Some Aspects of Eliminating Waste in Teaching," Ph.D.
   Teaching"   diss., Brown University, 1915

Introduction

1. J. W. Kenney, quoted in R. M. Kelly and V. P. Kelly, "Lillian Moller Gilbreth (1978–1972)." A. N. O'Connell and N. F. Russo, eds., *Women in Psychology: A Biobibliographic Sourcebook* (New York: Greenwood Press, 1990), 118–24. The lists include those in *Good Housekeeping,* December 1930, and the remark about Lillian's presidential potential appeared in "Dr. Gilbreth Has an Active Life," *Savannah, Georgia, Press,* October 5, 1937, which concluded, "At a women's meeting in Paris a couple of years ago her name was mentioned as one who deserved to be nominated as the first woman president of the United States." Clipping in archives of the General Federation of Women's Clubs.

2. Amelia Earhart, quoted by Virginia Whitney, in a letter to Frank Bunker Gilbreth Jr. (FBG Jr.), August 3, 1971, Frank and Lillian Gilbreth Collection, Purdue University, container c.4, File "Sympathy letters." (References to this collection will follow the form GC c.|container or box number], f.[folder] number or name; it is copyright 2004 by Ernestine Gilbreth Carey [EGC]. Quotations are reprinted with the permission of McIntosh and Otis, Inc.) Herbert

Hoover (subsequently HH) to EGC and FBG Jr., September 14, 1950, Herbert Hoover Presidential Library (subsequently HHPL), Post-Pres. Individual, Gilbreth, Lillian M.

3. FBG Jr. and ECG, *Cheaper by the Dozen* (New York: Thomas Crowell, 1948) (subsequently *Cheaper*). It has sold more than three million copies and is still selling. The hardcover version went into twenty-eight printings and sold 241,093 copies through bookstores in 1949. The Book-of-the-Month Club, which first issued the book in January 1949, sold 257,000 copies. Excerpts were published in the *Ladies' Home Journal* in January 1949 and in the *Reader's Digest* in March 1949. A paperback edition was issued in 1951 and has been selling steadily ever since. The most recent edition is under the Yearling imprint of Random House.

4. Ruth Schwartz Cowan, "Lillian Moller Gilbreth," in Barbara Sicherman et al., eds., *Notable American Women: The Modern Period: A Biographical Dictionary* (subsequently NAWMP) (Cambridge: Belknap Press of Harvard University Press, 1980), 271–73.

5. Jo Werne, "'Cheaper by Dozen' Mom Sidelined by Hip Injury," *Miami Herald* (February 12, 1971).

6. William J. Jaffe, "Dr. Lillian Moller Gilbreth: The One Best Life at Eighty: Dr. Lillian M. Gilbreth and the Unceasing Quest," in *The Gilbreth Story* (New York: Proceedings of the American Institute of Industrial Engineers, 1962), 6.

7. Gerda Lerner, "Priorities and Challenges in Women's History Research," *Perspectives* (April 1988): 17–20.

8. U.S. Department of Commerce, Bureau of the Census, *Historical Statistics of the United States, Colonial Times to 1970*, Part 1 (Washington, D.C., 1975), 131–34.

9. Edna Yost, *Frank and Lillian Gilbreth: Partners for Life* (New Brunswick, N.J.: Rutgers University Press, 1948), 10 (subsequently *Partners*). Lillian read the galleys and suggested a couple of changes; it is thus an "authorized" biography, though necessarily incomplete, as Lillian lived for almost twenty-five years after its publication and worked for more than twenty of those years. The only other biography was published by her son Frank B. Gilbreth Jr. and is called *Time Out for Happiness* (New York: Thomas Crowell, 1970; subsequently *Time Out*). Lillie Evelyn Moller (LEM), "Ben Jonson's Comedy of *Bartholomew Fair*: A Study" (M.Litt. thesis, University of California, 1902), 4.

10. It is impossible to know how many letters she destroyed. There are very few from her to her husband, Frank. For example, on February 7, 1918, Lillian wrote to him, "I have had a case of dysentery since yesterday morning. . . . it affected little Dan too, so as I had been wanting to talk to the Doctor for weeks about his food, I sent for him this morning. He advises weaning at once, as he is getting to be a little whale like all the rest. . . . [Weaning] is no fun until it is over. I hate to give him up, it seems as if my little baby was grown up." Lillian Moller Gilbreth (LMG) to Frank Bunker Gilbreth (FBG), c.C11. This paragraph was omitted from the version of the letter placed in the main collection, GC c.112, f.0813-8.

11. LMG, *As I Remember* (Norcross, Ga.; Engineering and Management Press, 1998), 127 (subsequently *AIR*). A tender is a bricklayer's helper. Frank had started work as a bricklayer and worked his way up to ownership of a large construction business. Lillian's remark is a pun, as she tenderly looks after Frank's interests, a very female role.

12. Jill Ker Conway, *Written by Herself: Autobiographies of American Women: An Anthology* (New York: Vintage, 1992), xi. See also Carolyn Heilbrun, *Writing a Woman's Life* (New York: Ballantine, 1988), and also Heilbrun, "Non-Autobiographies of 'Privileged' Women: England and America," in Bella Brodski and Celeste Schenck, eds., *Life/Lines: Theorizing Women's Autobiography* (Ithaca: Cornell University Press, 1988), 62–76.

13. Ruth Baker in the *Christian Science Monitor*, January 12, 1949, 14, quoted in *Book Review Digest 1949* (New York: H. H. Wilson, 1950), 345.

14. Lillian received a total of twenty-two honorary degrees between 1928 and 1964. Seventeen professional societies awarded her honorary memberships. She won twenty medals, all but two after *Cheaper by the Dozen* was published. On the subversive nature of some postwar domestic fiction, see Nancy A. Walker, "Humor and Gender Roles: The 'Funny' Feminism of the Post–World War II Suburbs," *American Quarterly* (Spring 1985): 98–113. One of the texts Walker deconstructs is Betty MacDonald's *The Egg and I* (Philadelphia: Lippincott, 1945). I read both *The Egg and I* and *Cheaper by the Dozen* as a child in postwar England; they colored my view of America while getting entangled in my memory. See also Jane F. Levey, "Imagining the Family in Postwar Popular Culture: The Case of *The Egg and I* and *Cheaper by the Dozen*," *Journal of Women's History* 13, no. 3 (Autumn 2001): 126–68.

15. Mary Brown Lawrence to author, January 24, 1996 (used with permission).

16. As Joanne Meyerowitz has noted in "Beyond *The Feminine Mystique:* A Reassessment of Postwar Mass Culture, 1946–1958," *Journal of American History* 79, no. 4 (March 1993): 1458, embedded in the popular culture of the postwar period "domestic ideals co-existed in ongoing tension with an ethos of individual achievement that celebrated nondomestic activity, individual striving, public service and public success." Betty Friedan's book *The Feminine Mystique* (New York: Norton, 1963) had a profound effect on many women. As some readers wrote to her, "It changed my life." See Friedan, *It Changed My Life: Writings on the Women's Movement* (New York: Random House, 1976). In recent years there has been a scholarly reexamination of Friedan's research methods and her findings. Notable revisions include Rachel Bowlby, "'The Problem with No Name': Rereading Friedan's *The Feminine Mystique*," *Feminist Review* 27 (September 1987); Joanne Meyerowitz, ed., *Not June Cleaver: Women and Gender in Postwar America, 1945–1960* (Philadelphia: Temple University Press, 1994).

1. GONE WEST

1. EGC, interview by the author, Paradise Valley, Ariz., October 25, 1998; Frank B. Gilbreth Jr. and Ernestine Gilbreth Carey, *Belles on Their Toes* (New York: Thomas Crowell, 1950), 2 (subsequently *Belles*).

2. "Proceedings of Meeting held June 13, 1924, at 3:30 P.M., in the Engineering Societies' Building, New York, of the PIMCO Committee on American Participation," GC c.120, f.0816-94.

3. Charles Lytle, "Frank Gilbreth—A Human Being," in *Gilbreth Centennial Reminiscences* (New York: ASME, 1969), 113.

4. Information in this and succeeding paragraphs is from the interview by the author with EGC on October 25, 1998; EGC to the author, November 7, 2001; and *AIR*, 191.

5. EGC interview, 1998; Daniel Bunker Gilbreth (DBG), interview by the author, West Caldwell, N.J., June 15, 1999.

6. *AIR*, 191; LMG to W. M. Newton, January 22, 1925, GC c.c11, f.letters. Dr. Lillian Powers arrived without her beloved squirrels, and for once there were no furry creatures nestling in her handbag. Information on Dr. Powers from "Houseful of Squirrels," *Newark Evening News*, June 9, 1923; "The Lady Doctor's Furry Friends," *San Francisco Chronicle*, April 24, 1958; and "The Actors Fed on Nuts," *San Francisco Chronicle*, April 25, 1958.

7. *AIR*, 192; Edna Yost, "Lillian Gilbreth As Known to Her Biographer," *Journal of Industrial Engineering*, Special Reprint (May 1962): 17–18.

8. Death Certificate, Department of Health, Montclair, N.J., dated June 16, 1924, and postmortem report, June 14, 1924, both found in GC c.c11, f.Insurance papers. Frank's brain does not seem to be at Harvard: an e-mail to the author from Lucretia McClure, of the Harvard Rare Books and Special Collections Department, dated April 24, 1997, stated, "I checked with the Warren Museum of Harvard Medical School and they have no brain specimens."

9. EGC interview, 1998. *AIR*, 192; *Cheaper*, 179.

10. *AIR*, 192.

11. EGC interview, 1998.

12. *AIR*, 192; much of the information in this and the next chapter is from the Ernestine Gilbreth Carey Papers, Sophia Smith Collection, Smith College, Northampton, Massachusetts (subsequently Carey Papers). I used the papers for background information, rather than citing them directly. The collection has been reprocessed since I first saw it and items relating to Lillian reclassified as the Lillian Moller Gilbreth Papers, so all file and folder numbers have been omitted on the advice of the archivists. Both collections are copyright 2004 Ernestine Gilbreth Carey. Quotations are reprinted with the permission of McIntosh and Otis, Inc.

13. *Cheaper*, 180; EGC interview, 1998.

14. *AIR*, 192.

15. "Mother of Eleven Manages Hubby's Business," *Providence Journal Bulletin*, July 11, 1924; "Gilbreth's Wife Carries on after Husband's Death," *New York World*, July 11, 1924.

16. John Dewey, *The School and Society* (Chicago: University of Chicago Press, 1899), 354–55.

17. LMG, *The Quest of the One Best Way* (1925; reprint, New York: Society of Women Engineers, 1990), 188 (subsequently *Quest*).

18. *AIR*, 190, 193; *SIE Bulletin* 6, no. 6 (June 1924): 3.

19. *AIR*, 192.

20. LMG, "To My Traveller," undated typescript, GC c.C11, f.LMG poetry/writings.

21. *Cheaper*, 235.

2. ONCE UPON A TIME

1. Details of this event were found in a letter from Annie Delger Moller to Lillie Delger, May 26, 1879. Annie's letters to her sister at boarding school, written over a period of four years, were saved and bound into four notebooks, which are now in the restricted Carey Papers at Smith College, though they were not apparently restricted when I saw them. These letters support Lillian's self-description as a nervous child in *As I Remember*, and some are referred to and summarized in this chapter.

2. J. M. Quinn, *History of California and Biographical Record of Oakland and Environs*, vol. 2 (1907), 827–29 (undated typescript from California State Library, Sacramento, without further attribution); "F. Delger Made His Fortune in Broadway Oaks," *Oakland Post Enquirer*, July 1, 1922, 18.

3. Quoted in *Partners*, 80–81.

4. The Delger girls were educated by the Sisters of the Holy Name in Oakland and later went as boarders to the convent of Notre Dame in San Jose. See Edgar J. Hinkel and William E. McCann, eds., *Oakland 1852–1938: Some Phases of the Social, Political and Economic History of Oakland, California* (Oakland: Oakland Public Library and the Works Progress Administration, 1939), 2: 459; 1: 493–95. See also LMG, "Autobiographical Fragment," n.d., probably 1941 (subsequently AF), GC c.3, f.LMG, 41; *Cheaper*, 87.

5. FBG Jr., *Ancestors of the Dozen* (Columbia, S.C.: privately printed in cooperation with the [Charleston, S.C.] *Post and Courier*, 1994), 20, 23 (subsequently *Ancestors*).

6. *AIR*, 3; "Record of Family Traits," GC c.136, f.0830-45.

7. *AIR*, 9–10. See Agnes Fine, "A Consideration of the Trousseau: A Feminine Culture," in Michele Perrot, ed., *Writing Women's History* (Oxford, Eng.: Blackwell, 1984): 118–45, and Ellen K. Rothman, *Hands and Hearts: A History of Courtship in America* (Cambridge: Harvard University Press, 1987).

8. *AIR*, 8, 3; *Ancestors*, 30.

9. *Ancestors,* 27; AF, 27; *AIR,* 10–11. According to records of the Green-Wood Cemetery, Brooklyn, Jacob J. Moller was interred on October 23, 1849, John J. Moller on November 1, 1851, and an unnamed child of John Moller on May 15, 1852. William Moller went into partnership with Robert Dalziel, a plumber and gas fitter and importer of gas fixtures. Dalziel and Company survived in San Francisco into the 1980s.

10. *AIR,* 12.

11. *AIR,* 37–38; AF, 57.

12. *AIR,* 19. See Nancy F. Cott, "Passionlessness: An Interpretation of Victorian Sexual Ideology, 1790–1850," *Signs* 4 (1978): 219–36; also Daniel Scott Smith, "Family Limitation, Sexual Control and Domestic Feminism in Victorian America," *Feminist Studies* 1 (Winter–Spring 1973): 40–47. See also Ann Douglas Wood, "'The Fashionable Diseases': Women's Complaints and Their Treatment in Nineteenth-Century America," in Judith Walzer Leavitt, ed., *Women and Health in America: Historical Readings* (Madison: University of Wisconsin Press, 1984), 222–38. Contemporary accounts include Catharine Beecher, "On Female Health in America" (1855), and Mary Putnam Jacobi, "On Female Invalidism," both in Nancy F. Cott, ed., *Root of Bitterness: Documents of the Social History of American Women,* 2d ed. (Boston: Northeastern University Press, 1996), 293–97, 334–37.

13. AF, 7; *AIR,* 12.

14. Photograph, GC c.15(a). Written on the back is "Lillie at 2 years 4 months." *AIR,* 13, 38.

15. *AIR,* 38.

16. AF, 5. Delger later relented and even provided his daughter with a house.

17. *AIR,* 15.

18. Ibid., 18. Matilda Brown never remarried. Tillie became president of the Ladies Relief Association and took over from her mother the leadership of the King's Daughters' Home for Incurables, which Matilda Brown financed. Annie Florence taught in the Oakland public schools and became president of Oakland's Board of Education. Everett became a judge. *Oakland Post Enquirer,* July 2, 1922, 18; Rockwell D. Hunt, ed., *California and Californians* (Chicago: Lewis, 1926), 3:466.

19. *AIR,* 38–39.

20. Ibid., 39–40.

21. The Moller house is described in an undated, unattributed newspaper clipping, "One Reason Why Mr. Moller Is Quietly Happy" [1895?], GC c.111, f.0811-2.

22. *AIR,* 39–40. See Jane Addams, "The Subjective Necessity for Social Settlements," in Henry C. Adams, ed., *Philanthropy and Social Progress* (New York: Thomas Crowell, 1893), and Addams, "The College Woman and the Family Claim," *Commons* 3 (1898): 3–7; Allen F. Davis, *American Heroine: The Life and Legend of Jane Addams* (New York: Oxford University Press, 1973), 83.

23. *AIR,* 19–21.

24. Frederick Delger bought his youngest daughter a house as a wedding gift; it is now in Oakland's Preservation Park. See Helaine Kaplan Prentice et al., *Through These Doors: Discovering Oakland at Preservation Park* (Oakland: Oakland Redevelopment Agency, 1996), 38–39. For Violette's death, see *AIR,* 19–20.

25. See *Melancholy Angels: An Intimate Portrait of Mountain View Cemetery* (Oakland: Board of Trustees, Mountain View Cemetery Association, 1996). Henriette Delger, who died of spinal meningitis at the age of four months, joined her sister less than three years later.

26. *AIR,* 24–25; AF, 36–37.

27. *AIR,* 31–32; AF, 37.

28. *AIR*, 4; AF, 37–38.

29. *AIR*, 32, 49.

30. AF, 13.

31. Ibid., 55. Although Alcatraz was a federal penitentiary for less than thirty years (1934–63), it had been used as a prison for military personnel, civilians, and Native Americans since 1850.

32. Photograph from GC c.15(a) 5. "Lillie Moller" is written on the back. *AIR*, 63–64.

33. *AIR*, 64; see John Kasson, *Amusing the Million: Coney Island at the Turn of the Century* (New York: Hill and Wang, 1978), 11–28, on the importance of the Midway in the development of American culture. The quotation is from *Rand-McNally Guide to the World's Fair* (Chicago, 1894), n.p., quoted in T. J. Jackson Lears, *No Place of Grace: Antimodernism and the Transformation of American Culture, 1880–1920*, 2d ed. (Chicago: University of Chicago Press, 1994), 116.

34. W. E. Hamilton, *The Time-Saver* (Chicago, 1893), quoted in John E. Findling, *Chicago's Great World Fairs* (Manchester, Eng.: University of Manchester Press, 1994), 29. The journalist William E. Hamilton sold 150,000 copies of his little book and made a handsome profit.

35. The Midway enabled the exposition to make a small profit for its investors. See Kasson, *Amusing the Million*, 24–25.

36. *AIR*, 51; see *Ancestors*, 27–28.

3. THE "ATHENS OF THE PACIFIC"

1. AF, 43; *Time Out*; AF, 46; *AIR*, 21; Conway, *Written by Herself*, ix. See Barbara Sicherman, "Sense and Sensibility: A Case Study of Women's Reading in Late-Victorian America," in Cathy N. Davidson, ed., *Reading in America: Literature and Social History* (Baltimore: Johns Hopkins University Press, 1989), 214, 224n.70.

2. *AIR*, 21–22. For Coolbrith see Edward T. James et al., eds., *Notable American Women 1607–1950: A Biographical Dictionary*, 3 vols. (Cambridge: Belknap Press of Harvard University Press, 1971; subsequently *NAW*), 1: 379–80. For reminiscences by the Steins, Duncan, and London, see Josephine DeWitt Rhodehamel and Raymond Francis Wood, *Ina Coolbrith: Librarian and Laureate of California* (Salt Lake City: Brigham Young University Press, 1973), 150–51. See also James D. Hart, *The Popular Book: A History of America's Literary Taste* (New York: Oxford University Press, 1950), 68–69, 73–78.

3. *AIR*, 22–23; *Time Out*, 190. See Burton J. Bledstein, *The Culture of Professionalism: The Middle Class and the Development of Higher Education in America* (New York: Norton, 1976), 77–78, which emphasizes the isolating nature of Victorian reading.

4. George Du Maurier, *Trilby* (1894; rept., New York: The Popular Library, 1963), 76. See John Higham, "The Reorientation of American Culture in the 1890s," in John Higham, *Writing American History* (Bloomington: Indiana University Press, 1970), 84–85.

5. *AIR*, 22; *NAW*, 3: 626; *Dictionary of Literary Biography* (Detroit: Gale Research, 1978), 42: 393–96.

6. *AIR*, 23; see Andrew Sanders, *The Victorian Historical Novel, 1840–1880* (New York: St. Martin's Press, 1979), 17.

7. *NAW*, 1: 529–31; *NAW*, 3: 355–59; Gertrude Stein, *The Autobiography of Alice B. Toklas* (1933; rept., London: Penguin, 1966), 82.

8. AF, 43–46; *AIR*, 23–24, 30–31.

9. Hinkel and McCann, *Oakland 1852–1938*, 497; *AIR*, 25; AF, 47–48.

10. *AIR*, 26; AF, 48; *Partners*, chapters 3 and 4; *Time Out*, chapter 2.

11. *AIR*, 41. See Leigh Eric Schmidt, *Consumer Rites: The Buying and Selling of American Holidays* (Princeton: Princeton University Press, 1995), which has a perceptive chapter, "St. Valentine's Day Greeting," which analyzes the tensions between commerce, gender, ritual, and material culture.

12. *AIR*, 57.

13. *AIR*, 49; AF, 49. Many early settlers in Oakland were German and created familiar institutions for themselves; see Hinkel and McCann, *Oakland 1852–1938*, 350–98. Lillie attended the local Turnverein, a mixture of militarism and German folk culture. See Harvey Green, *Fit for America: Fitness and Sport in American Society* (New York: Pantheon, 1986).

14. *AIR*, 50. Delsarte, a "scientific" system of dramatic training, was named after François Delsarte (1811–71), whose disciple Steele Mackaye brought it to America; see Genevieve Stebbins, *Delsarte System of Dramatic Expression* (New York: Edgar S. Werner, 1886), 5.

15. AF, 51–52; *California Teachers' Association Journal* (April 1956): 9. Stein's enthusiasm is quoted in John Malcolm Brinnin, *The Third Rose: Gertrude Stein and Her World* (Reading, Mass.: Addison-Wesley, 1959), 19, without attribution.

16. AF, 53; *AIR*, 58.

17. *Aegis 1896* (Oakland: Oakland High School Class of June Ninety Six, 1896), 29, 31.

18. Lillie E. Moller, "To the Class of June '96," *Aegis 1896*, 35.

19. *AIR*, 58; *Time Out*, 23–25.

4. IN SEARCH OF THE STRENUOUS LIFE

1. Higham, "Reorientation of American Culture," 87; Lears, *No Place of Grace;* Tom Lutz, *American Nervousness: An Anecdotal History* (Ithaca: Cornell University Press, 1991), 26, 20.

2. See Sean Dennis Cashman, *America in the Gilded Age* (New York: New York University Press, 1984; 3d ed., 1993), 313–80.

3. *AIR*, 154–59. On the Gibson Girl, see Lois W. Banner, *American Beauty: A Social History through Two Centuries of the America Idea, Ideal and Image of the Beautiful Woman* (New York: Random House, 1983): 154–59.

4. *AIR*, 66. See Barbara Miller Solomon, *In the Company of Educated Women: A History of Women and Higher Education in America* (New Haven: Yale University Press, 1985), 64, and Lynn D. Gordon, *Gender and Higher Education in the Progressive Era* (New Haven: Yale University Press, 1990), 20. In 1970, in her last publication, Lillian wrote that her father believed that "as his daughter, it would be most unlikely that I would have any need for professional training. He preferred to have me remain at home." "Lillian Moller Gilbreth," in Irving Stone, ed., *There Was Light: Autobiography of a University, 1868–1968* (Garden City, N.Y.: Doubleday, 1970), 83–89.

5. *AIR*, 66. On Dr. Powers, see "Houseful of Squirrels," "The Lady Doctor's Furry Friends," and "The Actors Fed on Nuts." See also Addams, "The College Woman and the Family Claim."

6. *AIR*, 67. Lillian's poem is a conventional piece of late-Victorian sentimentality; the second stanza reads: "My life grows bright and joyous for Love begins her reign / And sends from her new dominion all traces of doubt and pain. / The weary past is forgotten, its sorrows fade away, / For love has come through the darkness, 'tis day for my heart, 'tis day." *Sunrise* by John Metcalf, words by Lillie Evelyn Moller (Boston: Arthur Schmidt, 1898).

7. Shinn, "University of California," *Overland Monthly* 20 (October 1892): 362; quoted in Verne A. Stadtman, *The University of California, 1868–1968* (New York: McGraw-Hill, 1970), 118–19; Gordon, *Gender and Higher Education*, 56–59; for Mrs. Hearst (1842–1919) see *NAW*, 2: 171–73.

8. Martin Kellogg, quoted in Stadtman, *University of California*, 116.

9. Stadtman, *University of California*, 157, 159.

10. Rothman, *Hands and Hearts*, 211.

11. Studies of women and higher education include already cited works by Lynn Gordon and Barbara Miller Solomon. Other sources include Thomas Woody, *A History of Women's Education in the United States*, 2 vols. (New York: Science Press, 1929); Mabel Newcomer, *A Century of Higher Education for American Women* (New York: Harper and Bros., 1959); John Mack Faragher and Florence Howe, eds., *Women and Higher Education in American History* (New York: W. W. Norton, 1998); Geraldine Joncich Clifford, ed., *Lone Voyagers: Academic Women in Coeducational Institutions, 1870–1937* (New York: Feminist Press, 1989); Penina Migdal Glazer and Miriam Slater, *Unequal Colleagues* (New Brunswick, N.J.: Rutgers University Press, 1987); Helen Lefkowitz Horowitz, *Alma Mater: Design and Experience in the Women's Colleges from Their Nineteenth-Century Beginnings to the 1950s* (New York: Alfred A. Knopf, 1984); Jill Ker Conway, "Perspectives on the History of Women's Education in the United States," *History of Education Quarterly* 14 (Spring 1974): 1–12; Rosalind Rosenberg, "The Academic Prism: The New View of American Women," in Carol R. Berkin and Mary Beth Norton, eds., *Women of America: A History* (Boston: Houghton Mifflin, 1979), 318–41. Studies of the impact of higher education on women of the Gilded Age include Allen Davis on Jane Addams, *American Heroine*; Joyce Antler, *Lucy Sprague: The Making of a Modern Woman* (New Haven: Yale University Press, 1986); Sara Alpern, *Freda Kirchwey: A Woman of the Nation* (Cambridge: Harvard University Press, 1987); Kathryn Kish Sklar, *Florence Kelley and the Nation's Work* (New Haven: Yale University Press, 1995).

12. *The Occident*, University of California (November 1, 1900), quoted in Solomon, *Educated Women*, 84–85. See Carroll Smith-Rosenberg, "The New Woman as Androgyne: Social Disorder and Gender Crisis, 1870–1936," in *Disorderly Conduct: Visions of Gender in Victorian America* (New York: Oxford University Press, 1985), 245–96; Gordon, *Gender and Higher Education*, 4–5.

13. *AIR*, 66–68. This was not a special concession for Lillie; the University of California regularly made allowances for such "probationary" students who had not fulfilled all entry requirements. See *Time Out*, 29.

14. See *California Teacher's Association Journal* (April 1956): 9–19, 20; *AIR*, 69–71; LMG to Dean Carl Barus, Brown University, December 9, 1914, Lillian M. Gilbreth folder, University Archives, John Hay Library, Brown University. See also the preface to Lillian's unpublished dissertation, "Some Aspects of Eliminating Waste in Teaching" (Ph.D. diss., Brown University, 1915), viii (subsequently "Waste in Teaching"); Stone, *There Was Light*, 84.

15. Stadtman, *University of California*, 123; *AIR*, 68.

16. *AIR*, 68; Gordon, *Gender and Higher Education*, 38, 72–73. The cartoon can be found facing page 84 and was published in the *Pelican* c. 1911.

17. Interview with Jane Gilbreth Heppes (subsequently JGH), Longview, Washington, April 7, 2001. See reminiscences of alumnae in *The Prytaneans: An Oral History of the Prytanean Society, Its Members and Their University, 1901–1920*, 2 vols. (Berkeley: University of California Press, 1920), cited in Solomon, *Educated Women*, 233n.7. Lillie was able to skip the institution-building stage and go directly to building alliances with powerful men. See Estelle Freedman, "Separatism As Strategy: Female Institution Building and American Feminism, 1870–1930," *Feminist Studies* 5, no. 3 (Fall 1979): 445–59.

18. Stone, *There Was Light*, 81–89; *AIR*, 72. The two women who received the key were Adeline Belle Croyland, recipient of a master's degree, and Lillian's classmate Gertrude Eudora Allen '00. Lillian could, however, have been suggesting either that smart women could get jobs

teaching school (which is what Miss Croyland and Miss Allen did) with or without the key. According to an e-mail from William Roberts, University of California (Berkeley) archivist, October 4, 1997, distinguished alumnae were fairly regularly given keys after graduation.

19. *AIR*, 72.

20. Stadtman, *University of California*, 180, 185. See Benjamin Ide Wheeler, *The Abundant Life*, ed. Monroe E. Deutsch (Berkeley: University of California Press, 1926). The quotation is from his *Report of the President of the University* (1905): 9–11, quoted in Gordon, *Gender and Higher Education*, 70–71.

21. *AIR*, 73; "Student Orators to Speak at Graduation," *San Francisco Examiner* (April 21, 1900), and "Coeds Honored by President Wheeler," no source, found in GC c.135, f.0830-403.

22. *Oakland Tribune*, May 12, 1900, 6; *Blue and Gold* (Berkeley: University of California, 1900): 112.

23. *Oakland Tribune*, May 12, 1900, 2; *Blue and Gold* (1900): 114–15.

24. *AIR*, 73; *Oakland Enquirer*, May 16, 1900; clipping found in GC c.135, f.0830-403.

25. *AIR*, 73; program information and photographs from *Blue and Gold* (1900): 117 and between 44 and 45; summaries of the speeches from the *Oakland Enquirer*, May 16, 1900.

26. *AIR*, 72; *Oakland Enquirer*, May 16, 1900.

27. William James, *Essays in Pragmatism*, ed. and with an introduction by Alburey Castell (New York: Hafner Press, 1948), 146.

28. Theodore Roosevelt, "The Strenuous Life," in *The Strenuous Life: Essays and Addresses* (1900; rept., St. Clair Shores, Mich.: Scholastic Press, 1970), 1. The speech was delivered in 1898.

29. *Oakland Enquirer*, May 16, 1900; *AIR*, 73–75.

30. *AIR*, 73–75.

31. Ibid., 71.

32. See *NAW*, 3: 285–86 and 42–43. Peixotto became the first woman faculty member at the University of California in 1904; there was no official woman dean until Lucy Sprague arrived in 1906.

33. *AIR*, 71.

34. Ibid., 78.

35. Ibid., 75; *Time Out*, 35; *Catalogue* (New York: Columbia University 1900–1901): 117.

36. *Dictionary of American Biography* (*DAB*) 20 (1936), 478–81; *DAB* 12 (1933), 24–27; *AIR*, 72–73, 76; Columbia *Catalogue* (1900–1901): 67, 90.

37. *AIR*, 72–73, 76; Laurel Graham, *Managing on Her Own* (Norcross, Ga.: Engineering and Management Press, 1998), 56.

38. *AIR*, 73.

39. Ibid., 77.

40. LMG, *Twentieth Century Instruction Book: Artistic Ladies' Tailor System* (New York: Vienna Ladies' Tailoring Institute, 1902).

41. *AIR*, 77–78.

42. Ibid., 78; Colin Counsell, Introduction to Ben Jonson's *Bartholomew Fair* (London: Nick Hern Books, 1997), xvi. The play's reputation was revived in the mid-nineteenth century by Henry Morley in *Memoirs of Bartholomew Fair* (London: Frederick Warne, 1859). A generation later the poet Algernon Swinburne declared it was one of the "coarser masterpieces of comic art." See Frances Teague, *The Curious History of Bartholomew Fair* (Lewisburg, Pa.: Bucknell University Press, 1985), 107, 108.

43. LEM, "Ben Jonson's Comedy of Bartholomew Fair," 1, 3, 4, 96.

5. NOT LIKE ANY BOYS WE KNOW

1. "A Letter from Minnie Bunker," *Newsletter,* American School of Classical Studies at Athens (Spring 1983): 16–19; *AIR,* 81.

2. *AIR,* 80. Lillian's transcripts are in the John Hay Library, Brown University.

3. Jane Addams to Ellen Starr, July 11, 1883, quoted in Davis, *American Heroine,* 32.

4. Some feminist scholars argue that by traveling, women constructed a personal or national identity based on racial, class, or gender "superiority." I see Lillian's travels more as a personal escape, though empowerment followed. See Foster Rhea Dulles, *Americans Abroad: Two Centuries of European Travel* (Ann Arbor: University of Michigan Press, 1964), and Shirley Frost, *American Women Travellers to Europe in the Nineteenth and Early Twentieth Centuries* (Keele, Eng.: Keele University Press, 1994). Freud's suggestion, made in "A Disturbance of Memory on the Acropolis," is cited in William W. Stowe, *Going Abroad: European Travel in Nineteenth-Century American Culture* (Princeton: Princeton University Press, 1994), 223n.4.

5. Steven LaVoie, "Victorian-Era Oakland Sparked Women's Political Organizing," *Oakland Tribune,* November 8, 1992. The definitive study of the early years of the women's club movement is Karen Blair's *The Clubwoman As Feminist: True Womanhood Redefined, 1868–1914* (New York: Holmes and Meier, 1980). She maintains that literary clubs "served as a first step for feminists determined to improve their status. The significance of the development of sufficient audacity to strive for self-improvement in an era that defined ladies as selfless agents devoted to the well-being of others cannot be underrated" (58).

6. *AIR,* 81. Women's guides included the deliciously named Women's Rest Tour Association's *A Summer in England: A Handbook for the Use of American Women.* See Stowe, *Going Abroad,* 28–54. The best account of the San Francisco Chinese Mission is in Peggy Pascoe's *Relations of Rescue: The Search for Female Moral Authority in the American West, 1874–1939* (New York: Oxford University Press, 1990). The literature on settlements is extensive; Davis's biography of Jane Addams, *American Heroine,* and Sklar's *Florence Kelley and the Nation's Work* illuminate the role of middle-class women.

7. LMG, "Management's Place in the World Today," typescript dated July 7, 1961, GC c.2, f.Unrestricted papers FBG and LMG. Quotations in the next paragraphs are from letters written by Lillian, either to her family on June 30, 1903, or to her sister Josie on June 29, 1903; all these letters were found in GC c.17, "Just Us" album. Other quotations are from *AIR,* 82–89, unless otherwise indicated.

8. The murals were painted by the American artist Edwin Austin Abbey (1852–1911). Frank's car cost $2,500; a 1903 Model A cost $850 and a Cadillac cost $750. It is not clear who Mr. McWilliams was, nor what kind of car he drove.

9. FBG to LEM, June 26, 1904; GC series 2, box 4.

10. *Time Out,* 74. FBG to LEM, June 26, 1904.

11. *Time Out,* 37. The photograph of the stylish hat is in GC c.17, "Just Us" album.

12. FBG to LEM, February 24, 1904. FBG to LEM, May 12, 1904.

13. *AIR,* 89.

6. EVEN QUEST MAKERS CHANGE THEIR MINDS

1. Lillian's description of her grand tour and Frank's courtship is in *AIR,* 89–96.

2. Letters recalling Lillian's expression are from May 7 and 12, 1904; Frank's appendectomy was mentioned in letters from FBG to Martha Bunker Gilbreth (MBG), December 1903, and FBG to LEM, April 24, 1904.

3. *New York Times,* September 22, 1903, section 6:5; FBG to LEM, June 11, 1904. The engagement letters (December 29, 1903, to October 4, 1904) were found in GC series 2, c.4, f.FBG

Letters Sent. References in *AIR* suggest that Lillian's letters may have been available in 1941, as she describes Frank's daily letters and "equally long letters—but much more full of day dreams and wishful thinking, [which] went east" (91). These letters were not found at Purdue.

4. FBG to LEM, February 14, May 7, 1904.

5. *Ancestors*, 121; *Quest*, 23.

6. Stone, *There Was Light*, 86; FBG to LEM, June 30, 1904.

7. *AIR*, 95.

8. FBG to his mother and aunt, December 22, 24, 26, 28, 1903. GC c.11.

9. FBG to his mother, December 24, 1903.

10. FBG to his mother, December 26, 1903.

11. FBG to LEM, December 29, 1903, and January 24, 1904.

12. *Ancestors*, 44–46; *Quest*, 5–6; *Time Out*, 47–48; *Partners*, 15.

13. *Time Out*, 51; *Quest*, 8; *Ancestors*, 94.

14. *Time Out*, 53; *Ancestors*, 95.

15. *Time Out*, 52–53.

16. *Quest*, 10.

17. *Time Out*, 58; *Ancestors*, 96. The story of Martha's visit to the bank is almost certainly apocryphal, since she had relations in Boston, some of whom could have provided references or sureties. For nineteenth-century boardinghouses, see Joanne Meyerowitz, "Sexual Geography and Gender Economy: The Furnished Room Districts of Chicago, 1890–1930," in Barbara Melosh, ed., *Gender and American History Since 1890* (London: Routledge, 1993), 43–47. The impression the Gilbreths wanted to give was of middle-class respectability, not the arena for sexual experimentation described by Meyerowitz. As the 1880 and 1890 census enumerators' sheets were destroyed by fire, it is impossible to establish how many people, and of what occupations and sexes, lived in Martha's boardinghouse.

18. *Quest*, 12; George W. Coleman to Margaret Hawley (MH), June 15, 1928; William W. Lewis to MH, June 24, 1928. Hawley wrote to more than one hundred of Frank Gilbreth's former friends and colleagues in 1927–28 while preparing a master's thesis, "The Life and Work of Frank B. Gilbreth" (M.A. thesis, University of California, Berkeley, 1929). The replies were placed in GC c.111, f.0812-2 and are subsequently cited as [name] to MH. Frank was later a member of the Simplified Spelling Board, one of many Progressive-Era efforts at making life more efficient.

19. *Quest*, 15; George A. Titcomb to MH; Chas. H. Flood to MH.

20. See *Partners*, 50–51, 351; *Quest*, 15.

21. *Quest*, 17–21; *Partners*, 39–43, 190–91.

22. *Partners*, 72, 76, 108–14. His profit margin was usually between 8 and 10 percent.

23. *Time Out*, 76. The president of MIT, Henry Smith Pritchett, described Gilbreth as "an unusual and master builder," while the *Boston Evening Transcript* described the feat as a "marvel" of industrial planning and cooperation between labor and management.

7. A LONG-DISTANCE ENGAGEMENT

1. These letters are all in GC series 2, c.4, and date from between December 29, 1903, and October 4, 1904. Quotations from FBG in the succeeding paragraphs come from these letters unless otherwise noted.

2. *Oakland Tribune*, January 9, 1904, 7. All the press clippings about Lillian and Frank's engagement quoted in the next paragraphs were found pasted into the "Just Us" album (GC RF c.12); most of them have no identification beyond the name of the newspaper and the date.

3. *San Francisco Examiner*, April 15, 1904; "The Meddler" (April 16, 1904); "Announcement of Engagement Made at Tea This Afternoon" (April 14, 1904); *AIR*, 97.

4. *Oakland Tribune*, January 9, 1904, 7; "The Meddler" (April 16, 1904).

5. Walter Dill Scott, *The Theory of Advertising: A Simple Exposition of the Principles of Psychology in Relation to Successful Advertising* (Boston: Small, Maynard and Co., 1903).

6. MBG to LEM, October 10, 1904.

7. Lillian's description of the wedding is in *AIR*, 97–98; the photographs are in GC RF c.12, "Just Us" album.

8. *Oakland Tribune*, n.d.; *Oakland Herald*, n.d.; *AIR*, 97–98.

9. "Mollers Send Out Cards," *Oakland Tribune*, [October 1904].

10. *Time Out*, 98–99; Lillian M. Gilbreth, *Living with Our Children* (New York: W. W. Norton, 1928), 19, 21 (subsequently *Living*). Part memoir, part child-rearing manual, it was reprinted several times in the 1920s and reissued in a new edition, with an introduction by the author Dorothy Canfield Fisher, in 1951. References are to the 1928 edition.

11. FBG to LEM, October 4, 1904; *AIR*, 103.

8. The One Best Marriage

1. *Living*, 53–54.

2. Ibid., 5, 7.

3. Ibid., 33–34.

4. *Partners*, 6. Frances Mason, "Sons and Daughters of the Golden Bear: Lillian Moller Gilbreth '00," *California Alumni Fortnightly* 14, no. 8 (April 30, 1921): 183, 186.

5. *Living*, 43–44.

6. *Quest*, 33; Margaret W. Rossiter, *Women Scientists in America: Struggles and Strategies to 1940* (Baltimore: Johns Hopkins University Press, 1982), 143.

7. "Who Washes the Dishes When Ma Is Famous?" undated [1925] and unattributed clipping, GC N-File. For early-twentieth-century marital models see Margaret Marsh, "Suburban Men and Masculine Domesticity, 1870–1915," in Mark C. Carnes and Clyde Griffen, eds., *Meanings for Manhood: Constructions of Masculinity in Victorian America* (Chicago: University of Chicago Press, 1990). Marsh cites articles in *American Homes and Gardens* (1905) and *Cosmopolitan*, as well as books by Senator Albert Beveridge and the health publicist Bernarr Macfadden, all of which advocate sharing domestic responsibilities.

8. *Quest*, 32; *Time Out*, 100, 96; *Living*, 38.

9. MBG to LEM, September 23, 1904. GC series 2, box 11, f.LMB. Incoming correspondence. The present occupant kindly showed me around the apartment (which has been divided into two) in January 1999. The original floor plan was found in GC RF c.12, "Just Us" album.

10. MBG to LEM, September 23, 1904.

11. *AIR*, 104; *Time Out*, 100. According to Margaret Visser in *Much Depends on Dinner* (New York: Collier Books, 1986), 115, carving meat "has from time immemorial expressed not only family cohesion . . . but also hierarchy and difference. . . ."

12. *AIR*, 106; *Time Out*, 100.

13. *Living*, 34; MBG to LEM, September 23, 1904.

14. *Quest*, 34–35; FBG, *Concrete System* (New York: Engineering News Publishing, 1908) and *Bricklaying System* (New York: M. C. Clark, 1909).

15. *Partners*, 132–46; *AIR*, 107; *NAW*, I: 51–52.

16. *AIR*, 107, 112.

9. Planning a Family

1. Lillian described the first year of her marriage in *AIR*, 107–11. One of the babies was stillborn and one child died at age five.

2. C. B. Davenport, "The Eugenics Programme: Its Progress and Its Achievement," in *Eugenics: Twelve University Lectures* (New York: Dodd, Mead, 1914), 10–11.

3. Francis Galton, *Inquiries into Human Faculty and Its Development* (London: Macmillan, 1883). Holmes is quoted in Daniel J. Kevles, *In the Name of Eugenics: Genetics and the Uses of Human Heredity* (New York: Knopf, 1985), 111.

4. *Living*, 24–25, 29.

5. Harriot Stanton Blatch, "Voluntary Motherhood," in Rachel Foster Avery, ed., *Transactions* (Philadelphia: J. B. Lippincott, 1891), 282–83; quoted in Linda Gordon, *Women's Body, Women's Right*, rev. ed. (New York: Penguin, 1990), 126. Roosevelt, *The Strenuous Life*, 126.

6. ECG interview, Paradise Valley, Ariz., December 28, 1996. In her later years Lillian supported Margaret Sanger, perhaps because of a shared interest in eugenics. A copy of a letter from Sanger to LMG (July 18, 1952) asking "Planned Parenthood friends" to endorse a family planning conference, and LMG's reply doing so, can be found in the Carey Papers. See Margery Rex, "Last Baby Is Always Loved Most," *New York Evening Journal*, October 23, 1922.

7. Judith A. Merkle, *Management and Ideology: The Legacy of the International Scientific Management Movement* (Berkeley: University of California Press, 1980), 204n.58; *AIR*, 107.

8. This information on Anne's early days comes from an undated (but probably 1930s) speech by Lillian that was printed by the American Federation for Medical Research (AFMR) Manager Learning Center and found in the Carey Papers without full attribution.

9. See Alexander Francis Hamilton, *The Child: A Study in the Evolution of Man* (London and New York: Walter Scott Publishing, 1902); *AIR*, 109.

10. FBG to LMG, May 26, 1906.

11. *Partners*, 139, 143.

12. FBG to LMG, June [n.d.], May 26, September 5, 1906. There was a serious slump in 1907. Yost claims that Frank had between eight and ten thousand employees in the spring of 1906, though this is hard to verify, as the records do not seem to have survived. *Partners*, 137–38, 141–42.

13. FBG to LMG, June [n.d.] 1906.

14. *Quest*, 37. Information on the Mollers' education is from a genealogical form filled out by LMG, 1914; GC c.136, f.0830-45. FBG to LMG, [September] 1906.

15. FBG to LMG, September 1, 4, 1906.

16. The present owners (who had lived there for forty years) kindly showed me around in 1997 and told me about the pig farm. FBG to LMG, June, August 21, [late September] 1906.

17. FBG to LMG, September 10; [early September]; August 21; August 30; September [n.d.] 1906; *AIR*, 110.

18. FBG to LMG, September 11, 1906.

19. FBG to LMG, undated letter, 1906; *Partners*, 137–39, 143–44. James H. McGraw founded the McGraw-Hill Publishing Company.

20. *Partners*, 134. Frank's firm built the Wilson Building, the Boyd Building, the North Beach Electric Power Station, the Canadian Commerce Building, the Union Square Hotel, and the Pacific Grand Hotel.

21. *AIR*, 111.

22. See *Partners*, 142; *AIR*, 111–12.

10. MENTIONED FROM THE PLATFORM BY TAYLOR

1. Advertisement in "Apartment Houses of the Metropolis," n.d., framed in the lobby of the Hendrik Hudson Building, where I saw it in January 1999.

2. "Death Takes Boston Artist: Miss Caroline Bunker Dies at Providence, Oct. 3rd," undated and unattributed press clipping found in Carey Papers; *AIR*, 112; *Partners*, 149.

3. *Partners*, 137–38, 155–56; FBG Diaries, 1895–1924. Frank's engagement diaries were transcribed in 1941, and the quotations are from the transcribed version. GC c.109, f.808-3.

4. Taylor won, with his brother, the 1881 U.S. Lawn Tennis Association doubles championship using a spoon-shaped racket he had designed and patented. He also acted in amateur theatricals, often taking women's roles and deriving great pleasure from going into local shops, still dressed as a woman, to see if he fooled the shopkeepers. There is a photograph of a bewigged and begowned Taylor as "Lillian Gray" in Martha Banta's *Imaging American Women: Idea and Ideals in Cultural History* (New York: Columbia University Press, 1987), 271. Biographies of Taylor include Frank Barkley Copley, *Frederick W. Taylor: Father of Scientific Management* (New York: Harper and Bros., 1923), which is the "authorized" biography, having been commissioned and censored by the Taylor family; more recent works include Daniel Nelson, *Frederick W. Taylor and the Rise of Scientific Management* (Madison: University of Wisconsin Press, 1980), Sudhir Kakar, *Frederick Taylor: A Study in Personality and Innovation* (Cambridge: MIT Press, 1970), Marvin Weisbord, *Productive Workplaces* (San Francisco: Jossey-Bass, 1987), and Robert Kanigel, *The One Best Way* (New York: Viking, 1997).

5. Frederick W. Taylor, *The Principles of Scientific Management* (New York: Harper, 1911), 77; Samuel Haber, *Efficiency and Uplift: Scientific Management in the Progressive Era* (Chicago: University of Chicago Press, 1964), ix; Mary Barnett Gilson, *What's Past Is Prologue: Reflections on My Industrial Experience* (New York: Harper and Bros., 1940), 57; W. S. Ayres to MH.

6. Thompson to Taylor, November 24, 1908; Morris L. Cooke to Taylor, September 9, 1910, Taylor Collection, Stevens Institute of Technology, quoted in Milton J. Nadworny, "Frederick Taylor and Frank Gilbreth: Competition in Scientific Management," *Business History Review* 31 (Spring 1957): 25.

7. Frederick W. Taylor, *Shop Management* (New York: Harper, 1911), 22, 21; Taylor, *Principles*, 27, 26, 35–36, 25.

8. Frederick W. Taylor, *Scientific Management* (New York: Harper, 1947), 26–27.

9. Gilson, *Prologue*, 53.

10. Robert Kent to MH. Kent, a Plainfield neighbor of the Gilbreths and son of the mechanical engineer William Kent, became editor of the *Industrial Engineering and Engineering Digest*, which was to publish Lillian's University of California dissertation. Hugo Diemer to MH.

11. L. P. Alford, *Henry Laurence Gantt: Leader in Industry* (New York: ASME, 1934); Wallace Clark, *The Gantt Chart: A Working Tool for Management* (New York: Ronald Press, 1922). The Gantt chart is still used, though now it is computerized. *Quest*, 41 441 Lyndall Urwick, ed., *The Golden Book of Management: A Historical Record of the Life and Work of Seventy Pioneers* (London: Newman Neame, 1956), 43, 40. Dodge (1852–1915) was president of the ASME from 1902 to 1903.

12. LMG, interview with MH, May 6, 1927; quoted in Hawley, "Life and Work," 64.

13. *Partners*, 159–61. FBG, *Bricklaying System*.

14. MDG to Anne Gilbreth Cross (AGC), April 5, 1908, GC series 3, c.24, f.1.

15. *AIR*, 113–14; MBG to AGC, April 5, 1908; FBG Diaries, 1908.

16. FBG Diaries, 1908, 38; *Quest*, 38; *AIR*, 115.

17. EGC interview, 1998; comment by Edna Yost, *Partners*, 179.

18. EGC interview, 1998.

19. *AIR*, 114.

20. Ibid., 115, 118.

21. Institution of Mechanical Engineers, *Proceedings of Joint Meeting with American Society of Mechanical Engineers in England* (July 1910): 30. FBG to MBG, August 2, 1910.

22. *Partners*, 184. "The Meeting in England" (ASME, 1910), 1002–8. FBG to MBG, August 4, 1910; FBG to LMG, August 5, 1910.

23. LMG to MBG, August 4, 1910.

24. *Quest*, 44.

25. LMG interview with MH, May 6, 1927.

26. R. T. Kent to MH. *Partners*, 187; Kanigel, *One Best Way*, 432; *Quest*, 44. Frank had the brainstorm that lead to the formation of the Taylor Society on a river steamer in Canada at two o'clock in the morning.

27. Charles Going to MH; *Partners*, 203, 185–88.

28. Erwin H. Schnell, "The Gargantuan Nudge," *Journal of Industrial Engineering*, Special Reprint (May 1962): 24.

29. FBG, *Motion Study: A Method for Increasing the Efficiency of the Workman* (New York: D. Van Nostrand, 1911).

30. *American Magazine*, vols. 71–72; also reproduced in *The World's Work*, London edition, May, June, and July 1911; AIR, 118; FBG, *The Primer of Scientific Management* (New York: D. Van Nostrand, 1912). A second edition was published in 1914 and reprinted in 1973 by the Hive Publishing Co. in Easton, Pa. For an opinion on authorship, see Brian Price, "The Motion Study Controversy," in Daniel Nelson, ed., *A Mental Revolution* (Columbus: Ohio State University Press, 1992), 60. See Nancy F. Cott, "Two Beards: Co-authorship and the Concept of Civilization," *American Quarterly* 42, no. 2 (June 1990): 274.

31. AIR, 118.

32. Ibid., 127. See Clark, *The Gantt Chart*, 81–109.

33. Mayme Ober Peak, "She Conquers Fatigue—Woman's Greatest Enemy," *Beautiful Womanhood* (February 1923), n.p. Carey Papers.

34. LMG, *The Psychology of Management: The Function of the Mind in Determining, Teaching and Installing Methods of Least Waste* (New York. Sturgis and Walton, 1914), 137–38.

35. Quoted in Alford, *Gantt*, 239. See also Haber, *Efficiency and Uplift*, on Gantt's views.

36. LMG interview with MH, May 6, 1927.

37. *Addresses and Discussions at the Conference on Scientific Management Held October 12.13.14, Nineteen Hundred and Eleven* (Hanover, N.H.: Amos Tuck School of Administration and Finance, Dartmouth College, 1912), 356.

38. *Quest*, 36. *Partners*, 204.

11. DIVINE PROVIDENCE

1. Glass plates of color autochromes of the children playing under the Christmas tree are located in the Gilbreth Collection, Division of Engineering, Smithsonian Institution, Washington, D.C.

2. AIR, 119; *Partners*, 208–12. Taylor's testimony was printed in Taylor, *Scientific Management* (1947). Carl Fraenkel, an assistant to the great German bacteriologist Robert Koch, had developed an antitoxin in 1890; see Terra Ziporyn, *Disease in the Popular American Press: The Case of Diphtheria, Typhoid Fever and Syphilis, 1870–1920* (New York: Greenwood Press, 1988), 35–62. Interview with Irene Gilbreth, June 15, 1999. Mrs. Gilbreth said that her sister-in-law Anne Gilbreth Barney told her about the tracheotomy.

3. Carey Papers. Ernestine recollects that she wrote the poem when she was about sixteen and that it was later printed in the *Smith College Monthly*, which she edited. EGC to author, November 7, 2001.

4. EGC interview, 1998. Photograph of memorial stone in Fairfield, Maine, GC RF c.12, "Just Us" album.

5. AIR, 119; Anne Gilbreth Barney to EGC, August 5, 1982. Carey Papers.

6. AIR, 119; *Quest*, 36; Stone, *There Was Light*, 87. This story is impossible to verify because there is a gap in the minutes of the Graduate Council covering precisely the period in

which Lillian Gilbreth's case would have come up. FBG, "Here's to Lillian! Worth a Billion!" composed for LMG's forty-second birthday, May 1920, GC c.113, f.0813-12.

7. *Quest*, 48; Lillian cited Hugo Münsterberg's *American Problems from the Point of View of a Psychologist* (New York: Moffat, Yard & Co., 1910) in her dissertation. His *Psychology and Industrial Efficiency* (Boston: Houghton Mifflin, 1913) was an adaptation of his *Psychologie und Wirtschaftsleben* (Leipzig: J. A. Barth, 1912); although Lillian was fluent in German and could have read it, she had finished her dissertation before it was published in the United States.

8. *AIR*, 119–20. LMG, *Psychology of Management*.

9. Both Frank and Lillian and her former professor George Stratton stated it was somehow lost at Berkeley. Oddly, though Stratton chaired her committee, he claimed never to have seen her thesis, "so that I am sorry to say I can give you no judgment with regard to it. . . . I don't know how it came about that those to whom it was sent never submitted it in any way to me, but such is the case." G. M. Stratton to LMG, November 13, 1913, Lillian Gilbreth file, Brown University Archives. In the book she cited works on scientific management nearly one hundred times, with twenty-eight references to Taylor, seventeen to her own writings, and thirteen to Gantt. There were many fewer references to psychology; of the total of fifty-nine, thirteen were to her professor, George Stratton, twelve to William James, six to Hugo Münsterberg, six to Mary Calkins, who had been trained by William James and then taught at Wellesley, and five to Walter Dill Scott, whose book on the psychology of advertising Lillian had recommended to Frank during their engagement.

10. LMG, *Psychology of Management*, 221, 238, 252, 264.

11. Ibid., 328, 332.

12. *Quest*, 49; LMG, interview with MH, May 6, 1927.

13. "Dates in History of Y.W.C.A." typescript, Providence Young Women's Christian Association Records, Manuscripts Collection, Rhode Island Historical Society.

14. Anne Gilbreth married Fred Drew Cross in Boston in 1891; John Gilbreth Cross was born in 1897 and Caroline Cleveland Cross in 1901. Many elderly women remember their lessons at Mrs. Cross's Music School. Information is from interviews by the author with Eleanor Peckham, Providence, R.I., June 1, 1991; Marion Dunlop, Providence, R.I., March 6, 1994; Louise Aldrich Hoge, Providence, R.I., February 17, 1995; and EGC, Scottsdale, Ariz., December 28, 1996.

15. *AIR*, 121.

16. Ibid., 125; Dorothy W. Gifford, *Lincoln School: The First Century* (Providence, R.I.: Lincoln School, 1984), 7–9. I have a personal interest in the Lincoln School, having taught there for ten years.

17. Carey Papers; Peak, "She Conquers Fatigue."

18. Carey Papers.

19. Ibid.

20. *AIR*, 121.

21. Ibid., 131; EGC interview, 1998. The Gilbreths moved from 71 to 77 Brown Street after a couple of years; most of Ernestine's description here is of the second, larger house.

22. Helen Douglas Ladd to EGC, Christmas 1966, Carey Papers; also interview with Eleanor Peckham, June 1, 1991.

23. EGC interview, 1996; interview with Edward Winsor, Providence, R.I., June 1, 1991.

12. SCIENTIFICALLY MANAGING NEW ENGLAND BUTT

1. FBG to James F. Butterworth, May 18, 1912, GC c.117, f.0816-54.

2. "New England Butt Company Leading Maker of Braiding Machines," Wanskuck Company Records, f. 23, Manuscripts Collection, Rhode Island Historical Society.

3. *AIR*, 125.

4. *Partners*, 217; Frederick Taylor to Horace King Hathaway, September 2, 1912; Hathaway to Taylor, September 9, 1912, and February 19, 1914, quoted in Nadworny, "Frederick Taylor and Frank Gilbreth," 25.

5. Articles on the NEB installation in *Industrial Engineering and Engineering Digest* include "Micromotion Study" (January 1913); "The Use of the Route Model" (February 1913); "Motion Study for the Move-Man" (March 1913); and "Keeping Track of Work in the Shop" (November 1913).

6. Horace K. Hathaway, "Report to the New England Butt Company," June 8, 1912; Charles B. Going to MH.

7. FBG to Carl Barth, September 26, 1912; Carl Barth to FBG, October 9, November 12, 1912, GC c.117, f.0816-45. S. Edgar Whitaker (SEW) to FBG, August 28, October 11, November 15, 1912; January 10, 22, 19, March 19, 1913, GC c.159, f.0952-2. See Brian C. Price, "One Best Way: Frank and Lillian Gilbreth's Transformation of Scientific Management, 1885–1940" (Ph.D. diss., Purdue University, 1987), 165–66.

8. FBG to John Aldrich, September 8, 1913. In 1993, when I showed "The Original Films of Frank B. Gilbreth" to employees of Wardwell's, the firm that took over NEB in 1947, they expressed doubt about these figures and suggested that even if they were true, it was because of the production-line elements involved in assembling many identical machines. Nowadays, when machines are custom-made, such speeds would be impossible. My thanks to Jonathan Farnum for the chance to visit Wardwell's. The films are available in a compilation titled *The Original Films of Frank B. Gilbreth: The Quest for the One Best Way*, produced by Dr. Lillian M. Gilbreth and James S. Perkins.

9. Harry Hopkins to MH; John Aldrich, "Using Motion Pictures to Promote Business Efficiency," *New York Tribune*, February 9, 1913, quoted in Price, "One Best Way," 181.

10. LMG, *Psychology of Management*, 221; Joseph A. Piacitelli to MH.

11. Joseph A. Piacitelli, "The Gilbreths As I Have Known Them," *Journal of Industrial Engineering*, Special Reprint (May 1962): 12.

12. SEW to FBG, July 11, October 26, 1912.

13. Fred H. Colvin, "The Latest Developments in Motion Study," *American Machinist* (June 3, 1913); *Providence Journal*, December 22, 1912, section 5: 3–4; SEW to FBG, October 8, 15, 22, 29, 1912; January 21, February 11, 1913. "Waste in Teaching," 2–3.

14. LMG, *Psychology of Management*, 330.

15. SEW to FBG, July 4, 10, 1912. See SueEllen Hoy, *Chasing Dirt: The American Pursuit of Cleanliness* (New York: Oxford University Press, 1995), 137–49.

16. *Quest*, 57; H. R. Stronck, "A Report on the Operation of Scientific Management at the New England Butt Company, Providence," typescript (October 18, 1913), 7–8; GC c.117, f.0816-51, quoted in Price, "One Best Way," 176; FBG, 1914 Summer School. *Partners*, 238; "Anti-Fatigue Museum Started Here," *Providence Journal*, March 22, 1914, section 5: 8.

17. SEW to FBG, July 25, 31, August 28, 1912, February 13, 1913; FBG, *Primer of Scientific Management*, in William R. Spriegel and Clark E. Myers, *The Writings of the Gilbreths* (Homewood, Ill.: Richard D. Irwin, 1952), 120; *Partners*, 224.

18. Henry Hopkins to MH. See Joseph W. Sullivan, "'Every Shout a Cannon Ball': The IWW and Urban Disorders in Providence, 1912–1914," *Rhode Island History* 54, no. 1 (May 1996): 51–64.

19. SEW to FBG, August 16, 1912; Frederick Taylor to Horace King Hathaway, September 2, 1912; Taylor to Carl Barth, October 12, 1912, quoted in Price, "One Best Way," 209–11.

20. *Partners*, 236; SEW to FBG, September 1, 1913.

21. FBG to John Aldrich, September 8, 1913.

22. John G. Aldrich, "Ten Years of Scientific Management," *Management Engineering* 4, no. 2 (February 1923): 1.

13. THE GOOD EXCEPTION

1. *Time Out,* 177.

2. More complicated versions were called the chronocyclegraph, whereby the flow of electric current was interrupted and the resulting series of flashes showed the time and direction of the movements, and the stereochronocyclegraph, which created a three-dimensional image of motion by using two slightly offset cameras and viewing the prints through a stereopticon. The photograph is in the Smithsonian's Gilbreth Collection, 85–131.

3. Nadworny, "Frederick Taylor and Frank Gilbreth," 27; FBG Diaries, 1912, 74; Tom Scott, *The Story of Golf from Its Origins to the Present Day* (London: Arthur Barker, 1972), 60–64; Spriegel and Myers, *The Writings of the Gilbreths,* 292. A few seconds of the Giants' baseball film can be seen in *The Original Films of Frank B. Gilbreth.*

4. See Merkle, *Management and Ideology,* 178.

5. *AIR,* 129–30. Lillian's reference to certified milk might reflect her recent experiences in Rhode Island, where in 1913 the Providence Housewives' League led a pure milk campaign and investigated the corrupt licensing procedures in the city; they sent milk samples to be tested and found much of it was watered down and some was contaminated with dirt. The ensuing scandal led to the resignation of a corrupt milk inspector.

6. *Quest,* 53; *AIR,* 134; *Partners,* 213. A note in Lillian's file, "15 hrs + 7½ hrs = 22½ hrs," suggests that Brown allowed her to transfer credits from the University of California. Brown University: Report of Graduates, First Semester, 1913–14, ms IZ GR 1, Graduate Department Papers, University Archives. See also Brown University *Catalogue* (1913–14), 95, 195–96.

7. *AIR,* 133–34. FBG to LMG, November 5, 1914.

8. EGC interview, 1998.

9. FBG Diaries, 1912, 72; FBG to LMG, November 16, December 23, 1913.

10. FBG to LMG, May 25, September 20, October 1, 8, December 7, 17, 23, 25, 1914. See Albert Rees, *Real Wages in Manufacturing, 1890–1914* (Princeton: Princeton University Press, 1961).

11. Gifford, *Lincoln School,* 7; in 1912 the school moved to its present site, about a mile from the Gilbreths' Brown Street home; EGC interview, 1998.

12. Frederick Taylor to Carl Barth, July 28, 1914; Taylor to Horace King Hathaway, March 10, 14, 18, 1914; Hathaway to Taylor, May 16, 1914; Taylor to Professor Lionel S. Marks of Harvard, August 29, 1914; Taylor collection, all quoted in Nadworny, "Frederick Taylor and Frank Gilbreth," 28–30.

13. LMG, "Resolution," December 9, 1914, GC c.109, f 0805-2.

14. FBG to LMG, May 9, 1914; *Cheaper,* 29.

15. Merkle, *Management and Ideology,* chap. 4, "The Taylor System in Soviet Socialism"; FBG, "Motion Study As an Increase of National Wealth," *Annals of the American Association of Political and Social Science* 69, no. 148 (May 1915): 96–103.

16. FBG to LMG, May 14, 21, 15, 1914.

17. FBG to LMG, May 24, 1914.

18. *AIR,* 135–36.

19. FBG to LMG, May 13, 1914; *Cheaper,* 109–10; *AIR,* 133.

20. *AIR,* 137; FBG to LMG, August 31, 1914.

21. FBG Diary, September 18, 1914; FBG to LMG, September 21, October 1, 8, December 7, 1914, April 29, 195; *AIR,* 136.

14. A Second Dissertation

1. See E. Callaghan, *The Cult of Efficiency: A Study of the Social Forces That Have Shaped the Administration of Public Schools* (Chicago: University of Chicago Press, 1962); "Waste in Teaching," ix, 144.

2. "Waste in Teaching," xv, 118, xiv.

3. John B. Watson, "Psychology As the Behaviorist Views It," *Psychological Review* 20 (March 1913): 176, 158.

4. "Waste in Teaching," 20, 21.

5. Ibid., 60 f–g.

6. Ibid., Appendix E, 303–13; xii.

7. Ibid., xii, 91.

8. Ibid., xvi, xvii, xi, 179 h–j.

9. Ibid., 60 m–o.

10. Ibid., 151–54, 212. Lillian's interest in dress reform attracted the interest of the local press. In an article entitled "Should Women Wear Standardized Dress?" they reported that she answered, "Decidedly yes." The article explained that Lillian, a "Providence expert," had studied "suitable costumes for women in the trades," which should combine "simplicity, serviceability and comfortableness and at the same time be artistic." *Providence Journal*, April 6, 1916, section 5: 1.

11. "Waste in Teaching," xvi, 278.

12. See Elton Mayo, *The Social Problems of an Industrial Civilization* (Boston: Graduate School of Business Administration, Harvard University, 1945). The best recent account of Mayo's work is Richard Gillespie, *Manufacturing Knowledge: A History of the Hawthorne Experiments* (Cambridge, Eng.: Cambridge University Press, 1991).

13. FBG to LMG, April 7, 1915.

14. All the quotations in this and the next two paragraphs are taken from a letter from Lillian to her parents the day after her oral examination. LMG to Mr. and Mrs. W. Moller, May 24, 1915, GC series 2, c.9, f.LMG Letters Sent 1915–?

15. FBG to LMG, April 24, 1915.

16. LMG to her parents, May 24, 1915.

17. Frederick W. Taylor, who was almost universally referred to as Dr. Taylor, had only an honorary degree. "Crowds Attend 1915 Promenade," *Providence Journal*, June 15, 1915.

18. All the quotations about the 1915 Brown commencement are taken from letters from Mildred Gray to Mrs. William Moller, June 16, 1915, and LMG to her parents, June 17, 1915, GC c.11, f.precious LMG + FBG Papers. The brown gowns currently worn by Brown Ph.D.'s were adopted in the 1960s.

19. EGC interview, 1998.

20. FBG Diary, September 9, 1915, 79.

21. The death certificate of an unnamed Gilbreth daughter was found in Providence City Hall.

22. *Partners*, 6–7; Charles Colvin to FBG Jr., March 5, 1971; GC series 2, c.4, f.symphy letters.

23. See FBG Diary Notes for Lillian's travels.

15. Therbligs and Tonsils

1. *Applied Motion Study* [1917], in Spriegel and Myers, *The Writings of the Gilbreths*, 264.

2. The seventeen therbligs were search, find, select, grasp, position, assemble, use, disassemble, inspect, transport loaded, pre-position for next operation, release load, transport empty, wait unavoidably, wait avoidably, rest to overcome fatigue, plan.

3. See C. S. Myers, "The Efficiency Engineer and the Industrial Psychologist," *Journal of the National Institute of Industrial Psychology* 1 (1923): 170; FBG and LMG, "The Efficiency Engineer and the Industrial Psychologist," *Journal of the National Institute of Industrial Psychology* 2 (1924): 40–45.

4. Spriegel and Myers, *The Writings of the Gilbreths*, 292; FBG and LMG, "The Conservation of the World's Teeth: A New Occupation for Crippled Soldiers," *Scientific American Supplement* 83 (June 9, 1917): 260–61; a longer version appeared under the same title in *Trained Nurse and Hospital Review* (July 1917), n.p.; "Motion Study," *American Society of Mechanical Engineers Journal* 37, no. 2 (December 1915): 669–75; "Engineer and Cripple," *ASME Journal* 40, no. 1 (January 1918): 51–61; "Crippled Soldier," *Scientific American Supplement* 83 (April 28, 1917): 260–61; a longer version appeared under the same title in *Trained Nurse and Hospital Review* (May 1917): 255–60.

5. *AIR*, 142.

6. Ibid., 140, 144; FBG and LMG, *Fatigue Study: The Elimination of Humanity's Greatest Waste: A First Step in Motion Study* (New York: Sturgis and Walton, 1916). Another, revised edition appeared in September 1919 and Macmillan reprinted it in 1919 under both their names.

7. Spriegel and Myers, *The Writings of the Gilbreths*, 314.

8. *Cheaper*, 38; *AIR*, 138–39.

9. August Dvorak et al., *Typewriting Behavior: Psychology Applied to Teaching and Learning Typewriting* (New York: American Book Company, 1936), 149–50.

10. Ibid., 169–70.

11. LMG to FBG, January 17, 1918; Wednesday Club records, John Hay Library, Brown University Library, c.2, folders 27, 36, 38, 41, 42, c.3 Codex 4.

12. *AIR*, 144.

13. Ibid., 147.

14. See Urwick, *The Golden Book of Management*.

15. *AIR*, 147; EGC to author, November 7, 2001.

16. *AIR*, 147; EGC interview, 1998; *Cheaper*, 77–82.

17. EGC interview, 1998; *Cheaper*, 76–77, 110; FBG Diaries, 1917, 84; 1919, 94; *AIR*, 147.

18. Interview with Lillian Gilbreth Johnson (LGJ), April 24, 2000; *AIR*, 148; *Cheaper*, 59, 61.

19. *Cheaper*, 61–6?

20. Ibid., 55. Anne Gilbreth Barney to FBG Jr., May 11, 1970. GCu "Grusu" was the diminutive form of "Grossmutter."

21. *AIR*, 149.

22. FBG to LMG, August 24, 7, 1917.

23. *AIR*, 150; FBG Diary, April 6–9, June 1–2, 23, September 11, November 9, December 24, 1917; LMG to FBG, January 9, 1918.

24. FBG to Gilbreth family, December 23, 1917.

16. THE HOME FRONT

1. *Society of Industrial Engineers Bulletin* 3, no. 5 (May 1921): 2.

2. LMG to FBG, January 17, 1918.

3. LMG to FBG, January 17, February 1, 1918; FBG to LMG, January 7, 9, 10, 12, 15, 16, 18, 23, 25, February 2, 3, 1918.

4. See LMG to FBG, February 1, 1918. Lillian had a "convenient arrangement" with Clark, a photographer who had worked for the Gilbreths: he looked after their photo lab in return for the use of an enlarging lens, and she paid him "the worth of his time" for any Gilbreth photographic work he did.

5. LMG to FBG, January 18, 1918.

6. LMG to FBG, January 13, 14, 1918.

7. LMG to FBG, January 14, 1918.

8. LMG to FBG, January 17, 22, February 7, 1918.

9. *Cheaper,* 179; FBG to LMG, October 27, 1914; LMG to FBG, January 10, 1918.

10. LMG to FBG, January 10, 12, 1918.

11. A two-page outline of Lillian's lecture was found in the MIT Department of Business and Engineering Administration Records (AC 114), Institute Archives and Special Collections, MIT Libraries, Cambridge, Mass. For a discussion on class and gender issues in the engineering profession, see Carroll Pursell, "'Am I a Lady or an Engineer?' The Origins of the Women's Engineering Society in Britain, 1918–40," *Technology and Culture* 34, no. 1 (January 1993): 78–97.

12. LMG to FBG, January 17, 1918.

13. LMG to FBG, January 10, 1918.

14. LMG to FBG, January 18, 29, 1918.

15. LMG to FBG, February 2, 1918.

16. LMG to FBG, January 31, 1918.

17. LMG to FBG, February 2, 1, 10, 1918.

18. LMG to FBG, February 4, 1918.

19. LMG to FBG, February 4, 14, 27, 1918; *Providence Journal,* February 13, 1918, 3, and February 15, 1918, 14. See David M. Roth, *The Roth Memory Course: A Simple and Scientific Method of Improving the Memory and Increasing Mental Power* (New York: Independent Corporation, 1918).

20. LMG to FBG, January 18, February 12, 22, 1918.

21. *AIR,* 154.

22. *AIR,* 154–55; *Time Out,* 158. My thanks to Sue Englander, a Gilbreth scholar and former nurse, for insights into Frank's illness, in a conversation on March 22, 1997.

23. *AIR,* 155.

24. FBG, "Here's to Lillian! Worth a Billion!"

25. *AIR,* 154–56.

26. LMG, "Personal Record, March 4–April 10, 1918"; GC c.11; extracts were included in Lillian's memoirs, *AIR,* 157–59.

27. *AIR,* 160.

28. Ibid., 159; LMG to FBG, April 22, 1918.

29. FBG to LMG, June 11, 1918; LMG to FBG, April 24, 1918.

30. *AIR,* 160; FBG to LMG, May 26, 1918; LMG to FBG, June 7, 1918; FBG to LMG, May 28, 1918.

31. *AIR,* 161.

32. FBG to LMG, June 11, 14, 1918; LMG to FBG, June 14, 1918.

33. LMG to FBG, June 7, 1918; FBG to LMG, June [17?], 1919, GC c.113, f.0813-9.

34. FBG to LMG, June 9, 1918; LMG to FBG, June 24, 1918.

35. LMG to FBG, June 25, July 2, 1918.

36. LMG to FBG, July 5, 1918; EGC interview, 1998.

37. *AIR,* 62; LMG to FBG, July 2, 1918.

38. *AIR,* 165–66; 91–93.

39. Ibid., 164.

40. Sixteenth Annual Report of the Maria Mitchell Association, Nantucket, Mass., 1918; *AIR,* 165.

41. LMG to FBG, July 29, 1918.

42. *Cheaper,* 43; Montclair High School yearbooks, 1924–39. EGC interview, 1998.

43. *Cheaper,* 47; LMG to FBG, Friday, June 28, 1918.

44. *AIR,* 118; *Living,* 169.

17. THE GILBRETH FAMILY SYSTEM

1. LMG to FBG, December 18, October 30, 1918.

2. FBG to LMG, May 31, 1919. Old contracts, such as those with Remington, Regal Shoes, U.S. Rubber, and Eastman Kodak, were renewed several times; new contracts included California Loading Company in New Jersey, the Red Cross in Chicago, Lever Bros., Erie Steel and Forge, the (London) *Daily Mail,* Winchester (Mass.) Laundries, Stork (a tobacco machinery manufacturer in the Netherlands), American Radiator, Filene's department store, Barber Asphalt, Seamans Cobb, Wendel and Evans, and Heller and Merz. GC c.131, f.0813-9.

3. FBG to LMG, May 14, 31, 1919.

4. FBG to LMG, June 2, 1919; *Cheaper,* 24–25. A duster is a loose coverall reaching down to the ankles.

5. FBG to LMG, April 28, 1919.

6. *AIR,* 172; Anne Gilbreth Barney to FBG Jr., May 11, 1970, GC c.2, f.LMG Biography.

7. The house had rather a dramatic history. Built about 1900 by Herbert Bradley, a wealthy Englishman, it originally stood on sixteen acres. There was a small lake on the landscaped part, with fourteen acres reserved for deer. Mr. Bradley did not, however, enjoy his house for very long; on November 16, 1906, he was trying to put out a brushfire when one of the terrified deer gored him to death. His widow sold the fourteen acres but lived in the house until she remarried and rented it to the Gilbreths. (They later purchased it.) *Montclair Times,* October 10, 1949, Lillian Gilbreth clippings file, Montclair Public Library.

8. *AIR,* 169, 172–73.

9. *AIR,* 173; see Alford, *Gantt,* for an account of Gantt's life and sudden death in 1919 at the age of fifty-eight.

10. *AIR,* 175; *Partners,* 292.

11. FBG, "Here's to Lillian! Worth a Billion!"

12. *AIR,* 175–76. Lillian wore this gown for all her honorary doctorates, and grandchildren and great-grandchildren who earned doctorates have also worn it. LGJ interview, 2000.

13. *AIR,* 177; *Nantucket Inquirer,* July 5, 1919; conversation with Jane Richmond about her grandfather, William Ray, Nantucket, September 22, 1998.

14. *AIR,* 177. The *Lever Standard* is quoted in *AIR,* 179.

15. *AIR,* 178.

16. The Gilbreths subscribed to a press clipping service, and both the Gilbreth Collection at Purdue and the Lillian Gilbreth papers at Smith contain numerous examples. Headlines include "Mother of Dozen Children Is International Authority As Industrial Engineer," *Denver Post,* n.d., c. 1922; "Gilbreth Nantucket Laboratory," *Nantucket Inquirer,* September 8, 1923; "Mrs. Gilbreth Gives Formula for Happy Home" (n.s., n.d.); "Running a Home for Eleven Kids," *Colliers,* July 21, 1923; "Daddy and Mother of Eleven," *Philadelphia Evening Ledger,* July 25, 1922; "Mother of Dozen Finds Time to Run Two Businesses," *Boston Traveler,* October 25, 1922; "Mother of Thirteen," *Providence Journal,* November 20, 1922; "Woman Succeeds As Engineer: Raises 12 Children As Well," *New York Tribune,* October 20, 1922; "Mother of 11 Says Raising Children Is Life's Greatest Joy," *New York Evening Journal,* October 23, 1922. Almost every journalist who interviewed Lillian in the 1920s and 1930s (and there were dozens) had something to report on the Gilbreth family system.

17. *AIR,* 107. FBG to LMG April 24, 1917. Lillian had a love-hate relationship with John

D. Watson; although behaviorism influenced her 1915 doctoral dissertation, she later described throwing his book *The Psychological Care of Infant and Child* (New York: W. W. Norton, 1928) across the room, only to pick it up again and "read [it] most of the night." LMG, "The Psychological Implications of Economic Planning," speech to the Engineering Women's Club, New York, November 4, 1931, GC c.139, f.0839-130, 1.

18. *AIR*, 117; *Living*, 193.

19. Peak, "She Conquers Fatigue"; *AIR*, 112; Dewey, *The School and Society*, 354–55.

20. The store was probably Macy's, where Lillian was a long-term consultant; however, the children may be conflating aspects of the council before and after Frank's death, since the Gilbreths had few contacts with Macy's before 1924; *Cheaper*, 32–33.

21. *Cheaper*, 28.

22. *Living*, 215; *Cheaper*, 29.

23. Memorandum, September 8, 1923, GC c.109, f.0805-1.

24. *Living*, 138; *Cheaper*, 32.

25. *Living*, 214; *Time Out*, 129, 131; *Cheaper*, 129.

26. *Cheaper*, 121, 125.

27. FBG to LMG, February 20, 16, 1920.

28. JGH interview, 2001. EGC interview, April 4, 2001.

29. FBG to LMG, July 28, 31, 13, 1922, GC c.114, f.0813-15.

30. Carey Papers; *Living*, 230–31.

31. *Living*, 233. Standing order form, GC c.111, f.08091.

32. *Time Out*, 146–47.

33. Ibid., 147–48.

18. INDICTING THE STOPWATCH

1. LMG to FBG, March 6, 1920; FBG to LMG, March 7, 1920, GC c.113, f.0813-12; H. K. Hathaway, "Standards," *Bulletin of the Taylor Society* 5, no. 1 (February 1920): 12–42. The discrepancy between the date and Lillian's visit can be explained by the fact that the *Bulletin* seems often to have appeared later than the official publication date—not a good advertisement for an efficiency society.

2. Frank B. Gilbreth and L. M. Gilbreth, "An Indictment of Stop-Watch Time Study," *Bulletin of the Taylor Society* 6, no. 3 (June 1921): 100–108.

3. Carl G. Barth, Robert T. Kent, Morris L. Cooke, Thomas W. Mitchell, and Reynold A. Spaeth, "A Defense of the Stop Watch," *Bulletin of the Taylor Society* 6, no. 3 (June 1921): 108–17.

4. Frank B. Gilbreth and L. M. Gilbreth, "Closure," *Bulletin of the Taylor Society* 6, no. 3 (June 1921): 117–35.

5. H. R. Person, "Comment," *Bulletin of the Taylor Society* 6, no. 3 (June 1921): 97–99; *AIR*, 181.

6. "Get-Together Dinner," *SIE Bulletin* 3, no. 4 (May 1921): 2–3.

7. Ibid., 5; FBG to LMG, Wednesday, August 23, 1922.

8. FBG to LMG, March 3, 1922; *AIR*, 185.

9. Press release dated January 17, 1923, a "Preprint" from *American Machinist* (January 18, 1923), Carey Papers.

10. M. K. Wisehart, "Making One Hour Do the Work of Two," *American Magazine* 103 (March 1927): 43; *AIR*, 185.

11. *AIR*, 187.

12. Carey Papers.

13. EGC interview, 1996.

14. LMG to FBG, March 13, 1923, GC c.11, f.Precious LMG and FBG papers.

15. FBG to James F. Butterworth, March 20, 1923; LMG, "The American Paper," *The Woman Engineer,* Special Birmingham Conference Number 1, no. 15 (June 1923): 249–50.

16. *AIR,* 189–90.

17. *Quest,* 87.

19. "HERE I STAND, 'THE CASE!'"

1. "Who Washes the Dishes at Home When Ma Is Famous?"; "Can I Have a Family without Sacrificing My Career? Yes! Says Mrs. Lillian Gilbreth," *The World Magazine,* May 16, 1926; "Mother of 11 Has Achieved Success in the Business World," *Newark Reporter,* December 20, 1925; "Mother of Eleven Children Is International Engineer," *Newark Call,* August 8, 1926; Graham, *Managing on Her Own,* 107.

2. Will of Annie Delger Moller, County Clerk's office, Alameda County, Superior Court Records, reel 238, 1930; *AIR,* 195; conversations with LGJ, June 16, 1999, and April 24, 2000.

3. See LMG's activities in FBG Diaries. *Time Out,* 190; JGH interview, 2001.

4. LMG to Colonel Sheehan, June 16, 1924, GC c.135, f.0830-42.

5. *AIR,* 190, 194. Lillian's commissioned review of the conference was published in the *American Machinist* 61, no. 7 (August 7, 1924): 222.

6. LMG, *American Machinist,* 222; *AIR,* 194; FBG Diaries 1924, 113; Irene Witte, "How I Became Friends with Frank and Lillian Gilbreth," *Journal of Industrial Engineering,* Special Reprint (May 1962): 223–24.

7. *AIR,* 194; "History of Scientific Management in America," *Mechanical Engineering* 61, no. 9 (September 1939): 674.

8. *Report of the Proceedings of the First International Management Congress in Prague (PIMCO), July 20–24, 1924* (Prague: Masaryk Academy of Work, 1924): 53–54, quoted in Hawley, "Life and Work," 199; *AIR,* 194.

9. *AIR,* 196; FBG Diaries, which Lillian continued using for sixteen months after his death (LMG notes, 1924, 1–2). Carol Cross to EGC, n.d., Carey Papers.

10. *Cheaper,* 179; EGC interview, 1998; *AIR,* 196.

11. EGC interview, 1998; *AIR,* 199.

12. LMG, "Why Women Succeed in Business," *North American Review* 226 (August 1928): 165.

13. *AIR,* 199; *Time Out,* 192–93; Carol Cross to EGC, (n.d.), Carey Papers; LMG to EG, December 1, 1926, Carey Papers.

14. GC c.128, f.0817-4.

15. Unlike the ASME (in ASME *Transactions* 46 [1924]: 1300–1302) and the SIE (in SIE *Bulletin* 6, no. 6 [June 1924]: 203), which published detailed obituary notices, the Taylor Society's report was very brief (*Bulletin of the Taylor Society* 9, no. 3 [June 1924]: 156). *Quest,* vii, 31, 41–58.

16. *AIR,* 198. LMG interviewed by MH, May 6, 1927, in Hawley, "Life and Work," 202.

17. Wisehart, "Making One Hour Do the Work of Two," 43. Mimeographed circular describing the course, quoted in Hawley, "Life and Work," 204.

18. LMG, typescript of advertisement for Gilbreth, Inc., GC c.134, f.0830-20; *Belles,* 98–99. An undated typescript lists thirty-five people who attended the six motion study courses.

19. *AIR,* 202–3.

20. Piacitelli, "The Gilbreths As I Have Known Them," 13; *Belles,* 101–2.

21. Wednesday Club papers; LMG Diary, 8. She must have spoken well; the affirmative carried the vote on the merit of the debate, but lost on the merit of the question.

22. *Belles,* 96–98.

23. *Time Out,* 189.

24. Carol Cross to EGC, n.d., Carey Papers; Martha Gilbreth, "A Large Family," 171.

25. LMG to EG, October 25, 1928, "early autumn" 1925, March 8, 1926, December 15, 1925, Carey Papers.

26. *AIR,* 213-14, 207-8.

27. Between 1926 and 1928 she spoke at Columbia, Cornell, Stanford, U.C. Berkeley, University of Iowa, and University of Minnesota. Jane Callaghan to FBG Jr., August 11, 1970, GC c.2, f.LMG biography.

28. *AIR,* 202; "Efficiency in the Home," GC c.8, f.0030-8; "Ladies Night," GC c.131, f.0830-1.

29. *Boston Herald,* February 23, 1925. The Ford Hall Forum was started in Boston in 1908 by George W. Coleman, a Baptist lay leader, as a nonsectarian, nonpartisan public lecture movement.

30. *Boston Post,* December 11, 12, 1925.

31. Kathleen Halliday, "Take Chance on 'Nothing and Love,' Says Widowed Mother of Eleven Children, in Advice to Boston," *Boston Sunday Post,* December 13, 1925.

32. *AIR,* 209; Ellen Welles Page, "Mother of Eleven Is International Engineer," *Newark Call,* August 8, 1926.

33. English meetings were at the Medical Research Council, the National Institute of Industrial Psychology, and the Women's Engineering Society; *American Machinist,* August 5, 1926. See Nancy F. Cott, *The Grounding of Modern Feminism,* (New Haven: Yale University Press, 1987), chapter 6, for a detailed discussion of the 1920s debate over combining career, marriage, and motherhood.

34. LMG, "Reconciliation of Marriage and Profession," typescript of speech, with marginal notes in LMG's handwriting, 1926, GC c.135, f.0830-27. Lillian subscribed to a clippings service and her files contain many of these stories. Lillian continued to say similar things—on January 31, 1932, the *Philadelphia Public Ledger* headlined "Man's Place Is in the Home, Says Noted Woman Engineer"; (GC c.C11, f.Fragile clippings), and on May 12, 1932, the *St. Louis Post-Dispatch* discussed the fifty-fifty marriage under the headline "Eleven Children and a Career."

35. Frances Moran, "Lillian Moller Gilbreth '00," *California Alumni Fortnightly* 14, no. 8 (April 30, 1921): 183, 186; Zoe Beckley, "Mother of Dozen Children Is International Authority As an Industrial Engineer," *Denver Post,* [1921 or 1922], GC c.6, f.NAFDP.

20. AM I A LADY OR AN ENGINEER?

1. LMG, "Why Women Succeed in Business," 165.

2. See Rossiter, *Women Scientists in America,* 146-47; Ruth Oldenzeil, "Gender and Meanings of Technology," Ph.D. diss., Yale University, 1992, 258-80. Karl Drews, "Women Engineers: The Obstacles in Their Way," *Scientific American* Supplement 65 (March 7, 1908): 147-48; Alice Goff, *Women CAN Be Engineers* (Youngstown, Ohio: privately published, 1946).

3. *AIR,* 199-202. Laurel Graham, "Intertextual Analysis: Four Representations of Dr. Lillian Moller Gilbreth," in Carolyn Ellis and Michael G. Flaherty, eds., *Investigating Subjectivity: Research on Lived Experience* (Newbury Park, Calif.: Sage, 1992), 31-52. Graham points out that the children, particularly in *Belles on Their Toes,* were "less concerned with explaining what Lillian did to succeed than with explaining how [they] helped" (42). The fullest feminist treatment of Lillian's work is Graham's *Managing on Her Own.* Other accounts that privilege her "women's work" include Martha Moore Trescott, "Lillian Moller Gilbreth and the Founding of Modern Industrial Engineering," in Joan Rothschild, ed., *Machina Ex Dea: Feminist Perspectives in Technology* (New York: Pergamon, 1983), and Trescott, "Women in the Intellectual Development of Engineering," in G. Kass-Simon and Patricia Farnes, eds., *Women of Science: Righting the Record* (Bloomington: Indiana University Press, 1990).

4. "Notes on interview with Dr. (Mrs.) Lillian M. Gilbreth" [1937], GC c.11, f.Gilbreth articles, etc.; LMG, "Why Women Succeed in Business"; Ernest Groves, "The Personality Results of the Wage Employment of Women Outside the Home and Their Social Consequences," *Annals of the AAPSS* 143 (May 1929): 339–48.

5. The friend mentioned in the article was almost certainly Mrs. Roy Wright, who helped organize all the Gilbreth girls' weddings. Page, "Mother of Eleven Children Is International Engineer."

6. A series of articles by K. H. Condit, editor of the *American Machinist*, ran under the general heading "Management Methods and Principles of Frank B. Gilbreth, Inc." from January to August 1923. Two more articles appeared in April and June 1924 and a further two in April 1925. The quotation is from the first article; the photograph appeared in the last.

7. Graham, *Managing on Her Own,* 104; *Time Out,* 188; Frederick Waldron to LMG, August 15, 1925; F. R. Low to LMG, September 9, 1925, GC c.131, f.0830-1. Lillian's draft application, advice from Kent and Freeman, and the acceptance letter from Rice are in the same file.

8. Read at ASME Annual Meeting, New York, November 30–December 4, 1925, and published in *Mechanical Engineering* 47, no. 11a (mid-November 1925): 1039–42.

9. LMG to FBG, January 1, 17, 31, February 9, 26, 1918; see Sarah Deutsch, "Learning to Talk More Like a Man: Boston Women's Class-Bridging Organizations, 1870–1940," *American Historical Review* 97, no. 2 (April 1992): 379–404.

10. LMG to FBG, February 22, 1918.

11. Ibid.

12. LMG to FBG, June 24, 1918; see Pursell, "Am I a Lady or an Engineer?"

13. *Time Out,* 188; Elmer Sperry to LMG, October 1, 1927, GC c.136, f.0830-47. *AIR,* 210, 212, 216, 219.

14. Interview with Joseph Juran, June 14, 1999; Graham, *Managing on Her Own,* 103; the quote from Ellen Richards is in *NAW,* 3: 143.

15. *Partners,* 357–58

21. COUNTER CULTURES FOR WOMEN

1. *AIR,* 205.

2. Graham, *Managing on Her Own,* 130.

3. Ralph M. Hower, *History of Macy's of New York, 1858–1919* (Cambridge: Harvard University Press, 1943), 400; Eugenia Lies, "Motion Study: Principles and Case Illustrating Its Application in a Department Store," ASME *Transactions* (1927–28): 50–67A, and "Research As Applied to Retailing," paper presented to the Eastern Commercial Teachers' Association (April 6, 1928), GC c.94, f.0707.

4. Lies, "Research As Applied to Retailing," 22–23; also quoted in Frances R. Donovan, *The Saleslady* (1929; repr., New York: Arno Press, 1974), 247.

5. Donovan, *Saleslady,* 248. The verse appeared in *Sparks,* the staff magazine of Macy's, in January 1927.

6. LMG, "Why Women Succeed in Business," 159–60.

7. LMG, "What Does the Customer Want?" *Bulletin of the National Retail Dry Goods Association* 14 (March 1932): 155; T. J. Jackson Lears, "From Salvation to Self-Realization: Advertising and the Therapeutic Roots of the Consumer Culture, 1880–1930," in Richard Fox and T. J. Jackson Lears, eds., *The Culture of Consumption: Critical Essays in American History, 1880–1980* (New York: Pantheon, 1983), 4, 27; LMG's Chamber of Commerce speech, "Providence Can Take the Lead," *Providence Evening Bulletin,* February 14, 1929.

8. *AIR,* 205.

9. EGC interview, 1998.

10. *AIR*, 205; see Mrs. John Van Vorst and Marie Van Vorst, *The Woman Who Toils: Being the Experience of Two Gentlewomen As Factory Girls* (1903); Donovan, *The Saleslady;* LMG, "Hiring and Firing: Shall the Calendar Measure the Length of Service?" *Factory and Industrial Management* 72 (February 1930): 310–11.

11. LMG, "Industrial Fatigue," Commonwealth of Pennsylvania Conference on Women in Industry, December 8 and 9, 1925, Special Bulletin no. 10 (Harrisburg, Pa.: 1926), 72. See Susan Porter Benson, *Counter Cultures: Saleswomen, Managers and Customers in American Department Stores, 1890–1949* (Urbana: University of Illinois Press, 1988), 200–203. The title of this chapter pays homage to this excellent book.

12. *AIR*, 213.

13. An excellent account of the debate over protective labor legislation can be found in Alice Kessler-Harris, *Out to Work: A History of Wage-Earning Women in the United States* (New York: Oxford University Press, 1982), 181–214. See also William N. O'Neill, *Everyone Was Brave* (Chicago: Quadrangle, 1969), 274–94; J. Stanley Lemons, *The Woman Citizen: Social Feminism in the 1920s* (Urbana: University of Illinois Press, 1973), 184–99; Cott, *The Grounding of Modern Feminism,* 117–42.

14. LMG to Mary Anderson, U.S. Department of Labor, Women's Bureau papers on 1926 Women's Industrial Conference, c.3. *Life and Labor Bulletin,* Women's Trade Union League (February 1926): 2. The women staging this demonstration were prominent in the struggle for equal rights. Gail Laughlin (1868–1952) was a lawyer, feminist, suffragist, and first national president of the Business and Professional Women's Clubs. Mabel Vernon (1883–1975), a suffragist, feminist, and pacifist, is credited with one of the first acts of militancy during the suffrage campaign, when she interrupted Woodrow Wilson's speech of July 4, 1917. The third member of the group was Anita Pollitzer (1894–1975), a close colleague of Alice Paul, leader of the NWP. See *NAWMP,* 410–11, 711–12, 551–52.

15. U.S. Department of Labor Women's Bureau memo; GC c.129, f.0819-5. Other committee members were Sara Conboy of the American Federation of Labor, Mabel Leslie of the Women's Trade Union League, and Doris Stevens and Maud Younger of the NWP. During World War I Mary Van Kleeck headed the Women in Industry service within the Department of Labor, which was the forerunner of the permanent Women's Bureau. She served as director of the department of industrial studies at the Russell Sage Foundation from 1910 to 1918 and again from 1919 until she retired in 1948. See *NAWMP,* 707–9.

16. U.S. Department of Labor Women's Bureau memo; *AIR*, 206–17; Mary Anderson to Mary Van Kleeck, November 16, 1926, Mary Van Kleeck to LMG, November 17, 1926, Papers of the Women's Trade Union League and Its Principal Leaders, Schlesinger Library, Radcliffe Institute, Harvard University.

17. Kessler-Harris, *Out to Work,* 211. Sylvia Smith, "Mother of 11 Leads in Time-Saving," *The Newark Ledger,* June 16, 1935, 5B; HHPL, American Child Health Association (A.C.H.A.) Papers, Gilbreth, Lillian M.; "Dr. Gilbreth Opposes Section 213," *Equal Rights* (May 11, 1935), archives of Business and Professional Women of the United States of America.

18. *AIR*, 207.

19. Lillian's Johnson & Johnson study (subsequently J&J Report) is located in GC c.95, f.0704-2. Vern L. Bullough, in "Merchandising the Sanitary Napkin: Lillian Gilbreth's 1927 Survey," *Signs* 10, no. 1 (Spring 1985): 615–25, does little other than reprint part of Lillian's report. I am indebted to Laurel Graham's treatment of this topic in *Managing on Her Own,* 216–21.

20. LMG, J&J Report.

21. LMG, J&J Report; the remark about Lillian's indignation is from CWM-FRO 2, Menninger Archives, Topeka, Kans.

22. J&J Report.

23. Ibid.

24. Modess advertisement, quoted in Graham, *Managing on Her Own*, 220–21.

22. *THE HOME-MAKER AND HER JOB*

1. *AIR*, 209, 215; Lillian Moller Gilbreth, *The Home-maker and Her Job* (New York: Appleton, 1927; subsequently *Home-maker*). See also Martha Bensley Bruère and Robert W. Bruère, *Increasing Home Efficiency* (New York: Macmillan, 1912); Christine Frederick, *The New Housekeeping: Efficiency Studies in Home Management* (Garden City, N.Y.: Doubleday Page, 1913) and *Household Engineering: Scientific Management in the Home* (Chicago: American School of Home Economics, 1920).

2. *Home-maker*, 147, 151, 66. The classic statement of such an attitude to the use of time freed by mechanization of housework is contained in the title of Ruth Schwartz Cowan's article, "Two Washes in the Morning and a Bridge Party at Night: The American Housewife between the Wars," *Journal of Women's Studies* 3 (1976): 147–72.

3. FBG, "Scientific Management in the Household," *Journal of Home Economics* 4 (December 1912): 438–47; FBG, "Motion Study in the Household," *Scientific American* 106 (1912): 328.

4. One of the home economists in his 1912 audience was Dr. Louise Stanley, later head of the Bureau of Home Economics in the U.S. Department of Agriculture, who published an article on the "continuous kitchen" in 1916. Louise Stanley, "A Convenient Kitchen," *Journal of Home Economics* 8, no. 9 (September 1916): 493–94. See Bruère and Bruère, *Increasing Home Efficiency*, 291; FBG to Martha Van Rensselaer, July 19, 1912, GC c.117, f.0816-34.

5. FBG to LMG, April 6, 1916, GC c.111, f.0813-1; typescript, "Efficiency in the Home," November 29, 1922, GC c.111, f.0809-1. By the time Lillian's attention returned to kitchens in the mid-1920s, Christine Frederick had turned to advertising and was advising companies how to appeal to women. Her 1929 book, *Selling Mrs. Consumer*, was a product of this new direction. FBG to LMG, January 18, 1918; FBG, Foreword to Frederick, *Household Engineering*; Frederick, *The New Housekeeping*, 72. See Graham, *Managing on Her Own*, 167-68.

6. *Home-maker*, 150–52, 148.

7. LMG, address to the National Federation of Business and Professional Women's Clubs, New York Division, 1930.

8. *Home-maker*, 93, 94, 98, 101–2.

9. Ibid., 84–85, 59.

10. Ibid., 147, 120–21.

11. Ibid., 11, 58.

12. Ibid., 20, vii; for studies of housework see Ruth Schwartz Cowan, "The 'Industrial Revolution' in the Home: Household Technology and Social Change in the Twentieth Century," *Technology and Culture* 17 (January 1976): 17; Cowan, *More Work for Mother* (New York: Basic Books, 1987); Glenna Matthews, *"Just a Housewife": The Rise and Fall of Domesticity in America* (New York: Oxford University Press, 1987); Susan Strasser, *Never Done: A History of American Housework* (New York: Pantheon, 1982). See also Joann Vanek, "Household Technology and Social Status and Residence Differences in Housework," *Technology and Culture* 19 (July 1978): 361–75, and "Time Spent on Housework," *Scientific American* 231 (November 1974): 116–20.

13. *Home-maker*, 7, 14, 129, 90.

14. Ibid., 19.

15. Carey Papers.

16. "Man's Place Is in the Home"; see also *Home-maker,* 40–42, 140–41. See Christina Hardyment, *From Mangle to Microwave: The Mechanization of Household Work* (Cambridge, Eng.: Polity Press, 1988), 151–54, for a discussion of the evolution of dishwashers, which were becoming available in the 1920s. The Carol Cross anecdote is from the Carey Papers (n.d.).

17. *Home-maker,* 35, 29.

18. Edna Yost, "What Makes You Tired? Well, It's in Your Mind—Not in Your Body," *New York World* (April 4, 1926); *Home-maker,* 117.

19. *Home-maker,* 51–52. The best account of radical feminist domestic ideas is Dolores Hayden, *The Grand Domestic Revolution: A History of Feminist Designs for American Homes, Neighborhoods and Cities* (Cambridge: MIT Press, 1981).

20. Dorothy Budd, "Housekeeping—An Industry: An Interview with Lillian M. Gilbreth," *The Woman Citizen* 11 (July 1926): 41; *Home-maker,* 18.

21. See Halliday, "Take Chance on 'Nothing and Love'"; *Home-maker,* 12.

22. FBG and LMG, "Fatigue Study in the Home," paper presented to the Society of Industrial Engineers, Milwaukee, April 27, 1921; typescript, GC c.153, f.0896-3, 3. *Home-maker,* 47. "[words missing] Wants to Know—Can I Have a Family without Sacrificing My Career?" *The World Magazine* (May 16, 1926): 6–7; found in GC c.11, f.Fragile clippings.

23. *Home-maker,* 153–54.

23. THE KITCHEN AND THE OFFICE

1. Robert S. Lynd and Helen Merrell Lynd, *Middletown: A Study in Modern American Culture* (New York: Harcourt Brace Jovanovich, 1927).

2. Frederick Howe, review of "Homemaking As a Center for Research. Report of the Teachers College Conference on Homemaking," *Journal of Home Economics* 15, no. 1 (1928): 48.

3. LMG "Interruptions," typescript, GC c.C2, f."Interruptions."

4. *AIR,* 215.

5. LMG, "A Professional Summer in Europe: Observations on Meetings of Associations Concerned with Scientific Management and Human Relations in Industry," *Bulletin of the Taylor Society* 12, no. 4 (August 1927): 466.

6. *AIR,* 217, 221.

7. EGC, "Recollections about My Mother," Carey Papers.

8. *AIR,* 220–21. *Partners,* 342. The book was Charles Breasted, *Pioneer to the Past: The Story of James Henry Breasted, Archaeologist, Told by His Son* (New York: Charles Scribner's Sons, 1943).

9. Anne Gilbreth Barney to LMG, October 7, 1943, Carey Papers.

10. *AIR,* 221.

11. Ibid., 217.

12. LMG, "Report on the Katharine Gibbs School," 19, GC c.129, f.0819-5; *AIR,* 219.

13. Sonya F. Gray, "Katharine Ryan Gibbs," in *Women in Rhode Island History—Making a Difference* (Providence: Providence Journal Co., 1994), 14.

14. LMG to Katharine Gibbs (KG), March 19, 1928, GC c.134, f.0830-13. Chase Going Woodhouse, "Married College Women in Business and the Professions," Women in the Modern World: *AAAPSS* 143 (May 1929): 325–38. There was one outlier, a successful realtor (with a bachelor's degree rather than a doctorate) earning twenty thousand dollars a year.

15. KG to LMG, March 21, 1928, GC c.134, f.0830-13; LMG, "Report on the Katharine Gibbs School," 7.

16. LMG to KG, March 11, 1929.

17. LMG, "Report on the Katharine Gibbs School," 15, 17.

18. *AIR,* 219; LMG, "Skills and Satisfactions," undated (but 1928 or 1929) typescript circulated by the People's Gas Light and Coke Co.; GC c.C11, f."Gilbreth articles, etc." Quotations in the following paragraphs are from this source.

19. Graham, *Managing on Her Own,* 180; LMG, list of model kitchens, etc., GC c.88, f.0655-8. The Kitchen Practical was the prototype of kitchens built for the Narragansett Electric Light Company in Providence and for housing conferences in Santa Barbara and Berlin, all in 1930.

20. "The Kitchen Practical: The Story of an Experiment" (Brooklyn Borough Gas Company, 1931), GC c.88, f.0655-8. Lillian started work there in 1929.

21. *Time Out,* 209, 211–12.

22. LMG, "The Kitchen Practical."

23. EGC interview, 1998.

24. Ibid.; Marguerite Martyn, "Eleven Children and a Career," *St. Louis Post-Dispatch Daily Magazine,* May 12, 1932.

25. See *NAW,* 2: 525–26, for Meloney's career.

26. See Susan Quinn, *Marie Curie: A Life* (New York: Simon and Schuster, 1995), 382–99, for an account of Missy Meloney's campaign to buy Marie Curie a gram of radium.

27. See Ellis W. Hawley, "Herbert Hoover, the Commerce Secretariat and the Vision of the 'Associative State,' 1921–28," *Journal of American History* 61 (June 1974): 133–34.

28. *NAW,* 2: 525–26.

29. Elizabeth H. Russell, "Saving Steps in the Kitchen," *The American Home* (1930): 559.

30. See "The *New York Herald Tribune* Institute Presents Four Model Kitchens," 3d ptg. (New York: *New York Herald Tribune* Institute, September 1931), GC c.11, f.Gilbreth articles, misc. Beneath the title in Lillian's handwriting was the phrase "modeled and planned by Dr. Lillian M. Gilbreth."

24. This Home Is for Hoover

1. *AIR,* 217–18.

2. "Thirty-Seven Leading Women Tell Why They Will Vote for Herbert Hoover," advertisement in the *Delineator,* October 1928, 3; Charlotte Kellogg, "Herbert Hoover As Women See Him," *Commonweal* (March 14, 1928): 176, Hoover Institution on War, Revolution and Peace, Stanford University, (subsequently HI), GC c.222, f."HH As Women See Him"; Kathleen Norris, "A Woman Looks at Hoover," *Colliers,* May 5, 1928, 8. See *NAWMP,* 509–11.

3. LMG to Herbert Hoover (subsequently HH), August 28, September 12, 1928; HH to LMG, August 31, 1928, HHPL C&T—Gen.Corres., Gilbreth, Lillian M. The photograph appeared in the *New York Herald Tribune;* the undated clipping was found in GC c.134, f.0831-19, "Lou Henry Hoover." Other reports appeared in the *New York Evening Post,* October 22, 1928, and the *Oakland Chronicle,* October 22, 1928. For Lou Henry Hoover (1874–1944) see *NAW,* 2: 217–18; Helen B. Pryor, *Lou Henry Hoover: Gallant First Lady* (New York: Dodd, Mead, 1969); Dale C. Mayer, ed., *Lou Henry Hoover: Essays on a Busy Life* (Worland, Wyo.: High Plains Publishing, 1994).

4. LMG to HH, November 10, 1928. LMG to Lou Henry Hoover (subsequently LHH), November 10, 1928, GC c.134, f.0830-19, "Women's Committee for Hoover."

5. LHH to LMG, April 11, 1931, HHPL, LHH Papers—Pers. Corres., 1929–33, Gilbreth, Lillian, August 18, 1929; HHPL, Presidential Secretary's File, Gilbreth, Dr. Lillian M.; *AIR,* 218; LMG's account of the visit (found in GC c.14, f.0830-19) is quoted in succeeding paragraphs.

6. Mrs. Reed Smoot, "A Guest at the White House Talks," *The Improvement Era* (October 1930): 33–41. MacDonald was in the United States to discuss the London Naval Treaty. It

was almost completed and Hoover wanted the final details settled. For an account of visitors to Camp Rapidan, see Darwin Lambert, *Herbert Hoover's Hideaway* (Luray, Va.: Shenandoah Natural History Association, 1971), 66–67.

7. Lambert, *Hideaway*, 42; *Belles*, 191–92.

8. LHH to LMG, April 11, 1931.

9. *Belles*, 190–202.

10. Conversation with Mary Elizabeth Freeman's niece, Anne Freeman Giraud, March 11, 2000.

11. *Japan Advertiser*, October 28, 1929, GC c.136, f.0830-47.

12. LMG, "Impressions of Tokio Congress," *Iron Age* (January 16, 1929): 224–25, contains photographs of the opening session. LMG, "The World Engineering Congress in Tokyo As Seen Through American and Japanese Eyes," *Bulletin of the Taylor Society* 15, no. 1 (February 1920): 40.

13. LMG, "World Engineering Congress," 41; LMG, "The Management Movement in Japan," *Management Review* (February 1930): 40; "Prince Hears Talks on Many Problems in Technical World," *Japan Advertiser*, November 1, 1929. Speakers during Lillian's session included Professors Francesco Mauro of Italy, Georg Schlesinger of Germany, John Roe and Harrington Emerson of the United States, Stanislav Spacek of Czechoslovakia, and Toichiro Araki and Vice Admiral Tadao Hatanio of Japan.

14. LMG to Charles A. Beard, November 22, 1930. POUR box 1, entry 21. Beard's response was not found. Mary Elizabeth Pidgeon, *Women in the Economy of the United States of America: A Summary Report,* Women's Bureau Bulletin 152 (Washington, D.C.: Government Printing Office, 1937).

15. "Women in Engineering," *California Monthly,* undated clipping, c. 1930, GC c.136, f.0830-47; LMG, "The Management Movement in Japan," *Iron Age* 125 (January 23, 1929): 298. Clara Bell Woolworth, "America's Leading Woman Engineer Looks at Home Economics in Japan," *Practical Home Economics* (April 1930): 110, 114.

16. LMG, "Impressions of Tokyo Congress," 225.

17. LMG, "Impressions of Industrial Japan" and "Furthering Business with Japan," *Iron Age* (February 6, 1929): 373–74, 443.

18. LMG, "World Engineering Congress," 41; "Tributes to Gilbreths," *Montclair Times,* December 5, 1968.

25. A DOLLAR-A-YEAR WOMAN IN WASHINGTON

1. M. H. Jones to FBG Jr., January 31, 1971, GC c.C4, f.Sympathy letters.

2. *AIR,* 218; *Time Out,* 218.

3. LHH to Mrs. Brady, April 14, 1930, HHPL, LHH papers—Girl Scouts, Admin. Corres., Brady, Genevieve Garvin. Lillian served on personnel and financial committees and attended international conventions in Switzerland, Poland, and Sweden. She also did motion study analysis for the Scouts, advising them on efficient use of space at their national headquarters. See Edna Yost, "First Lady of Engineering," *The American Girl* (September 1943); LMG to her family, July 22, 1930, GC series 2, c.9, f.LMG Letters Sent.

4. LMG to her family, June 11, 1930 (also quoted in subsequent paragraphs). See Michael Rowlinson, "The Early Application of Scientific Management by Cadbury," *Business History* 30, no. 4 (October 1988), for a discussion of the conflicts felt by Edward Cadbury in the 1900s and 1910s as he introduced elements of Taylorism while remaining a pro-union employer. See also Charles Delheim, "The Creation of a Company Culture: *Cadburys, 1861–1931,*" *American Historical Review* 92, no. 1 (February 1987): 13–43. Delheim's description of Cadbury's

efforts at worker empowerment resemble the Gilbreths' schemes at New England Butt, which suggests why they sent Bill Sanderson to be trained by Lillian Gilbreth in the late 1920s.

5. J. Crosfield, *Cadbury Family Book* n.p., n.d., 372–74.

6. A tweeny was a servant who assisted the cook in the kitchen and the housemaids in the rest of the house. The rank of a tweeny was low. Kenneth G. Wilson, *The Columbia Guide to Standard American English* (New York: Columbia University Press, 1993).

7. LMG to family, July 22, 1930; Catharine Wright Menninger, "In Memory of Dr. Lillian Moller Gilbreth," October 6, 1972, Menninger Archives, CWM-PRO 2. Lillian and Mrs. Wright later worked on Dwight Morrow's campaign for governor of New Jersey. EGC, *Rings Around Us* (Boston: Little, Brown, 1956), 19–27.

8. Will of Annie Delger Moller. It is not clear exactly when the trust was dissolved.

9. Telegram from Arthur Woods to LMG, October 24, 1930, National Archives, President's Organization for Unemployment Relief, records relating to activities of officials of Women's Division (subsequently POUR), box 1, entry 22. Arthur Woods to HH, November 21, 1930, President's Emergency Committee for Employment (subsequently PECE) papers, quoted in Irving Bernstein, *A History of the American Worker, 1920–33: The Lean Years* (Boston: Houghton Mifflin, 1960), 303. HH, radio address, December 22, 1930, in HHPL, POUR, f.Mobilization of Relief Resources. Critical accounts of PECE and POUR can be found in Bernstein, *The Lean Years,* 303–11, 460–62; Albert U. Romasco, *The Poverty of Abundance: Hoover, the Nation and the Depression* (New York: Oxford University Press, 1965). Bruce Bustard's unpublished seminar paper "President Hoover, Colonel Arthur Woods and the President's Emergency Committee for Employment, 1930–31" takes a more sympathetic view; my thanks to Mr. Bustard for sending me a copy.

10. "Secretary Hoover's Address, September 26, 1921," in *Report of the President's Conference on Unemployment* (Washington, D.C.: Government Printing Office, 1921), 28. White House press release, October 17, 1930.

11. Ida M. Tarbell, "Ida Tarbell Lists Fifty Foremost Women," *New York Evening World,* September 13, 1930; *Good Housekeeping,* March 1931, 17, 42.

12. Sue McNamara, "Mother of Eleven Summoned to Aid Job Relief Program," undated, unattributed clipping, GC.

13. Ellis W. Hawley's work on Hoover and the Associative State is useful, notably *The Great War and the Search for a Modern Order* (New York: St. Martin's Press, 1979); also Hawley, "Herbert Hoover, the Commerce Secretariat and the Vision of the Associative State", and Hawley's untitled essay in Joseph Huthmacher and Warren I. Susman, eds., *Herbert Hoover and the Crisis of American Capitalism* (Cambridge: Schenkman, 1973), 3–34. See Annette K. Baxter's preface to Blair, *The Clubwoman As Feminist,* xi; and Anne Firor Scott, *Natural Allies: Women's Associations in American History* (Urbana: University of Illinois Press, 1991).

14. POUR, box 1, entry 22, "Itinerary." LMG Memorandum for Mr. Hunt, December 5, 1930, POUR, Reading File, Oct. 29, 1930–April 29, 1931, box 1, entry 21.

15. LMG Memorandum for Mr. Hunt.

16. LMG, "The Job of Motherhood," typescript of talk, probably a radio address, undated, POUR, Activities of Officers, box 1, entry 22. Other cooperating groups were the Junior League, the Girl Scouts, the American Woman's Association, the National Council of Catholic Women, the National Council of Jewish Women, the Business and Professional Women's Clubs, the Association of Bank Women, the Daughters of 1812, the United Daughters of the Confederacy, the League of Women Voters, the Association for Childhood Education, the American Federation of Teachers, and the American War Mothers. "Activities of the Women's Division of PECE," POUR, General Records, box 1, 5–6; LMG radio address, December 15,

1930, and LMG, Report of the Women's Division, December 12, 1930, 4, POUR Reading File, box 1, entry 21.

17. LMG, Report of the Women's Division, December 12, 1930, 4.

18. LMG to the National Retail Dry Goods Association, November 8, 1930, POUR, box 21, f.00637. LMG to Florence Nesbitt, Assistant Superintendent, United Charities of Chicago, December 6, 1930; cable from LMG to Bertha E. Nettleton, Chairman, New York Group of American Home Economics Association.

19. Craig Lloyd, in *Aggressive Introvert: Herbert Hoover and Public Relations Management, 1912–1933* (Columbis: Ohio State University Press, 1973), suggests that the use of PR and mass communications is crucial to an understanding of Hoover's career. A reprint of the *Delineator* article was found in the League of Women Voters papers, C.II: 135, f.B. misc., Library of Congress Manuscript Division. LMG, "What Women Can Do to Aid Employment Conditions," radio address on the Columbia Broadcasting System, November 14, 1930, POUR, General Records, box 4.

20. LMG to EGC, undated, but late November 1930, Carey Papers. Tony Sarg (1880–1942) was a German-born puppeteer who arrived in the United States at the beginning of World War I. He put on shows as well as window displays.

21. LMG to Alice Dickson, January 5, 1931. POUR, box 1, entry 22. Mrs. Roosevelt did eventually speak; Amelia Earhart's speech was missing from the POUR files, which contained all the others. Lillian's undated letter (probably January 5, 1931) was in POUR, box 1, entry 22. Examples of articles and interviews include LMG, "Your Job for the Jobless," editorial in the *Women's Journal,* December 15, 1930; LMG, "Spruce Up Your Home," *New York Herald Tribune,* December 28, 1930, 17, 21; "Head of Women's Board on Unemployment Tells How All May Give Relief," undated clipping found in GC c.139, f.0830-139. The quotation is from Paul Harrison, "A Woman's War on the Depression," *Newark Ledger,* April 17, 1932.

22. LMG to Elizabeth McCauseland, December 13, 1930, and LMG Memorandum to Mr. Hunt, November 19, 1930, POUR, box 1, entries 2, 21.

23. Alice M. Dickson to Dorothy Frooks, February 27, 1931, POUR, box 1, entry 21.

24. See Kessler-Harris, *Out to Work,* 250–58, and Lois Scharf, *To Work and to Wed: Female Employment, Feminism and the Great Depression* (Westport, Conn.: Greenwood Press, 1980), chapter 3, for the Depression-era debate over married women's jobs.

25. LMG, "Spruce Up Your Home," 17, 21; Elizabeth Haskell, President, Rhode Island State Federation of Women's Clubs, March 6, 1931, to Alice M. Dickson, POUR, box 21, f.1. The Commerce Department also issued a "Spruce Up Your Garden" pamphlet (Washington, D.C.: Government Printing Office, 1931). The copy found in GC c.C11, f.Gilbreth articles, includes a note in Lillian's handwriting: "Planned and Outlined by LMG."

26. LMG, "Women and Industry," typescript of radio address, NBC, January 27, 1931, POUR, box 8. Goldmark, publications secretary of the NCL, amassed the data used by her brother-in-law Louis Brandeis in preparing his brief for *Muller v. Oregon* in 1908. She published *Fatigue and Efficiency* (New York: Russell Sage Foundation) in 1912, which took a very similar line to the Gilbreths' work. In the 1920s she researched nurses' training, another topic of interest to Lillian. See *NAW,* 2: 60–61.

27. Bernstein, *The Lean Years,* 462.

28. Memo from LMG to Arthur Woods, April 1931; LMG to Louise Stanley, April 25, 1931, PECE, series 3, box 25, f.LMG biog. file. Arthur Woods to LMG, May 6, 1931, GC c.139, f.0830-139; Arthur Woods to Alice Dickson, April 31, 1931, PECE, series 3, box 25, f.LMG biog. file.

29. LMG to Mrs. John F. Sippel, April 27, 1931, POUR, box 1, entry 21; Ellen Woodward, head of the Women's and Professional Projects for the Works Progress Administration, Federal

Emergency Relief Administration (FERA) press release, November 16, 1933, quoted in Susan Ware, *Beyond Suffrage: Women in the New Deal* (Cambridge: Harvard University Press, 1981), 106. Part of Franklin D. Roosevelt's New Deal, FERA, under its administrator Harry Hopkins, allocated $500 million toward direct relief; states had to provide matching funds for half of the allocated money.

26. WOMAN POWER

1. LMG, "Work and Leisure," in Charles Beard, ed., *Toward Civilization* (New York: Longmans, Green, 1930), 242.

2. LMG, "Acceptance of Medal," *SIE Bulletin* 13 (November 1931): 10.

3. LMG, "Hiring and Firing: Shall the Calendar Measure the Length of Service?" *Factory and Industrial Management* 72 (February 1930): 310–11.

4. "Activities of Women's Division, The President's Emergency Committee for Employment," 14, POUR, General Records, box 1; Bryn Mawr research proposal, "Our New Research Project," *Independent Woman* 10 (April 1931): 156, 186; "60,000 Working Girls Asked to 'Tell All' to Provide 'Case Histories' for Vocational Guidance in Survey," *New York World-Telegram,* April 8, 1931.

5. Harriet A. Byrne, *The Age Factor As It Relates to Women in Business and the Professions* (Washington, D.C.: Government Printing Office, 1934); LMG, "Research Committee," *Independent Woman* 11 (July 1932): 268.

6. See Mary Anderson, "The Fallacy of the Pin Money Theory," typescript, September 20, 1929, League of Women Voters papers, c.II:191, f.U.S. Labor Dept., Library of Congress.

7. LMG, "Economic Trends and the Worker," typescript (marked in Lillian's handwriting, "old draft") POUR, box 1, entry 22. "Man's Place Is in the Home."

8. LMG to Edgar Rickard, June 15, 1932, January 4, 1933, HHPL, American Child Health Association Papers, Gilbreth, Lillian M.

9. *Who's Who* (1930) for Nicholas Brady; *AIR,* 231.

10. LMG, radio address, 1932, quoted in *Partners,* 334; LMG, "How Can Federal Expenditures Be Reduced?" *AAAPSS* 165 (January 1933): 125–30.

11. The Congress of Women was inspired by Anna Garlin Spencer (1851–1931), a minister and noted social reformer, who had attended a conference on philanthropy at the previous Chicago exposition in 1893 with her friend Susan B. Anthony and realized that the Women's Pavilion there had publicized the movement for women's rights more effectively than decades of agitation. Mrs. Spencer was to die before the 1933 exposition opened. See Lisa Sergio, *A Measure Filled: The Life of Lena Madesin Phillips* (New York: Robert B. Luce, 1972), 102–3, 116–20; LMG, "Work and Leisure," 233–52; Nancy F. Cott, ed., *A Woman Making History: Mary Ritter Beard Through Her Letters* (New Haven, Conn.: Yale University Press, 1991), 105–10.

12. Sergio, *A Measure Filled,* 116–17; Mary R. Beard, "Struggling Towards Civilization," and Paul R. Douglas, "The Economic Collapse," in *Our Common Cause: Civilization, Report of the International Congress of Women* (New York: National Council of Women of the United States, 1933), 23–38. Delegates included Baroness Shidzue Ishimoto, "Japan's leading feminist"; Christine Galitzine, director of Romania's Public Assistance Program; Margaret Bondfield, Britain's first woman cabinet member; Dame Rachel Crowdy, former Chief of Social Questions and Opium Traffic Section of the League of Nations; Muthulakshmi Reddy, Deputy-President of Madras, "the Jane Addams of India"; and Rosa Manus, a Dutch suffrage leader. The American delegates included Henry T. Rainey, Speaker of the House of Representatives, and Ernest Gruening, editor of *The Nation.*

13. LMG, "Can the Machine Pull Us Out?" *Our Common Cause,* 39–48.

14. All the quotations in this paragraph were taken from "Planned Motion in the Home, Saves: Time—Energy—Money," GC c.11, f.Gilbreth articles/misc. See Saul Engelbourg, *International Business Machines: A Business History* (New York: Arno Press, 1976), especially chapter 11, "Bucking the Depression." Letter from LMG to Thomas J. Watson, May 14, 1940, GC c.3, f.Correspondence IBM 1940. A photograph taken by Century of Progress official photographers Kaufmann-Fabry was found in GC c.88, f.0655-8. Curators at the Smithsonian Institution searched in vain for a Gilbreth management desk to include in their section on "Dr. Gilbreth's Kitchen" for the permanent exhibit "On Time" and finally made one based on IBM specifications.

27. PROFESSOR GILBRETH

1. Frank B. Gilbreth Jr., *I'm a Lucky Guy* (New York: Thomas Y. Crowell, 1951), 30, 2, 93.
2. Ibid., 94, 97–98.
3. LMG, "Work Centers," *America's Little House* (New York, n.d.), GC c.88, f.06557.
4. Ibid.
5. LMG, "Is Your Home a Hazard?" Typescript of radio talk on Columbia Network, GC c.86, f.0655-1.
6. "Homemaker," *American Magazine* 119 (March 1935): 37.
7. LMG, "Planning the Kitchen," in *The Model Kitchen is Remodeled* (New York: *New York Herald Tribune* Home Institute, 1935), 7–12, GC c.87, f.0655-3. Marjorie Shuler, "In Family Council Asse . . ." [half of headline missing], *Christian Science Monitor,* June 19, 1935. Janey incident, Carey Papers. The Eleanor Roosevelt advertisement appeared in *Good Housekeeping,* June 1930.
8. See Susan Ware, *Still Missing: Amelia Earhart and the Search for Modern Feminism* (New York: W. W. Norton, 1994), 94.
9. *Providence Journal,* March 6, 1935, 14; Sylvia Smith, "Mother of 11 Leads in Time-Saving"; Scrapbook, Amelia Earhart Collection, Schlesinger Library, Radcliffe Institute, Harvard University; Virginia Whitney to FBG Jr., August 3, 1971, GC c.C4, f.Sympathy letters.
10. LMG to Eleanor Roosevelt, April 6, 1936, and J. M. Helm to LMG, April 10, 1936, FDR Library, Social Entertainments box 216, f.Correspondence Pa–Pen.
11. "Notes on Interview with Dr. (Mrs.) Lillian M. Gilbreth," undated, but 1936; GC c.11 f.Gilbreth articles etc.
12. Ibid.; Andrey A. Potter, "Reminiscences of the Gilbreths," *Journal of Industrial Engineering,* Special Reprint (May 1962): 30–31; "Purdue Institute of American Policy and Technology," GC series 3, c.25, f.LMG biography.
13. *Partners,* 339–40; James Gage to EGC, April 2, 1982, and Jerry Nadler to EGC, October 1978, Carey Papers.

28. A SUPERANNUATED BACHELOR GIRL GOES TO WAR

1. *Time Out,* 221; *AIR,* 226–29; other biographical details are from a typescript of a talk by Jack Gilbreth to Dunworkin Club, Montclair, 1993, Carey Papers. Dan graduated from the Wharton School at the University of Pennsylvania, Jack from Princeton, Bob from the University of North Carolina, and Jane from the University of Michigan.
2. *Time Out,* 228. Interview with DBG and Jack Gilbreth, June 15, 1999.
3. *Time Out,* 228.
4. Martha Gilbreth, "A Large Family," 171–73.
5. *Belles,* 207–8.
6. *AIR,* 230.

7. Ibid., 229–31. Interviews with Brookes Barnes, Plymouth, Mass., April 19, 2000, and JGH, April 6, 2001.

8. Martha Gilbreth, "A Large Family," 173. *AIR,* 227.

9. Martha Gilbreth, "A Large Family," 171–73; JGH interview, 2001; *Time Out,* 226–27.

10. *Time Out,* 229–30.

11. It was the Oak Park, Illinois, chapter of the Society of Industrial Engineering. See *The Original Films of Frank B. Gilbreth.*

12. Ibid.

13. The Twentieth Century Fund has been renamed the Century Foundation. LMG, memo to President Elliott, March 4, 1941; GC c.135, f.0830-32.

14. "Newark Engineering College Adds Dr. Gilbreth to Faculty," *Newark Evening News,* August 31, 1941.

15. Dorothy Stratton to EGC, July 10, 1978, Carey Papers.

16. "Newark College of Engineering Names First Woman to Professorship in Field," *New York Times,* August 21, 1941, 4D; LMG, "Women in Engineering," *Mechanical Engineering* 64, no. 12 (December 1942): 856–57, 859.

17. *Time Out,* 223; *American Women at War,* with a foreword by Mrs. William Brown Meloney (New York: National Association of Manufacturers, 1942); Mary Anderson to LMG, January 9, 1942, and LMG to Mary Anderson, January 6, 1942, National Archives, Women's Bureau correspondence, c.21; Mary V. Robinson, "Recreation and Housing for Women War Workers: A Handbook on Standards," *Bulletin of the Women's Bureau* no. 190 (Washington, D.C.: U.S. Department of Labor, 1942), 38.

18. *Time Out,* 223–34.

19. Margaret Hickey, "Wider Development of In-Plant Counseling Services Recommended," National Archives, Records of War Manpower Commission, Women's Advisory, WAC Issuances 1942–45. *Partners,* 343.

20. Dorothy K. Newman, *Employing Women in Shipyards,* Bulletin of the Women's Bureau no. 192-6 (Washington, D.C.: Government Printing Office, 1944), 1, 44.

21. Nell Giles, "They Are Dependable," in *American Women at War,* 18; "Dr. Lillian Gilbreth declares . . ." *Oakland Tribune,* September 13, 1944, 13; Edna Yost in collaboration with Dr. Lillian M. Gilbreth, *Normal Lives for the Disabled* (New York: Macmillan, 1944), 201, v, viii.

22. Elizabeth Eckhardt May, "Lillian Moller Gilbreth, 1878–1972," *Journal of Home Economics* (April 1972): 13–16.

23. Peter Kihss, "Dr. Lillian M. Gilbreth Battles Inertia and Fatigue to Increase Productivity of Nation's Industry," *New York World-Telegram,* January 23, 1942, 2: 19, GC series 3, c.25, f.LMG Biographical Material.

24. Ibid.

25. *Partners,* 345, 351.

29. As Resilient As a Good Rubber Band

1. Joseph Juran interview, 1999.

2. *New York Herald Tribune* Institute, *America's Housekeeping Book* (New York: Charles Scribner's Sons, 1941).

3. EGC, "Eloise Davidson and Missy Her Boss," Carey Papers.

4. Margaret C. Lewis, "Leaders of Handicapped Girl Scouts Confer," *Girl Scout Leader* (November 1948): 5–6.

5. Ruth Frick, "Reminiscences of LMG," March 3, 1979, and anecdote about Dr. Lillian Gilbreth from Martha Davis Coe, February 1979, Carey Papers.

6. Jane Callaghan to James Landis, March 11, 1966, GC Frank and Lillian Gilbreth Papers, series 1, box 1, f.LMG Scrapbook of Activities, 1966–67.

7. Harold Smalley first met Lillian when he was an undergraduate at the University of Alabama, and it was she who inspired him to attend graduate school at Purdue, where she was then a professor. They later worked together in the application of industrial engineering to the health care field. Harold E. Smalley to EGC, June 26, 1978; Harold E. Smalley, *Hospital Management Engineering: A Guide to the Improvement of Hospital Management Systems* (1966; rev. ed., Englewood Cliffs, N.J.: Prentice-Hall, 1982), 64. See LMG, "Time and Motion Study," *Modern Hospital* 65, no. 3 (September 1945): 53–54; LMG, "Management Engineering and Nursing," *American Journal of Nursing* 50, no. 2 (December 1950): 780–81; conversation with Helen Belcher, Plymouth, Mass., April 19, 2000.

8. Pauline Rehder, "Trends in Management," unpublished term paper, Mechanical Engineering 180, University of Wisconsin, Madison, undated but post-1952. GC c.11, f.Gilbreth articles, Misc. Eva von Baur Hansl (1889–1978) was a journalist, radio director, and writer. Eva Hansl, "The Woman with a Dual Job," typescript of speech, undated, but late 1950s, Carey Papers.

9. LMG, "Teamwork Today," in *The Humanities at Scripps College: Views and Reviews* (Los Angeles: Ward Richie Press, 1952), 44–45.

10. Ibid.

11. Jane Callaghan, March 11, 1966; *Heart of the Home* (New York: American Heart Association, 1950), GC series 3, c.25, f.Articles on LMG.

12. LMG, "You Can Be a Time-Saving Expert, Too!" *Better Homes and Gardens*, June 1950, 78–81.

13. LMG in *Where There's a Will*, John L. Schwab and Associates, for the School of Home Economics, University of Connecticut, and the Office of Vocational Rehabilitation, 1955; 16mm film, in University of Connecticut library.

14. Lillian M. Gilbreth, Orpha Mae Thomas, and Eleanor Clymer, *Management in the Home: Happier Living Through Saving Time and Energy* (New York: Dodd, Mead, 1955), 1.

15. Ibid., 2, 6, 214.

16. Hansl, "Dual Job."

30. Cheaper by the Dozen

1. EGC, *Rings Around Us,* 117. EGC interview, Providence, R.I., March 12, 1991; Marion McInery, "Life 'Cheaper by the Dozen' for Fabulous Gilbreths," *San Francisco Examiner,* March 13, 1949.

2. EGC interview, 1998; FBG Jr., *Lucky Guy,* 220–39.

3. Jack Gilbreth, transcript of talk given to Dunworkin Club in 1993, Carey Papers; Alice Dixon Bond, "Gilbreths Have Made Good Use of Time, the Essence of Life," *Boston Herald,* March 20, 1949; Anne Gilbreth Barney to EGC, December 18, 29, 1948, Carey Papers.

4. LMG to EGC, undated letter, Carey Papers; *Cheaper,* n.p.

5. Reviews included J. A. Wadowick, "Dozen's Author Points Out Drawback of Home Council," *Cleveland Plain Dealer,* October 31, 1950; Ruth Baker, "Fun with a Family," *Christian Science Monitor,* October 11, 1949.

6. Information on best-sellers from Betsey Dexter, *You Must Remember This: 1949* (New York: Warner Books, 1995). The *World Almanac and Book of Facts* (New York: Press Publishing Co., 1950) names Frances Parkinson Keyes's *Dinner at Antoine's* as the top-selling fiction book. "Arthur Miller defines aim of 'true tragedy,'" *New York Herald Tribune,* March 16, 1949; Ruth Baker in the *Christian Science Monitor,* January 12, 1949, 14; *Book Review Digest, 1949* (New York: H. H. Wilson Co., 1950).

7. EGC interview, 1998.

8. *Time Out,* 240–41.

9. Ibid., 237.

10. Otis L. Guernsey Jr., "'Cheaper by the Dozen,'" *New York Herald Tribune,* April 1, 1950; "'Cheaper by the Dozen' Is Webb, not Gilbreth," *New York World Telegraph,* April 1, 1950.

11. C. B. Burnett, *Christian Science Monitor,* October 14, 1950, 14; Lisle Bell, "They Remember Mama—All Eleven Gilbreths Do," *New York Herald Tribune,* October 1, 1950.

12. *Time Out,* 243.

13. Philip Wylie, *Generation of Vipers* (New York: Pocket Books, 1942). This book had been reprinted twenty times by 1955. Ferdinand Lundberg and Marynia F. Farnham, *Modern Woman: The Lost Sex* (New York: Harper and Brothers, 1947), 370–71; Ruth Pollock to EGC, February 28, 1978, Carey Papers.

14. "Lillian Gilbreth wins international award," April 1954; page from unattributed journal, probably of Society of American Management, found in GC c.11, f.Gilbreth articles/misc.

15. Washington Award Commission, program for Award Dinner, April 7, 1954, National Federation of Business and Professional Women's Clubs Archives; "At 75, 'The Greatest,'" *Newsweek,* April 19, 1954, 83–84.

16. The Hoover Medal has been awarded sixty times between 1930 and 2002; Lillian Gilbreth is the only woman recipient. The full citation can be found on the ASME Web site, http://www.asme.org/member/awards/hoover_medal/past.html (accessed October 10, 2003).

17. Fanny M. Sweeney, quoted in *Occupations* 27 (December 1948): 214.

18. "New Jersey's Mother of the Year," *Advance* (May 17, 1957), 25, and "Mother of the Century," *Industrial Management* 1, no. 5 (May 1959), GC Series 3, c.21A, f.Articles on LMG and f Materials on LMG.

19. Marion Mackin, "'Cheaper by Dozen' Heroine Visits Port," *Ozaukee Press,* June 23, 1955, 10, GC series 3, box 22, f.Misc. clippings.

31. Work, for the Night Is Coming

1. LMG, "Unemployment," GC c.11, f.LMG poetry/writings.

2. Marta Navia Kinder et al., "Four Decades of the Society of Women Engineers," reprinted in *SWE: Magazine of the Society of Women Engineers* (January/February 2000).

3. Phyllis Bailey Chisholm to EGC, March 12, 1983, Carey Papers.

4. Mary Murphy, quoted in Kinder et al., "Four Decades," 20, 22; Chisholm to EGC, March 12, 1983, Dot Merrill, transcript of talk about LMG, Carey Papers.

5. Merrill transcript.

6. Margaret Hyndman, "Reminiscences of LMG," transcript of tape (Fall 1978), 3, Carey Papers; John Schwab to EGC, undated extract, Carey Papers; Jerry Nadler, "Reflections," *SWE* (January/February 2000), 86.

7. Jerome Barnum, "The Most Unforgettable Character of All," in *Journal of Industrial Engineering,* Special Reprint (May 1962): 26–28.

8. "Daniel M. Braum receives Gilbreth Medal," GC series 1, c.1, f.LMG Scrapbook of Activities, 1966–67. LMG, "Integration and Integrity in Managing," typescript of speech, June 28, 1956, GC c.11, f.Gilbreth articles/misc.

9. *Time Out,* 244.

10. Sir Walter Scott to EGC, April 24, 1979, Carey Papers.

11. An e-mail from the National Chen Kung University, formerly the Tainan Engineering College, listing the lectures, was forwarded to the author by Eddie Chaonan Chen, Academia Sinica, Taiwan, February 23, 2000.

12. Mary Cushing Niles to "Dear Friends," January 28, 1954, GC.

13. Ibid.

14. Catharine Menninger to Eve[?], 1964, CWM-PRO 2, Menninger Archives; *Time Out,* 245.

15. See *Time Out,* chapter 20; LMG to family, September 15, 1954.

16. E. M. Chervenik, "Reminiscences of Lillian M. Gilbreth," transcript of interview, August 1, 1978, Carey Papers; John Dutton, "Woman Who Combined Careers Tells Students, 'You Have to Work All Your Life,'" *Madison State Journal,* February 8, 1955.

17. LMG, "Integration and Integrity in Management."

18. Articles by Joseph Piacitelli, Erwin Schell, Jerome Barnum, B. W. Berenschott, Bo Casten Carlberg, Walter Scott, Anne G. Shaw, and Andrey Potter, all in *Journal of Industrial Engineering,* Special Reprint (May 1962): 20–36.

19. Shaw, *Journal of Industrial Engineering,* 36.

20. Joseph Rich, quoted in Jaffe, "The One Best Life at Eighty," 9.

32. "IT DOESN'T TAKE LONG TO GET BACK FROM RANGOON"

1. "Dedication," *The Gilbreth Story* (New York: Proceedings of the American Institute of Industrial Engineers, 1962).

2. Jane Callaghan, "After Eighty: The Quest Continues"; Marie Sealey, quoted in Jaffe, "The One Best Life at Eighty," 10, 9.

3. Transcription of letter from Paris from LMG to EGC, August 15, 1961, Carey Papers.

4. Robert Cromie, "*Cheaper by the Dozen* Mother a Swinger at 88," *Chicago Tribune,* November 8, 1966, GC series 1, c.1, f.LMG Scrapbook of activities 1966–67.

5. Jane Callaghan to FBG Jr., July 18, 1980, GC c.2, f.LMG Biography; *Time Out,* 247.

6. Jane Callaghan to Eva Hansl, May 5, 1967, GC c.2, f.LMG Biography. *Time Out,* 246–47.

7. Jane Callaghan to Lady Scott, GC series 2, c.9, f.LMG Letters Sent 1967.

8. Ibid.; LMG to family, September 11, 12, 14, 1967.

9. LMG to family, September 19, 21, 1967.

10. LMG to "Dear Friends," December 16, 1967; Frankie Glynn, "Dr. Gilbreth's Touring Days May Be Nearing an End," *Huntsville [Ala.] Times,* December 12, 1967.

11. Ellen Hawley Jones to FBG Jr., January 31, 1971, GC series 2, c.4, f.Sympathy letters.

12. LMG to Margaret [Hyndman?], March 28, 1968, and LMG to Donald M. Rosenberger, March 25, 1968, GC series 2. c.9, f.LMG Letters Sent 1967–68.

13. *Time Out,* 253–54.

14. Bill Gilbreth to family, April 21, 1969, GC c.25, f.LMG Funeral and Valley Memorial Information.

15. Conversation with LGJ, April 24, 2000. FBG Jr. to Lawrence W. Wallace, March 18, 1971, and FBG Jr. to Beth Russler, November 17, 1971, GC c.4, f.Sympathy letters.

16. Bill Gilbreth to family, April 21, 1969, GC c.25, f.LMG Funeral.

17. EGC interview, 1998.

18. Rev. N. Wesley Haynes, Memorial service for LMG, January 9, 1972, typescript, GC c.4, f.Sympathy letters, and telephone interview, June 28, 1999.

19. Albin Krebs, obituary in *New York Times,* January 3, 1972.

20. *Ancestors,* 136.

21. Ibid., 137.

Index